Fodor's

BARCELONA

WELCOME TO BARCELONA

The capital of Catalonia is a banquet for the senses, with its beguiling mix of ancient and modern architecture, tempting cafés and markets, and sun-drenched Mediterranean beaches. A stroll along La Rambla and through waterfront Barceloneta, as well as a tour of Gaudí's majestic Sagrada Família and his other unique creations, are part of a visit to Spain's second-largest city. Modern art museums and chic shops call for attention, too. Barcelona's vibe stays lively well into the night, when you can linger over regional wine and cuisine at buzzing tapas bars.

TOP REASONS TO GO

★ **Gaudí:** The iconic Sagrada Família, undulating Casa Batlló, and playful Park Güell.

★ **Food:** From the Boqueria market's bounty to tapas bars to avant-garde restaurants.

★ **Museums:** Museu Picasso and the Museu Nacional d'Art de Catalunya lead the list.

★ **Architecture:** Roman and medieval in the Barri Gòtic, Moderniste in the Eixample.

★ **Shopping:** Stylish fashion boutiques and innovative design emporia tempt buyers.

★ **Beautiful Beaches:** Sandy havens and surfing hubs delight urban sun worshippers.

Fodor's BARCELONA

Editorial: Douglas Stallings, *Editorial Director*; Salwa Jabado and Margaret Kelly, *Senior Editors*; Alexis Kelly, Jacinta O'Halloran, and Amanda Sadlowski, *Editors*; Teddy Minford, *Associate Editor*; Rachael Roth, *Content Manager*

Design: Tina Malaney, *Art Director*

Photography: Jennifer Arnow, *Senior Photo Editor*

Maps: Rebecca Baer, *Senior Map Editor*; David Lindroth, Mark Stroud (Moon Street Cartography), *Cartographers*

Production: Jennifer DePrima, *Editorial Production Manager*; Carrie Parker, *Senior Production Editor*; Elyse Rozelle, *Production Editor*; David Satz, *Director of Content Production*

Business & Operations: Chuck Hoover, *Chief Marketing Officer*; Joy Lai, *Vice President and General Manager*; Stephen Horowitz, *Head of Business Development and Partnerships*

Public Relations: Joe Ewaskiw, *Manager*

Writers: Jared Lubarsky, Malia Politzer, Elizabeth Prosser, Steve Tallantyre

Editor: Rachael Roth

Production Editor: Elyse Rozelle

Production Design: Liliana Guia

6th Edition

ISBN 978–1–101–87982–5

ISSN 1554–5865

All details in this book are based on information supplied to us at press time. Always confirm information when it matters, especially if you're making a detour to visit a specific place. Fodor's expressly disclaims any liability, loss, or risk, personal or otherwise, that is incurred as a consequence of the use of any of the contents of this book.

PRINTED IN THE UNITED STATES OF AMERICA

10 9 8 7 6 5 4 3 2 1

CONTENTS

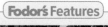

MAPS

ABOUT THIS GUIDE

Fodor's Recommendations

Everything in this guide is worth doing—we don't cover what isn't—but exceptional sights, hotels, and restaurants are recognized with additional accolades. Fodor's Choice ★ indicates our top recommendations. Care to nominate a new place? Visit Fodors.com/contact-us.

Trip Costs

We list prices wherever possible to help you budget well. Hotel and restaurant price categories from **$** to **$$$$** are noted alongside each recommendation. For hotels, we include the lowest cost of a standard double room in high season. For restaurants, we cite the average price of a main course at dinner or, if dinner isn't served, at lunch. For attractions, we always list adult admission fees; discounts are usually available for children, students, and senior citizens.

Hotels

Our local writers vet every hotel to recommend the best overnights in each price category, from budget to expensive. Unless otherwise specified, you can expect private bath, phone, and TV in your room. For expanded hotel reviews, visit Fodors.com.

Top Picks

- ★ Fodor's Choice

Listings

- ✉ Address
- 📨 Branch address
- ☎ Telephone
- 📠 Fax
- 🌐 Website
- 📧 E-mail
- 🎟 Admission fee
- 🕒 Open/closed times
- [M] Subway
- ✥ Directions or Map coordinates

Hotels & Restaurants

- 🏨 Hotel
- 🛏 Number of rooms
- 🍽 Meal plans
- ✕ Restaurant
- ✍ Reservations
- 👔 Dress code
- 💳 No credit cards
- [$] Price

Other

- ⇨ See also
- ☞ Take note
- ⛳ Golf facilities

Restaurants

Unless we state otherwise, restaurants are open for lunch and dinner daily. We mention dress code only when there's a specific requirement and reservations only when they're essential or not accepted. For expanded restaurant reviews, visit Fodors.com.

Credit Cards

The hotels and restaurants in this guide typically accept credit cards. If not, we'll say so.

EUGENE FODOR

Hungarian-born Eugene Fodor (1905–91) began his travel career as an interpreter on a French cruise ship. The experience inspired him to write *On the Continent* (1936), the first guidebook to receive annual updates and discuss a country's way of life as well as its sights. Fodor later joined the U.S. Army and worked for the OSS in World War II. After the war, he kept up his intelligence work while expanding his guidebook series. During the Cold War, many guides were written by fellow agents who understood the value of insider information. Today's guides continue Fodor's legacy by providing travelers with timely coverage, insider tips, and cultural context.

EXPERIENCE
BARCELONA

BARCELONA TODAY

Capital of the autonomous Community of Catalonia, bilingual Barcelona (Catalan and Spanish) is the unrivaled visitor destination in Spain, and with good reason: dazzling art and architecture, creative cuisine, great weather, and warm hospitality are just part of what the city offers. Barcelona is proud of its cultural past and confident about its future.

A Tale of Two Cities

Restive for centuries in the shadow of Madrid, where Spain ruled from the center—more often than not, with an iron hand—Barcelona has a drive to innovate and excel that stems largely from a determination to eclipse its longtime rival. A powerful sense of national identity (Catalans consider themselves a "nation" and decidedly not a province of Spain) motivates designers, architects, merchants, and industrialists to ever-higher levels of originality and achievement. Especially since the success of the 1992 Olympic Games, national pride and confidence have grown stronger and stronger, and today nearly half the Catalan population believes the nation would be better served—whatever implications that might have for membership in the European Union—by complete independence.

Cuisine: Haute and Hot

Since Ferran Adrià's northern Catalonian phenomenon elBulli closed, *chef d'auteur* successes in Barcelona have proliferated. Some two dozen superb restaurants (and more on the way) have won international recognition, so keeping abreast of the city's culinary rock stars can be a dizzying pursuit. Here's a quick primer: Adrià disciples Sergi Arola at his eponymous Arola Restaurant in the Hotel Arts, and Carles Abellán at BRAVO24 in the W Barcelona remain at the frontiers of Adrià-inspired molecular gastronomy. Rising stars such as Jordi Artal of Cinc Sentits, Jordi Vilà of Alkimia, the Torres twins at Dos Cielos, and Jordi Herrera of Manairó, join established masters Carles Gaig and Mey Hofmann in a dazzling galaxy of gastronomical creativity. Meanwhile, the Roca brothers from Girona, Raül Balam from Sant Pol de Mar, and Martin Berasategui from San Sebastián have opened award-winning hotel restaurants in, respectively, the Omm (Moo), the Mandarin Oriental (Moments), and the Condes de Barcelona (Lasarte). Add to this list up-and-comers like Xavier Franco of the restaurant Saüc (in the

WHAT WE'RE TALKING ABOUT

Barcelona already has a higher percentage of five-star accommodations than even London or Paris, and luxury operations are eager to add even more. In 2015, however, newly elected mayor Ada Colau imposed a short-term moratorium on new billets, part of an effort to limit growth of the city's tourist industry. Residents are generally happy with the idea, while hoteliers are not.

The Sagrada Família, Gaudí's masterpiece that's been in the works since 1882, is finally nearing completion, expected to be finished by the centenary of Gaudí's death, 2026. The basilica was consecrated by Pope Benedict XVI in 2010, and today the nave and transept of the interior are open to visitors. Drawing some 3 million visitors a year, it is Barcelona's most iconic structure.

Ohla Hotel), Dani Lechuga of Caldeni, and Oriol Ivern of Hisop, and you begin to appreciate what a gastronomic haven Barcelona has become.

Design, Architecture, Fashion, Style

Barcelona's cutting-edge achievements in interior design and couture continue to threaten the traditional dominance of Paris and Milan, while "starchitect" landmarks like Jean Nouvel's Torre Agbar, Norman Foster's communications tower on the Collserola skyline, and Ricardo Bofill's W Barcelona hotel (nicknamed Vela: the Sail) on the waterfront transform the city into a showcase of postmodern visual surprises.

Fútbol Nirvana

The FC Barcelona soccer juggernaut seemed as if it had peaked in 2006 when Brazilian import Ronaldinho led the team to its second European title—but the best was yet to come. Former star-midfielder-turned-coach Pep Guardiola and an almost entirely homegrown team of stars amazed the world in 2009, winning—for the first time in La Liga history—a *triplete*, or Triple Crown: the Liga league championship, the King's Cup, and the UEFA Champions League European title, which they won again in 2015. With the talent of star player Leo Messi as well as the farm system used (most players are trained at the club's "La Masia" youth academy), the team continues to strengthen.

Breaking New Ground

With a new airport terminal, a behemoth new convention center complex, and a new AVE high-speed train connection to Madrid, Barcelona is again on the move. City planners predict that the recent redesign of Plaça de les Glòries will someday shift the city center eastward, and that the new Barcelona hub will surround the Torre Agbar and the Fòrum at the Mediterranean end of the Diagonal.

Can FC Barcelona continue to dominate world *fútbol*? When beloved coach Pep Guardiola left the team for German Bundesliga club Bayern Munich in 2012, Barça faltered for awhile; three coaches later, Guardiola protegé Luis Enrique (who retired at the end of the 2016–2017 season) brought the team back as the Liga powerhouse.

Visitors can marvel at Catalan Modernisme masterworks: Puig i Cadafalch's landmark Casa de les Punxes, and Gaudí's Casa Vicens are now open to the public; the restoration of Domènech i Montaner's Hospital de Sant Pau (now Europe's largest Art Nouveau architectural complex, rechristened the Sant Pau Recinte Modernista) is complete.

BARCELONA PLANNER

When to Go

For optimal weather and fewer tourists, visit Barcelona, Catalonia, and Bilbao from April through June and mid-September through mid-December. Expect traffic at the start and end of August when locals leave for vacation. Major cities are relaxed and empty except for tourists in August, though Gràcia's Festa Major in Barcelona and Semana Grande in Bilbao keep these two cities alive during summer. Some shops and restaurants shut down for part of the month, but museums remain open, and music and theater festivals ensure that there's never a cultural lull.

Barcelona summers can be very hot, but temperatures rarely surpass 100°F (38°C), and air-conditioning is becoming more widespread. Dining alfresco on a warm summer night is one of northern Spain's finest pleasures. Spring and fall offer the best temperatures at both ends of the Pyrenees. Barcelona winters—chilly, but never freezing—are ideal for fireside dining and hearty cuisine.

Getting Around

The best way to get around Barcelona is on foot; though subway, taxi, or tram rides can save you time. The FGC (Ferrocarril de la Generalitat de Catalunya) trains that run up the center of the city from Plaça de Catalunya to Sarrià put you within 20- to 30-minute walks of nearly everything. The metro and the FGC close before 12 am Monday-Thursday and Sunday, and at 2 am on Friday; on Saturday, the metro runs all night. You need a taxi or the metro to reach Montjuïc (Miró Foundation, MNAC, Mies van der Rohe Pavilion, CaixaForum, and Poble Espanyol), most easily accessed from Plaça Espanya; Park Güell above Plaça Lesseps; and the Auditori at Plaça de les

Glòries. You can reach Gaudí's Sagrada Família by two metro lines (L2 and L5), or walk from the FGC's Provença stop; the half-hour jaunt passes by Palau Baró de Quadras, Casa Terrades (les Punxes), and Casa Macaia.

Sarrià and Pedralbes are easily explored on foot. The Torre Bellesguard and the Col·legi de les Teresianes are uphill treks; you might want to take a cab. Stroll from Sarrià down through the Jardins de la Vil·la Cecilia and Vil·la Amèlia to the Cátedra Gaudí (the pavilions of the Finca Güell, with Gaudí's wrought-iron dragon gate); from there, you can get to the Futbol Club Barcelona through the Jardins del Palau Reial de Pedralbes and the university campus, or catch a two-minute taxi.

All of Ciutat Vella (Barri Gòtic, Rambla, El Raval, Born-Ribera, and Barceloneta) is walkable. If you stay in Barceloneta for dinner (usually not more than €25), have the restaurant call you a taxi to get back to your hotel.

A city bus lets you view the city, but the metro is faster and more comfortable. The tramway offers a quiet ride from Plaça Francesc Macià out Diagonal past the Futbol Club Barcelona and beyond to Cornellà and Sant Feliu de Llobregat, or from the Vila Olimpica terminus in Poblenou, behind the Ciutadella Park, out to Glòries and the Fòrum at the east end of Diagonal, continuing on across the Besòs River to neighboring Sant Adrià.

Barcelona's Discount Cards

MUSEUM DISCOUNTS

The **Articket BCN** (AKA the Art Passport ⊕ *www.articketbcn.org*), valid for a year, gives you half-price admission to the Museu Picasso, the Fundació Antoni Tapies, the CCCB Barcelona Centre de

Cultura Contemporània, the MACBA Museum of Contemporary Art, the Fundació Joan Miró, and the MNAC Museu Nacional d'Art de Catalunya, and lets you skip the long lines (€28.50 at participating museums). The **Arqueo-ticket** (€14.50), valid for a year, grants free entry to the Museu d'Arqueologia de Catalunya, the Museu Egipci de Barcelona, the Museum of the History of the City and the historical buildings of the Plaça del Rei, and the Born Centre de Cultura i Memòria. Available at any of the four museums.

TRANSPORTATION DISCOUNTS

The **Barcelona Card** (valid three days €45, four days €55), gives you access to all public transportation, and free or discounted admissions to various museums, sites, and tours: ⊕ *www.barcelonaturisme.com*. The Modernisme Route Guidebook (€12), available at bookstores and at the Centro del Modernismo in the Güell Pavillions, features 120 Catalan Art Nouveau architectural sites in the city, and includes a book of discount vouchers. The **T-10 Metro Card** (€9.95), from the ticket dispensers at all subway stations, is good for 10 rides on any of the city's public transportation systems: metro, bus, tram, and FGC. You can transfer from any one to another free (within 75 minutes)—and the card can be shared. Fares on the hop-on, hop-off double-decker **Barcelona Bus Turistic** (€29 for one day, €39 for two consecutive days) include a voucher booklet of discounts to a number of cultural sites, attractions, shows, and restaurants. Purchase tickets at any tourist information office, kiosks in the city center, or on the bus.

Catalan for Beginners

Catalan is derived from Latin and Provençal French, whereas Spanish borrows from Arabic vocabulary and phonetics. For free half-hour language exchanges of English for Catalan or Spanish (*intercambios*), check the bulletin board at the Central University Philosophy and Letters Faculty or any English bookstore. It's a great way to get free private lessons or meet locals.

Top Festivals and Events

Carnaval (*Carnestoltes*) which rivals its more flamboyant counterpart in Sitges, arrives just before Lent in February or March and travels down the coast.

Semana Santa (Holy Week), the week before Easter, is Spain's most important celebration everywhere but Barcelona, as the locals depart in droves for vacations elsewhere.

La Diada de Sant Jordi (April 23) is Barcelona's Valentine's Day, celebrated with gifts of flowers and books in observance of International Book Day and to honor the deaths of Miguel de Cervantes and William Shakespeare.

La Fira de Sant Ponç brings farmers to town for an open-air market in the Raval on May 11. **La Verbena de Sant Joan** celebrates the summer solstice and Midsummer's Eve with fireworks and all-night beach parties on June 23.

La Festa Major de Gràcia honors Santa Maria with street dances and concerts in Barcelona's village-turned-neighborhood, Gràcia, in mid-August.

Festes de La Mercé honors Barcelona's patron saint, Nostra Senyora de la Mercé, for a week in late September.

WHAT'S WHERE

1 La Rambla. The city's most emblematic promenade was once a seasonal watercourse that flowed along the outside of the 13th-century city walls. A stroll on La Rambla—where tourists mix with pickpockets, buskers, street performers, and locals—passes the Boqueria market, the Liceu opera house, and, at the port end, Drassanes, the medieval shipyards. Just off La Rambla is Plaça Reial, a stately neoclassical square; off the other side is Gaudí's masterly Palau Güell.

2 Barri Gòtic. The medieval Gothic Quarter surrounds the Catedral de la Seu on the high ground that the Romans settled in the 1st century BC. The medieval Jewish quarter, the antiquers' row, Plaça Sant Jaume, and the Sant Just neighborhood are quintessential Barcelona.

3 El Raval. Once a slum, this area west of La Rambla has brightened considerably, thanks partly to the Barcelona Museum of Contemporary Art, designed by Richard Meier. Behind the Boqueria market is the stunning Antic Hospital de la Santa Creu, with its high-vaulted Gothic Biblioteca de Catalunya reading room; just steps away is Sant Pau del Camp, Barcelona's earliest church.

4 Sant Pere, La Ribera, and El Born. Northeast of La Rambla, Sant Pere is the city's old textile neighborhood. The narrow cobblestone streets of La Ribera and El Born are filled with interesting shops and restaurants; this area is known for the grand urban palaces of Barcelona's medieval nobles and merchant princes—five of which linked together now house the Picasso Museum. Find shops and saloons in Passeig del Born, once the medieval jousting ground.

5 Barceloneta. This waterfront neighborhood, just east of Born-Ribera, was open water until the mid-18th century, when it was filled in to provide housing for those displaced by the construction of Ciutadella—at the time the largest fortress in Europe and a symbol of the hated Bourbon regime. Some of the city's best seafood restaurants make Barceloneta a favorite for Sunday-afternoon paella gatherings.

6 The Eixample. The Eixample (Expansion) is the post-1860 grid square of city blocks uphill from Ciutat Vella containing most of Barcelona's Moderniste (Art Nouveau) architecture, including Gaudí's unfinished work, the Sagrada Família church. Passeig de Gràcia is the city's premier shopping street. It also offers more Gaudí at Casa Batlló, Casa Milà (La Pedrera), and Casa Calvet.

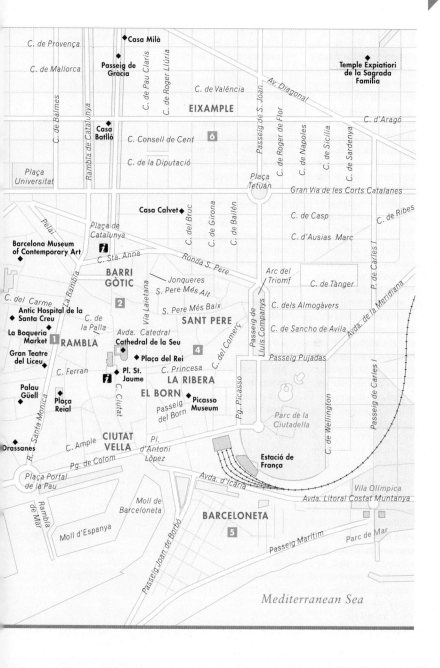

C. de Provença

◆ **Casa Milà**

C. de Mallorca

◆

Passeig de Gràcia

C. de Pau Claris

C. de Roger Llúria

C. de València

Av. Diagonal

Passeig de S. Joan

Temple Expiatori de la Sagrada Família ◆

C. d'Aragó

C. de Balmes

EIXAMPLE

Rambla de Catalunya

◆ **Casa Batlló**

C. Consell de Cent

C. de la Diputació

C. de Roger de Flor

C. de Nápoles

C. de Sicília

C. de Sardenya

6

Plaça Universitat

Plaça Tetuán

Gran Via de les Corts Catalanes

Casa Calvet ◆

C. del Bruc

C. de Girona

C. de Ballén

C. de Casp

C. de Ribes

Plaça de Catalunya

C. d'Ausias Marc

P. de Carles I

Pelai

Barcelona Museum of Contemporary Art ◆

C. Sta. Anna

Ronda S. Pere

Arc del Triomf

C. de Tànger

Avda. de la Meridiana

BARRI GÒTIC

La Rambla

Jonqueres

S. Pere Més Alt

Via Laietana

S. Pere Més Baix

2

C. del Carme

Antic Hospital de la Santa Creu ◆

C. de la Palla

Avda. Catedral

SANT PERE

Passeig de Lluís Companys

C. dels Almogàvers

C. de Sancho de Avila

Passeig de Carles I

La Boqueria Market ◆

1

RAMBLA

Cathedral de la Seu

4

C. del Comerç

Gran Teatre del Liceu ◆

C. Ferran

◆ **Plaça del Rei**

Pl. St. Jaume

C. Princesa

LA RIBERA

Passeig Pujadas

Palau Güell ◆

C. Ciutat

EL BORN

◆ **Picasso Museum**

Pg. Picasso

R. Santa Mònica

◆ **Plaça Reial**

Passeig del Born

Parc de la Ciutadella

C. de Wellington

CIUTAT VELLA

C. Ample

Pl. d'Antoni López

◆ **Drassanes**

Pg. de Colom

Avda. d'Icària

Estació de França

Plaça Portal de la Pau

Rambla de Mar

Moll de Barceloneta

Avda. Litoral Costat Muntanya

Vila Olímpica

Moll d'Espanya

BARCELONETA

5

Passeig Joan de Borbó

Passeig Marítim

Parc de Mar

Mediterranean Sea

WHAT'S WHERE

7 Gràcia. This former outlying village begins at Gaudí's playful Park Güell and continues past his first commissioned house, Casa Vicens, through two markets and various pretty squares such as Plaça de la Vila de Gràcia (formerly Plaça de Rius i Taulet) and Plaça del Sol. Carrer Gran de Gràcia, though narrow and noisy, is lined with buildings designed by Gaudí's assistant Francesc Berenguer i Mestres.

8 Sarrià and Pedralbes. Sarrià was an independent village until it was incorporated into the burgeoning metropolis in 1927. It still feels very much like a village, though present-day gentrification has endowed it with a gratifying number of gourmet shops and fine restaurants. Nearby is the Monestir de Pedralbes, a 14th-century architectural gem with a rare triple-tiered cloister; not far away are Gaudí's Col·legi de les Teresianes and his Torre Bellesguard.

9 Tibidabo, Vallvidrera, and the Collserola Hills. Tibidabo, Barcelona's perch, has little more to offer at the summit than its retro kitschy amusement park—but do take the *Tramvia Blau* (Blue Tram) at least to the lower end of the funicular that goes up to the park: the square in front of the terminus has

restaurants and bars with views over the city. Even better is the Collserola forest and park on the far side of the hill, accessible by the FGC train out to the Baixador de Vallvidrera. Vallvidrera is a sleepy village with a good restaurant (Can Trampa), a Moderniste funicular station, and views west to the Montserrat massif.

10 Montjuïc. Located on the western edge of the city, Montjuïc is Barcelona's playground: a sprawling complex of parks and gardens, sports facilities, open-air theater spaces, and museums. Among the latter are the Museu Nacional d'Art de Catalunya (MNAC) in the Palau Nacional, repository of a thousand years of Catalonia's artistic treasures; the Joan Miró Foundation collection of contemporary art and sculpture; the Mies van der Rohe Barcelona Pavilion; and the CaixaForum.

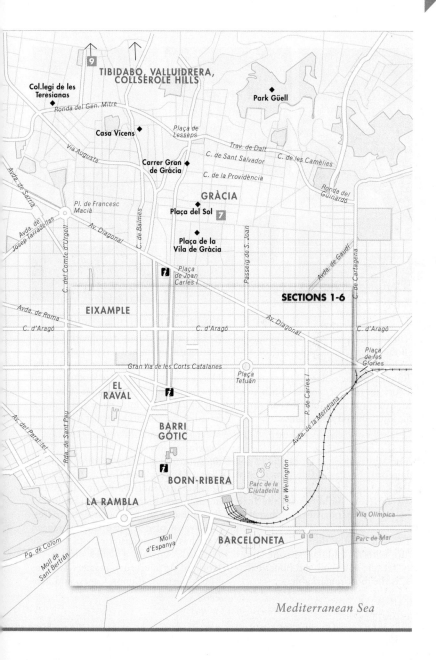

TIBIDABO, VALLUIDRERA,
COLLSEROLE HILLS

Col.legi de les
Teresianas
♦
Park Güell ♦

Ronda del Gen. Mitre

Casa Vicens ♦
Plaça de
Lesseps

Via Augusta
Trav. de Dalt
C. de Sant Salvador
C. de les Camèlies

Carrer Gran
de Gràcia ♦
C. de la Providència

GRÀCIA
♦
*Ronda del
Guinardó*

Pl. de Francesc
Macià ♦
Plaça del Sol 🔲7

Avda. de Sarrià

*Avda. de
Josep Tarradellas*

C. del Comte d'Urgell
Av. Diagonal
C. de Balmes
Plaça de la
Vila de Gràcia

Passeig de S. Joan
Avda. de Gaudí
C. de Cartagena

Plaça
de Joan
Carles I
🔵

SECTIONS 1-6

Avda. de Roma
EIXAMPLE
Av. Diagonal

C. d'Aragó
C. d'Aragó
C. d'Aragó

Plaça
de les
Glories

Gran Via de les Corts Catalanes
Plaça
Tetuán

EL
RAVAL
🔵
P. de Carles I

Rda. de Sant Pau
BARRI
GÓTIC

Avda. de la Meridiana

Av. del Paral·lel
🔵
BORN-RIBERA
Parc de la
Ciutadella

C. de Wellington

LA RAMBLA
Vila Olímpica

Pg. de Colom
Moll
d'Espanya
BARCELONETA
Parc de Mar

*Moll de
Sant Bertrán*

Mediterranean Sea

BARCELONA TOP ATTRACTIONS

The Boqueria Market

(A) The oldest market of its kind in Europe, the Boqueria market is a labyrinth of stalls in a Moderniste wrought-iron shell just off La Rambla, selling edibles of every imaginable sort: the must-see source of fish, fowl, meat, fruits, and vegetables for Barcelona's home kitchens and restaurants.

Casa Batlló and the Manzana de la Discòrdia

(B) The Manzana de la Discòrdia (Apple of Discord) on Passeig de Gràcia is so called for its row of astonishing but vastly different buildings by the three most famous Moderniste architects—Domènech i Montaner, Puig i Cadafalch, and Gaudí. Of the three, Gaudí's Casa Batlló, with its undulating roof, multicolor facade, and skull-and-bones balconies, is the most remarkable.

Gaudí's Sagrada Família

(C) The city's best-known landmark, Gaudí's soaring still-unfinished Temple Expiatori de la Sagrada Família (Expiatory Temple of the Holy Family) draws lines of visitors around the block. With the completion of the interior in 2010, the lofty nave and transept have become the city's premier sight.

Museu Nacional d'Art de Catalunya (MNAC)

(D) Atop the stairway leading up from Plaça d'Espanya, MNAC is Barcelona's answer to Madrid's Prado. It houses an unmatched collection of Catalonia's Romanesque art, from altarpieces to frescoes, most of it rescued from Pyrenean churches and monasteries and lovingly restored. Separate galleries display the work of 19th-century masters such as Marià Fortuny, Ramón Casas, and Santiago Rusiñol.

Museu Picasso

(E) Pablo Picasso's connection to Barcelona, where he spent key formative years and first showed his work in 1900, eventually bore fruit when his manager Jaume Sabartés donated his collection to the city in 1962. Nearly as stunning as the 3,500 Picasso works on display are the five medieval palaces that house them.

Palau de la Música Catalana

(F) Often described as the flagship of Barcelona's Modernisme, this dizzying tour de force by architect Lluís Domènech i Montaner is a showcase of Art Nouveau crafts and decorative techniques—every detail and motif symbolic of the Catalan cultural identity. Much criticized during the aesthetically somber 1939–75 Franco regime, the city's longtime prime concert venue is an exciting place to hear music.

Park Güell

(G) Gaudí's playful park in Gràcia was originally developed as a residential community. Gaudí's patron and principal investor in the project, Count Eusebi Güell, must have been disappointed when the idea failed to catch on; only two of the houses planned for this whimsical garden were built. What did get built were Moderniste gems: the gingerbread gatehouses, the dazzling central staircase, and the undulating ceramic tile bench around the central square.

Santa Maria del Mar Basilica

(H) For Mediterranean Gothic at its best, Santa Maria del Mar is the Sagrada Família's opposite. Burned back to its stone shell in a fire at the start of the Spanish Civil War in 1936, it was restored by post-Bauhaus architects who saw the purity of Berenguer de Montagut's 1329 design and maintained his spare, elegant lines.

LIKE A LOCAL

If you want to get a sense of local culture, start with these few highlights in the rituals of daily life—activities and events you can share with the leisure-loving inhabitants of this most dynamic of cities.

Grazing: Tapas and Wine Bars

Few pastimes in Barcelona are more satisfying than wandering, tippling, and tapas hunting. By day or after dark, exploring Barri Gòtic, Gràcia, Barceloneta, or the Born-Ribera district offers an endless selection of taverns, cafés, bars, and restaurants, where you ballast your drinks with little portions of fish, sausage, cheese, peppers, wild mushrooms, or *tortilla* (potato omelet), lovingly prepared on the premises. If you find yourself on Passeig de Gràcia or La Rambla in a bar that serves microwaved tapas, know this: you're missing out. The areas around Passeig del Born, Santa Maria del Mar, Plaça de les Olles, and the Picasso Museum are the prime *tapeo* (tapa-tasting) and *txikiteo* (tippling) grounds.

Openings, Presentations, Lectures, and Musical Events

Check listings in the daily newspapers *El País* or *La Vanguardia*, or the online edition of *Barcelona Time Out* (⊕ *www.timeout.com/barcelona*) to find announcements for art-gallery openings, book presentations, and free public concerts. Often serving *cava* (Catalan sparkling wine) and canapés, these little gatherings welcome visitors (if it's announced in the papers, you're invited). Famous authors from Richard Ford to Paul Auster to Martin Amis or local stars such as Javier Marías or Carlos Ruiz Zafón may be presenting new books at the British Institute or at bookstores like La Central. Laie Libreria holds jazz performances in its café; the travel bookstore Altair has frequent book signings and talks by prominent travel authors. Events in the town hall's Saló de Cent are usually open to the public.

Soccer: FC Barcelona

If FC Barcelona is playing while you're in town, get thee to a sports bar—the bigger the flat-screen TV, the better. The pubs down around La Rambla with fútbol on the tube are usually packed with foreign tourists; the taverns and cafés in Barceloneta, El Raval, Gràcia, and Sarrià are generally local *penyas* (fan clubs), where passions run high. Learn the club song in Catalan so you can join in when Barça scores. To watch in person, head to Camp Nou stadium—though tickets can be pricy.

Sunday Sardanas, Puppets, and Castellers

The Sunday-morning papers carry announcements for local neighborhood celebrations, flea markets and produce fairs, puppet shows, storytelling sessions for children, *sardana* folk-dancing, bell-ringing concerts, and the fascinating *castellers*. The castellers, complex human pyramids sometimes reaching as high as 10 stories, are a quintessentially Catalan phenomenon that originated in the Penedés region west of Barcelona; they're performed at neighborhood fiestas or on major holidays. Most Sunday-morning events are over by 2 pm, when lunchtime officially reigns supreme, so get an early start. The Barcelona town hall in Plaça Sant Jaume is a frequent venue for *castellers* and *sardanas,* as is the Plaça de la Catedral.

GREAT ITINERARIES

Ciutat Vella, Quintessential Barcelona

Stroll La Rambla and see the colorful Boqueria market before cutting over to the Catedral de la Seu in Barri Gòtic, unrivaled for the density and number of its surviving medieval buildings and monuments. Detour through stately Plaça Sant Jaume where the Palau de la Generalitat, Catalonia's seat of government, faces the Ayuntamiento (City Hall). The Gothic Plaça del Rei and the neoclassical Plaça Reial—not to be confused—are short walks from Plaça Sant Jaume. The Museu Picasso is five minutes from the loveliest example of Catalan Gothic architecture, the basilica of Santa Maria del Mar. An evening concert at the Palau de la Música Catalana after a few tapas and before a late dinner is an unbeatable way to end the day.

Budget a whole day for the Raval, behind the Boqueria, for the Museu d'Art Contemporani de Barcelona, the medieval Antic Hospital de la Santa Creu, the Sant Pau del Camp church, and the medieval shipyards at Drassanes Reiales. Palau Güell, just off the lower Rambla, is an important Gaudí work. A short hike away, the waterfront Barceloneta neighborhood is a prime venue for a paella.

The Post-1860 Checkerboard Eixample

A morning touring the Eixample starts early and begins at Gaudí's magnum opus, the Temple Expiatori de la Sagrada Família (while there, include a side trip up Avinguda Gaudí to the Hospital de Sant Pau—if you buy your tickets to the Sagrada Família online ahead of time, you can avoid the inevitable lengthy queue. After, head to the central Passeig de Gràcia; en route swing past Moderniste architect Puig i Cadafalch's Casa

Terrades and his Palau Baró de Quadras. Spend the afternoon in the Eixample with the undulating facades and stunning interiors of Casa Milà and Casa Batlló. Other Eixample masterpieces include Gaudí's Casa Calvet, not far from Plaça de Catalunya, the Fundació Tàpies, and more far-flung Moderniste gems such as the Casa Golferichs, and the Casa de la Papallona (the "Butterfly House") out toward Plaça de Espanya. Parallel to the Passeig de Gràcia is the Rambla Catalunya, a tree-shaded promenade lined with shops and cafés.

Upper Barcelona: Gràcia and Sarrià

For a more rustic and restful excursion, try the formerly outlying towns of Gràcia and Sarrià. Gràcia is home to Gaudí's first private residential commission, Casa Vicens, and his playful Park Güell above Plaça Lesseps; the tree-lined lower reaches of this bustling neighborhood are filled with houses by Gaudí's right-hand man, Francesc Berenguer. Sarrià is a village long since absorbed by the ever-expanding city, an intimate warren of narrow streets, neighborhood shops, and restaurants. A bit removed from the village itself are the Monestir de Pedralbes, with its superb Gothic cloister, Gaudí's Torre Bellesguard, and his Col·legi de les Teresianes (a convent school, not open to the public).

Art in Montjuïc

Montjuïc is the site of the Museu Nacional d'Art de Catalunya; the nearby Fundació Miró features Catalan artist Joan Miró's colorful paintings and textiles, and a stellar Calder mobile. Down the stairs toward Plaça d'Espanya are the Mies van der Rohe Barcelona Pavilion and the restored Casaramona textile mill, now the CaixaForum cultural center and gallery.

A WALK AROUND LA RAMBLA

It's a Mediterranean thing: many towns have that one street in town, or barrio, that runs from the town hall to the church, or from the main street to the port, where everyone comes to hang out. These streets are dedicated to the long tradition of the promenade, where you move slower (don't walk, stroll) and take in your surroundings, where you go to see and be seen, and where you share a table with friends at an outdoor café. In Barcelona, that's La Rambla.

La Rambla: Rite of Passage

Start from the top, at **Plaça de Catalunya.** La Rambla changes names and personalities as you descend toward the sea, bringing you first to **Rambla de Canaletes** (drink from the fountain here, and the inscription on the base promises that you will return to Barcelona, no matter how far away you go), then to **Rambla dels Ocells**—the old bird market now given over to ice-cream vendors and souvenir stands—past Carrer de Portaferrissa to the flower stalls along **Rambla de les Flors.** (The **Boqueria market** is off to the right here.) From the **Liceu opera house, Rambla de Santa Mónica** takes you past the Plaça Reial on the left to the end of your promenade at Drassanes.

The Boqueria: Horn of Plenty

There's a stall in the Mercat de Sant Josep, popularly known as **La Boqueria,** for any and every imaginable ingredient in a Barcelona kitchen. Highlights are **Pinotxo,** the legendary dozen-stool gourmet counter, **Quim de la Boqueria,** with its famous *ous esclafats amb llanqueta* (eggs with tiny fish), and **Petràs,** the world-renowned wild mushroom stand at the back.

The Medieval Hospital: Gothic Splendor

Behind the Boqueria and through Plaça de la Gardunya is the medieval **Antic Hospital de la Santa Creu,** founded in the 13th century by King Martí l'Humà (Martin the Humane), now housing the archives and library of the Biblioteca de Catalunya. The library, well worth a visit, is up the stairway under the breathtaking Gothic stone arches of the courtyard, to the right.

Moderniste Raval: Gaudí and Domènech i Montaner

From the Hospital, walk back along Carrer Hospital to Plaça de Sant Agustí, and cut through Carrer de l'Arc de Sant Agustí to the **Hotel España,** a Moderniste masterpiece by architect Lluís Domènech i Montaner. The mermaid murals in the dining room and the marble fireplace in the bar are highlights. From here, Carrer Sant Pau brings you to the **Liceu**—Barcelona's magnificent opera house.

An alternative detour off Rambla des Ocells also brings you to this point. (Why not do both?) Turn left on Carrer de Portaferrissa, and take the second right, down Carrer Petritxol (art galleries and to-die-for chocolate shops) into the square in front of **Santa Maria del Pi,** and admire this 14th-century masterpiece. Then return to La Rambla via Carrer Cardenal Casañas, which brings you out just in front of the Liceu. Farther down, the first street to the right is Carrer Nou de la Rambla; Gaudí's **Palau Güell** is 50 yards down the street. Directly across the Rambla here is the entrance to the neoclassical **Plaça Reial.**

1

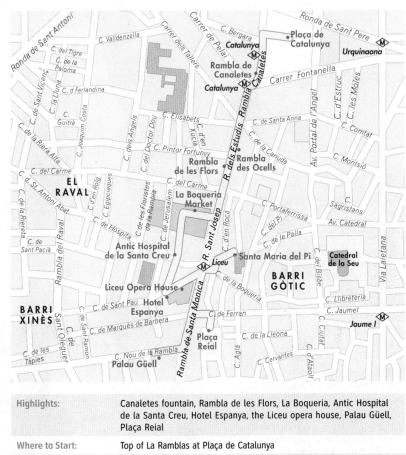

Highlights:	Canaletes fountain, Rambla de les Flors, La Boqueria, Antic Hospital de la Santa Creu, Hotel Espanya, the Liceu opera house, Palau Güell, Plaça Reial
Where to Start:	Top of La Ramblas at Plaça de Catalunya
Length:	Three hours with time for browsing through the Boqueria; 2 miles in all
Where to Stop:	Plaça Reial
Best Time to Go:	Before 2 pm, when everything is open and the market is at its busiest
Worst Time to Go:	Between 2 pm and 4 pm, when the market starts to slow down
Where to Refuel:	Café Viena for the famous *flautas de jamón ibérico* (Iberico ham sandwiches); Bar Pinotxo, Quim de la Boqueria or Kiosko Universal in La Boqueria

GAUDÍ

ARCHITECTURE
THROUGH
THE LOOKING
GLASS

(left) The undulating rooftop of Casa Batlló. (top) Right angles are notably absent in the Casa Milà façade.

Before his 75th birthday in 1926, Antoni Gaudí was hit by a trolley car while on his way to Mass. The great architect—initially unidentified—was taken to the medieval Hospital de la Santa Creu in Barcelona's Raval and left in a pauper's ward, where he died two days later without regaining consciousness. It was a dramatic and tragic end for a man whose entire life seemed to court the extraordinary and the exceptional.

Gaudí's singularity made him hard to define. Indeed, eulogists at the time, and decades later, wondered how history would treat him. Was he a religious mystic, a rebel, a bohemian artist, a Moderniste genius? Was he, perhaps, all of these? He certainly had a rebellious streak, as his architecture stridently broke with tradition. Yet the same sensibility that created the avant-garde benchmarks Park Güell and La Pedrera also created one of Spain's greatest shrines to Catholicism, the *Temple Expiatori de la Sagrada Família* (Expiatory Temple of the Holy Family), which architects agree is one of the world's most enigmatic structures; work on the cathedral continues to this day. And while Gaudí's works suggest a futurist aesthetic, he also reveled in the use of ornamentation, which 20th century architecture largely eschewed.

What is no longer in doubt is Gaudí's place among the great architects in history. Eyed with suspicion by traditionalists in the 1920s and 30s, vilified during the Franco regime, and ultimately redeemed as a Barcelona icon after Spain's democratic transition in the late 70s, Gaudí has finally gained universal admiration.

THE MAKING OF A GENIUS

Gaudí was born in 1852 the son of a boilermaker and coppersmith in Reus, an hour south of Barcelona. As a child, he helped his father forge boilers and cauldrons in the family foundry, which is where Gaudí's fascination with three-dimensional and organic forms began. Afflicted from an early age with reoccuring rheumatic fever, the young architect devoted his energies to studying and drawing flora and fauna in the natural world. In school Gaudí was erratic: brilliant in the subjects that interested him, absent and disinterested in the others. As a seventeen-year-old architecture student in Barcelona, his academic results were mediocre. Still, his mentors agreed that he was brilliant.

Unfortunately being brilliant didn't mean instant success. By the late 1870s, when Gaudí was well into his twenties, he'd only completed a handful of projects, including the Plaça Reial lampposts, a flower stall, and the factory and part of a planned workers' community in Mataró. Gaudí's career got the boost it needed when, in 1878, he met Eusebi Güell, heir to a textiles fortune and a man who, like

Gaudí, had a refined sensibility. (The two bonded over a mutual admiration for the visionary Catalan poet Jacint Verdaguer.) In 1883 Gaudí became Güell's architect and for the next three decades, until Güell's death in 1918, the two collaborated on Gaudí's most important architectural achievements, from high-profile endeavors like Palau Güell, Park Güell, and Pabellones Güell to smaller projects for the Güell family.

(top) Interior of Casa Batlló. (bottom) Chimneys on rooftop of Casa Milà recall helmeted warriors or veiled women.

GAUDÍ TIMELINE

1883–1884

Gaudí builds a summer palace, *El Capricho* in Comillas, Santander for the brother-in-law of his benefactor, Eusebi Güell. Another gig comes his way during this same period when Barcelona ceramics tile mogul Manuel Vicens hires him to build his town house, *Casa Vicens*, in the Gràcia neighborhood.

El Capricho

1884–1900

Gaudí whips up the Pabellones Güell, Palau Güell, the Palacio Episcopal of Astorga, Barcelona's Teresianas school, the Casa de los Botines in León, Casa Calvet, and Bellesguard. These have his classic look of this time, featuring interpretation of Mudéjar (Moorish motifs), Gothic, and Baroque styles.

Palacio Episcopal

BREAKING OUT OF THE T-SQUARE PRISON

If Eusebi Güell had not believed in Gaudí's unusual approach to Modernisme, his creations might not have seen the light of day. Güell recognized that Gaudí was imbued with a vision that separated him from the crowd. That vision was his fascination with the organic. Gaudí had observed early in his career that buildings were being composed of shapes that could only be drawn by the compass and the T-square: circles, triangles, squares, and rectangles—shapes that in three dimensions became prisms, pyramids, cylinders and spheres. He saw that in nature these shapes are unknown. Admiring the structural efficiency of trees, mammals, and the human form, Gaudí noted ". . . neither are trees prismatic, nor bones cylindrical, nor leaves triangular." The study of natural forms revealed that bones, branches, muscles, and tendons are all supported by internal fibers. Thus, though a surface curves, it is supported from within by a fibrous network that Gaudí translated into what he called "ruled geometry," a system of inner reinforcement he used to make hyperboloids, conoids, helicoids, or parabolic hyperboloids.

These tongue-tying words are simple forms and familiar shapes: the femur is hyperboloid; the way shoots grow off a

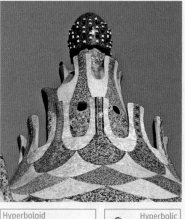

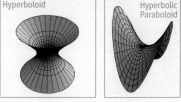

Hyperboloid

Hyperbolic Paraboloid

The top of the gatehouse in Park Güell at the main entrance; note the mushroom-like form.

branch is helicoidal; the web between your fingers is a hyperbolic paraboloid. To varying degrees, these ideas find expression in all of Gaudí's work, but nowhere are they more clearly stated than in the two masterpieces La Pedrera and Park Güell.

1900–1917

Gaudí's Golden Years—his most creative, personal, and innovative period. Topping each success with another, he tackles Park Güell, the reform of Casa Batlló, the Güell Colony church, Casa Milà (La Pedrera), and the Sagrada Família school.

Casa Batlló's complex chimneys

1918–1926

A crushing blow: Gaudí suffers the death of his assistant, Francesc Berenguer. Grieving and rudderless, he devotes himself fully to his great unfinished opus, la Sagrada Família—to the point of obsession. On June 10th, 1926, he's hit by a trolley car. He dies two days later.

La Sagrada Família

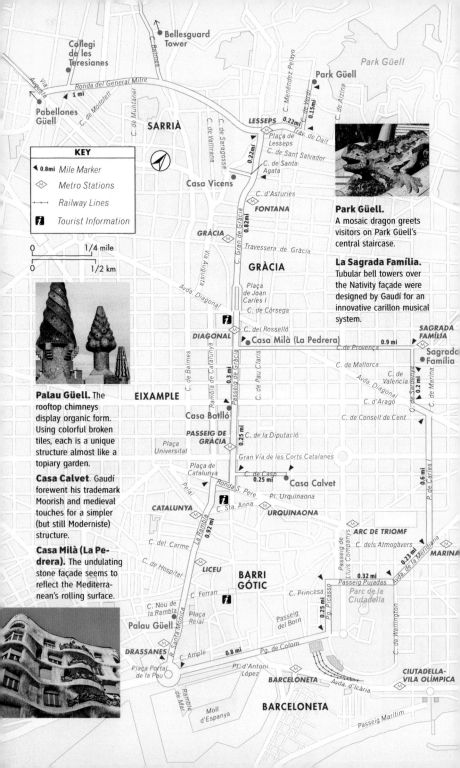

Bellesguard Tower

Collegi de les Teresianes

Park Güell

Park Güell

Ronda del General Mitre
1 mi

Pabellones Güell

SARRIÀ

LESSEPS 0.22mi

Plaça de Lesseps
C. de Sant Salvador
C. de Santa Agata

Casa Vicens

FONTANA

KEY

◀ 0.8mi *Mile Marker*

◇ *Metro Stations*

┼ *Railway Lines*

ℹ *Tourist Information*

0   1/4 mile
0   1/2 km

GRÀCIA

Travessera de Gràcia

GRÀCIA

Plaça de Joan Carles I

C. de Còrsega

ℹ

DIAGONAL

C. del Rosselló

● Casa Milà (La Pedrera)

Park Güell.
A mosaic dragon greets visitors on Park Güell's central staircase.

La Sagrada Família.
Tubular bell towers over the Nativity façade were designed by Gaudí for an innovative carillon musical system.

SAGRADA FAMÍLIA

Sagrada Família

C. de Provença 0.9 mi

C. de Mallorca

C. de València

Avda. Diagonal

C. d'Aragó

C. de Consell de Cent

Palau Güell. The rooftop chimneys display organic form. Using colorful broken tiles, each is a unique structure almost like a topiary garden.

Casa Calvet. Gaudí forewent his trademark Moorish and medieval touches for a simpler (but still Moderniste) structure.

Casa Milà (La Pedrera). The undulating stone façade seems to reflect the Mediterranean's rolling surface.

EIXAMPLE

Casa Batlló

PASSEIG DE GRÀCIA

Plaça Universitat

Plaça de Catalunya

Plaça de Catalunya

Ronda S. Pere

C. de la Diputació 0.25 mi

Gran Vía de les Corts Catalanes

C. de Casp 0.25 mi

Casa Calvet

Pl. Urquinaona

ℹ C. Sta. Anna

CATALUNYA

URQUINAONA

ARC DE TRIOMF

C. dels Almogàvers

MARINA

Passeig de Lluís Companys

C. del Carme

C. de Hospital

LICEU

BARRI GÒTIC

C. Ferran

C. Princesa

Passeig del Born

Parc de la Ciutadella

Passeig Pujades 0.32 mi

C. Nou de la Rambla

Plaça Reial

Palau Güell

DRASSANES

C. Ample 0.8 mi

Pg. de Colom

Plaça Portal de la Pau

Pl. d'Antoni López

BARCELONETA

CIUTADELLA-VILA OLÍMPICA

Moll d'Espanya

BARCELONETA

Avda. d'Icària

Passeig Marítim

HOW TO SEE GAUDÍ IN BARCELONA

Few architects have left their stamp on a major city as thoroughly as Gaudí did in Barcelona. Paris may have the Eiffel Tower, but Barcelona has Gaudí's still unfinished masterpiece, the **Temple Expiatori de la Sagrada Família**, the city's most emblematic structure. Dozens of other buildings, parks, gateways and even paving stones around town bear Gaudí's personal Art Nouveau signature, but the continuing progress on his last and most ambitious project makes his creative energy an ongoing part of everyday Barcelona life in a unique and almost spectral fashion.

(top) The serpentine ceramic bench at Park Güell, designed by Gaudí collaborator Josep Maria Jujol, curves sinuously around the edge of the open square. (bottom) Sculptures by Josep María Subirachs grace the temple of the Sagrada Família.

In Barcelona, nearly all of Gaudí's work can be visited on foot or, at most, with a couple of metro or taxi rides. A walk from **Palau Güell** near the Mediterranean end of the Rambla, up past **Casa Calvet** just above Plaça Catalunya, and on to **Casa Batlló** and **Casa Milà** is an hour's stroll, which, of course, could take a full day with thorough visits to the sites. **Casa Vicens** is a half hour's walk up into Gràcia from **Casa Milà**. **Park**

Güell is another thirty- to forty-minute walk up from that. **La Sagrada Família**, on the other hand, is a good hour's hike from the next nearest Gaudí point and is best reached by taxi or metro. The **Teresianas** school, the **Bellesguard Tower**, and **Pabellones Güell** are within an hour's walk of each other, but to get out to Sarrià you will need to take the comfortable Generalitat (FGC) train.

FLAVORS OF BARCELONA

Chockablock with celebrity chefs and starred restaurants, Catalonia has become a foodie's dream destination. But long before that, there was traditional country cooking: a lush palette of tastes and textures, including sausages and charcuterie, wild mushrooms, spring onions with romescu sauce, and hams from acorn-fed pigs from southwestern Spain, all happily paired with sparkling wines from the Penedès, or rich reds from nearby Montsant and Priorat. These are the quintessential flavors of this city.

Calçots

One of Catalonia's most beloved and authentic feasts is the winter *calçotada*: a celebration of the sweet, long-stemmed, twice-planted spring onions called *calçots*. These delicacies were originally credited to a 19th-century farmer named Xat Benaiges, who discovered a technique for extending the scallions' edible portions by packing soil around the base, giving them stockings or shoes (*calçats*), so to speak. Valls and the surrounding region now produce upward of 5 million calçots annually. Calçot feasts take place in restaurants and homes between January and March, though the season is getting longer on both ends. On the last weekend of January, the town of Valls itself holds a public calçotada, hosting as many as 30,000 people who come to gorge on onions, sausage, lamb chops, and young red wine.

Casa Félix (⊠ *Ctra. N240, Km 17, north of Tarragona* ☎ *977/601350* ⊕ *www.felixhotel.net*) is the classic Valls calçotada restaurant, with small private dining rooms encased entirely in enormous wine barrels.

L'Antic Forn (⊠ *Pintor Fortuny 28* ☎ *93/412–0286* ⊕ *www.lanticforn.com*) serves calçots in the middle of Barcelona a few steps from Plaça de Catalunya.

Restaurant Masia Bou (⊠ *Ctra. de Lleida, Km 21.5* ☎ *977/600427* ⊕ *www.masia-bou.com*) offers typical calçotades in a sprawling Valls *masia* (farmhouse) an hour and a half from Barcelona by car.

Cava

Catalan sparkling wine, called *cava*, is produced mainly in the Penedès region, 40 km (25 miles) southwest of Barcelona. Cava was created in 1872 by local winemaker Josep Raventós after the Penedès vineyards had been devastated by the phylloxera plague and the predominantly red varietals were being replaced by vines producing white grapes. Impressed with the success of the Champagne region, Raventós decided to make his own dry sparkling wine, which has since become the region's runaway success story. Cava comes in different degrees of dryness: *brut nature, brut* (extra dry), *seco* (dry), *semiseco* (medium), and *dulce* (sweet). The soil and microclimate of the Penedès region, along with the local grape varietals, give cava a slightly earthier, darker taste than its French counterpart, with larger and zestier bubbles.

La Vinya del Senyor (⊠ *Pl. de Santa Maria 5* ☎ *93/310–3379*) offers top cavas and wines by the glass from a continually changing list.

Ibérico Ham

Jamón ibérico de bellota, or ham from free-range acorn-fed Ibérico pigs, descendant from the *Sus mediterraneus* that once roamed the Iberian Peninsula, has become Spain's modern-day caviar. The meat is dark and red, and tastes of the roots, herbs, spices, tubers, and wild mushrooms of southwestern Spain. The defining characteristic of this free-range pig is its ability to store monounsaturated fats from acorns in streaks or marbled layers that run through its muscle tissue. This is one of the few animal fats scientifically proven to fight the cholesterol that clogs arteries. The tastes and aromas, after two years of aging, are so complex—so nutty, buttery, earthy, and floral—that Japanese enthusiasts have declared Ibérico ham *umami,* a word used to describe a fifth dimension in taste, in a realm somewhere beyond delicious. In addition, jamón ibérico de bellota liquefies at room temperature, so it literally melts in your mouth.

Caveats: *Jamón serrano* refers to mountain-cured ham (from *sierra*) and should never be confused with jamón ibérico de bellota. What is commercialized in the United States as Serrano ham comes from white pigs raised on cereals and slaughtered outside of Spain. *Pata negra* means "black hoof." Not all ibérico pigs have black hooves, and some pigs with black hooves are not purebred ibéricos. *Jabugo* refers only to ham from the town of Jabugo in Huelva in the Sierra de Aracena. The term has been widely and erroneously applied to jamón ibérico de bellota in general.

For heavenly ham, try one of these spots: **Café Viena** (⊠ *Rambla 115* ☎ *93/317–1492*) is famous for its *flauta de jamón ibérico* (flute or slender roll filled with tomato drizzlings and Ibérico ham), described by the *New York Times* as "the best sandwich in the world." **Mesón Cinco Jotas** (⊠ *Rambla de Catalunya 91–93* ☎ *93/487–8942*) serves a complete selection of ham and charcuterie from the famous Sánchez Carvajal artisans in the town of Jabugo, Huelva.

Sausage

Catalonia's variations on this ancient staple cover a wide range of delicacies. Typically, ground pork is mixed with black pepper and other spices, stuffed into casings, and dried to create a protein-rich, easy-to-conserve meat product. If Castile is the land of roasts and Valencia is the Iberian rice bowl and vegetable garden, Catalonia may produce the greatest variety of sausages. Below are some of the most common:

Botifarra: pork sausage seasoned with salt and pepper. Grilled and served with stewed white beans and *allioli* (garlic mayonnaise). Variations include botifarra with truffles, apples, wild mushrooms, and even chocolate.

Botifarra Blanca: typical of El Vallès Oriental just north of Barcelona, made of tripe and pork jowls, seasoned and boiled. Served as a cold cut.

Botifarra Catalana Trufada: a tender, pink-hued sausage, seasoned and studded with truffles.

Botifarra de Huevo: egg sausage with ingredients similar to botifarra but with egg yolks added.

Botifarra dolça: cured with sugar instead of salt and seasoned with spices such as cinnamon and nutmeg; served as a semi-dessert, this sausage is typical of the Empordà region.

Botifarra negra: Catalan blood sausage made with white bread soaked in pig blood with fat, salt, and black pepper.

Fuet: means "whip" for its slender shape; made of 60/40 lean meat to fat, also known as *secallona, espetec,* and *somalla.*

Llonganissa: classic pork sausage, made with 85/15 lean meat to fat, and ample salt and pepper.

Ready to cook? Try these markets:

La Botifarreria de Santa Maria (✉ *Carrer de Santa Maria 4* ☎ *93/319–9123*) next to the Santa Maria del Mar basilica stocks a compendium of Catalonia's sausages and charcuterie, along with top hams from all over Spain.

La Masia de la Boqueria (✉ *Mercat de la Boqueria* ☎ *93/317–9420*) is one of the finest charcuterie and ham specialists in the Boqueria market.

Xarcuteria Margarit (✉ *Cornet i Mas 63, Sarrià* ☎ *93/203–3323*) up in the village of Sarrià has an excellent charcuterie (*xarcuteria* or *cansaladeria* in Catalan) on Cornet i Mas just below Plaça Sant Vicenç and another in the Sarrià market on Reina Elisenda.

Wild Mushrooms

Wild mushrooms are a fundamental taste experience in Catalan cuisine: the better the restaurant, the more chanterelles, moreis, black trumpets, or mushrooms of a dozen standard varieties are likely to appear on the menu. Wild mushrooms (in Spanish *setas*, in Catalan *bolets*) are valued for their aromatic contribution to gastronomy; they impart a musty, slightly gamey taste of the forest floor—a dark flavor of decay—to the raw materials such as meat or eggs with which they are typically cooked. Many locals are proficient wild-mushroom stalkers and know how to find, identify, and prepare up to half a dozen kinds of bolets, from *rovellones* (*Lactarius deliciosus*) sautéed with parsley, olive oil, and a little garlic, to *camagrocs* (*Cantharellus lutescens*) scrambled with eggs. Wild mushrooms flourish in the fall, but different varieties appear in the spring and summer, and dried and reconstituted mushrooms are available year-round. Panlike Llorenç

Petràs retired in 2010, but his Fruits del Bosc (Forest Fruits) stall at the back of the Boqueria market is still the place to go for a not-so-short course in mycology. Petràs and his sons supply the most prestigious chefs in Barcelona and around Spain with whatever they need; if morels are scarce this year in Catalonia but abundant in, say, Wisconsin, the Petràs family will dial them in. Llorenç's book *Cocinar con Setas* (Cooking with Wild Mushrooms) is a runaway best seller presently in its 10th edition.

Petràs—Fruits del Bosc. This shop (✉ *Mercat de la Boqueria, stands 867–870 and 962–965* ☎ *93/302–5273* ⊕ *www.boletspetras. com*) in the back of the Boqueria shows and sells the finest wild-mushroom collection in Barcelona.

EXPLORING BARCELONA

Updated by
Jared Lubarsky

Between the infinite variety of street life, the nooks and crannies of the medieval Barri Gòtic, the ceramic tile and stained glass of Art Nouveau facades, and the art, music, and incredible food, one way or another, Barcelona commands your full attention.

The Catalonian capital greets the new millennium with a cultural and industrial rebirth comparable only to the late-19th-century Renaixença (Renaissance) that filled the city with its flamboyant Moderniste (Art Nouveau) buildings. An exuberant sense of style—from cutting-edge interior design to the extravagant visions of famed Postmodern architects—gives Barcelona a vibe like no other city in the world. Barcelona is Spain's most-visited city, and it's no wonder: it's a 2,000-year-old master of perpetual novelty.

What sinks in first about Barcelona is its profoundly human scale—its dogged attention, in all matters of urban development, to the quality of life. Corner buildings in the Eixample are chamfered, leaving triangles of public space at the intersections for people to stop and schmooze, and survey the passing scene. Arteries like La Rambla, Diagonal, and Rambla de Catalunya send the vehicle traffic flowing down both sides of broad leafy pedestrian promenades. Benches and pocket parks are everywhere, often with a striking piece of sculpture. You have to look hard for a building more than nine stories high: locals are reluctant to live too far up away from the street, where all the action is.

And the action never stops. Families with baby strollers are a common sight on La Rambla until well after midnight. Restaurants don't even begin to fill up for dinner until 9 or 10 pm. At 2 am, the city's bar and club scene is barely in first gear. Creative, acquisitive, and playful in equal doses, barcelonins seem to have learned to do without much sleep; they stay up late and get up early—buying and selling, planning, building, and working in fields from medical research, to "smart city" green technologies, to hospitality, in which Catalonia has established itself at the frontier.

Barcelona's present boom began on October 17, 1987, when Juan Antonio Samaranch, president of the International Olympic Committee, announced that his native city had been chosen to host the 1992 Olympics. This single masterstroke allowed Spain's so-called second city to throw off the shadow of Madrid and its 40-year "internal exile" under Franco, and resume its rightful place as one of Europe's most dynamic destinations. The Catalan administration lavished millions in subsidies from the Spanish government on the Olympics, then used the Games as a platform to broadcast the news about Catalonia's cultural and national identity from one end of the planet to the other. Madrid? Where's that? Calling Barcelona a second city of anyplace is playing with fire; its recent past as a provincial outpost is well behind it, and the city looks to the future with more creativity and raw energy than ever. More Mediterranean than Spanish, historically closer and more akin to Marseille or Milan than to Madrid, Barcelona has always been ambitious, decidedly modern (even in the 2nd century), and quick to accept the most recent innovations. (The city's electric light system, public gas system, and telephone exchange were among the first in the world.) Its democratic form of government is rooted in the so-called Usatges Laws instituted by Ramon Berenguer I in the 11th century, which amounted to a constitution. This code of privileges represented one of the earliest known examples of democratic rule; Barcelona's Consell de Cent (Council of 100), constituted in 1274, was Europe's first parliament and one of the cradles of Western democracy. The center of an important seafaring commercial empire, with colonies spread around the Mediterranean as far away as Athens, when Madrid was still a Moorish outpost on the arid Castilian steppe; it was Barcelona that absorbed new ideas and styles first. It borrowed navigation techniques from the Moors. It embraced the ideals of the French Revolution. It nurtured artists like Picasso and Miró, who blossomed in the city's air of freedom and individualism. Barcelona, in short, has always been ahead of the curve.

It must be in the air. The temperature here is almost always just right; the sky is impossibly blue; the light dazzles and transforms. Every now and then a breeze from the sea reminds you that Barcelona is, after all, a beach city and one of the great ports of Europe, still flourishing—and bewitching visitors as it has for centuries.

LA RAMBLA

Sightseeing
★★★★★
Nightlife
★★★★
Dining
★★★
Lodging
★★★★
Shopping
★★★

The promenade in the heart of pre-modern Barcelona was originally a watercourse, dry for most of the year, that separated the walled Ciutat Vella from the outlying Raval. In the 14th century, the city walls were extended and the arroyo was filled in, so it gradually became a thoroughfare where peddlers, farmers, and tradesmen hawked their wares. (The watercourse is still there, under the pavement. From time to time a torrential rain will fill it, and the water rises up through the drains.) The poet-playwright Federico García Lorca called this the only street in the world he wished would never end—and in a sense, it doesn't.

Down the watercourse now flows a river of humanity, gathered here and there around the mimes, acrobats, jugglers, musicians, puppeteers, portrait artists, break dancers, rappers, and rockers competing for the crowd's attention. Couples sit at café tables no bigger than tea trays while nimble-footed waiters dodge traffic, bringing food and drink from kitchens. With the din of taxis and motorbikes in the traffic lanes on either side of the promenade, the revelers and rubberneckers, and the Babel of languages, the scene is as animated at 3 am as it is at 3 pm.

From the rendezvous point at the head of La Rambla at Café Zurich to the Boqueria produce market, the Liceu opera house, or La Rambla's lower reaches, there is something for everyone along this spinal column of Barcelona street life.

TOP ATTRACTIONS

Fodor's Choice
★

Gran Teatre del Liceu. Barcelona's opera house has long been considered one of the most beautiful in Europe, a rival to La Scala in Milan. First built in 1848, this cherished cultural landmark was torched in 1861, later bombed by anarchists in 1893, and once again gutted by an accidental fire in early 1994. During that most recent fire, Barcelona's soprano Montserrat Caballé stood on La Rambla in tears as her beloved venue was consumed. Five years later, a restored Liceu, equipped for modern productions, opened anew. Even if you don't see an opera, you can take a tour of the building; some of the Liceu's most spectacular halls and rooms, including the glittering foyer known as the Saló dels Miralls (Room of Mirrors), were untouched by the fire of 1994, as were those of Spain's oldest social club, El Círculo del Liceu—an art deco

2

tour de force established in 1847 and restored to its pristine original condition after the fire. The Espai Liceu downstairs in the annex has a cafeteria; a gift shop with a wide selection of opera-related books and recordings; and a 50-seat video theater, where you can see a documentary history of the Liceu and a media library of recordings and films of past productions. ⊠ *La Rambla 51–59, La Rambla* ☎ *93/485–9914 express and guided tour information and reservations, 93/485–9931 premium visit reservations* ⊕ *www.liceubarcelona.cat* ⊠ *50-min guided tour €16, 45-min express tour €9, premium tours for groups up to 25 persons €550* Ⓜ *L4 Liceu.*

Fodor's Choice **La Boqueria.** Barcelona's most spectacular food market, also known as
★   the Mercat de Sant Josep, is an explosion of life and color with small tapas bar/restaurants. A solid polychrome wall of fruits, herbs, vegetables, nuts, candied fruits, cheeses, hams, fish, and poultry greets you as you turn in from La Rambla. Within this steel hangar the market occupies a neoclassical square built in 1840. The Ionic columns around the edges of the market were uncovered in 2001. Highlights include the sunny greengrocer's market outside, along with Pinotxo (Pinocchio), just inside to the right, which serves some of the best food in Barcelona. The Kiosko Universal and Quim de la Boqueria both offer delicious alternatives. Don't miss the *fruits del bosc* (fruits of the forest) stand at the back of La Boqueria, with its display of wild mushrooms, herbs, nuts, and berries. ⊠ *La Rambla 91, La Rambla* ☎ *93/318–2017 information desk, Tues.–Thurs. 8–3, Fri. and Sat. 8–5, 93/318–2584* ⊕ *www.boqueria.info* ☾ *Closed Sun.* ☞ *No entry for tour groups of 15 or more on Fri. and Sat. 8 am–3 pm* Ⓜ *Liceu.*

FAMILY **Museu Marítim.** The superb Maritime Museum is housed in the 13th-
Fodor's Choice century Drassanes Reials (Royal Shipyards), at the foot of La Rambla
★   adjacent to the harbor front. This vast covered complex launched the ships of Catalonia's powerful Mediterranean fleet directly from its yards into the port. Today these are the world's largest and best-preserved medieval shipyards. On the Avinguda del Paral·lel side of Drassanes is a completely intact section of the 14th- to 15th-century walls—Barcelona's third and final ramparts—that encircled El Raval along the Paral·lel and the Rondas de Sant Pau, Sant Antoni, and Universitat. Though the shipyards seem more like a cathedral than a naval construction site, the Maritime Museum is filled with vessels, including a spectacular collection of ship models. Perhaps the most impressive display is the life-size reconstruction of the galley of Juan de Austria, commander of the Spanish fleet in the Battle of Lepanto. Headphones and infrared pointers provide a first-rate self-guided tour. ⊠ *Av. de les Drassanes s/n, La Rambla* ☎ *93/342–9920 Ext. 121 for reservations at Norai* ⊕ *www.mmb.cat* ⊠ *€5; free Sun. after 3* Ⓜ *L3 Drassanes.*

Fodor's Choice **Palau Güell.** Gaudí built this mansion in 1886–89 for textile baron Count
★   Eusebi de Güell Bacigalupi, his most important patron. The dark facade is a dramatic foil for the brilliance of the inside, where spear-shape Art Nouveau columns frame the windows, rising to support a series of detailed and elaborately carved wood ceilings. The basement stables are famous for the "fungiform" (mushroomlike) columns carrying the weight of the whole building. Don't miss the figures of the faithful hounds, with the

Getting Oriented

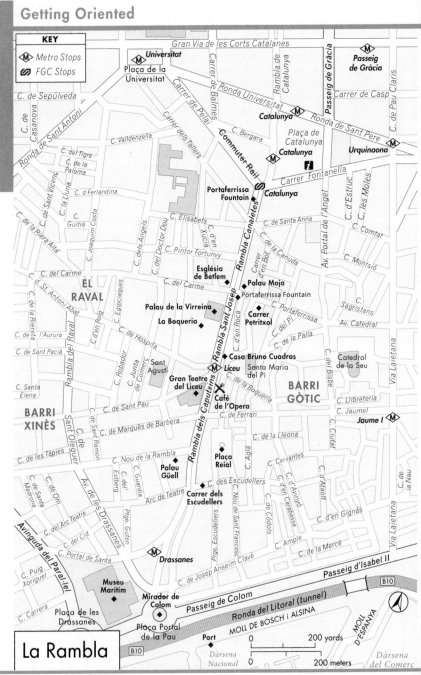

KEY

Ⓜ *Metro Stops*

Ⓕ *FGC Stops*

Gran Via de les Corts Catalanes

Universitat
Plaça de la
Universitat

C. de Sepúlveda

Ronda Universitat

Rambla de Catalunya

Passeig de Gràcia

Passeig de Gràcia

Carrer de Casp

C. de Pau Claris

C. de Casanova

Ronda de Sant Antoni

Carrer de Balmes

Carrer de Pelai

Carrer dels Tallers

Catalunya

Ronda de Sant Pere

C. Bergara

Plaça de Catalunya

Urquinaona

C. del Tigre
C. de la Paloma

C. Valldenzella

Catalunya

Carrer Fontanella

C. d'Estruc
C. les Moles

C. d Ferlandina

Portaferrissa Fountain

Catalunya

C. de Santa Anna

C. Comtat

C. de Sant Vicenç
C. la Lluna

C. Guitrè

Rambla Canaletes

Carrer d'en Bot

C. de la Canuda

C. Montsió

C. de la Riera Alta

C. Joaquim Costa

C. dels Angels

C. del Doctor Dou

C. Elisabets

C. d'en Xuclà

Av. Portal de l'Angel

EL RAVAL

C. del Carme

C. de St. Antoni Abat

C. d'en Roig

C. Egipciaques

Església de Betlem

C. del Carme

Palau Moja

Portaferrissa Fountain

C. Sagristans

C. de la Riereta

C. de l'Aurora

C. de Hospita

C. d'en Roca

Rambla Sant Josep

Palau de la Virreina

La Boqueria

Carrer Petritxol

C. Portaferrissa

C. del Pi

Av. Catedral

C. de Sant Pacià

Rambla del Raval

C. de Comerç

C. de le Palla

C. del Bisbe

Via Laietana

C. Santa Elena

C. Robador

C. Junta de Comerç

Casa Bruno Cuadros

Liceu

Santa Maria del Pi

Catedral de la Seu

BARRI GÒTIC

C. Llibreteria

Sant Agustí

Gran Teatre del Liceu

Rambla dels Caputxins

C. de la Boqueria

C. Jaumel

Jaume I

BARRI XINÈS

C. de Sant Pau

Café de l'Opera

C. de Ferran

C. de la Lleona

C. Ciutat

C. de Sant Oleguer

C. de Sant Ramon

C. de Marquès de Barbera

C. Aglà

C. Cervantes

C. d'en Carabassa

C. d'en Avinyó

C. de les Tàpies

Av. de les Drassanes

C. Nou de la Rambla

Plaça Reial

Palau Güell

C. des Escudellers

C. de Còdols

C. de la Nau

C. de Santa Madrona

C. del Estbng

C. de Guardia

Arc de Teatre

Carrer dels Escudellers

Pge. Escudellers

C. Nou de Sant Francesc

C. d'en Gignàs

Pge. Guten

C. de l'Arc Teatre

C. del Cid

Avinguda del Paral·lel

C. Portal de Santa

Drassanes

C. Ample

C. de la Mercè

Via Laietana

C. Puig Xoriguer

Museu Marítim

C. de Josep Anselm Clavé

Passeig d'Isabel II

B10

C. Carrera

Plaça de les Drassanes

Mirador de Colom

Passeig de Colom

Ronda del Litoral (tunnel)

MOLL D'ESPANYA

Plaça Portal de la Pau

B10

Port

Dàrsena Nacional

MOLL DE BOSCH i ALSINA

Dàrsena del Comerç

0   200 yards

0   200 meters

La Rambla

TIMING

Allow three to four hours, including stops, for exploring La Rambla. The best times to find things open are 9 am-2 pm and 4 pm-8 pm, although this popular promenade has a life of its own 24 hours a day. Not all museums remain open through the lunch hour—go online or ask at your nearest Tourist Information office to check. Most church hours are 9 am-1:30 pm and 4:30 pm-8 pm.

GETTING HERE

The Plaça de Catalunya metro stop will put you at the head of La Rambla in front of the Café Zurich, Barcelona's most famous rendezvous point. From here it's just a few steps down to the fountain on the right side of La Rambla de Canaletes.

QUICK BITES

Café de l'Opera. Across La Rambla from the Liceu opera house, Café de l'Opera is a favorite Barcelona hangout. The waiters are seasoned pros, the tapas come in ample portions, and the Thonet chairs and etched mirrors give the café historic charm. Always bustling, especially when a performance lets out at the Liceu, this is a place to keep a close eye on your belongings. ✉ *La Rambla 74, La Rambla* ☎ *93/317-7585* ⊕ *www.cafeoperabcn.com* Ⓜ *Liceu.*

A shipshape collection of nautical wonders is on display at the Museu Marítim.

rings in their mouths for hitching horses, or the wooden bricks laid down in lieu of cobblestones in the entryway upstairs. The passageway built toward La Rambla was all that came of a plan to buy an intervening property and connect three houses into one grand structure, a scheme that never materialized. Gaudí is most himself on the roof, where his playful, polychrome ceramic chimneys seem like preludes to later works like the Park Güell and La Pedrera. ✉ *Nou de la Rambla 3–5, La Rambla* ☎ *93/472–5771, 93/472–5775* ⊕ *www.palauguell.cat/en* ✉ *€12; free first Sun. of the month, 5–8 pm* ⊗ *Closed Mon.* ☞ *Guided tours (1 hr) in English Fri. at 2 pm at no additional cost* Ⓜ *L3 Drassanes, Liceu.*

Plaça Reial. Nobel Prize–winning novelist Gabriel García Márquez, architect and urban planner Oriol Bohigas, and Pasqual Maragall, former president of the Catalonian Generalitat, are among the many famous people said to have acquired apartments overlooking this elegant square, a chiaroscuro masterpiece in which neoclassical symmetry clashes with big-city street funk. Plaça Reial is bordered by stately ocher facades with balconies overlooking the wrought-iron **Fountain of the Three Graces,** and an array of lampposts designed by Gaudí in 1879. Cafés and restaurants—several of them excellent—line the square. Plaça Reial is most colorful on Sunday morning, when collectors gather to trade stamps and coins; after dark it's a center of downtown nightlife for the jazz-minded, the young, and the adventurous (it's best to be streetwise touring this area in the late hours). Bar Glaciar, on the uphill corner toward La Rambla, is a booming beer station for young international travelers. Tarantos has top flamenco performances, and Jamboree offers world-class jazz. ✉ *La Rambla* Ⓜ *L3 Liceu.*

Portaferrissa Fountain. Both the fountain and the ceramic representation of Barcelona's second set of walls and the early Rambla are worth studying carefully. If you can imagine pulling out the left side of the ceramic scene and looking broadside at the amber yellow 13th-century walls that ran down this side of the Rambla, you will see a clear picture of what this spot looked like in medieval times. The sandy Rambla ran along outside the walls, while the portal looked down through the ramparts into the city. As the inscription on the fountain explains, the Porta Ferrica, or Iron Door, was named for the iron measuring stick attached to the wood and used in the 13th and 14th centuries to establish a unified standard for measuring goods. The fountain itself dates to 1680; the ceramic tiles are 20th century. ⊠ *Rambla and Carrer Portaferrissa, La Rambla* Ⓜ *L3 Pl. Catalunya, Liceu.*

WORTH NOTING

Carrer dels Escudellers. Named for the *terrissaires* (earthenware potters) who worked here making *escudellas* (bowls or stew pots), this colorful loop is an interesting subtrip off La Rambla. Go left at Plaça del Teatre and you'll pass the landmark **Grill Room** at No. 8, an Art Nouveau saloon with graceful wooden decor and an ornate oak bar; next is **La Fonda Escudellers,** another lovely, glass- and stone-encased dining emporium. (Alas, the food is not especially good at either.) At Nos. 23–25 is Barcelona's most comprehensive ceramics display, **Art Escudellers.** Farther down, on the right, is **Los Caracoles,** once among the most traditional of Barcelona's restaurants and now mainly the choice of tourists with deep pockets. Still, the bar and the walk-through kitchen on the way in are picturesque, as are the dining rooms and the warren of little stairways between them. Another 100 yards down Carrer Escudellers is **Plaça George Orwell,** named for the author of *Homage to Catalonia,* a space created to bring light and air into this formerly iffy neighborhood. The little flea market that hums along on Saturday is a great place to browse.

Take a right on on the narrow Carrer de la Carabassa—a street best known in days past for its houses of ill fame, and one of the few remaining streets in the city still entirely paved with cobblestones. It is arched over with two graceful bridges that once connected the houses with their adjacent gardens. At the end of the street, looming atop her own basilica, is **Nostra Senyora de la Mercè** (Our Lady of Mercy). This giant representation of Barcelona's patron saint is a 20th-century (1940) addition to the 18th-century Església de la Mercè; the view of La Mercè gleaming in the sunlight, babe in arms, is one of the Barcelona waterfront's most impressive sights. As you arrive at Carrer Ample, note the **15th-century door** with a winged Sant Miquel Archangel delivering a backhand blow to a scaly Lucifer; it's from the Sant Miquel church, formerly part of City Hall, torn down in the early 19th century. From the Mercè, a walk out Carrer Ample (to the right) leads back to the bottom of La Rambla. The *colmado* (grocery store) on the corner as you make the turn, **La Lionesa** (Carrer Ample 21), is one of Barcelona's best-preserved 19th-century shops: a prime location for Spanish wines

CLOSE UP

Barcelona's Lovers' Day

One of the best days to spend in Barcelona is April 23: St. George's Day, La Diada de Sant Jordi, Barcelona's "Valentine's Day." A day so sweet and playful, so goofy and romantic, that 6 million Catalans go giddy from dawn to dusk.

Legend has it that the patron saint of Catalonia, the knight-errant St. George (Sant Jordi in Catalan) slew a dragon that was about to devour a beautiful princess in the little village of Montblanc, south of Barcelona. From the dragon's blood sprouted a rosebush, from which the hero plucked the prettiest blossom for the princess. Hence the traditional Rose Festival celebrated in Barcelona since the Middle Ages, to honor chivalry and romantic love, and a day for men to present their true loves with roses. In 1923 the festival merged with International Book Day to mark the anniversary of the all-but-simultaneous deaths of Miguel de Cervantes and William Shakespeare, on April 23, 1616; it then became the custom for the ladies to present their flower-bearing swains with a book in return.

More than 4 million roses and half a million books are sold in Catalonia on Sant Jordi's Day. In Barcelona, bookstalls run the length of nearly every major thoroughfare, and although it's an official workday, nearly everybody manages to duck out for at least awhile and go browsing. There is a 24-hour reading of *Don Quixote*. Authors come to bookstalls to sign their works. Given Barcelona's importance as a publishing capital, the literary side of the holiday gets special attention.

A Roman soldier martyred for his Christian beliefs in the 4th century, St. George is venerated as the patron saint of 15 European countries—England, Greece, and Romania among them. Images of St. George are everywhere in Barcelona—most notably, perhaps, on the facade of the Catalonian seat of government, the Generalitat. Art Nouveau sculptor Eusebi Arnau depicted Sant Jordi skewering the unlucky dragon on the facade of the Casa Amatller, and on the corner of Els Quatre Gats café. Gaudí referenced the story with an entire building, the Casa Batlló, with the saint's cross implanted on the scaly roof and the skulls and bones of the dragon's victims framing the windows.

Sant Jordi's Day roses are tied with a spike of wheat (for his association with springtime and fertility) and a little red and yellow *senyera*, the Catalonian flag.

In Sarrià there are displays of 45 varieties of rose, representing 45 different kinds of love, from impossible to unrequited, from platonic to filial and maternal. In the Plaça Sant Jaume the Generalitat, its patio filled with roses, opens its doors to the public. Choral groups sing love songs in the Barri Gòtic; jazz combos play in Plaça del Pi. La Rambla is packed solid from the Diagonal to the Mediterranean, with barcelonins basking in the warmth of spring and romance. Rare is the woman anywhere in town without a rose in hand, bound with a red-and-yellow ribbon that says "t'estimo": I love you.

Summer days bring strollers to Barcelona's main thoroughfare, La Rambla.

and liquors, artisanal cheeses and *charcuterie*. At No. 7 is the **Calçats Artesans Solé** shoe store, known for nearly a century for its handmade footwear. You might recognize Plaça Medinaceli, next on the left, from Pedro Almodóvar's film *Todo Sobre Mi Madre* (*All About My Mother*). ✉ *Carrer dels Escudellers* Ⓜ *L3 Drassanes*.

Carrer Petritxol. Just steps from La Rambla and one of Barcelona's most popular streets, lined with art galleries, *xocolaterías* (chocolate shops), and stationers, this narrow passageway dates back to the 15th century, when it was used as a shortcut through the backyard of a local property owner. Working up Petritxol from Plaça del Pi, stop to admire the late-17th-century *sgraffito* design (mural ornamentation made by scratching away a plaster surface), some of the city's best, on the facade over the **Ganiveteria Roca** knife store, *the* place for cutlery in Barcelona. Next on the right at Petritxol 2 is the 200-year-old **Dulcinea**, with a portrait of the great Catalan playwright Àngel Guimerà (1847–1924) over the fireplace; drop in for the house specialty, the *suizo* ("Swiss" hot chocolate and whipped cream). Also at Petritxol 2 is the **Llibreria Quera,** one of the city's best hiking and mountaineering bookstores.

Note the plaque to Àngel Guimerà over No. 4 and the **Art Box** gallery at Nos. 1–3 across the street. At No. 5 is **Sala Parès,** founded in 1840, the dean of Barcelona's art galleries, where major figures like Isidre Nonell, Santiago Russinyol, and Picasso have shown their work, and its affiliated **Galeria Trama,** which shows more contemporary work. **Xocoa** at No. 9 is another popular chocolate shop. Look carefully at the "curtains" carved into the wooden door at No. 11 and the floral ornamentation around the edges of the ceiling inside; the store is **Granja**

la Pallaresa, yet another enclave of chocolate and *ensaimada* (a light-looking but deadly sweet Majorcan pastry, with confectioner's sugar dusted on top). Finally on the left at No. 17 is the **Rigol** fine arts supply store. ✉ *Carrer Petrixol* Ⓜ *L3 Liceu, Pl. Catalunya.*

Casa Bruno Cuadros. Like something out of an amusement park, this former umbrella shop was whimsically designed (assembled is more like it) by Josep Vilaseca in 1885. A Chinese dragon with a parasol, Egyptian balconies and galleries, and a Peking lantern all reflect the Eastern style that was very much in vogue at the time of the Universal Exposition of 1888. Now housing a branch office of the Banco Bilbao Vizcaya Artentaria, this prankster of a building is much in keeping with Art Nouveau's eclectic playfulness, though it has never been taken very seriously as an expression of Modernisme and is generally omitted from most studies of Art Nouveau architecture. ✉ *La Rambla 82, La Rambla* Ⓜ *L3 Liceu.*

Església de Betlem. The Church of Bethlehem is one of Barcelona's few baroque buildings, and hulks stodgily on La Rambla just above Rambla de les Flors. Burned out completely at the start of the Civil War in 1936, the church is unremarkable inside; the outside, spruced up, is made of what looks like quilted stone. If you find this less than a must-see, worry not: you have all of Barcelona for company, with the possible exception of Betlem's parishioners. This was where Viceroy Amat claimed the hand of the young Virreina-to-be when in 1780 she was left in the lurch by the viceroy's nephew. In a sense, Betlem has compensated the city with the half-century of good works the young widow was able to accomplish with her husband's fortune. The Nativity scenes on display down the stairs at the side entrance on La Rambla at Christmastime are an old tradition here, allegedly begun by St. Francis of Assisi, who assembled the world's first such creche in Barcelona in the early 13th century. ✉ *Carrer del Carme 2, La Rambla* ☎ *93/318–3823* Ⓜ *Pl. Catalunya.*

Mirador de Colom (*Columbus Monument*). This Barcelona landmark to Christopher Columbus sits grandly at the foot of La Rambla along the wide harbor-front promenade of Passeig de Colom, not far from the very shipyards (Drassanes Reials) that constructed two of the ships of his tiny but immortal fleet. Standing atop the 150-foot-high iron column—the base of which is a swirl with gesticulating angels—Columbus seems to be looking out at "that far-distant shore" he discovered; in fact he's pointing, with his 18-inch-long finger, in the general direction of Sicily. The monument was erected for the 1888 Universal Exposition to commemorate the commissioning of Columbus's voyage in Barcelona by the monarchs Ferdinand and Isabella, in 1491. Since the royal court was at that time itinerant (and remained so until 1561), Barcelona's role in the discovery of the New World is at best circumstantial. In fact, Barcelona was consequently excluded from trade with the Americas by Isabella, so Catalonia and Columbus have never really seen eye to eye. For a bird's-eye view of La Rambla and the port, take the elevator to the small viewing platform (*mirador*) at the top of the column. The entrance is on the harbor side. ✉ *Pl. Portal de la Pau s/n, Port Olímpic* ☎ *93/302–5224* 💶 *€6* Ⓜ *L3 Drassanes.*

Palau de la Virreina (*La Virreina Centre de la Imatge*). The baroque Virreina Palace, built by a viceroy to Peru in the late 18th century, is now a major center for themed exhibitions of contemporary art, film, and photography. The **Tiquet Rambles** office on the ground floor, run by the city government's *Institut del Cultura* (ICUB), open daily 10–8:30, is the place to go for information and last-minute tickets to concerts, theater and dance performances, gallery shows, and museums. The portal to the palace, and the pediments carved with elaborate floral designs, are a must-see. ⊠ *Rambla de les Flors 99, La Rambla* ☎ *93/316–1000* ⊕ *lavirreina.bcn.cat* ⊠ *Free; €3 charge for some exhibits* ⊗ *Closed Mon.* Ⓜ *Liceu.*

Palau Moja. The first palace to occupy this corner on La Rambla was built in 1702 and inhabited by the Marquès de Moja. The present austere palace was completed in 1784 and, with the Betlem church across the street, forms a small baroque-era pocket along La Rambla. Now housing offices of the Cultural Heritage Department of the Catalan Ministry of Culture (with a Tourist Information Center on the ground floor), the Palau is normally open to the public only on rare occasions, such as special exhibitions, when visitors also have the chance to see the handsome mural and painted ceiling by Francesc Pla, the 18th-century painter known as El Vigatà (meaning "from Vic," a town 66 km (40 miles) north of Barcelona, where he was born). In the late 19th century the Palau Moja was bought by Antonio López y López, Marquès de Comillas, and it was here that Jacint Verdaguer, Catalonia's national poet and chaplain of the marquess's shipping company, the Compañia Transatlántica, wrote his famous patriotic epic poem "L'Atlàntida." ⊠ *Carrer de la Portaferrissa 1, La Rambla* ☎ *93/316–2740* Ⓜ *Pl. Catalunya.*

Port. Beyond the Columbus monument—behind the ornate Duana (now the Barcelona Port Authority headquarters)—is **La Rambla de Mar,** a boardwalk with a drawbridge designed to allow boats into and out of the inner harbor. La Rambla de Mar extends out to the **Moll d'Espanya,** with its Maremagnum shopping center, IMAX theater, and the excellent **Aquarium.** Next to the Duana you can board a Golondrina boat for a tour of the port and the waterfront or, from the Moll de Barcelona on the right, take a cable car to Montjuïc or Barceloneta. Trasmediterránea and the fleeter Buquebus passenger ferries leave for Italy and the Balearic Islands from the Moll de Barcelona; at the end of the quay is Barcelona's World Trade Center and the Eurostars Grand Marina Hotel. ⊠ *Port Olímpic* Ⓜ *Drassanes.*

THE BARRI GÒTIC

Sightseeing
★★★★★
Nightlife
★★
Dining
★★★★
Lodging
★★★
Shopping
★★★★

No city in Europe has an ancient quarter to rival Barcelona's Barri Gòtic in its historic atmosphere and the sheer density of its monumental buildings. It's a stroller's delight, where you can expect to hear the strains of a flute or a classical guitar from around the next corner. Thronged with sightseers by day, the quarter can be eerily quiet at night, a stone oasis of silence at the eye of the storm.

A labyrinth of medieval buildings, squares, and narrow cobblestone streets, the Barri Gòtic comprises the area around the Catedral de la Seu, built over Roman ruins you can still visit and filled with the Gothic structures that marked the zenith of Barcelona's power in the 15th century. On certain corners you feel as if you're making a genuine excursion back in time.

The Barri Gòtic rests squarely atop the first Roman settlement. Sometimes referred to as the *rovell d'ou* (the yolk of the egg), this high ground the Romans called Mons Taber coincides almost exactly with the early 1st- to 4th-century fortified town of Barcino. Sights to see here include the Plaça del Rei, the remains of Roman Barcino underground beneath the Museum of the History of the City, the Plaça Sant Jaume and the area around the onetime Roman Forum, the medieval Jewish Quarter, and the ancient Plaça Sant Just.

TOP ATTRACTIONS

Ajuntament de Barcelona. The 15th-century city hall on Plaça Sant Jaume faces the Palau de la Generalitat, with its mid-18th-century neoclassical facade, across the square once occupied by the Roman Forum. The Ajuntament is a rich repository of sculpture and painting by the great Catalan masters, from Marès to Gargallo to Clarà, from Subirachs to Miró and Llimona. Inside is the famous Saló de Cent, from which the Consell de Cent, Europe's oldest democratic parliament, governed Barcelona between 1373 and 1714. The Saló de les Croniques (Hall of Chronicles) is decorated with Josep Maria Sert's immense black-and-burnished-gold murals (1928) depicting the early-14th-century Catalan campaign in Byzantium and Greece under the command of Roger de Flor. Sert's perspective technique makes the paintings seem to follow you around the room. The city hall is open to visitors on Sunday mornings 10–1:30, with guided visits in English at 10; on local holidays; and for occasional concerts or events in the Saló de Cent. ⊠ *Pl. Sant Jaume 1, Barri Gòtic* ☎ *93/402-7000* ⊕ *ajuntament.barcelona.cat/en* ➡ *Free* Ⓜ *L4 Jaume I, L3 Liceu.*

Baixada de Santa Eulàlia. Down Carrer Sant Sever from the side door of the cathedral cloister, past Carrer Sant Domènec del Call and the Església de Sant Sever, is a tiny shrine, in an alcove overhead, dedicated to the 4th-century martyr Santa Eulàlia, patron saint of the city. Down this hill, or *baixada* (descent), Eulàlia was rolled in a barrel filled with—as the Jacint Verdaguer verse in ceramic tile on the wall reads—*glavis i ganivets de dos talls* (swords and double-edged knives), the final of the 13 tortures to which she was subjected before her crucifixion at Plaça del Pedró. ⊠ *Carrer Sant Sever s/n, Barri Gòtic* Ⓜ *Liceu, Jaume I.*

Casa de l'Ardiaca (*Archdeacon's House*). The interior of this 15th-century building, home of the Municipal Archives (upstairs), has superb views of the remains of the 4th-century Roman watchtowers and walls. Look at the Montjuïc sandstone carefully, and you will see blocks taken from other buildings carved and beveled into decorative shapes, proof of the haste of the Romans to fortify the site as the Visigoths approached from the north, when the Pax Romana collapsed. The marble letter box by the front entrance was designed in 1895 by Lluís Domènech i Montaner for the Lawyer's Professional Association; as the story goes, it was meant to symbolize, in the images of the doves, the lofty flight to the heights of justice and, in the images of the turtles, the plodding pace of administrative procedures. In the center of the lovely courtyard here, across from the Santa Llúcia chapel, is a fountain; on the day of Corpus Christi in June the fountain impressively supports *l'ou com balla,* or "the dancing egg," a Barcelona tradition in which eggs are set to bobbing atop jets of water in various places around the city. ⊠ *Carrer de Santa Llúcia 1, Barri Gòtic* ☎ *93/256-2255* Ⓜ *L3 Liceu, L4 Jaume I.*

Fodor's Choice ★ **Catedral de la Seu.** Barcelona's cathedral is a repository of centuries of the city's history and legend—although as a work of architecture visitors might find it a bit of a disappointment. Don't miss the beautifully carved choir stalls of the Knights of the Golden Fleece; the intricately and elaborately sculpted organ loft over the door out to Plaça Sant Iu (with its celebrated Saracen's Head sculpture); the series of 60-odd wood sculptures of evangelical figures along the exterior lateral walls of the choir; the cloister with its fountain and geese in the pond; and, in the crypt, the tomb of Santa Eulàlia. Among the two dozen ornate and gilded chapels in the basilica, pay due attention to the **Capilla de Lepanto,** dedicated to Santo Cristo de Lepanto. The leafy, palm tree–shaded **cloister** surrounds a tropical garden, and a pool populated by 13 snowwhite geese, one for each of the tortures inflicted upon St. Eulàlia in an effort to break her faith. ⊠ *Pl. de la Seu s/n, Barri Gòtic* ☎ *93/342-8262* ⊕ *www.catedralbcn.org* ➡ *Free weekdays 8–12:45 and 5:45–7:30, Sat. 8–12:45 and 5:15–8, Sun. 8–1:30 and 5:15–8; €7 donation weekdays 1–5:30, Sat. 1–5, Sun. 2–5; choir €3; rooftop €3* Ⓜ *L4 Jaume I.*

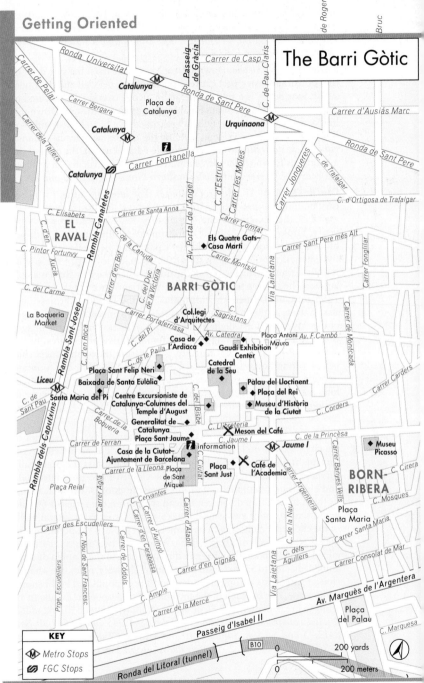

Getting Oriented

The Barri Gòtic

KEY

Ⓜ Metro Stops

Ⓢ FGC Stops

TIMING

Exploring the Barri Gòtic should take about three hours, depending on how often you stop and how long you linger. Allow another hour or two for the Museum of the History of the City. Plan to visit before 1:30 or after 4:30, or you'll miss a lot of street life; some churches are closed mid-afternoon as well.

GETTING HERE

The best way to get to the Barri Gòtic and the cathedral is to start down La Rambla from the Plaça de Catalunya metro stop. Take your first left on Carrer Canuda and walk past Barcelona's Ateneu Barcelonès at No. 6, through Plaça Villa de Madrid and its Roman tombstones, then through Passatge and Carrer Duc de la Victoria and out Carrer Boters (where the boot makers were located in medieval times) to Plaça Nova.

QUICK BITES

Café de l'Acadèmia. With its brick arches and exposed-beam ceilings, the Café de l'Acadèmia is an intimate, relaxing place for lunch or dinner, popular with government workers from nearby Plaça Sant Jaume and visitors alike. ⊠ *Carrer Lledo 1, Barri Gòtic* ☎ *93/319–8253* ⊘ *Closed weekends* Ⓜ *L4 Jaume I.*

Mesón del Café. For a coffee or tapas, look for the Mesón del Café, an amiable (if pricey) gingerbread-house-like hole in the wall steps from the Plaça Sant Jaume. ⊠ *Carrer de la Llibreteria 16, Barri Gòtic* ☎ *93/315–0754* Ⓜ *L4 Jaume I.*

TOP ATTRACTIONS

Catedral de la Seu

Els Quatre Gats–Casa Martí

Museu d'Història de la Ciutat

Plaça Sant Felip Neri

Plaça Sant Jaume

Columns of the Temple of 'Augustus

TOP EXPERIENCES

Exploring the Casa de l'Ardiaca and its 4th-century Roman walls

Wandering through El Call, the Jewish Quarter

Listening to a guitarist behind the cathedral

Lingering over a coffee at the historic Els Quatre Gats–Casa Martí

Watching *sardanas* in the Plaça de la Catedral

WHERE TO EAT (CH. 3)

Agut

Café de l'Acadèmia

Cuines Santa Caterina

La Palma

Koy Shunka

HAPPENING NIGHTLIFE (CH. 5)

Milk

Sidecar Factory Club

AREA SHOPS (CH. 7)

Art Escudellers

Ganiveteria Roca

El Call: The Jewish Quarter

Barcelona's Jewish Quarter, El Call (a name derived from the Hebrew word qahal, or "meeting place"), is just to the Rambla side of the Palau de la Generalitat. Carrer del Call, Carrer de Sant Domènec del Call, Carrer Marlet, and Arc de Sant Ramón del Call mark the heart of the medieval ghetto. Confined by law to this area at the end of the 7th century (one reason the streets in Calls or Aljamas were so narrow was that their inhabitants could only build into the streets for more space), Barcelona's Jews were the private bankers to Catalonia's sovereign counts (only Jews could legally lend money). The Jewish community also produced many leading physicians, translators, and scholars in medieval Barcelona, largely because the Jewish faith rested on extensive Talmudic and textual study, thus promoting a high degree of literacy. The reproduction of a plaque bearing Hebrew text on the corner of Carrer Marlet and

Arc de Sant Ramón del Call was the only physical reminder of the Jewish presence here until the medieval synagogue reopened as a historical site in 2003.

The **Sinagoga Major de Barcelona** (⊠ *Carrer Marlet 2, Barri Gòtic* ⊕ *www.calldebarcelona.org* ☎ *€2.50* ⊙ *weekdays 11–5:30, weekends 11–3*), the restored original synagogue at the corner of Marlet and Sant Domènec del Call, is virtually all that survives of the Jewish presence in medieval Barcelona. Tours are given in English, Hebrew, and Spanish, and a booklet in English (€3) explains the history of the community.

The story of Barcelona's Jewish community came to a bloody end in August 1391, when during a time of famine and pestilence a nationwide outbreak of anti-Semitic violence reached Barcelona, with catastrophic results: nearly the entire Jewish population was murdered or forced to convert to Christianity.

Columnes del Temple d'August (*Columns of the Temple of Augustus*). The highest point in Roman Barcelona is marked with a circular millstone at the entrance to the Centre Excursionista de Catalunya, a club dedicated to exploring the mountains and highlands of Catalonia on foot and on skis. Inside the entryway on the right are some of the best-preserved 1st- and 2nd-century Corinthian Roman columns in Europe. Massive, fluted, and crowned with the typical Corinthian acanthus leaves in two distinct rows under eight fluted sheaths, these columns remain only because Barcelona's early Christians elected, atypically, not to build their cathedral over the site of the previous temple. The Temple of Augustus, dedicated to the Roman emperor, occupied the northwest corner of the Roman Forum, which coincided approximately with today's Plaça Sant Jaume. ⊠ *Centre Excursionista de Catalunya, Carrer Paradís 10, Barri Gòtic* ☎ *93/315–2311 Centre Excursionista* Ⓜ *L4 Jaume I.*

Els Quatre Gats–Casa Martí. Built by Josep Puig i Cadafalch for the Martí family, this Art Nouveau house, a three-minute walk from the cathedral, was the fountainhead of bohemianism in Barcelona. It was here in 1897

The ornate Gothic interior of the Catedral de la Seu is always enclosed in shadows, even at high noon.

that four friends, notable dandies all—Ramon Casas, Pere Romeu, Santiago Russinyol, and Miguel Utrillo—started a café called the Quatre Gats (Four Cats), meaning to make it *the* place for artists and art lovers to gather and shoot the breeze, in the best Left Bank tradition. (One of their wisest decisions was to mount a show, in February 1900, for an up-and-coming young painter named Pablo Picasso, who had done the illustration for the cover of the menu.) The exterior was decorated with figures by sculptor Eusebi Arnau (1864–1934), a darling of the Moderniste movement—notice the wrought-iron St. George and the dragon (that no Puig i Cadafalch project ever failed to include) over the door. Inside, Els Quatre Gats hasn't changed one iota: the tile and stained glass are as they were; the bar is at it was; the walls are hung with copies of work by the original owners and their circle. (Pride of place goes to the Casas self-portait, smoking his pipe, comically teamed up on a tandem bicycle with Romeu.) Drop in for a café au lait and you just might end up seated in Picasso's chair. Venture to the dining room in back, with its unusual gallery seating upstairs; this room where Miró used to produce puppet theater is charming, but the food is nothing to rave about. *Quatre gats* in Catalan is a euphemism for "hardly anybody," but the four founders were each definitely somebody. ⊠ *Carrer Montsió 3 bis, Barri Gòtic* ☎ *93/302–4140* ⊕ *www.4gats.com* Ⓜ *Pl. Catalunya, L4 Jaume I, L4 Urquinaona.*

Generalitat de Catalunya. Opposite city hall, the Palau de la Generalitat is the seat of the autonomous Catalan government. Seen through the front windows of this ornate 15th-century palace, the gilded ceiling of the Saló de Sant Jordi (St. George's Hall), named for Catalonia's dragon-slaying patron saint, gives an idea of the lavish decor within. Carrer del Bisbe, running along the right side of the building from the square to the Cathedral, offers a favorite photo op: the ornate gargoyle-bedecked Gothic bridge overhead, connecting the Generalitat to the building across the street. The Generalitat opens to the public on the second and fourth weekends of the month, with free one-hour guided tours in English (request in advance), through the Generalitat website. The building is also open to visitors on Día de Sant Jordi (St. George's Day: April 23), during the Fiesta de la Mercé in late September, and on the National Day of Catalonia (September 11). There are carillon concerts here on Sunday at noon, another opportunity to see inside. ⊠ *Pl. de Sant Jaume 4, Barri Gòtic* ☎ *93/402–4600* ⊕ *www.gencat.cat* Ⓜ *L4 Jaume I, L3 Liceu.*

Fodor'sChoice
★ **Museu d'Història de la Ciutat** (*Museum of the History of the City (MUHBA)*). This fascinating museum just off Plaça del Rei traces Barcelona's evolution from its first Iberian settlement through its Roman and Visigothic ages and beyond. The Romans took the city during the Punic Wars, and you can tour underground remains of their Colonia Favencia Julia Augusta Paterna Barcino (Favored Colony of the Father Julius Augustus Barcino) via metal walkways. Some 4,000 square meters of archaeological artifacts, from the walls of houses, to mosaics and fluted columns, workshops (for pressing olive oil and salted fish paste) and street systems, can be found in large part beneath the Plaça. See how the Visgoths and their descendents built the early medieval walls on top of these ruins, recycling chunks of Roman stone and concrete, bits of columns, and even headstones. In the ground floor gallery is a striking collection of marble busts and funerary urns discovered in the course of the excavations. The price of admission to the museum includes entry to the other treasures of the **Plaça del Rei,** including the **Palau Reial Major,** the splendid **Saló del Tinell,** and the chapel of **Santa Àgata.** Also included are visits to other antiquarian sites maintained by the Museum: the Temple of Augustus, the Door of the Sea (the largest of the Roman-era city gates) and Dockside Thermal Baths, including the Roman Funeral Way in the Plaça de la Vila de Madrid, and the Call (medieval Barcelona's Jewish quarter). ⊠ *Palau Padellàs, Pl. del Rei s/n, Barri Gòtic* ☎ *93/256–2100* ⊕ *www.museuhistoria.bcn.cat* ⬛ *€7, includes admission to Monestir de Pedralbes, Centre d'Interpretació (Casa del Guarda) del Park Güell, Centre d'Interpretació del Call, Centre d'Interpretació Històrica, Refugi 307, and Museu-Casa Verdaguer (free with Barcelona Card, the 1st Sun. of the month and all other Sundays after 3 pm)* ⊘ *Closed Mon.* Ⓜ *L4 Jaume I, L3 Liceu.*

Fodor'sChoice
★ **Plaça del Rei.** This little square is as compact a nexus of history as any-thing the Barri Gòtic has to offer. Long held to be the scene of Colum-bus's triumphal return from his first voyage to the New World—the precise spot where Ferdinand and Isabella received him is purportedly on the stairs fanning out from the corner of the square (though evidence indicates that the Catholic monarchs were at a summer residence in the Empordá)—the **Palau Reial Major** was the official royal residence in Barcelona. The main room is the **Saló del Tinell,** a magnificent banquet

hall built in 1362. To the left is the **Palau del Lloctinent** (Lieutenant's Palace); towering overhead in the corner is the dark 15th-century **Torre Mirador del Rei Martí** (King Martin's Watchtower). The 14th-century **Capilla Reial de Santa Àgueda** (Royal Chapel of St. Agatha) is on the right side of the stairway, and behind and to the right as you face the stairs is the **Palau Clariana-Padellàs,** moved to this spot stone by stone from Carrer Mercaders in the early 20th century and now the entrance to the **Museu d'Història de la Ciutat.** ⊠ *Pl. del Rei s/n, Barri Gòtic* 🔁 *Included in the €7 entrance fee for the Museu d'Història de Barcelona (MUHBA). Free the 1st Sun. of the month and all other Sundays after 3 pm* Ⓜ *L3 Liceu, L4 Jaume I.*

Plaça Sant Felip Neri. A tiny square just behind **Plaça de Garriga Bachs** off the side of the cloister of the Catedral de la Seu, this was once a burial ground for Barcelona's executed heroes and villains, before all church graveyards were moved to the south side of Montjuïc, the present site of the municipal cemetery. The church of San Felip Neri here is a frequent venue for classical concerts. Fragments of a bomb that exploded in the square during the Civil War made the pockmarks on the walls of the church. ⊠ *Pl. Sant Felip Neri, Barri Gòtic* Ⓜ *L3 Liceu, L4 Jaume I.*

Plaça Sant Jaume. Facing each other across this oldest epicenter of Barcelona (and often on politically opposite sides as well) are the seat of Catalonia's regional government, the Generalitat de Catalunya, in the **Palau de La Generalitat,** and the City Hall, the Ayuntamiento de Barcelona, in the **Casa de la Ciutat.** This square was the site of the Roman forum 2,000 years ago, though subsequent construction filled the space with buildings. The square was cleared in the 1840s, but the two imposing government buildings are actually much older: the Ayuntamiento dates back to the 14th century, and the Generalitat was built between the 15th and mid-17th century. ⊠ *Barri Gòtic* 🕙 *Closed weekdays* ☞ *Tours of the Ayuntamiento (in English) weekends at 11; tours of the Generalitat on 2nd and 4th weekends of the month 10:30–1, by reservation only* Ⓜ *Jaume I.*

Santa Maria del Pi (*St. Mary of the Pine*). Sister church to Santa Maria del Mar and to Santa Maria de Pedralbes, this early Catalan Gothic structure is perhaps the most fortress-like of all three: hulking, dark, and massive, and perforated only by the main entryway and the mammoth rose window, said to be the world's largest. Try to see the window from inside in the late afternoon to get the best view of the colors. The church was named for the lone *pi* (pine tree) that stood in what was a marshy lowland outside the 4th-century Roman walls. An early church dating back to the 10th century preceded the present Santa Maria del Pi, which was begun in 1322 and finally consecrated in 1453. The interior compares poorly with the clean and lofty lightness of Santa Maria del Mar, but there are two interesting things to see: the original wooden choir loft, and the Ramón Amadeu painting *La Mare de Deu dels Desamparats* (*Our Lady of the Helpless*), in which the artist reportedly used his wife and children as models for the Virgin and children. The church is a regular venue for classical guitar concerts by well-known soloists. Tours of the basilica and bell tower are available in English, by reservation.

The adjoining squares, **Plaça del Pi** and **Plaça de Sant Josep Oriol,** are two of the liveliest and most appealing spaces in the Ciutat Vella, filled with much-frequented outdoor cafés and used as a venue for markets selling natural products or paintings, or as an impromptu concert hall for musicians. The handsome entryway and courtyard at No. 4 Plaça de Sant Josep Oriol across from the lateral facade of Santa Maria del Pi is the **Palau Fivaller,** now seat of the Agricultural Institute, an interesting patio to have a look through. Placeta del Pi, tucked in behind the church, has outdoor tables and is convenient for a coffee or tapas. ⊠ *Pl. del Pi 7, Barri Gòtic* ☎ *93/318–4743* ⊕ *www.basilicadelpi.com* 🔖 *Basilica and treasury-museum €4; guided tour (including the bell tower) €8.50, night visit €16* Ⓜ *L3 Liceu.*

WORTH NOTING

Col·legi d'Arquitectes. Barcelona's College of Architects, designed by Xavier Busquets and opened in 1962, houses three important gems: a superb library located across the street, where for a small fee the college's bibliographical resources are at your disposal for research; a bookstore specializing in architecture, design, and drafting supplies; and a decent restaurant (one of the city's best-kept secret lunch options for the weary explorer). The Picasso friezes on the facade of the building were designed by the artist in 1960; inside are two more, one a vision of Barcelona and the other dedicated to the *sardana,* Catalonia's traditional folk dance. The glass-and-concrete modernity of the building itself raises hackles: how could *architects,* of all people, be so blithely unconcerned—even contemptuous—about the aesthetics of accommodation to the Gothic setting around it? ⊠ *Pl. Nova 5, Barri Gòtic* ☎ *93/301–5000, 93/306–7803* ⊕ *www.coac.net* ☉ *Closed Sun.* Ⓜ *L3 Jaume I.*

Gaudí Exhibition Center (*Casa de la Pia Almoina–Museu Diocesà de Barcelona*). Set virtually into the city's ancient Roman wall, this 11th-century Gothic building, now a museum, once served soup to the city's poor; hence its popular name, the "House of Pious Alms." The museum (originally housing a collection of religious sculpture, paintings, and liturgical implements) is now dedicated to the works of the master architect Antoni Gaudí. For a tour of the Roman walls, consult the excellent relief map/scale model of Roman Barcelona in the vestibule; copies of the map and model are for sale in the nearby **Museu d'Història de la Ciutat** (Museum of the History of the City). Inside, Roman stones are clearly visible in this much-restored structure, the only octagonal tower of the 82 that ringed 4th-century Barcino. The museum is behind the massive floral iron grate in the octagonal Roman watchtower to the left of the stairs of the Catedral de la Seu. ⊠ *Av. de la Catedral 4, Barri Gòtic* ☎ *93/315–2213* ⊕ *www.gaudiexhibitioncenter.com* 🔖 *€15 (€17 with virtual reality/hologram headset and commentary)* Ⓜ *L4 Jaume I.*

Palau del Lloctinent (*Lieutenant's Palace*). The three facades of the Palau face Carrer dels Comtes de Barcelona on the cathedral side, the Baixada de Santa Clara, and Plaça del Rei. Typical of late Gothic–early

The Barri Gòtic actually sits on top of the first Roman settlement. Roman walls are visible around the edges of the neighborhood.

Renaissance Catalan design, it was constructed by Antoni Carbonell between 1549 and 1557, and remains one of the Gothic Quarter's most graceful buildings. The heavy stone arches over the entry, the central patio, and the intricately coffered wooden roof over the stairs are all good examples of noble 16th-century architecture. The door on the stairway is a 1975 Josep Maria Subirachs work portraying scenes from the life of Sant Jordi and the history of Catalonia. The Palau del Lloc-tinent was inhabited by the king's official emissary or viceroy to Barcelona during the 16th and 17th centuries; it now houses the historical materials of the Archivo de la Corona de Aragón (Archive of the Crown of Aragon), and offers an excellent exhibit on the life and times of Jaume I, one of early Catalonia's most important figures. The patio also occasionally hosts early music concerts, and during the Corpus Christi celebration is one of the main venues for the *ou com balla,* when an egg "dances" on the fountain amid an elaborate floral display. ⊠ *Carrer dels Comtes de Barcelona 2, Barri Gòtic* ☎ *93/485–4285 archives office* ⊕ *www.mecd.gob.es* Ⓜ *L4 Jaume I.*

Plaça Sant Just. Off to the left side of city hall down Carrer Hèrcules (named for the mythical founder of Barcelona) are this square and the site of the Església de Sant Just i Pastor, one of the city's oldest Christian churches. Unfortunately, nothing remains of the original church, founded in 801 by King Louis the Pious; the present structure dates to 1342. Christian catacombs are reported to have been found beneath Plaça. The Gothic fountain was built in 1367 by the patrician Joan Fiveller, then Chief Minister of the city administration. (Fiveller's major claim to fame was to have discovered a spring in the Collserola hills and had the water piped straight to Barcelona.) The fountain in the square bears an image of St. Just, and the city and sovereign count-kings' coats of arms, along with a pair of falcons. The excellent entryway and courtyard to the left of Carrer Bisbe Caçador is the Palau Moixó, the town house of an important early Barcelona family; down Carrer Bisbe Caçador is the Acadèmia de Bones Lletres, the Catalan Academy of Arts and Letters. The church is dedicated to the boy martyrs Just and Pastor; the Latin inscription over the door translates into English as "Our pious patron is the black and beautiful Virgin, together with the sainted children Just and Pastore."⊠ *Pl. Sant Just, Barri Gòtic* Ⓜ *Jaume I.*

EL RAVAL

Sightseeing
★★★★
Nightlife
★★★
Dining
★★★
Lodging
★★
Shopping
★★★

El Raval (from *arrabal*, meaning "suburb" or "slum") is the area to the west of La Rambla, on the right as you walk toward the port. Originally a rough quarter outside the second set of city walls that ran down the left side of La Rambla, El Raval was once notorious for its Barri Xinès (or Barrio Chino) red-light district, the lurid attractions of which are known to have fascinated a young Pablo Picasso.

Gypsies, acrobats, prostitutes, and *saltimbanques* (clowns and circus performers) who made this area their home soon found immortality in the many canvases Picasso painted of them during his Blue Period. It was the ladies of the night on Carrer Avinyó, not far from the Barri Xinès, who may have inspired one of the 20th-century's most famous paintings, Picasso's *Les Demoiselles d'Avignon*, an important milestone on the road to Cubism. Not bad for a city slum.

El Raval, though still rough and tumble, has been gentrified and much improved since 1980, largely as a result of the construction of the Museu d'Art Contemporani de Barcelona (MACBA) and other cultural institutions nearby, such as the Centre de Cultura Contemporània (CCCB) and the Convent dels Àngels. La Rambla del Raval has been opened up between Carrer de l'Hospital and Drassanes, bringing light and air into the streets of the Raval for the first time in a thousand years. The medieval Hospital de la Santa Creu, Plaça del Pedró, the Mercat de Sant Antoni, and Sant Pau del Camp are highlights of this funky, rough-edged part of Barcelona. The only area to consider avoiding is the lower part between Carrer de Sant Pau and the back of the Drassanes Reials shipyards on Carrer del Portal Santa Madrona.

TOP ATTRACTIONS

Fodor'sChoice
★

Antic Hospital de la Santa Creu i Sant Pau. Founded in the 10th century as one of Europe's earliest medical complexes, the mostly 15th- and 16th-century complex contains some of Barcelona's most impressive Gothic architecture. From the entrance, the first building on the left is the 18th-century **Reial Acadèmia de Cirurgia i Medecina** (Royal Academy of Surgery and Medicine). Across the way on the right is the gateway into the patio of the **Casa de la Convalescència,** where patients were moved for recuperation; it now houses the Institute for Catalan

Getting Oriented

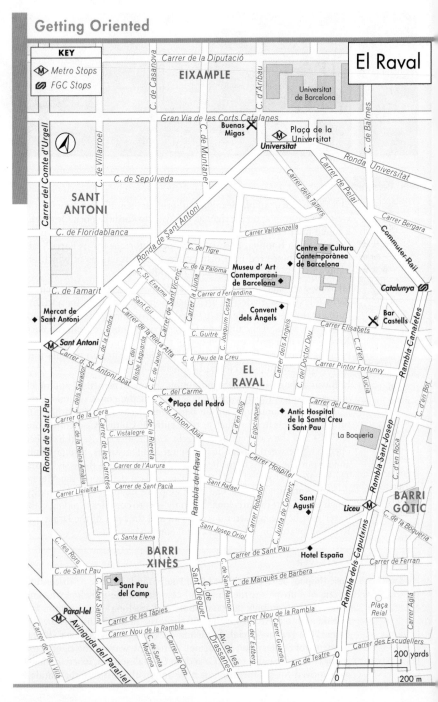

KEY
Ⓜ Metro Stops
🚇 FGC Stops

El Raval

Carrer de la Diputació

C. de Casanova

EIXAMPLE

C. d'Aribau

Universitat de Barcelona

C. de Balmes

Carrer del Comte d'Urgell

C. de Villarroel

Gran Via de les Corts Catalanes

Buenas Migas

Plaça de la Universitat

Ⓜ Universitat

Ronda Universitat

Carrer de Pelai

Carrer dels Tallers

C. de Muntaner

C. de Sepúlveda

Carrer Bergara

Commuter Rail

SANT ANTONI

C. de Floridablanca

Ronda de Sant Antoni

Carrer Valldenzella

Centre de Cultura Contemporànea de Barcelona

Catalunya 🚇

C. de Tamarit

C. del Tigre

C. de la Paloma

Museu d' Art Contemporani de Barcelona

C. St. Erasme

C. de Sant Vicenç

C. de la Lluna

Carrer d'Ferlandina

Mercat de Sant Antoni

Sant Gil

Carrer de la Riera Alta

C. de Joaquim Costa

Convent dels Àngels

Bar Castells

Carrer Elisabets

Rambla Canaletes

Ⓜ **Sant Antoni**

Carrer d. St. Antoni Abat

C. de la Cendra

Bisbe Laguarda

C. E. de Janer

C. Guitrè

C. d. Peu de la Creu

Carrer dels Àngels

C. d'en Dou

Carrer Pintor Fortunvy

C. d'en Bot

C. de Salvador

EL RAVAL

C. del Doctor Dou

Rambla de Sant Josep

C. del Carme

Plaça del Pedró

C. d. St. Antoni Abat

Antic Hospital de la Santa Creu i Sant Pau

Carrer del Carme

C. d'en Roig

Carrer de la Cera

C. d'en Roca

Carrer de la Reina Amàlia

C. de la Riereta

C. Vistalegre

C. Espicaques

La Boqueria

Carrer de les Carretes

Carrer de l'Aurura

Carrer Hospital

Carrer Lleialtat

Carrer de Sant Pacià

Rambla del Raval

Sant Rafael

Carrer Robador

Carrer Junta de Comerç

Sant Agustí

Liceu Ⓜ

BARRI GÒTIC

C. de la Boqueria

Sant Josep Oriol

C. Santa Elena

BARRI XINÈS

Sant Josep Oriol

Carrer de Sant Pau

Hotel España

Carrer de Ferran

C. de Sant Pau

Sant Pau del Camp

C. Abat Safont

C. de Sant Ramon

Sant Oleguer

C. de Sant Ramon

C. de Marquès de Barbera

Plaça Reial

Carrer Aglà

Paral·lel Ⓜ

Avinguda del Paral·lel

Carrer de les Tàpies

Carrer Nou de la Rambla

Av. de les Drassanes

C. del Esberg

Carrer Guàrdia

Carrer des Escudellers

Carrer de Vila i Vilà

Carrer Nou de la Rambla

C. de Santa Madrona

Carrer de Om

Arc de Teatre

0   200 yards

0   200 m

TIMING

The Raval covers a lot of ground. Plan on a four-hour walk or break your exploration into multiple two-hour hikes. The cloister of Sant Pau del Camp, not to be missed, is closed Monday morning, Saturday afternoon, and all day Sunday, except for during Mass.

GETTING HERE

Begin at Plaça de Catalunya, with its convenient metro stop. Walk down La Rambla and take your first right into Carrer Tallers, working your way through to the MACBA.

QUICK BITES

Bar Castells. Enjoy tapas, coffee, and other light items at Bar Castells, which has a lovely marble counter and a gorgeous wood-framed mirror behind the bar. ⊠ *Pl. Bonsuccés 1, El Raval* 🕾 *93/302–1054* ⊙ *Closed Sun.* Ⓜ *Catalunya, Liceu.*

Buenas Migas. With a tree-shaded terrace a block in from the Rambla, Buenas Migas—one of a chain of casual shops specializing in *focaccia*, salads, and pastries (the chocolate cake is to die for)—is open daily 8 am–11 pm, and until midnight on Saturdays. (*Migas* means crumbs, and the expression *hacer buenas migas* refers to new friends hitting it off.) ⊠ *Pl. Bonsuccés 6, El Raval* 🕾 *93/318–3708* Ⓜ *Catalunya, L3 Liceu.*

Skateboarders enjoy practicing in front of the Museu d'Art Contemporani de Barcelona.

Studies. Through a gate to the left of the Casa de Convalescència is the garden-courtyard of the hospital complex, the **Jardins de Rubió i Lluc,** centered on a baroque cross and lined with orange trees. On the right is the **Biblioteca de Catalunya,** Catalonia's national library. Outside, the next set of doors to the left leads to the 15th-century **Capella** (Chapel) of the Hospital, an interesting art space well worth a visit, now a showcase for promising young artists. ✉ *Carrer Hospital 56 (or Carrer del Carme 45), El Raval* ☎ *93/317–1686 Reial Acadèmia de Medecina, 93/270–2300 Biblioteca de Catalunya* ⊕ *www.bnc.cat* 🖃 *€8 per person (Royal Academy of Medicine); €25 per group (up to 25 persons) for guided tours of the Biblioteca de Catalunya* Ⓜ *L3 Liceu.*

Centre de Cultura Contemporània de Barcelona (*CCCB*). Just next door to the MACBA, this multidisciplinary gallery, lecture hall, and concert and exhibition space offers a year-round program of cultural events and projects. The center also has a remarkable film archive of historic shorts and documentaries, free to the public. Housed in the restored and renovated Casa de la Caritat, a former medieval convent and hospital, the CCCB, like the Palau de la Música Catalana, is one of the city's shining examples of contemporary flare added to traditional architecture and design. A smoked-glass wall on the right side of the patio, designed by architects Albert Villaplana and Helio Piñon, reflects out over the rooftops of El Raval to Montjuïc and the Mediterranean beyond. ✉ *Carrer Montalegre 5, El Raval* ☎ *93/306–4100* ⊕ *www.cccb.org* 🖃 *Exhibitions €6; Sun. 3–8, free. Admission to the CCCB Film Archive is free* ☉ *Closed Mon.* Ⓜ *L1/L2 Universitat, Catalunya.*

FAMILY
Fodor's Choice
★

Museu d'Art Contemporani de Barcelona (*Barcelona Museum of Contemporary Art, MACBA*). Designed by American architect Richard Meier in 1992, this gleaming explosion of light and geometry in El Raval houses a permanent collection of contemporary art, and regularly mounts special thematic exhibitions of works on loan. Meier gives a nod to Gaudí (with the Pedrera-like wave on one end of the main facade), but his minimalist building otherwise looks unfinished. That said, the MACBA is unarguably an important addition to the cultural capital of this once-shabby neighborhood. The MACBA's 20th-century art collection (Calder, Rauschenberg, Oteiza, Chillida, Tàpies) is excellent, as is the guided tour in English (daily at 4 pm, and at 4 and 6 pm on Mondays): a useful introduction to the philosophical foundations of contemporary art as well as the pieces themselves. The museum also offers wonderful workshops and activities for kids. ⊠ *Pl. dels Àngels 1, El Raval* ☎ *93/412–0810* ⊕ *www.macba.es* ☞ *€10 (valid for 1 month)* ☉ *Closed Tues.* Ⓜ *L1/L2 Universitat, L1/L3 Catalunya.*

Sant Agustí. This unfinished church is one of Barcelona's most unusual structures, with jagged stone sections projecting down the left side, and the upper part of the front entrance on Plaça Sant Agustí waiting to be covered with a facade. The church has had an unhappy history: Originally part of an Augustinian monastery, it was first built between 1349 and 1700. It was later abandoned and rebuilt only to be destroyed in 1714 during the War of the Spanish Succession, rebuilt again, then burned in the anti-religious riots of 1825 when the cloisters were demolished. The church was looted and torched once more in the closing days of the Civil War. Sant Agustí comes alive on May 22, feast day of Santa Rita, patron saint of *"los imposibles,"* meaning lost causes. Unhappily married women, unrequited lovers, and all-but-hopeless sufferers of every sort form long lines through the square and down Carrer Hospital. Each carries a rose that will be blessed at the chapel of Santa Rita on the right side of the altar. ⊠ *Pl. Sant Agustí s/n, El Raval* ☎ *93/318–3863* Ⓜ *L3 Liceu.*

Fodor's Choice
★

Sant Pau del Camp. Barcelona's oldest church was originally outside the city walls (*del camp* means "in the fields") and was a Roman cemetery as far back as the 2nd century, according to archaeological evidence. What you see now was built in 1127 and is the earliest Romanesque structure in Barcelona. Elements of the church—the classical marble capitals atop the columns in the main entry—are thought to be from the 6th and 7th centuries. The hulking mastodonic shape of the church is a reminder of the church's defensive posture in the face of intermittent Roman persecution and later, Moorish invasions and sackings. Check carefully for musical performances here, as the church is an acoustical gem. The tiny stained-glass window high on the facade facing Carrer Sant Pau may be Europe's smallest, a bookend to Santa Maria del Pi's largest. The tiny cloister is Sant Pau del Camp's best feature, and one of Barcelona's semisecret treasures. ⊠ *Carrer de Sant Pau 101, El Raval* ☎ *93/441–0001* ☞ *Free admission when Masses are celebrated; guided tour of the church and cloister €3* ☉ *Cloister closed Sun. during Mass; no tours on Sun. in mid-Aug.* Ⓜ *L3 Paral.lel.*

One of the earliest medical complexes in Europe is the Antic Hospital de la Santa Creu i Sant Pau.

WORTH NOTING

Convent dels Àngels (*La Capella*). This former Augustinian convent directly across from the main entrance to the MACBA, built by Bartolomeu Roig in the middle of the 16th century, has been converted into additional exhibition space for the MACBA, with a performing arts venue and an exhibition hall (El Fòrum dels Àngels) rented out on occasion for special events. The Fòrum dels Àngels is an impressive space, with magnificent Gothic arches and vaulted ceilings. ⊠ *Pl. dels Àngels 5, El Raval* ☎ *93/412–0810, 93/481–7922* ⊕ *www.macba.cat* Ⓜ *Pl. Catalunya, L3 Liceu.*

Hotel España. Just off La Rambla behind the Liceu Opera House on Carrer Sant Pau is the Hotel España, remodeled in 1904 by Lluís Domènech i Montaner, architect of the Moderniste flagship Palau de la Música Catalana. Completely refurbished in 2010, the interior is notable for its Art Nouveau decor. The sculpted marble Eusebi Arnau fireplace in the bar, the Ramon Casas undersea murals in the salon (mermaids singing each to each), and the lushly ornate dining room are the hotel's best artistic features. The España is so proud of its place in the cultural history of the city—and justly so—it opens to the public for 40-minute guided tours, usually twice a week. Check their website for times. (Note that tours are usually in Spanish or Catalan, but English can be requested.) ⊠ *Carrer Sant Pau 9–11, El Raval* ☎ *93/550–0000* ⊕ *www. hotelespanya.com* 🎫 *Tour €5* Ⓜ *L3 Liceu.*

Mercat de Sant Antoni. A mammoth hangar at the junction of Ronda de Sant Antoni and Comte d'Urgell, designed in 1882 by Antoni Rovira i Trias, the Mercat de Sant Antoni is considered the city's finest example of wrought iron architecture. The Greek-cross-shaped market covers an entire block on the edge of the Eixample, and some of the best Moderniste stall facades in Barcelona distinguish this exceptional space. Fully functioning as of 2017 after years of painstaking restoration to incorporate medieval archaeological remains underneath, the market is a foodie paradise of fruit, vegetables, fish, cheeses, and more. On Sunday morning, visit Sant Antoni, and wander the outdoor stalls of the weekly flea market full of stamps and coins, comic books and trading cards, VHS, CDs, vinyl, and vintage clothing. ⊠ *Carrer Comte d'Urgell s/n, El Raval* ☎ *93/426–3521* ⊕ *www.mercatdesantantoni. com* ⊗ *Closed Sun.* Ⓜ *L2 Sant Antoni.*

Plaça del Pedró. This landmark in medieval Barcelona was the dividing point where ecclesiastical and secular paths parted. The high road, Carrer del Carme, leads to the cathedral and the seat of the bishopric; the low road, Carrer de l'Hospital, heads down to the medieval hospital and the Boqueria market, a clear choice between body and soul. Named for a stone pillar, or *pedró* (large stone), marking the fork in the road, the square became a cherished landmark for Barcelona Christians after Santa Eulàlia, co-patron of Barcelona, was crucified there in the 4th century after suffering the legendary 13 ordeals designed to persuade her to renounce her faith—which, of course, she heroically refused to do. As the story goes, an overnight snowfall chastely covered her nakedness with virgin snow. The present version of Eulàlia and her cross was sculpted by Barcelona artist Frederic Marès and erected in 1951. The bell tower and vacant alcove at the base of the triangular square belong to the **Capella de Sant Llàtzer** church, originally built in the open fields in the mid-12th century and used as a leper hospital and place of worship after the 15th century when Sant Llàtzer (Saint Lazarus) was officially named patron saint of lepers. Flanked by two ordinary apartment buildings, the Sant Llàtzer chapel has a tiny antique patio and apse visible from the short Carrer de Sant Llàtzer, which cuts behind the church between Carrer del Carme and Carrer Hospital. ⊠ *Pl. del Pedró, El Raval* Ⓜ *L2 Sant Antoni.*

SANT PERE AND LA RIBERA

Sightseeing
★★★★★
Nightlife
★★★★★
Dining
★★★★★
Lodging
★★★★
Shopping
★★★★★

The textile and waterfront neighborhoods are home to some of the city's most iconic buildings, from the Gothic 14th-century basilica of Santa Maria del Mar to the over-the-top Moderniste Palau de la Música Catalana. At the Museu Picasso, works of the 20th-century master are displayed in five adjoining Renaissance palaces.

Sant Pere, Barcelona's old textile neighborhood, is centered on the church of Sant Pere. A half mile closer to the port, the Barri de la Ribera and the former market of El Born, now known as the Born-Ribera district, were at the center of Catalonia's great maritime and economic expansion of the 13th and 14th centuries. Surrounding the basilica of Santa Maria del Mar, the Born-Ribera area includes Carrer Montcada, lined with 14th- to 18th-century Renaissance palaces; Passeig del Born, where medieval jousts were held; Carrer Flassaders and the area around the early mint; the antiques shop- and restaurant-rich Carrer Banys Vells; Plaça de les Olles; and Pla del Palau, where La Llotja, Barcelona's early maritime exchange, housed the fine-arts school where Picasso, Gaudí, and Domènech i Montaner all studied, as did many more of Barcelona's most important artists and architects.

Long a depressed neighborhood, La Ribera began to experience a revival in the 1980s; now replete with intimate bars, cafés, and trendy boutiques, it continues to enjoy the blessings of gentrification. An open excavation in the center of El Born, the onetime market restored as a multipurpose cultural center, offers a fascinating view of pre-1714 Barcelona, dismantled by the victorious troops of Felipe V at the end of the War of the Spanish Succession. The Passeig del Born, La Rambla of medieval Barcelona, is once again a pleasant leafy promenade.

TOP ATTRACTIONS

Fossar de les Moreres (*Cemetery of the Mulberry Trees*). This low marble monument runs across the eastern side of the church of Santa Maria del Mar. It honors defenders of Barcelona who gave their lives in the final siege that ended the War of the Spanish Succession on September 11, 1714. The inscription (in English: "in the cemetery of the mulberry trees no traitor lies") refers to the graveyard keeper's story. He refused to bury those on the invading side, even when one turned out to be his son. This is the traditional gathering place for the most radical elements of Catalonia's nationalist (separatist) movement, on the Catalonian national day, which celebrates the heroic defeat.

From the monument, look back at Santa Maria del Mar. The lighter-color stone on the lateral facade was left by the 17th-century Pont del Palau (Palace Bridge), erected to connect the Royal Palace in the nearby Pla del Palau with the Tribuna Real (Royal Box) over the right side of the Santa Maria del Mar altar, so that nobles and occupying military officials could get to Mass without the risk of walking in the streets. The bridge, regarded as a symbol of imperialist oppression, was finally dismantled in 1987. The steel arch with its eternal flame was erected in 2002. ⊠ *Pl. de Santa Maria, Born-Ribera* Ⓜ *L4 Jaume I.*

La Llotja (*Maritime Exchange*). Barcelona's maritime trade center, the Casa Llotja de Mar, was designed to be the city's finest example of civil architecture, built in the Catalan Gothic style between 1380 and 1392. At the end of the 18th century the facades were (tragically) covered in the neoclassical uniformity of the time, but the interior, the great Saló Gòtic (Gothic Hall), remained unaltered, and was a grand venue for balls and celebrations throughout the 19th century. The Gothic Hall was used as the Barcelona stock exchange until 1975, and until late 2001 as the grain exchange. The hall, with its graceful arches and columns and floors of light Carrara and dark Genovese marble, has now been brilliantly restored. The building, which is not typically open to the general public, now houses the Barcelona Chamber of Commerce.

The Escola de Belles Arts (School of Fine Arts) occupied the southwestern corner of the Llotja from 1849 until 1960. Many illustrious Barcelona artists studied here, including Gaudí, Miró, and Picasso. The **Reial Acadèmia Catalana de Belles Arts de Sant Jordi** (Royal Catalan Academy of Fine Arts of St. George) still has its seat in the Llotja, and its museum is one of Barcelona's semisecret collections of art, from medieval paintings by unknown artists to modern works by members of the Academy itself; a 17th-century *Saint Jerome* by Joan Ribalta is especially fine. To slip into the Saló Gòti, walk down the stairs from the museum to the second floor, then take the marble staircase down and turn right. Guided visits to the museum collection (free) are offered for groups of 10–25 persons. ⊠ *Casa Llotja, Passeig d'Isabel II, 1, Born-Ribera* ☎ *93/319–2432 Reial Acadèmia, 670/466260 guided visits to museum* ⊕ *www.racba.org* 🎫 *Free* ⊙ *Museum closed weekends* Ⓜ *L4 Barceloneta.*

Mercat de Santa Caterina. This marketplace, a splendid carnival of colors with a roller-coaster rooftop, was restored by the late Enric Miralles, whose widow Benedetta Tagliabue finished the project in 2005. Undulating wood and colored-ceramic mosaic ceilings redolent of both Gaudí and Miró cover a bustling and dramatically illuminated market which features the must-try restaurant, Cuines de Santa Caterina (☎ 93/268–9918), and several good bars and cafés. The archaeological section of the building is at the eastern end, showing Visigothic remains and sections of the 13th-century church and convent that stood here until the early 18th century. ⊠ *Av. Francesc Cambó 16, Born-Ribera* ☎ *93/319–5740* ⊕ *www.mercatsantacaterina.com* Ⓜ *L4 Jaume I, Urquinaona.*

Getting Oriented

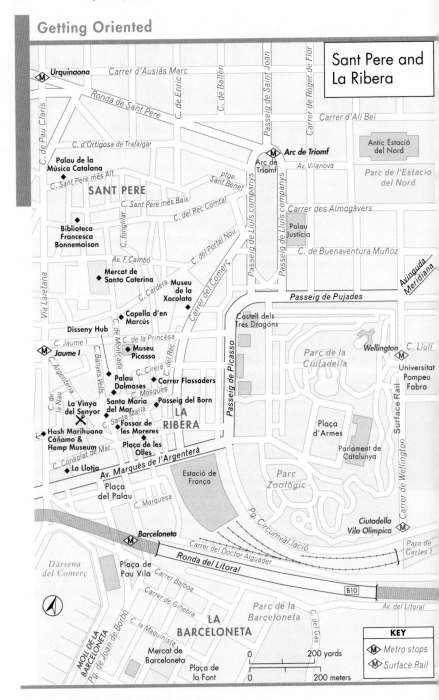

Sant Pere and La Ribera

Ⓜ Urquinaona
Carrer d'Ausiás Marc
Ronda de Sant Pere
C. de Enric
C. de Ballen
Passeig de Sant Joan
Carrer de Roger de Flor

C. de Pau Claris
C. d'Ortigosa de Trafalgar
Carrer d'Alí Bei

◆ Palau de la
Música Catalana
C. Sant Pere més Alt

SANT PERE

Arc de
Triomf
Ⓜ **Arc de Triomf**
Av. Vilanova

Antic Estació
del Nord

Parc de l'Estacio
del Nord

ptge.
Sant Benet
C. Sant Pere més Baix
C. del Rec Comtal

◆ Biblioteca
Francesca
Bonnemaison

C. Jongillar

C. del Portal Nou

Passeig de Lluís companys
Passeig de Lluís companys

Carrer des Almogàvers

Palau
Justícia

Av. F. Cambó

C. de Buenaventura Muñoz

Via Laietana

◆ Mercat de
Santa Caterina

C. Carders

Museu
de la
Xocolata

Passeig de Pujades

Avinguda
Meridiana

◆ Capella d'en
Marcús

Castell dels
Tres Dragóns

Wellington   Ⓜ   C. Llull

Disseny Hub

C. de la Princèsa

◆ Museu
Picasso

C. del Rec

Passeig de Picasso

Parc de la
Ciutadella

Universitat
Pompeu
Fabra

Ⓜ Jaume I
C. Jaume I
C. Argenteria
C. Banyes Vells

C. Cirera

◆ Palau
Dalmases

◆ Carrer Flassaders

C. de la Nau

C. Mosques

C. Montcada

La Vinya
del Senyor ✕
Santa Maria
del Mar

Passeig del Born

**LA
RIBERA**

Plaça
d'Armes

◆ Hash Marihuana
Cáñamo &
Hemp Museum

C. Santa Maria

◆ Fossar de
les Moreres

Surface Rail

Parlament de
Catalunya

C. Consolat de Mar

Plaça de les
Olles

Ciutadella
Vila Olimpica   Ⓜ

Carrer de Wellington

◆ La Llotja

Av. Marquès de l'Argenterá

Estació de
França

Parc
Zoològic

Parc de
Carles I

Plaça
del Palau

C. Marquesa

Pg. Circumval.lació

Ⓜ Barceloneta

Carrer del Doctor Aiguader

B10

Av. del Litoral

Dàrsena
del Comerç

Plaça de
Pau Vila

Carrer Balboa

Ronda del Litoral

Ronda del Litoral

Carrer de Ginebra

Parc de la
Barceloneta

C. del Gas

MOLL DE LA
BARCELONETA

Pg. de Joan de Borbó

C. la Maquinista

**LA
BARCELONETA**

Mercat de
Barceloneta

Plaça de
la Font

0   200 yards
0   200 meters

KEY	
Ⓜ	*Metro stops*
Ⓜ	*Surface Rail*

TIMING

Depending on the number of museum visits and stops, exploring these neighborhoods can take a full day. Count on at least four hours of actual walking time. Catching Santa Maria del Mar open is key (it's closed daily 1:30–4:30). If you make it to Cal Pep for tapas before 1:30, you might get a place at the bar; if you don't, it's well worth the wait. The Picasso Museum is at least a two-hour visit.

GETTING HERE

From the central Plaça de Catalunya metro hub, it's a 10-minute walk over and down to the Palau de la Música Catalana for the beginning of this tour. The yellow L4 metro stop at Jaume I is closer to Santa Maria del Mar, but it's a hassle if you have to change trains; Plaça de Catalunya is close enough, and makes for a pleasant stroll.

QUICK BITES

La Vinya del Senyor. Relax on the patio of La Vinya del Senyor and sample top wines from around the world. Must-tries include Spanish reds from Montsant, Priorat and Rioja, best enjoyed by the glass, along with light tapas like the Ibérico ham. ⊠ *Pl. de Santa Maria 5, Born-Ribera* ☎ *93/310–3379* Ⓜ *L4 Jaume I.*

TOP ATTRACTIONS

Museu Picasso

Palau de la Música Catalana

Santa Maria del Mar

TOP EXPERIENCES

Grazing on counter food at Cal Pep

Feasting your eyes at the Mercat de Santa Caterina

Going to a concert in the Palau de la Musica Caterina

Browsing for exotic foodstuffs at the 150-year-old Casa Gispert

Attending a requiem Mass in Santa Maria del Mar

WHERE TO EAT (CH. 3)

Cal Pep

El Passadís d'en Pep

La Báscula de la Cerería

Sagardi

HAPPENING NIGHTLIFE (CH. 5)

Paspartu

Rubi Bar

2

FAMILY **Museu de la Xocolata.** The elaborate, painstakingly detailed chocolate sculptures, which have included everything from La Sagrada Família to Don Quixote's windmills, delight both youthful and adult visitors to this museum, set in an imposing 18th-century former monastery and developed by the Barcelona Provincial Confectionery Guild. Other exhibits here touch on Barcelona's centuries-old love affair with chocolate, the introduction of chocolate to Europe by Spanish explorers from the Mayan and Aztec cultures in the New World, and both vintage and current machinery and tools used to create this sweet delicacy. The beautiful shop and café offers rich hot and cold chocolate drinks, boxes and bars of artisanal chocolate, and house-made cakes and pastries. Classes on making and tasting chocolate are offered, too. ⊠ *Carrer del Comerç 36, Born-Ribera* ☎ *93/268–7878* ⊕ *www.museuxocolata.cat* 🎟 *€6* Ⓜ *L4 Jaume 1, L1 Arc de Triomf.*

Fodor'sChoice **Museu Picasso** (*Picasso Museum*). The Picasso Museum is housed in five
★ adjoining palaces on Carrer Montcada, a street known for Barcelona's most elegant medieval palaces. Picasso spent his key formative years in Barcelona (1895–1904), and this collection, while it does not include a significant number of the artist's best paintings, is particularly strong on his early work. Displays include childhood sketches, works from Picasso's Rose and Blue periods, and the famous 1950s Cubist variations on Velázquez's *Las Meninas* (in Rooms 22–26). The lower-floor sketches, oils, and schoolboy caricatures and drawings from Picasso's early years in A Coruña are perhaps the most fascinating part, showing the facility the artist seemed to possess almost from the cradle. On the second floor are works from his Blue Period in Paris, a time of loneliness, cold, and hunger for the artist. ■TIP→ **Admission is free the first Sunday of the month. Arrive early to avoid the long lines and crowds.** ⊠ *Carrer Montcada 15–19, Born-Ribera* ☎ *93/256–3000, 93/256–3022 guided tour and group reservations* ⊕ *www.museupicasso.bcn.cat* 🎟 *€11; free Sun. 3–7, and 1st Sun. of month all day* ⊙ *Closed Mon.* ⟳ *Guided tours of permanent collection (in English) Sun. at 11 (except Aug.) free with admission* Ⓜ *L4 Jaume I, L1 Arc de Triomf.*

Palau Dalmases. If you can get through the massive wooden gates that open onto Carrer Montcada (at the moment, the only opportunity is when the first-floor café-theater Espai Barroc is open) you'll find yourself in Barcelona's best 17th-century Renaissance courtyard, built into a former 15th-century Gothic palace. Note the door knockers up at horseback level; then take a careful look at the frieze of "The Rape of Europa" running up the stone railing of the elegant stairway at the end of the patio. It's a festive abduction: Neptune's chariot, cherubs, naiads, dancers, tritons, and musicians accompany Zeus, in the form of a bull, as he carries poor Europa up the stairs and off to Crete. The stone carvings in the courtyard, the 15th-century Gothic chapel, with its reliefs of angelic musicians, and the vaulting in the reception hall and salon, are all that remain of the original 15th-century palace. Espai Barroc, on the ground floor, is a café-theater (flamenco, jazz, opera *concertante*) with baroque-era flourishes, period furniture, and musical performances. ⊠ *Carrer Montcada 20, Born-Ribera* ☎ *93/310–0673 Espai Barroc* ⊕ *palaudalmases.com* 🎟 *Shows €25 (includes 1 drink)* Ⓜ *L4 Jaume I.*

FodorśChoice **Palau de la Música Catalana.** One of the world's most extraordinary
★ music halls, with facades that are a riot of color and form, the Music
Palace is a landmark of Carrer Amadeus Vives, set just across Via
Laietana, a five-minute walk from Plaça de Catalunya. The Palau is
a flamboyant tour de force designed in 1908 by Lluís Domènech i
Montaner. Originally conceived by the Orfeó Català musical society
as a vindication of the importance of music at a popular level—as
opposed to the Liceu opera house's identification with the Catalan
aristocracy—the Palau and the Liceu were for many decades opposing crosstown forces. The exterior is remarkable in itself. The Miquel
Blay sculptural group is Catalonia's popular music come to life, with
everyone included from St. George the dragon slayer to women and
children, fishermen, and every strain and strata of popular life and
music. The Palau's over-the-top decor overwhelms the senses even
before the first note of music is heard. ⊠ *Carrer Sant Pere Més Alt
4–6, Sant Pere* ☎ *93/295-7200, 902/442882 box office* ⊕ *www.pal-
aumusica.cat* ◺ *Tour €18* Ⓜ *L1/L4 Urquinaona.*

FodorśChoice **Passeig del Born.** Once the site of medieval jousts and autos-da-fé of
★ the Inquisition, the passeig, at the end of Carrer Montcada behind the
church of Santa Maria del Mar, was early Barcelona's most important
square. Late-night cocktail bars and miniature restaurants with tiny
spiral stairways now line the narrow, elongated plaza. The numbered
cannonballs under the public benches are the work of the "poet of
space"—a 20th-century specialist in combinations of letters, words, and
sculpture—the late Joan Brossa. The cannonballs evoke the 1714 siege
of Barcelona that concluded the 14-year War of the Spanish Succession, when Felipe V's conquering Castilian and French troops attacked
the city ramparts at their lowest, flattest flank. After their victory, the
Bourbon forces obliged residents of the Barri de la Ribera (Waterfront
District) to tear down nearly a thousand of their own houses, some 20%
of Barcelona at that time, to create fields of fire so that the occupying
army of Felipe V could better train its batteries of cannon on the conquered populace and discourage any nationalist uprisings. Thus began
Barcelona's "internal exile" as an official enemy of the Spanish state.

Walk down to the Born itself—a great iron hangar, once a produce
market designed by Josep Fontseré, in the Plaça Comercial, across the
street from the end of the promenade. The initial stages of the construction of a public library in the Born uncovered the remains of the lost
city of 1714, complete with blackened fireplaces, taverns, wells, and
the canal that brought water into the city. The Museu d'Història de la
Ciutat opened a museum here in 2013, the El Born Centre de Cultura
i Memòria, kicking off a year of events concluding with the September
11, 2014, commemoration of Barcelona's defeat. The streets of the
14th- to 18th-century Born-Ribera lie open in the sunken central square
of the old market; around it, on the ground level, are a number of new
multifunctional exhibition and performance spaces; these give the city
one of its newest and liveliest cultural subcenters. ⊠ *Passeig del Born,
Born-Ribera* ☎ *93/256-6851 El Born Centre de Cultura i Memòria*
⊕ *elbornculturaimemoria.barcelona.cat* ◺ *Free to upper galleries, €6
to the archaeological site* ⊙ *Closed Mon.* Ⓜ *L4 Jaume I/Barceloneta.*

A wooden door leads to Barcelona's best 17th-century patio in the Palau Dalmases.

Fodor's Choice **Santa Maria del Mar.** The most beautiful example of early Catalan Gothic
★ architecture, Santa Maria del Mar is extraordinary for its unbroken
lines and elegance. The lightness of the interior is especially surprising
considering the blocky exterior. The site was home to a Christian cult
from the late 3rd century. Built by a mere stonemason who chose, fitted,
and carved each stone hauled down from a Montjuïc quarry, the church
is breathtakingly and nearly hypnotically symmetrical. The medieval
numerological symbol for the Virgin Mary, the number eight (or mul-
tiples thereof) runs through every element of the basilica. Although anticlerical anarchists burned the basilica in 1936, it was restored after the
end of the Spanish civil war by Bauhaus-trained architects. Set aside at
least a half hour to see Santa Maria del Mar. *La Catedral del Mar (The
Cathedral of the Sea)* by Ildefonso Falcons chronicles the construction
of the basilica and 14th-century life in Barcelona. Check the schedule for concerts. ⊠ *Pl. de Santa Maria 1, Born-Ribera* ☎ *93/310–2390*
⊕ *www.santamariadelmarbarcelona.org* ⌑ *Guided tour €10, includes
rooftop and crypt* Ⓜ *L4 Jaume I.*

WORTH NOTING

Biblioteca Francesca Bonnemaison (*Women's Public Library*). Barcelona's
(and probably the world's) first library established exclusively for
women, the *Biblioteca Popular de la Dona* was founded in 1909, evidence of the city's early-20th-century progressive attitudes and tenden-
cies. Over the opulently coffered main reading room, the stained-glass
skylight reads "Tota dona val mes quan letra apren" (Any woman's
worth more than she learns how to read), the first line of a ballad by

Picasso's Barcelona

The city's claim to Pablo Picasso (1881–1973) has been contested by Málaga (the painter's birthplace), as well as by Madrid, where *La Guernica* hangs, and by the town of Gernika, victim of the 1937 Luftwaffe saturation bombing that inspired the famous canvas. Fervently anti-Franco, Picasso refused to return to Spain after the Civil War; in turn, the regime allowed no public display of his work until 1961, when the artist's *Sardana* frieze on Barcelona's Architects' Guild building was unveiled. Picasso never set foot on Spanish soil for his last 39 years.

Picasso spent a sporadic but formative period of his youth in Barcelona between 1895 and 1904, after which he moved to Paris. His father was an art professor at the Reial Acadèmia de Belles Arts in La Llotja—where his son, a precocious draftsman, began advanced classes at the age of 15. The 19-year-old Picasso first exhibited at Els Quatre Gats, a tavern on Carrer Montsió that looks today much as it

did then. His early Cubist painting *Les Demoiselles d'Avignon* was inspired not by the French town but by the Barcelona street Carrer d'Avinyó, then infamous for its brothels. After moving to Paris, Picasso returned occasionally to Barcelona until his last visit in 1934. Considering the artist's off-and-on tenure, it is remarkable that the city and Picasso should be so intertwined in the world's perception. The Picasso Museum, deservedly high on the list of the city's must-see attractions, is perhaps fourth (after the Miró, the MNAC, and the MACBA) on any connoisseur's roster of Barcelona art collections.

Iconoserveis Culturals (✉ *Av. Portal de l'Àngel 38, 4°–2ª, Born-Ribera* ☎ *93/410–1405* ⊕ *www.iconoser-veis.com*) will arrange walking tours through the key spots in Picasso's Barcelona life, covering studios, galleries, family apartments, and the painter's favorite haunts and hangouts.✍ *Groups up to 25: €237 plus museum entrance fees.*

the 13th-century Catalan troubadour Severí de Girona. Once Franco's Spain composed of church, army, and oligarchy had restored law and order after the Spanish civil war, the center was taken over by Spain's one legal political party, the Falange, and women's activities were reoriented toward more domestic pursuits such as sewing and cooking. Today the library complex includes a small theater and offers a lively program of theatrical and cultural events. ✉ *Centro de Cultura, Carrer Sant Pere Més Baix 7, Sant Pere* ☎ *93/268–7360* ⊕ *www.barcelona.cat/bibfbonnemaison.cat* ⊙ *Closed Sun.* Ⓜ *L1/L4 Urquinaona.*

Capella d'en Marcús (*Marcús Chapel*). This Romanesque hermitage looks as if it had been left behind by some remote order of hermit-monks who meant to take it on a picnic in the Pyrenees. The tiny chapel, possibly—along with Sant Llàtzer—Barcelona's smallest religious structure, and certainly one of its oldest, was originally built in the 12th century on the main Roman road into Barcelona, the one that would become Cardo Maximo just a few hundred yards away as it passed through the walls at Portal de l'Àngel. Bernat Marcús, a wealthy merchant concerned with public welfare and social issues, built a hospital here for poor travelers; the hospital chapel that bears his name was dedicated to the Mare de Déu de la Guia (Our Lady of the Guide). As a result of its affiliation, combined with its location on the edge of town, the chapel eventually became the headquarters of the Confraria del Correus a Cavall (Brotherhood of the Pony Express), also known as the *troters* (trotters), that made Barcelona the key link in overland mail between the Iberian Peninsula and France. ⊠ *Carrer Carders 2 (Placeta d'en Marcús), Born-Ribera* ☎ *93/310–2390* Ⓜ *Jaume I.*

Carrer Flassaders. Named for the weavers and blanket makers whom this street belonged to in medieval times, Carrer Flassaders begins on Carrer Montcada opposite La Xampanyet, one of La Ribera's most popular bars for tapas and cava. Duck into the short, dark Carrer Arc de Sant Vicenç; at the end you'll find yourself face to face with **La Seca,** the Royal Mint (officially, the *Reial Fàbrica de la Moneda de la Corona d'Aragó*), where money was manufactured until the mid-19th century. Coins bearing the inscription, in Castilian, "Principado de Cataluña" (Principality of Catalonia) were minted here as late as 1836. La Seca has been exquisitely restored, with the original wooden beams, pillars, and brickwork intact; it's now home to a small avant-garde repertory theater company called Espai Brossa. Adjacent is the studio and showroom of internationally acclaimed sculptor Manel Alvarez.

Turn left on Carrer de la Seca to Carrer de la Cirera; overhead to the left is the image of **Santa Maria de Cervelló**, one of the patron saints of the Catalan fleet, on the back of the Palau Cervelló on Carrer Montcada. Turn right on Carrer de la Cirera past the Otman shop and tearoom, and arrive at the corner of **Carrer dels Flassaders.** Walk left past several shops—**Re-Born** at Flassaders 23; cozy **La Báscula** café in the former candy factory at No. 30; the upbeat food court **Mercat Princesa** at No. 21; and the gourmet **Montiel** restaurant at No. 19. Wander down Flassaders through a gauntlet of elegant clothing, furnishings, and jewelry design boutiques, and you'll pass the main entry to La Seca at No. 40, with the gigantic Bourbon coat of arms over the imposing archway. At No. 42 is **Loisaida** (vintage clothing and curios: the name is Spanglish for the Lower East Side in New York City). The stylish Cortana clothing store is across the street. Look up to your right at the corner of the gated Carrer de les Mosques, famous as Barcelona's narrowest street. The mustachioed countenance peering down at you was once a medieval advertisement for a brothel. **Hofmann,** at No. 44, is the excellent pastry shop of famous Barcelona chef Mey Hofmann, whose cooking school is over on nearby Carrer Argenteria. (Don't pass up the mascarpone croissants.) A right on Passeig del Born will take you back to Santa Maria del Mar. ⊠ *Carrer Flassaders, Born-Ribera* Ⓜ *Jaume I.*

Fodor's Choice ★ **Disseny Hub.** This center of activity represents the efforts of Barcelona's urban planners to put all the city's designer eggs in one basket and to plant an eye-catching architectural anchor in the long-delayed renewal project on Plaça de les Glòries. The new building is home to no less than four museum collections: the **Museu de Arts Tèxtil i Indumentària** (Textiles and Clothing Museum) of fashion, embroidery, jewelry, and accessories from ancient times to modern *haute couture*;

the **Museu de Ceràmica** (Ceramics Museum), tracing the evolution of ceramic arts from 13th-century Moorish influences to the present, with a number of pieces by Miró and Picasso; the **Museu de les Arts Decoratives** (Museum of Decorative Arts), devoted mainly to the historical high arts of furniture and furnishings; and the **Gabinet de les Arts Gràfiques** (Graphic Arts Collection) of posters, packaging, typographic styles, and printed papers. The DHUB store has a fine selection of books on design as well as reproductions that make great gifts to take home. The building itself, by MBM Arquitectes (Oriol Bohigas, doyen of the firm, was the prime mover in much of Barcelona's makeover for the 1992 Olympics), juts out like a multistoried wedge into the Plaça de les Glòries, anchoring a traffic hub where the Diagonal meets the Avenida Meridiana. Originally built to be the new city center, the Glòries (designed by Eixample architect Ildefons Cerdà) had been run-down and unnavigable for decades. Next door to the Hub is the **Mercat dels Encants** open-air flea market (open Monday, Wednesday, Friday, and Saturday 9–8), Barcelona's biggest, reborn in the same project that produced the museum, with a whimsical, undulating mirrored roof. The Mercat is prime grazing land for old furniture, vintage clothing, and bric-a-brac of all sorts. ⊠ *Edific DHUB, Pl. de les Glòries Catalans 37–8, Sant Martí* ☏ *93/256–6800* ⊕ *www.museudeldisseny.cat* ✉ *€6, valid for 2 days; free Sun. 3–8 and all day 1st Sun. every month; 30% discount with Bus Turistic tickets* ⊘ *Closed Mon.* Ⓜ *L1 Glòries.*

Hash Marihuana Cáñamo & Hemp Museum. Legendary Dutch cannabis pioneer Ben Dronkers acquired the historic Palau Mornau, in the Gothic Quarter, and opened it in 2012 after a major renovation as the world's largest museum devoted to this controversial crop. The building alone makes this a must-visit: a 16th-century noble palace later reconfigured in exuberant Modernista style by architect Manuel Raspell, a contemporary of Guadí and student of both Domenech i Muntaner and Puig i Cadafalch, with jewel box-like details of stained glass, carved wood door lintels, coffered ceilings, and ceramic tile. The museum collection of art and artifacts celebrates the history, cultivation, processing, and consumption of hemp in all its industrial, medicinal, and recreational aspects. Alas: no take-away samples. ⊠ *Carrer Ample 35, Born-Ribera* ☏ *93/319–7539* ⊕ *hashmuseum.com* ✉ *€9* Ⓜ *L4 Jaume 1.*

Plaça de les Olles. This pretty little square named for the makers of *olles*, or pots, has been known to host everything from topless sunbathers to elegant Viennese waltzes to the overflow from the popular nearby tapas bar Cal Pep. Notice the balconies at No. 6 over Café de la Ribera, oddly with colorful blue and yellow tile on the second and top floors. The house with the turret over the street on the right at the corner leading out to Pla del Palau (at No. 2 Plaça de les Olles) is another of Enric Sagnier i Villavecchia's retro-Moderniste works. ⊠ *Pl. de les Olles, Born-Ribera* Ⓜ *L4 Jaume I/Barceloneta.*

LA CIUTADELLA AND BARCELONETA

Sightseeing
★★★★★
Nightlife
★★★
Dining
★★★★★
Lodging
★★★
Shopping
– – –

Now Barcelona's central downtown park, La Ciutadella was originally the site of a fortress built by the conquering troops of the Bourbon monarch Felipe V after the fall of Barcelona in the 1700–1714 War of the Spanish Succession. Barceloneta has always been a little seedy: the people who live here hang their washing out over the narrow streets; they will cheerfully direct you to the nearest tattoo parlor, or the eclectic bar around the corner that serves a great paella; they rent their flats to the rowdiest of low-budget visitors; they thumb their noses a bit at the fancy yachts in the marina across the Passeig Joan de Borbó—but like the folks in the Born, they are not immune to the recent siren song of gentrification.

Barceloneta and La Ciutadella fit together historically. In the early 18th century, some 1,000 houses in the Barrio de la Ribera, then the waterfront neighborhood around Plaça del Born, were ordered torn down, to create fields of fire for the cannon of La Ciutadella, the newly built fortress that kept watch over the rebellious Catalans. Barceloneta, then a marshy wetland, was filled in and developed almost four decades later, in 1753, to house the families who had lost homes in La Ribera.

Open water in Roman times, and gradually silted in only after the 15th-century construction of the port, it became Barcelona's fishermen's and stevedores' quarter. Originally composed of 15 longitudinal and three cross streets and 329 two-story houses, this was Europe's earliest planned urban development, built by the military engineer Juan Martin Cermeño under the command of El Marquès de la Mina, Juan Miguel de Guzmán Dávalos Spinola (1690–1767). Barceloneta was always sort of a safety valve, a little fishing village next door where locals could go to escape the formalities and constraints of city life, for a Sunday seafood lunch on the beach and a stroll through what felt like a freer world. With its tiny original apartment blocks, and its history of seafarers and gypsies, Barceloneta even now maintains its spontaneous, carefree flavor.

Getting Oriented

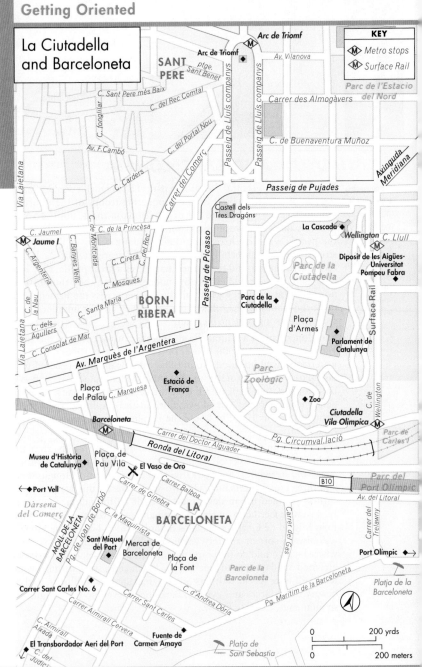

La Ciutadella
and Barceloneta

KEY
- Metro stops
- Surface Rail

SANT PERE

Arc de Triomf
Arc de Triomf
ptge. Sant Benet
Av. Vilanova
C. Sant Pere més Baix
C. del Rec Comtal
Carrer des Almogàvers
Parc de l'Estacio del Nord
Av. F.Cambó
C. del Portal Nou
C. de Buenaventura Muñoz
C. Carders
Passeig de Lluís companys
Passeig de Lluís companys
Avinguda Meridiana
Passeig de Pujades
Via Laietana
Carrer del Comerç
Castell dels Tres Dragóns
La Cascada
Wellington
C. Llull
C. Jaumel
C. de la Princèsa
Jaume I
C. de Montcada
C. del Rec
Diposit de les Aigües-Universitat Pompeu Fabra
C. Banyes Vells
C. Cirera
Parc de la Ciutadella
C. Argentería
C. Mosques
Passeig de Picasso
C. de la Nau
C. Santa Maria
BORN-RIBERA
Parc de la Ciutadella
C. dels Agullers
Plaça d'Armes
Surface Rail
C. Consolat de Mar
Parlament de Catalunya
Av. Marquès de l'Argentera
Parc Zoològic
Plaça del Palau
C. Marquesa
Estació de França
Zoo
C. de Wellington
Ciutadella Vila Olimpica
Barceloneta
Carrer del Doctor Aiguader
Pg. Circumval.lació
Parc de Carles I
Ronda del Litoral
Museu d'Història de Catalunya
Plaça de Pau Vila
El Vaso de Oro
Parc del Port Olímpic
Port Vell
Carrer Balboa
B10
Av. del Litoral
Dàrsena del Comerç
Carrer de Ginebra
LA BARCELONETA
Carrer del Trelawny
MOLL DE LA BARCELONETA
Pg. de Joan de Borbó
C. la Maquinista
Sant Miquel del Port
Mercat de Barceloneta
Plaça de la Font
Carrer del Gas
Port Olímpic
Carrer Sant Carles No. 6
Parc de la Barceloneta
Platja de la Barceloneta
Carrer Sant Carles
C. d'Andrea Dória
Pg. Marítim de la Barceloneta
C. Aimirall Cervera
C. Aimirall Arkada
Fuente de Carmen Amaya
Platja de Sant Sebastia
El Transbordador Aeri del Port
C. del Judici

0   200 yrds
0   200 meters

TIMING

Exploring Ciutadella Park and Barceloneta can take from three to four hours. Add at least another hour if you're stopping for lunch. Try to time your arrival in Barceloneta so you catch the local market in full swing at midday (until 3) and work your way through the neighborhood to a beachside table for paella. Can Manel la Puda serves paella until 4 pm.

GETTING HERE

The Barceloneta stop on the metro's yellow line (L4) is the closest subway stop; there's lots to see on a walk to the beach through the Barri Gòtic from Plaça de Catalunya, but it could leave you a little footsore. For La Ciutadella, the Arc de Triomf stop on the red line (L1) is closest.

QUICK BITES

El Vaso de Oro. Friendly El Vaso de Oro is a famous tapas specialist, always full of grazers, local and otherwise. Don't miss the foie gras—or the restaurant's own microbrewery beer. ✉ *Carrer de Balboa 6, Barceloneta* ☎ *93/319–3098* ⊕ *vasodeoro.com* Ⓜ *L4 Barceloneta.*

TOP ATTRACTIONS

Carrer Sant Carles No. 6

Estació de França

Museu d'Història de Catalunya

Sant Miquel del Port church

TOP EXPERIENCES

Dining at the edge of the sand

Joining a Sunday drum fest in Ciutadella Park

Renting a windsurfer and catching a breeze

Walking the beachfront from W Hotel Barcelona to the Hotel Arts

WHERE TO EAT (CH. 3)

Agua

Barceloneta

Can Majó

El Vaso de Oro

La Mar Salada

HAPPENING NIGHTLIFE (CH. 5)

Eclipse Bar

Pacha

Shôko

City strollers hit the beach on summer days.

TOP ATTRACTIONS

Carrer Sant Carles No. 6. The last Barceloneta house left standing in its original 1755 two-story entirety, this low, boxlike structure was planned as a single-family dwelling with shop and storage space on the ground floor and the living space above. Overcrowding soon produced split houses and even quartered houses, with workers and their families living in tiny spaces. After nearly a century of living under Madrid-based military jurisdiction, Barceloneta homeowners were given permission to expand vertically, and houses of as many as five stories began to tower over the lowly original dwellings. The house is not open to the public. ⊠ *Carrer Sant Carles 6, Barceloneta* Ⓜ *Barceloneta.*

OFF THE BEATEN PATH

Dipòsit de les Aigües–Universitat Pompeu Fabra. The Ciutadella campus of Barcelona's private Universitat Pompeu Fabra contains a contemporary architectural gem worth seeking out. It's two blocks up from the Ciutadella–Vil·la Olímpica metro stop, just beyond where the tramline out to the Fòrum begins. Once the hydraulic cistern for the Ciutadella waterworks, built in 1880 by Josep Fontseré, the Dipòsit de les Aigües was converted to the school's Central Library in 1999 by the design team of Lluís Clotet and Ignacio Paricio. The massive, 3-foot-thick walls, perforated and crowned with tall brick arches, are striking; the trompe-l'oeil connecting corridor between the reading rooms is a brilliant touch. Even in humble Barceloneta, there are opportunities for really gifted architects to take a historical property in hand and work magic. ⊠ *Ramon Trias Fargas 25–27, La Ciutadella* ☎ *93/542–1709* ⊕ *www.upf.edu/campus/en/ciutadella/aigues.html* ✉ *Free* Ⓜ *L4 Ciutadella–Vil.la Olímpica.*

Estació de França. Barcelona's main railroad station until about 1980, and still in use, the elegant Estació de França is outside the west gate of the Ciutadella. Rebuilt in 1929 for the International Exhibition and restored in 1992 for the Olympics, this mid-19th-century building sits on Estació de Sants, the city's main intercity and international terminus. The marble and bronze, the Moderniste decorative details, and the delicate tracery of its wrought-iron roof girders make this one of the most beautiful buildings of its kind. Stop in for a sense of the bygone romance of European travel. ⊠ *Av. Marquès de l'Argentera s/n, La Ciutadella* ☎ *902/320230 RENFE office, 902/240505 ticket sales and reservations* Ⓜ *L4 Barceloneta.*

Museu d'Història de Catalunya. Established in what used to be a port warehouse, this state-of-the-art interactive museum makes you part of Catalonian history, from prehistoric times to the contemporary democratic era. After centuries of "official" Catalan history dictated from Madrid (from 1714 until the mid-19th century Renaixença, and from 1939 to 1975), this offers an opportunity to revisit Catalonia's autobiography. Explanations of the exhibits appear in Catalan, Castilian, and English. Guided tours are available Sunday at noon and 1 pm. The rooftop restaurant has excellent views over the harbor and is open to the public (whether or not you visit the museum itself) during museum hours. ⊠ *Pl. de Pau Vila 3, Barceloneta* ☎ *93/225–4700* ⊕ *www.en.mhcat.net* ⊠ €4.50 ⊘ *Closed Mon.* Ⓜ *L4 Barceloneta.*

WORTH NOTING

Arc del Triomf. This exposed-redbrick arch was built by Josep Vilaseca as the grand entrance for the 1888 Universal Exhibition. Similar in size and sense to the traditional triumphal arches of ancient Rome, this one refers to no specific military triumph anyone can recall. In fact, Catalonia's last military triumph of note may have been Jaume I el Conqueridor's 1229 conquest of the Moors in Mallorca—as suggested by the bats (always part of Jaume I's coat of arms) on either side of the arch itself. The Josep Reynés sculptures adorning the structure represent Barcelona hosting visitors to the exhibition on the western side (front), while the Josep Llimona sculptures on the eastern side depict the prizes being given to its outstanding contributors. ⊠ *Passeig de Sant Joan, La Ciutadella* Ⓜ *L1 Arc de Triomf.*

El Transbordador Aeri del Port (*port cable car*). This hair-raising cable-car ride over the Barcelona harbor from Barceloneta to Montjuïc (with a midway stop in the port) is an adrenaline rush with a view. The rush comes from being packed in with 18 other people (standing-room only) in a tiny gondola swaying a hundred feet or so above the Mediterranean. The cable car leaves from the tower at the end of Passeig Joan de Borbó and connects the Torre de San Sebastián on the Moll de Barceloneta, the tower of Jaume I in the port boat terminal, and the Torre de Miramar on Montjuïc. Critics maintain, not without reason, that the ride is expensive, the maintenance is so-so, and the queues can seem interminable. On the positive side, this is undoubtedly the slickest way to connect Barceloneta and Montjuïc. The Torre de Altamar restaurant in the tower at the Barceloneta end serves excellent food and wine. ⊠ *Passeig Joan de Borbó 88, Barceloneta* ☎ *93/441–4820* ⊕ *www.telefericodebarcelona.com* ⌑ *€16.50 round-trip, €11 one-way* Ⓜ *L4 Barceloneta.*

Fuente de Carmen Amaya (*Carmen Amaya Fountain*). Down at the eastern end of Carrer Sant Carles, where Barceloneta joins the beach, is the monument to the famous Gypsy flamenco dancer Carmen Amaya (1913–63). Amaya was born in the Gypsy settlement known as Somorrostro, part of Barceloneta until 1920 when development sent the Gypsies farther east to what is now the Fòrum grounds (from which they were again displaced in 2003). Amaya achieved universal fame in 1929 at the age of 16, when she performed at Barcelona's International Exposition. Amaya made triumphal tours of the Americas and starred in films such as *La hija de Juan Simón* (1934) and *Los Tarantos* (1962). The fountain, and its high-relief representations of cherubic children as flamenco performers (two guitarists, three dancers—in the nude, unlike real flamenco dancers), has been poorly maintained since it was placed here in 1959, but it remains an important reminder of Barceloneta's roots as a rough-and-tumble romantic enclave of free-living sailors, stevedores, Gypsies, and fishermen. This Gypsy ambience all but disappeared when the last of the *chiringuitos* (ramshackle beach restaurants specializing in fish and rice dishes) fell to the wreckers' ball shortly after the 1992 Olympics. ⊠ *Carrer Sant Carles s/n, Barceloneta* Ⓜ *L4 Barceloneta.*

La Cascada. The sights and sounds of Barcelona seem far away when you stand near this monumental creation by Josep Fontseré, presented as part of the 1888 Universal Exhibition. The waterfall's somewhat overwrought arrangement of rocks was the work of a young architecture student named Antoni Gaudí—his first public work, appropriately natural and organic, and certainly a hint of things to come. ⊠ *Parc de la Ciutadella, La Ciutadella* Ⓜ *L1 Arc de Triomf.*

FAMILY **Parc de la Ciutadella** (*Citadel Park*). Once a fortress designed to consolidate Madrid's military occupation of Barcelona, the Ciutadella is now the city's main downtown park. The clearing dates from shortly after the War of the Spanish Succession in the early 18th century, when Felipe V demolished some 1,000 houses in what was then the Barri de la Ribera to build a fortress and barracks for his soldiers and a *glacis* (open space) between rebellious Barcelona and his artillery positions. The fortress walls were pulled down in 1868 and replaced by gardens laid out by Josep Fontseré. In 1888 the park was the site of the Universal Exposition that put Barcelona on the map as a truly European city; today it is home to the Castell dels Tres Dragons, built by architect Lluís Domènech i Montaner as the café and restaurant for the exposition (the only building to survive that project, now a botanical research center), the Catalan parliament, and the city zoo. ⊠ *Passeig de Picasso 21, La Ciutadella* Ⓜ *L4 Barceloneta, Ciutadella–Vila Olímpica, L1 Arc de Triomf.*

Parlament de Catalunya. Once the arsenal for the Ciutadella—as evidenced by the thickness of the building's walls—this is the only surviving remnant of Felipe V's fortress. For a time it housed the city's

Downtown's main park, the Parc de la Ciutadella

museum of modern art, before it was repurposed to house the unicameral Catalan Parliament. Under Franco, the Generalitat—the regional government—was suppressed, and the Hall of Deputies was shut fast for 37 years. Call or go online (⊕ *eeducativa@parlament.cat*) to book and schedule a free 45-minute guided tour of the building; the website makes it a bit complicated to register for a booking, but the grand "Salon Rose" is worth a visit in itself. ⊠ *Pl. de Joan Fiveller, Parc de la Ciutadella s/n, La Ciutadella* ☎ *93/304–6500, 93/304–6645 guided visits* ⊕ *www.parlament.cat/document/cataleg/48179.pdf* ⊠ *Free* Ⓜ *L4 Ciutadella/Vila Olímpica.*

Port Olímpic. Filled with yachts, restaurants, tapas bars, and mega-restaurants serving reasonably decent fare continuously from 1 pm to 1 am, the Olympic Port is 2 km (1 mile) up the beach from Barceloneta, marked by the mammoth shimmering goldfish sculpture in its net of girders by starchitect Frank Gehry. In the shadow of Barcelona's first real skyscraper, the Hotel Arts, the Olympic Port draws thousands of young people of all nationalities on Friday and Saturday nights, especially in summer, to the beach at Nova Icària, generating a buzz redolent of spring break in Cancún. ⊠ *Port Olímpic, Port Olímpic* Ⓜ *L4 Ciutadella/Vila Olímpica.*

Port Vell (*Old Port*). From Pla del Palau, cross to the edge of the port, where the Moll d'Espanya, the Moll de la Fusta, and the Moll de Barceloneta meet. (*Moll* means docks.) Just beyond the colorful Roy Lichtenstein sculpture in front of the post office, the modern Port Vell complex—an IMAX theater, aquarium, and Maremagnum shopping mall—stretches seaward to the right on the Moll d'Espanya. The

Palau de Mar, with rows of somewhat pricey, tourist-oriented quay-side terrace restaurants (try La Gavina, the Merendero de la Mari, or El Magatzem), stretches down along the Moll de Barceloneta to the left. Key points in the Maremagnum complex are the grassy hillside (popular on April 23, Sant Jordi's Day) and the *Ictineo II*, a replica of the world's first submarine created by Narcis Monturiol (1819–85), launched in the Barcelona port in 1862. ⊠ *Port Vell, Barceloneta* Ⓜ *L4 Barceloneta.*

Sant Miquel del Port. Have a close look at this baroque church with its modern (1992), pseudo-bodybuilder version of the winged archangel Michael himself, complete with sword and chain, in the alcove on the facade. (The figure is a replica; the original was destroyed in 1936.) One of the first buildings to be completed in Barceloneta, Sant Miquel del Port was begun in 1753 and finished by 1755 under the direction of architect Damià Ribes. Due to strict orders to keep Barceloneta low enough to fire La Ciutadella's cannon over, Sant Miquel del Port had no bell tower and only a small cupola until Elies Rogent added a new one in 1853. Interesting to note are the metopes: palm-sized gilt bas-relief sculptures around the interior cornice and repeated outside at the top of the facade. These 74 Latin-inscribed allegories each allude to different attributes of St. Michael. For example, the image of a boat and the Latin inscription "iam in tuto" (finally safe), alludes to the saint's protection against the perils of the sea. To the right of Sant Miquel del Port at No. 41 Carrer de Sant Miquel is a house decorated by seven strips of floral *sgraffiti* and a plaque commemorating Fernando de Lesseps, the engineer who built the Suez Canal, who lived in the house while serving as French consul to Barcelona. In the square by the church, take a close look at the fountain, with its Barcelona coat of arms, and Can Ganassa, on the east side, a worthy tapas bar. ⊠ *Carrer de Sant Miquel 39, Barceloneta* ☎ *93/221–6550* Ⓜ *L4 Barceloneta.*

FAMILY **Zoo.** Barcelona's zoo occupies the whole eastern end of the Parc de la Ciutadella. There's a superb reptile house and a full assortment of African animals. The dolphin show is a visitor favorite. ⊠ *Parc de la Ciutadella s/n, La Ciutadella* ☎ *902/457545* ⊕ *www.zoobarcelona.cat/en/home* 🎫 *€19.90 adults, €11.95 children* Ⓜ *L4 Ciutadella–Vila Olímpica, Barceloneta; L1 Arc de Triomf.*

THE EIXAMPLE

Sightseeing
★★★★★

Nightlife
★★★★★

Dining
★★★★★

Lodging
★★★★★

Shopping
★★★★★

Barcelona's most famous neighborhood, this late 19th-century urban development is known for its dazzling Art Nouveau architecture. Called the "Expansion" in Catalan, the district appears on the map as a geometric grid laid out north above the Plaça de Catalunya. The upscale shops, the art galleries, the facades of the Moderniste town houses, and the venues for some of the city's finest cuisine are the main attractions here.

The Eixample (ay-shompla) is an open-air Moderniste museum. Designed as a grid, in the best Cartesian tradition, the Eixample is oddly difficult to find your way around in; the builders seldom numbered the buildings and declined to alphabetize the streets, and even Barcelona residents can get lost in it. The easiest orientation to grasp is the basic division between the well-to-do Dreta, to the right of Rambla Catalunya looking inland, and the more working-class Ezquerra to the left. Eixample locations are also either *mar* (on the ocean side of the street) or *muntanya* (facing the mountains).

The name of Eixample's most famous block of houses, Mazana de la Discordia, is a pun on the Spanish word *manzana,* which means both "apple" and "city block," alluding to the three-way architectural counterpoint on this street and to the classical myth of the Apple of Discord, which played a part in that legendary tale about the Judgment of Paris and the subsequent Trojan War. The houses here are spectacular and encompass three monuments of Modernisme—Casa Lleó Morera, Casa Amatller, and Casa Batlló—in significantly different styles.

The Eixample was created when the Ciutat Vella's city walls were demolished in 1860, and Barcelona embarked on a vast expansion, financed by the return of rich colonials from the Americas, aristocrats who had sold their country estates, and the city's industrial magnates. They expected their investment to trumpet not only their own wealth and influence, but also the resurgence of Barcelona itself and its unique cultural heritage—not Spanish, but Catalan, and modern European. The grid was the work of engineer Ildefons Cerdà, and much of the construction was done in the peak years of the Moderniste movement by a who's who of Art Nouveau architects, starring Gaudí, Domènech i Montaner, and Puig i Cadafalch; rising above it all is Gaudí's Sagrada Família church. The Eixample's principal thoroughfares are La Rambla de Catalunya and the Passeig de Gràcia, where many of the city's most elegant shops occupy the ground floors of the most interesting Art Nouveau buildings.

Getting Oriented

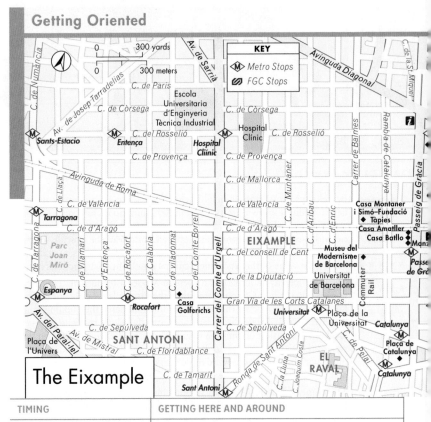

| 0 | 300 yards |
| 0 | 300 meters |

KEY

Ⓜ Metro Stops
Ⓕ FGC Stops

The Eixample

TIMING	GETTING HERE AND AROUND
Exploring the Eixample can take days, but three hours will be enough to cover the most important sites. Add another two or three hours (including the wait in line) for the Sagrada Família. Look for the *passatges* (passageways) through some of the Eixample blocks; Passatge Permanyer, Passatge de la Concepció, and Passatge Mendez Vigo are three of the best. Beware of the tapas emporia on Passeig de Gràcia; almost all of them microwave previously prepared bits and are not the best.	The metro stops at Plaça de Catalunya and Provença nicely bracket this quintessential Barcelona neighborhood; the Diagonal and Passeig de Gràcia stations are right in the center. Barcelona's unnumbered Eixample (Expansion), the post-1860 grid, is a perfect place to get lost, but fear not: the Eixample is vertebrate. Carrer Balmes divides the working-class *Esquerra* (left, looking uphill) from its bourgeois *Dreta* (right). Even the blocks are divided by flats *davant* (front) or *darrera* (behind). The sides of the streets are either *mar* (seaward) or *muntanya* (facing the mountain).

TOP ATTRACTIONS

Casa Milà

Casa Montaner i Simó–Fundació Tàpies

Temple Expiatori de la Sagrada Família

TOP EXPERIENCES

Exploring the art galleries on Consell de Cent

Strolling down the leafy promenade of La Rambla de Catalunya

Walking the rooftop of Casa Milà

WHERE TO EAT (CH. 3)

Bar Mut

Restaurant Gaig

Casa Calvet

Cinc Sentits

L'Olivé

Tragaluz

Yaya Amelia

DISCOUNT TICKETS

The Ruta del Modernisme (Moderniste Route) packet offers a book of discount coupons and a guide to 120 Moderniste buildings, including homes and palaces, shops, restaurants, parks, and theaters, in and around Barcelona. For €18, you get a manual and a set of maps in various languages (with a carry-bag) that allows you to self-guide through the city's Art Nouveau treasures. You can only buy the complete packet (the guidebook alone is available at most bookstores) at the **Pavellons de la Finca Güell** (⊠ Av. de Pedralbes 7) or at the Institut Municipal del Paisatge Urbá (⊠ Av. de las Drassanes 6–8, Edifici Colon 21F).

TOP ATTRACTIONS

Casa Amatller. The neo-Gothic Casa Amatller was built by Josep Puig i Cadafalch in 1900, when the architect was 33 years old. Eighteen years younger than Domènech i Montaner and 15 years younger than Gaudí, Puig i Cadafalch was one of the leading statesmen of his generation. Puig i Cadafalch's architectural historicism sought to recover Catalonia's proud past, in combination with eclectic elements from Flemish and Dutch architectural motifs. Note the Eusebi Arnau sculptures—especially his St. George and the Dragon, and the figures of a drummer with his dancing bear. The first-floor apartment, where the Amatller family lived, opened as a museum in 2015, after a four-year restoration, with the original furniture and decor (guided tours are offered in English daily at 11 am). The small gallery on the first floor, which mounts various exhibitions related to Modernisme, is open to the public free of charge. ✉ *Passeig de Gràcia 41, Eixample* ☎ *93/216–0175, 93/461–7460 tour info and ticket sales* ⊕ *www.en.fundacionamatller.org* ⌨ *Museum €14, guided tour €17; combined ticket for Casa Amatller and the Museum of Modernism (Carrer Balmes 48), €24* Ⓜ *L2/L3/L5 Passeig de Gràcia, FGC Provença.*

FAMILY **Casa Batlló.** Gaudí at his most spectacular, the Casa Batlló is actually a makeover: it was originally built in 1877 by one of Gaudí's teachers, Emili Sala Cortés, and acquired by the Batlló family in 1900. Batlló wanted to tear down the undistinguished Sala building and start over, but Gaudí persuaded him to remodel the facade and the interior, and the result is astonishing. The facade—with its rainbow of colored glass and *trencadís* (polychromatic tile fragments) and the toothy masks of the wrought-iron balconies projecting outward toward the street—is an irresistible photo op. Nationalist symbolism is at work here: the scaly roof line represents the Dragon of Evil impaled on St. George's cross, and the skulls and bones on the balconies are the dragon's victims, allusions to medieval Catalonia's code of chivalry and religious piety. Gaudí is said to have directed the composition of the facade from the middle of Passeig de Gràcia, calling instructions to workmen on the scaffolding. Inside, the translucent windows on the landings of the central staircase light up the maritime motif and the details of the building, all whorls and spirals and curves; here, as everywhere in his oeuvre, Gaudí opted for natural shapes and rejected straight lines.

Budget-conscious visitors can take in the view from outside the Casa Batlló; the admission fee is ridiculously high, and you won't see much inside that you can't also see in the Casa Milà, up the Passeig de Gràcia on the opposite side. ✉ *Passeig de Gràcia 43, Eixample* ☎ *93/216–0306* ⊕ *www.casabatllo.es* ⌨ *€23.50, "Fast Pass" to skip the queue €28.50, "Open Date" pass €30.50, "Theatrical Visit" dramatized guided tour €36* Ⓜ *L2/L3/L4 Passeig de Gràcia, FGC Provença.*

Fodor'sChoice **Casa Milà.** Usually referred to as *La Pedrera* (The Stone Quarry), with ★ a wavy, curving stone facade that undulates around the corner of the block, this building, unveiled in 1910, is one of Gaudí's most celebrated yet initially reviled designs. Seemingly defying the laws of gravity, the exterior has no straight lines, and is adorned with winding balconies

DID YOU KNOW?

Josep Puig i Cadafalch designed Casa Amatller to mix Catalonian influences with Flemish motifs like the stepped rooftop.

covered with wrought-iron foliage sculpted by Josep Maria Jujol. Inside, the handsome **Espai Gaudí** (Gaudí Space) in the attic has excellent critical displays of Gaudí's works from all over Spain. The Pis de la Pedrera apartment is an interesting look into the life of a family that lived in La Pedrera in the early 20th century. Guided tours are offered during the week and must be booked in advance by emailing *grupslapedrera@ oscatalunyacaixa.com*. On Nits d'Estiu (aka weekend summer nights June 20–September 10, Friday and Saturday) the Espai Gaudí and the roof terrace are open for drinks and jazz concerts (€27). ✉ *Passeig de Gràcia 92, Eixample* ☎ *902/202138* ⊕ *www.lapedrera.com/en/home* 🎟 *€22, Premium tour (no queue) €29. Gaudí's Pedrera: The Origins tour €34. Jazz concerts €28* Ⓜ *L2/L3/L5 Diagonal, FGC Provença.*

Palau Baró de Quadras. The neo-Gothic and plateresque (intricately carved in silversmith-like detail) facade of this house built for textile magnate Baron Manuel de Quadras and remodeled (1902–1905) by Moderniste starchitect Puig i Cadafalch, has one of the most spectacular collections of Eusebi Arnau sculptures in town (other Arnau sites include the Palau de la Música Catalana, Quatre Gats–Casa Martí, and Casa Amatller). Look for the theme of St. George slaying the dragon once again, this one in a spectacularly vertiginous rush of movement down the facade. Don't miss the intimate-looking row of alpine chalet–like windows across the top floor. The Palau currently houses the Institut Ramon Llull, a nonprofit organization dedicated to spreading the knowledge of Catalan culture worldwide. ✉ *Av. Diagonal 373, Eixample* ☎ *93/467–8000* ⊕ *www.llull.cat* 🎟 *Group guided tours €10/ person* Ⓜ *L2/L3/L5 Diagonal.*

Plaça de Catalunya. Barcelona's main bus-and-metro hub is the frontier between the Old City and the post-1860 Eixample. Fountains and statuary, along with pigeons and backpackers in roughly equal numbers, make the Plaça de Catalunya an open space to scurry across on your way to somewhere quieter, shadier, and gentler on the senses. Across the street on the west side is **Café Zurich**, the classic Barcelona rendezvous point at the top of La Rambla, by the steps down to the metro. The block behind the Zurich, known as El Triangle, houses a collection of megastores, chief among them FNAC (for electronics, books, and music) and Massimo Dutti (for designer garb). Corte Inglés, the department store on the northeast side of the square, offers quality goods at decent prices—if you can get the attention of one of their famously indifferent salespeople. ✉ *Pl. de Catalunya, Eixample* Ⓜ *Pl. Catalunya.*

Fodor's Choice
★

Recinte Modernista de Sant Pau. Set in what was one of the most beautiful public projects in the world—the Hospital de Sant Pau—the Modernist Complex is a UNESCO World Heritage Site that's extraordinary in its setting, style, and the idea that inspired it. Architect Lluís Domènech i Montaner believed that trees, flowers, and fresh air were likely to help people recover from what ailed them more than anything doctors could do in emotionally sterile surroundings. The hospital wards were set among gardens, their brick facades topped with polychrome ceramic tile roofs in extravagant shapes and details. Domènech also believed in the therapeutic properties of form and color, and decorated the hospital with Pau Gargallo sculptures and colorful mosaics, replete with motifs of hope and healing and healthy growth. Begun in 1900, this monumental production won Domènech i Montaner his third Barcelona "Best Building" award in 1912. Tours are offered in English daily at 11 am. ✉ *Carrer Sant Antoni Maria Claret 167, Eixample* ☎ *93/553–7801* ⊕ *www.santpaubarcelona.org/en* ✏ *€13, guided tour €19; 20% off with BCN and Bus Turistic cards; free 1st Sun. of the month* Ⓜ *L5 Sant Pau/Dos de Maig.*

Fodor'sChoice **Temple Expiatori de la Sagrada Família.** Barcelona's most emblematic archi-
★ tectural icon, Antoni Gaudí's Sagrada Família, is still under construction 130 years after it was begun. This striking and surreal creation was conceived as a gigantic representation of the entire history of Christianity. Begun in 1882 under architect Francesc Villar and passed on in 1891 to Gaudí (until his death in 1926), it is still thought to be 15 or 20 years from completion. No building in Barcelona and few in the world are more deserving of the investment of a few hours to the better part of a day. The current lateral facades will one day be dwarfed by the main Glory facade and central spire, to be crowned by an illuminated polychrome ceramic cross. Take an elevator up the bell towers for spectacular views. The museum displays Gaudí's scale models and photographs showing the progress of construction. The architect is buried to the left of the altar in the crypt. ■ TIP➔ Lines to enter the church can stretch around the block. Buy your tickets online, with a reserved time of entry, and jump the queue. ✉ *Pl. de la Sagrada Família, Carrer Mallorca 401, Eixample* ☎ *93/207–3031, 93/208–0414 visitor info* ⊕ *www.sagradafamilia.cat* ✏ *€15, €22 with audio guide; €24 guided tour, €29 with audio guide and tower access by elevator* Ⓜ *L2/L5 Sagrada Família.*

WORTH NOTING

Casa Calvet. This exquisite but more conventional town house (for Gaudí, anyway) was the architect's first commission in the Eixample (the second was the dragon-like Casa Batlló, and the third, and last—he was never asked to do another—was the stone quarry–esque Casa Milà). Peaked with baroque scroll gables over the unadorned (no ceramics, no color, no sculpted ripples) Montjuïc sandstone facade, Casa Calvet compensates for its structural conservatism with its Art Nouveau details, from the door handles to the benches, chairs, vestibule, and spectacular glass-and-wood elevator. Built in 1900 for the textile baron Pere Calvet, the house includes symbolic elements on the facade, ranging from the owner's stylized letter "C" over the door to the cypress, symbol of hospitality, above. The wild mushrooms on the main (second) floor reflect Pere Calvet's (and perhaps Gaudí's) passion for mycology, while the busts at the top of the facade represent St. Peter, the owner's patron saint, and St. Genis of Arles and St. Genis of Rome, patron saints of Vilassar, the Calvet family's hometown in the coastal Maresme north of Barcelona. The only part of the building accessible to visitors is the ground-floor **Casa Calvet** restaurant, originally the suite of offices for Calvet's textile company, with its exuberant Moderniste decor. ✉ *Carrer Casp 48, Eixample* ⊕ *www.casacalvet.es (restaurant)* Ⓜ *L1/L4 Urquinaona.*

Continued on page 99

TEMPLE EXPIATORI DE LA
SAGRADA FAMÍLIA

Antoni Gaudí's striking and surreal masterpiece was conceived as nothing short of a Bible in stone, an arresting representation of the history of Christianity. Today this Roman Catholic church is Barcelona's most emblematic architectural icon. Looming over Barcelona like a mid-city massif of grottoes and peaks, the Sagrada Família strains skyward in piles of stalagmites. Construction is ongoing and continues to stretch toward the heavens.

CONSTRUCTION, PAST AND PRESENT

"My client is not in a hurry," was Gaudí's reply to anyone curious about his project's timetable ... good thing, too, because the Sagrada Família was begun in 1882 under architect Francesc Villar, passed on in 1891 to Gaudí, and is still thought to be more than a decade from completion. Gaudí added Art Nouveau touches to the crypt and in 1893 started the Nativity facade. Conceived as a symbolic construct encompassing the complete story and scope of the Christian faith, the church was intended by Gaudí to impress the viewer with the full sweep and force of the Gospel. At the time of his death in 1926 only one tower of the Nativity facade had been completed.

By 2026, the 100th anniversary of Gaudí's death, after 144 years of construction in the tradition of the great medieval and Renaissance cathedrals of Europe, the Sagrada Família may well be complete enough to call finished. Architect Jordi Bonet continues in the footsteps of his father, architect Lluís Bonet, to make Gaudí's vision complete as he has since the 1980s.

(left) Sagrada Família interior. (top) Shepherds gather to witness the birth of Christ in the Nativity facade.

BIBLE STUDIES IN STONE: THE FACADES

Gaudí's plans called for three immense facades. The northeast-facing **Nativity facade** and the southwest-facing **Passion facade** are complete. The much larger southeast-facing **Glory facade**, the building's main entry, is still under construction. The final church will have **eighteen towers:** The four **bell towers** over each facade represent the twelve apostles; the four **larger towers** represent the evangelists Mark, Matthew, John, and Luke; the **second-highest tower** in the reredos behind the altar honors the Virgin Mary; and in the center the **Torre del Salvador** (Tower of the Savior) will soar to a height of 564 feet.

THE NATIVITY FACADE

Built during Gaudí's lifetime, this facade displays his vision and sculptural style, the organic or so-called "melting wax" look that has become his signature. The facade is crowned by **four bell towers,** representing the apostles Barnabas, Jude, Simon, and Matthew and divided into three sections around the doors of **Charity** in the center, **Faith** on the right, and **Hope** on the left.

(left) The ornamental Nativity facade. (above, top right) A figure in the Portal of Faith. (above, center right) The spiraling staircase. (above, bottom right) A decorative cross.

The focal point in the Nativity facade: Joseph and Mary presenting the infant Jesus.

by Joseph, with the Holy Spirit represented as a dove.

THE PASSION FACADE

On the **Passion facade**, Gaudí intended to dramatize the abyss between the birth of a child and the death of a man. In 1986 Josep Maria Subirachs, an artist known for his atheism and his hard-edged and geometrical sculptural style, was commissioned to finish the Passion facade. The contrast is sharp, in content and in sculptural style, between this facade and the Nativity facade. Framed by leaning columns of tibia-like bones, the Passion facade illustrates the last days of Christ and his Resurrection. The scenes are laid out chronologically in an S-shape path beginning at the bottom left and ending at the upper right.

At bottom left is the **Last Supper**, the disciples' faces contorted in confusion and anguish, most of all Judas clutching his bag of money behind his back over a reclining hound, the contrasting symbol of fidelity. To the right is the Garden of Gethsemane and Peter awakening, followed by the **Kiss of Judas**. To the right of the door is **Peter's Third Denial** of

Over the central **Portal of Charity** is the birth of Christ, with a representation of the Annunciation overhead in an ice grotto, another natural element. Above that are the signs of the zodiac for the Christmas sky at Bethlehem, with two babies representing the Gemini, and the horns of a bull for Taurus. The evergreen cypress tree rising above symbolizes eternity, with the white doves as souls seeking life everlasting.

The **Portal of Faith** on the right shows Christ preaching as a youth. Higher up are the Eucharistic symbols of grapes and wheat, and a hand and eye, symbols of divine Providence.

The **Portal of Hope** on the left shows a series of biblical scenes including the slaughter of the innocents, the flight into Egypt, Joseph surrounded by his carpenter's tools looking down at his infant son, and the marriage of Joseph and Mary with Mary's parents, Joaquin and Anna, looking on. Above is a boat, representing the Church, piloted

Judas kissing Jesus while a cryptogram behind contains a numerical combination adding up to 33, the age of Christ's death.

The stark, geometric Passion facade.

Christ "ere the cock crows." Farther to the right are **Pontius Pilate and Jesus** with the crown of thorns.

Above on the second tier are the **Three Marys** and Simon helping Jesus lift the cross. Over the center, **Jesus carries the cross**. To the left, Gaudí himself is portrayed, pencil in hand, the evangelist in stone, while farther left a **mounted centurion** pierces the side of the church with his spear, the church representing the body of Christ. At the top left, **soldiers gamble for Christ's clothing** while at the top center is the **crucifixion**, featuring Subirachs's controversial (in 1971 when it was unveiled) naked and anatomically complete Christ. Finally to the right, Peter and Mary grieve at **Christ's entombment**, an egg overhead symbolizing rebirth and the resurrection. At a height of 148 feet are the four Apostles on their bell towers. Bartholomew, on the left, looks upward toward the 26-foot risen Christ between the four bell towers at a height of 198 feet.

THE GLORY FACADE

The Glory facade, still under construction, will have a wide stairway and esplanade or porch leading up to three portals dedicated, as in the other facades, to Charity, Faith, and Hope. The doors are inscribed with the Lord's Prayer in bronze in fifty different languages with the Catalan version in the center in relief. Carrer Mallorca will be routed underground and the entire city block across the street will be razed to make space for the esplanade and park. Present predictions are between 2026 and 2030 for the completion of this phase.

A new element in the Sagrada Família: the bronze doorway of the Glory facade.

THE INTERIOR: "TEMPLE OF HARMONIOUS LIGHT"

(top) Above the altar, supporting columns form a canopy of light. (below) Towering columns and stained-glass windows keep the interior bright.

Until 2010, The Sagrada Família was able to be adequately appreciated without going inside. But since the interior was completed for the Papal consecration, it's become Barcelona's most stunning space, comparable to the breathtaking upsweep of the finest soaring Gothic architecture but higher, brighter, and carved in a dazzling fusion of hard-edged Subirachs over organic Gaudí.

DESIGN

The floor plan for the church is laid out in the form of a **Latin cross** with five longitudinal naves intersected by three transepts. The **apse** has space for 15,000 people, a choir loft for 1,500, and is large enough to encompass the entire Santa Maria del Mar basilica. From the Glory Façade, the Baptistry Chapel is to the left and the Chapel of the Sacrament and Penitence is to the right. The Chapel of the Assumption is at the back of the apse. Over the main altar is the figure of the crucified Christ, suspended in mid-air under a diaphanous canopy.

LIGHT

The main nave and the apse of the basilica create an immense and immaculate space culminated by the highest point: the hyperboloid skylight over the main altar 75 meters (247.5 ft) above the floor. The vaulting is perforated with 288 skylights admitting abundant light. The sharp-edged, tree-like leaning columns shape the interior spaces and will support the six towers being built above them. Vaults are decorated with green and gold Venetian mosaics that diffuse the light as if they were leaves in a forest, making the basilica, in the words of Gaudí, "the temple of harmonious light."

DETAILS TO DISCOVER: THE EXTERIOR

GAUDÍ IN THE PASSION FACADE

Subirachs pays double homage to the great Modern-iste master in the Passion facade: Gaudí himself appears over the left side of the main entry making notes or drawings, the evangelist in stone, while the Roman soldiers are modeled on Gaudí's helmeted, Star Wars–like warriors from the roof of La Pedrera.

Gaudí in the Passion facade

TOWER TOPS

Break out the binoculars and have a close look at the pinnacles and peaks of the Sagrada Família's towers. Sculpted by Japanese artist Etsuro Sotoo, these clusters of grapes and different kinds of fruit are symbols of fertility, of rebirth, and of the Resurrection of Christ.

SUBIRACHS IN THE PASSION FACADE

At Christ's feet in the entombment sculpture is a blocky figure with a furrowed brow, thought to be a portrayal of the agnostic's anguished search for certainty. This figure is generally taken as a self-portrait of Subirachs, characterized by the sculptor's giant hand and an "S" on his massive right arm.

Sotoo's ornamental fruit

DONKEY ON THE NATIVITY FACADE

On the left side of the Nativity facade over the Portal of Hope is a *burro*, a small donkey, known to have been modeled from a donkey that Gaudí saw near the work site. The *ruc català* (Catalan donkey) is a beloved and iconic symbol of Catalonia, often displayed on Catalonian bumpers as a response to the Spanish fighting bull.

THE ROSE TREE DOOR

The richly sculpted Rose Tree Door, between the Nativity facade and the cloisters, portrays Our Lady of the Rose Tree with the infant Jesus in her arms, St. Dominic and St. Catherine of Siena in prayer, with three angels dancing overhead. The sculptural group on the wall known as "The Death of the Just" portrays the Virgin and child comforting a moribund old man, the Spanish prayer "Jesús, José, y María, asistidme en mi última agonía" (Jesus, Joseph, and María, help me in my final agony). The accompanying inscriptions in English, "Pray for us sinners now and at the hour of our death, Amen" are the final words of the Ave María prayer.

The donkey in the Nativity facade

The heavily embelished Rose door

COLUMN FROM THE PORTAL OF CHARITY

The column, dead center in the Portal of Charity, is covered with the genealogy of Christ going back through the House of David to Abraham. At the bottom of the column is the snake of evil, complete with the apple of temptation in his mouth, closed in behind an iron grate, symbolic of Christianity's mission of neutralizing the sin of selfishness.

The column in the Portal of Charity

FACELESS ST. VERONICA

Because her story is considered legendary, not historical fact, St. Veronica appears faceless in the Passion facade. Also shown is the veil she gave Christ to wipe his face with on the way to Calvary that was said to be miraculously imprinted with his likeness. The veil is torn in two overhead and covers a mosaic that Subirachs allegedly disliked and elected to conceal.

St. Veronica with the veil

STAINED-GLASS WINDOWS

The stained-glass windows of the Sagrada Família are work of Joan Vila-Grau. The windows in the west central part of the nave represent the light of Jesus and a bubbling fountain in a bright chromatic patchwork of shades of blue with green and yellow reflections. The main window on the Passion facade represents the Resurrection. Gaudí left express instructions that the windows of the central nave have no color, so as not to alter the colors of the tiles and trencadis (mosaics of broken tile) in green and gold representing palm leaves. These windows will be clear or translucent, as a symbol of purity and to admit as much light as possible.

Stained-glass windows

TORTOISES AND TURTLES

Nature lover Gaudí used as many elements of the natural world as he could in his stone Bible. The sea tortoise beneath the column on the Mediterranean side of the Portal of Hope and the land turtle supporting the inland Portal of Faith symbolize the slow and steady stability of the cosmos and of the church.

SAINT THOMAS IN THE BELL TOWER

Above the Passion facade, St. Thomas demanding proof of Christ's resurrection (thus the expression "doubting Thomas") and perched on the bell tower is pointing to the palm of his hand asking to inspect Christ's wounds.

CHRIST RESURRECTED ABOVE PASSION FACADE

High above the Passion facade, a gilded Christ sits resurrected, perched between two towers.

Christ resurrected

MAKING THE MOST OF YOUR TRIP

The Nativity facade

WHEN TO VISIT

To avoid crowds, come first thing in the morning. Save your trip for a sunny day so you can admire the facades at length.

WHAT TO WEAR AND BRING

Visitors are encouraged not to wear shors and to cover bare shoulders. It's a good idea to bring binoculars to absorb details all the way up.

TIMING

If you're just walking around the exterior, an hour or two is plenty of time. If you'd like to go inside to the crypt, visit the museum, visit the towers, and walk down the spiraling stairway, you'll need three to four hours.

HIGHLIGHTS

The Passion facade, the Nativity facade, the Portal of Faith, the Portal of Hope, and the main altar.

BONUS FEATURES

The museum displays Gaudí's scale models and shows photographs of the construction. The crypt holds Gaudí's remains. For €2 (and a 45-minute wait in line), you can take an elevator to the top of the bell towers for spectacular views.

TOURS

English-language tours are given daily at 11 AM, 1 PM, 3 PM, and 5 PM and cost €4.

VISITOR INFORMATION

✉ Pl. de la Sagrada Família, Eixample ☎ 93/207-3031 ⊕ www.sagradafamilia.org 💳 €11, bell tower elevator €2, audio guides €4 🕐 Oct.–Mar., daily 9–6; Apr.–Sept., daily 9–8 Ⓜ Sagrada Família.

TOWERS

Climbing the towers is no longer permitted, and lines for the elevator are long. Only the Passion Facade may be descended on foot, which is highly recommended for a close look at some of the figures, including that of Gaudí himself.

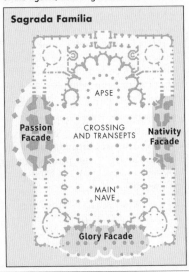

Sagrada Família

APSE

Passion Facade

CROSSING AND TRANSEPTS

Nativity Facade

MAIN NAVE

Glory Facade

2

Casa de les Punxes (*House of the Spikes*). Also known as Casa Terrades for the family that owned the house and commissioned Puig i Cadafalch to build it, this extraordinary cluster of six conical towers ending in impossibly sharp needles is another of Puig i Cadafalch's northern European inspirations, this one rooted in the Gothic architecture of Nordic countries. One of the few freestanding Eixample buildings, visible from 360 degrees, this ersatz Bavarian or Danish castle in downtown Barcelona is composed entirely of private apartments, some of them built into the conical towers themselves on three circular levels, connected by spiral stairways. The ground floor, first level, terrace, and towers are now open to the public; check the website for the schedule of guided tours in English. Interestingly, Puig i Cadafalch also designed the Terrades family mausoleum, albeit in a much more sober style. ✉ *Av. Diagonal 416–420, Eixample* ☎ *93/018–5242* ⊕ *www. casadelespunxes.com* ✉ *€12.50 (with audio guide), €20 guided tour* Ⓜ *L4/L5 Verdaguer, L3/L5 Diagonal.*

Casa Golferichs (*Golferichs Civic Center*). Gaudí disciple Joan Rubió i Bellver built this extraordinary house, known as El Xalet (The Chalet), for the Golferichs family when he was not yet 30. The rambling wooden eaves and gables of the exterior enclose a cozy and comfortable dark-wood-lined interior with a pronounced verticality. The top floor, with its rich wood beams and cerulean walls, is often used for intimate concerts; the ground floor exhibits paintings and photographs. The building serves now as the quarters of the Golferichs Centre Civic, which offers local residents a range of conferences and discussions, exhibitions and adult education courses, and organizes various thematic walking tours of the city. ✉ *Gran Via 491, Eixample* ☎ *93/323–7790* ⊕ *www.golferichs.org* ⊙ *Closed Sun.* Ⓜ *L1 Rocafort, Urgell.*

Casa Macaya (*Palau Macaya*). This graceful Puig i Cadafalch building constructed in 1901 was the former seat of the *Obra Social "la Caixa,"* a deep-pocketed, far-reaching cultural and social welfare organization funded by Spain's major (and most civic-minded) savings bank. It now houses the foundation's *Espai Caixa* cultural center, organizing a range of conferences, discussion forums, and presentations on current social and political issues. Look for the Eusebi Arnau sculptures over the door depicting, somewhat cryptically, a man mounted on a donkey and another on a bicycle, reminiscent of the similar Arnau sculptures on the facade of Puig i Cadafalch's Casa Amatller on Passeig de Gràcia. ✉ *Passeig de Sant Joan 108, Eixample* ☎ *93/457–9531* ⊕ *obrasociallacaixa.org* ⊙ *Closed weekends* Ⓜ *L4/L5 Verdaguer.*

Casa Montaner i Simó–Fundació Tàpies. Built in 1880, this former publishing house, and the city's first building to incorporate iron supports, has been handsomely converted to hold the work of preeminent contemporary Catalan painter Antoni Tàpies, and a collection of works by many important modern artists that he acquired over this lifetime. Tàpies, who died in 2012, was an abstract painter, but was also influenced by surrealism, which accounts for the *Núvol i cadira* (*Cloud and Chair*) sculpture atop the structure. The modern airy split-level gallery also has a bookstore that's strong on Tàpies, Asian art, and Barcelona art and architecture. ✉ *Carrer Aragó 255, Eixample* ☎ *93/487–0315* ⊕ *www.fundaciotapies.org* 🎫 *€7* ⊙ *Closed Mon.* Ⓜ *L2/L3/L4 Passeig de Gràcia.*

OFF THE BEATEN PATH

Museu Egipci de Barcelona. Presumably you came to Barcelona to learn about Catalonia, not ancient Egypt, but you might be making a mistake by skipping this major collection of art and artifacts. This museum takes advantage of state-of-the-art curatorial techniques, with exhibitions showcasing everything from mummies to what the ancient Egyptian had for dinner. The museum offers free guided tours, but only in Catalan or Spanish. ✉ *Fundació Arqueòlogica Clos, Valencia 284, Eixample* ☎ *93/488–0188* ⊕ *www.museuegipci.com* 🎫 *€11* Ⓜ *L2/L3/L4 Passeig de Gràcia.*

Museu del Modernisme de Barcelona (*Museum of Catalan Modernism: MMBCN*). Unjustly bypassed in favor of rival displays in the Casa Milà, Casa Batlló, and the DHUB Design Museum in Plaça de les Glòries, this museum houses a small but rich collection of Moderniste furnishings, paintings and posters, sculpture (including works by Josep Limona), and decorative arts. Don't miss the section devoted to Gaudí-designed furniture. ✉ *Carrer Balmes 48, Eixample* ☎ *93/272–2896* ⊕ *www.mmbcn.cat* 🎫 *€10* ⊙ *Closed Mon.* Ⓜ *L1/ L2 Universitat.*

Passatge Permanyer. Cutting through the middle of the block bordered by Pau Claris, Roger de Llúria, Consell de Cent, and Diputació, this charming, leafy mid-Eixample sanctuary is one of 46 *passatges* (alleys or passageways) that cut through the blocks of this gridlike area. Inspired by John Nash's neoclassical Regent's Park terraces in London (with their formal and separate town houses), Ildefons Cerdà originally envisioned many more of these utopian mid-block gardens, but Barcelona never endorsed his vision. Once an aristocratic enclave and hideaway for pianist Carles Vidiella and poet, musician, and illustrator Apel·les Mestre, Passatge Permanyer is, along with the nearby Passatge Méndez Vigo, the best of these through-the-looking-glass downtown Barcelona alleyways. ✉ *Passatge Permanyer, Eixample* Ⓜ *L2/L3/L4 Passeig de Gràcia.*

GRÀCIA

Sightseeing
★★★
Nightlife
★★★★
Dining
★★★★
Lodging
★★
Shopping
★★

Gràcia is a state of mind. More than a neighborhood, it is a village republic that has periodically risen in armed rebellion against city, state, and country; its jumble of streets have names (Llibertat, Fraternitat, Progrès) that invoke the ideological history of this fierce little progressive, working-class enclave.

Lying above the Diagonal from Carrer de Còrsega all the way up to Park Güell, Gràcia is bound by Via Augusta and Carrer Balmes to the west and Carrer de l'Escorial and Passeig de Sant Joan to the east. Today the area is filled with hip little bars and trendy restaurants, movie theaters, outdoor cafés, gourmet shops and designer boutiques, and the studios of struggling artists: this is where Barcelona's young cohort, want to live, and come to party. Mercé Rodoreda's novel *La Plaça del Diamant* (translated by the late David Rosenthal as *The Time of the Doves*) begins and ends in Gràcia during the August Festa Major, a festival that fills the streets with the rank-and-file residents of this always lively, intimate little pocket of general resistance to Organized Life.

TOP ATTRACTIONS

Fodor'sChoice
★

Casa Vicens. Antoni Gaudí's first important commission as a young architect began in 1883 and finished in 1889. For this house Gaudí still used his traditional architect's tools, particularly the T square. The historical eclecticism (that is, borrowing freely from past architectural styles around the world) of the early Art Nouveau movement is evident in the Orientalist themes and Mudejar (Moorish-inspired) motifs lavished throughout the design. The client, Don Manuel Vicens Montaner, owned a brick and tile factory—which explains the lavish use of the green and yellow ceramic tiles, in checkerboard and floral patterns, that animate the facade. (Casa Vicens was in fact the first polychromatic facade to appear in Barcelona.) The chemaro palm leaves decorating the gate and surrounding fence are thought to be the work of Gaudí's assistant Francesc Berenguer; the comic iron lizards and bats oozing off the facade are Gaudí's playful version of the Gothic gargoyle.

Getting Oriented

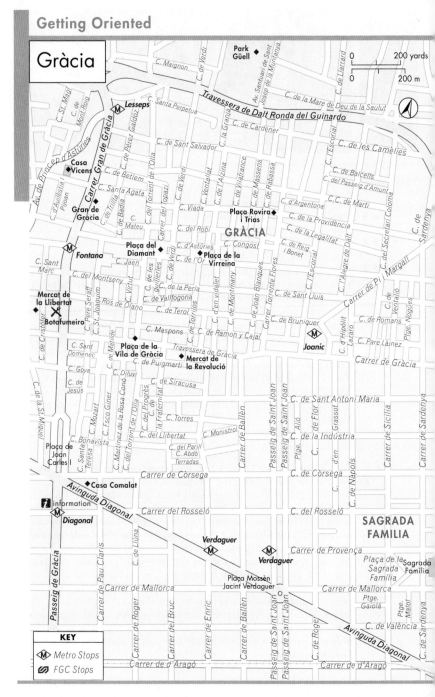

Gràcia

Park Güell

C. Maignon

C. de Verdi

Av. Santuari de Sant Josep de la Muntanya

C. de Llarrad

C. de la Mare de Déu de la Salut

0   200 yards

0   200 m

Travessera de Dalt Ronda del Guinardó

Lesseps

C. Santa Perpetua

C. de la Graciela

C. de Cardener

C. l'Escorial

C. de les Camèlies

C. St. Magi

C. de Mont Roig

C. de Pérez Galdós

Carrer Gran de Gràcia

C. de Sant Salvador

Casa Vicens

C. de Betlem

C. del Torrent de l'Olla

C. de Verdi

C. de l'Alzina

C. de Vilafrance

C. de Massens

C. de Rabassa

C. de Balcells

C. del Passeig d'Amunt

Av. de Princep d'Astúries

C. d'Aullèstia i Pijoan

C. Santa Agata

C. de Topazi

C. d'Argentona

C.C. de Marti

C. de Sardenya

Gran de Gràcia

C. de Trilla

C. de Badia

C. Viada

C. del Robí

Plaça Rovira i Trias

C. de la Providència

C. Mateu

GRÀCIA

C. de la Legalitat

C. Congost

C. de Reig i Bonet

C. d'Alegre de Dalt

C. del Secretari Coloma

Fontana

Plaça del Diamant

C. d'Astúries

C. de l'Or

Plaça de la Virreina

C. Jaén

C. de les Guilleries

C. de Verdi

C. l'Escorial

C. Sant Marc

C. del Montseny

C. Virtut

C. de la Perla

C. d'en Vidalet

C. de Montmany

C. de Joan Blanques

C. Torrent Flores

C. de Pi i Margall

C. de Ventalló

Mercat de la Llibertat

Pere Serafí

Ros de Olano

C. de Vallfogona

C. de Sant Lluis

C. de Romans

Ptge. Nogues

Botafumeiro

St. Joaquim

C. de Terol

C. de Torrijos

C. de Bruniquer

C. d'Hipòlit Lazaro

C. Pare Làinez

C. de Cristòfol

C. Maspons

C. de Ramon y Cajal

Joanic

C. de Crist

C. Sant Domenec

Plaça de la Vila de Gràcia

Travessera de Gràcia

Mercat de la Revolució

Carrer de Gràcia

C. Goya

C. de Matilde

C. de Puigmarti

C. Diluvi

C. de Jesús

C. Mozart

C. Fco Giner

C. de Siracusa

C. de la Rosa Coral

C. del Progrés

C. de Sant Antoni Maria

C. de Sardenya

Plaça de Joan Carles I

C. Bonavista

C. Santa Teresa

C. Martinez de la Rosa

C. del Torrent de l'Olla

C. de la Fraternitat

C. Torres

C. del Llibertat

C. Monistrol

Carrer de Ballèn

C. del Parill

C. Abdó Terradas

Passeig de Sant Joan

Passeig de Sant Joan

Ptge. Alió

C. de Flor

C. d'en Grassot

C. de la Indústria

Carrer de Sicília

Casa Comalat

Carrer de Córsega

C. de Córsega

C. de Nàpols

Avinguda Diagonal

Carrer del Rosseló

C. del Rosseló

SAGRADA FAMILIA

information

Diagonal

C. de Lluna

Verdaguer

Verdaguer

Carrer de Provença

Plaça de la Sagrada Família

Sagrada Família

Passeig de Gràcia

Carrer de Pau Claris

Carrer de Roger

Carrer del Bruc

Carrer de Enric

Carrer de Ballèn

Passeig de Sant Joan

Passeig de Sant Joan

Plaça Mossèn Jacint Verdaguer

Carrer de Mallorca

Carrer de Mallorca

Ptge. Gaiolà

Ptge. Matot

C. de Roger

Avinguda Diagonal

C. de València

C. de Sardenya

Carrer de d'Aragó

Carrer de d'Aragó

KEY

M   *Metro Stops*

🅖   *FGC Stops*

TIMING

Exploring Gràcia is at least a several-hours outing, or an entire day if you want to get the full feel of the neighborhood. Evening sessions at the popular Verdi cinema (showing films in their original languages) usually get out just in time for a late-night supper in any of a number of bars and restaurants, including Botafumeiro, which closes at 1 am. Park Güell is best in the afternoon, when the sun spotlights the view east over the Mediterranean. Exploring Gràcia when the Llibertat and Revolució markets are closed would be a major loss, so plan to get here before 2 pm.

GETTING HERE

By metro, the Gràcia stop on the FGC (Ferrocarril de la Generalitat de Catalunya) trains that connect Sarrià, Sabadell, Terrassa, and Sant Cugat with Plaça de Catalunya is your best option. The metro's green line (L3) stations at Fontana and Lesseps put you in the heart of Gràcia and in hiking distance of Park Güell, respectively. The yellow line (L4) stop at Joanic is a short walk from Gràcia's northeast side.

QUICK BITES

Nou Candanchú. A refreshing stop, this bar runs tables inside and out until early morning, serving a variety of tapas, sandwiches, salads, and seafood dishes. Weather permitting, take a table out on the square and order a paella. ✉ *Pl. de la Vila de Gràcia 9, Gràcia* ☎ *93/237–7362* ✆ *Closed Tues.* Ⓜ *Gràcia (FGC).*

Botafumeiro. For an upscale treat, Botafumeiro never disappoints; the counter is the place to be for icy Albariño white wine and *pop a feira* (octopus on potato slices with smoked paprika), a Galician favorite. ✉ *Carrer Gran de Gràcia 81, Gràcia* ☎ *93/218–4230* ⊕ *botafumeiro.es/en* Ⓜ *Gràcia (FGC), L3 Fontana.*

In 1900 the house was sold to Antonio Jover, a prominent local doctor, and remained in the family until 2014, when it was sold to the Andorra-based MoraBank; the bank established a foundation to preserve this remarkable historic property, and opened it to the public in 2017. The interior is even more surprising than the outside, with its trompe-l'oeil birds painted on the walls and intricately carved ceilings; the fantasmic Moorish design and cupola in the little smoking alcove on the main floor is enough to make you wonder what folks back then were putting in their pipes. In any case, it is a must-visit.

Gaudí's second commission, built in 1885, was in the little town of Comillas in Santander, for the Marquès de Comillas, Antonio López y López, a shipping magnate and the most powerful man of his time. Not surprisingly, the two houses bear a striking resemblance to each other. ⊠ *Carrer de les Carolines 24–26, Gràcia* ⊕ *www.casavicens.org* Ⓜ *L3 Fontana, Lesseps.*

Gran de Gràcia. This highly-trafficked central artery up through Gràcia is lined with buildings of great artistic and architectural interest, beginning with the hotel **Can Fuster**. Built between 1908 and 1911 by Palau de la Música Catalana architect Lluís Domènech i Montaner in collaboration with his son Pere Domènech i Roure, the building shows a clear move away from the chromatically effusive heights of Art Nouveau. More powerful, and somehow less superficial, than much of that style of architecture, it uses the winged supports under the balconies and the floral base under the corner tower as important structural elements instead of as pure ornamentation, as Domènech i Montaner the elder might have. As you move up Gran de Gràcia, probable Francesc Berenguer buildings can be identified at No. 15; No. 23, with its scrolled cornice; and Nos. 35, 49, 51, 61, and 77. Officially attributed to a series of architects—Berenguer lacked a formal degree, having left architecture school to become Gaudí's "right hand"—these Moderniste masterworks have long inspired debate over Berenguer's role. ⊠ *Gran de Gràcia, Gràcia* Ⓜ *L3 Fontana, Lesseps; FGC Gràcia.*

Mercat de la Llibertat. This uptown version of the Rambla's Boqueria market is one of Gràcia's coziest spaces, a food market big enough to roam in and small enough to make you feel at home. Built by Francesc Berenguer between 1888 and 1893, the Llibertat market reflects, in its name alone, the revolutionary and democratic sentiment strong in Gràcia's traditionally blue-collar residents. Look for Berenguer's decorative swans swimming along the roof line and the snails surrounding Gràcia's coat of arms. ⊠ *Pl. Llibertat 27, Gràcia* ☎ *93/217–0995* ⊕ *www.bcn. es/mercatsmunicipals* ⊘ *Closed Sun.* Ⓜ *FGC Gràcia.*

Mercat de la Revolució. Officially the Abaceria Central, the market got its early name from the nearby Plaça de la Revolució de Setembre de 1868 just a block away up Carrer dels Desamparats. Browse your way through, and consider having something delicious such as a plate of wild mushrooms or a *tortilla de patatas* (potato omelet) at the bar and restaurant at the far corner on the lower east side. ⊠ *Travessera de Gràcia 186, Gràcia* ☎ *93/213–6286* ⊕ *www.mercatabaceria.com* Ⓜ *L4 Joanic, FGC Gràcia.*

FAMILY
Fodor's Choice
★

Park Güell. Alternately shady, green, floral, or sunny, this park is one of Gaudí's, and Barcelona's, most visited venues. Named for and commissioned by Gaudí's main patron, Count Eusebi Güell, it was originally intended as a gated residential community based on the English Garden City model, with a covered marketplace. The pillars of the market support the main public square above it, where impromptu dances and plays were performed. Only two of the houses were ever built (one of which, designed by Gaudí assistant Francesc Berenguer, became Gaudí's home from 1906 to 1926 and now houses the park's Gaudí museum). Gaudí highlights include the gingerbread gatehouses; the **Casa-Museu Gaudí,** where the architect lived; the Room of a Hundred Columns; and the fabulous serpentine polychrome bench that snakes along the main square by Gaudí assistant Josep Maria. Tickets can be booked online up to three months in advance. ⊠ *Carrer d'Olot s/n, Gràcia* ☎ *902/200302* ⊕ *www.parkguell.cat/en* ⚐ *€8 (€7 online)* Ⓜ *L3 Lesseps, Vallcarca.*

Plaça de la Vila de Gràcia. Originally named (until 2009) for the memorable Gràcia mayor Francesc Rius i Taulet, this is the town's most emblematic and historic square, marked by the handsome clock tower in its center. The tower, built in 1862, is just over 110 feet tall. It has water fountains around its base, royal Bourbon crests over the fountains, and an iron balustrade atop the octagonal brick shaft stretching up to the clock and belfry. The symbol of Gràcia, the clock tower was bombarded by federal troops when Gràcia attempted to secede from the Spanish state during the 1870s. Always a workers' neighborhood and prone to social solidarity, Gràcia was mobilized by mothers who refused to send their sons off as conscripts to fight for the crumbling Spanish Imperial forces during the late 19th century, thus requiring a full-scale assault by Spanish troops to reestablish law and order. Today sidewalk cafés prosper under the leafy canopy here. The Gràcia Casa de la Vila (town hall) at the lower end of the square is yet another Francesc Berenguer opus. ⊠ *Pl. de la Vila de Gràcia, Gràcia* Ⓜ *L3 Fontana, Gràcia (FGC).*

WORTH NOTING

Casa Comalat. At the bottom of Gràcia between the Diagonal and Carrer Còrsega, this often overlooked Moderniste house (not open to the public) built in 1911 is worth stopping by to view the exterior. For a look at the best side of this lower Gràcia Art Nouveau gem, cut down past Casa Fuster at the bottom of Gran de Gràcia, take a left on Bonavista, then a right on Santa Teresa down to Casa Comalat just across Carrer Còrsega. This Salvador Valeri i Pupurull creation is one of Barcelona's most interesting Moderniste houses, with its undulating polychrome ceramic balconies and its Gaudí-on-steroids columned arches on the ground level. Look for the curious wooden galleries, and the turret on the Carrer Corsega side of the building, clad in green ceramic tiles. Don't miss a look into the excellent Bar Mut at Pau Claris 192 just across the street. ⊠ *Av. Diagonal 442, Gràcia* ☎ *93/285–3834* Ⓜ *L3/L5 Diagonal.*

DID YOU KNOW?

Park Güell was originally built to be a private garden community. One of the houses built here became Gaudí's residence from 1906 to 1926.

BERENGUER: GAUDÍ'S RIGHT HAND

Francesc Berenguer's role in Gaudí's work and the Moderniste movement, despite his leaving architecture school prematurely to work for Gaudí, was significant (if not decisive), and has been much debated by architects and Art Nouveau scholars. If Barcelona was Gaudí's grand canvas, Gràcia was Berenguer's. Though he was not legally licensed to sign his projects, Berenguer is known to have designed nearly every major building in Gràcia, including the Mercat de la Llibertat. The house at Carrer de l'Or 44 remains one of his greatest achievements, a vertical tour de force with pinnacles at the stress lines over rich stacks of wrought-iron balconies. The Gràcia Town Hall in Plaça Rius i Taulet and the Centre Moral Instructiu de Gràcia at Carrer Ros de Olano 9 are confirmed as his; the buildings on Carrer Gran de Gràcia at Nos. 15, 23, 35, 49, 51, 61, 77, and 81 are all either confirmed or suspected Berenguer designs. Even Gaudí's first domestic commission, Casa Vicens, owes its palm-leaf iron fence to Berenguer. When Berenguer died young in 1914, at the age of 47, Gaudí said he had "lost his right hand." Indeed, in his last 12 years, Gaudí worked on nothing but the Sagrada Família and, in fact, made little progress there.

Casa-Museu Gaudí. Up the steps of **Park Güell** and to the right is the whimsical Alice-in-Wonderland-esque house where Gaudí lived with his niece from 1906 to his death in 1926. Now a small museum, exhibits include Gaudí-designed furniture and decorations, drawings, and portraits and busts of the architect. Stop by if you are in the area, but the museum is not worth traveling far for. ✉ *Park Güell, Carretera del Carmel 23A, Gràcia* ☎ *93/219–3811* ⊕ *www.casamuseugaudi.org* ✉ *€5.50* Ⓜ *L3 Lesseps, Vallcarca.*

Plaça de la Virreina. The much-damaged and oft-restored church of Sant Joan de Gràcia in this square stands where the Palau de la Virreina once stood, the mansion of the same *virreina* (wife, or in this case, widow of a viceroy) whose 18th-century palace, the Pallau de la Virreina, stands on the Ramblas. (The Palau is now a prominent municipal museum and art gallery.) The story of La Virreina, a young noblewoman widowed at an early age by the death of the elderly viceroy of Peru, is symbolized in the bronze sculpture in the center of the square: it portrays Ruth of the Old Testament, represented carrying the sheaves of wheat she was gathering when she learned of the death of her husband, Boaz. Ruth is the Old Testament paradigm of wifely fidelity to her husband's clan, a parallel to La Virreina—who spent her life doing good deeds with her husband's fortune.

The rectorial residence at the back of the church is the work of Gaudí's perennial assistant and right-hand man Francesc Berenguer. Just across the street, the house at Carrer de l'Or 44 was built in 1909, also by Berenguer. Giddily vertical and tightly packed into its narrow slot, it demonstrates one of his best tricks: putting up town houses that share walls with adjacent buildings. ✉ *Pl. de la Virreina, Gràcia* Ⓜ *L3 Fontana.*

Plaça del Diamant. This little square is of enormous sentimental importance in Barcelona as the site of the opening and closing scenes of 20th-century Catalan writer Mercé Rodoreda's famous 1962 novel *La Plaça del Diamant*. Translated by the late American poet David Rosenthal as *The Time of the Doves*, it is the most widely translated and published Catalan novel of all time: a tender yet brutal story of a young woman devoured by the Spanish civil war and, in a larger sense, by life itself. An angular and oddly disturbing steel and bronze statue in the square, by Xavier Medina-Campeny, portrays Colometa, the novel's protagonist, caught in the middle of her climactic scream. The bronze birds represent the pigeons that Colometa spent her life obsessively breeding; the male figure on the left pierced by bolts of steel is Quimet, her first love and husband, whom she met at a dance in this square and later lost in the war. Most of the people taking their ease at the cafés in the square will be unaware that some 40 feet below them is one of the largest air-raid shelters in Barcelona, hacked out by the residents of Gràcia during the bombardments of the civil war. ✉ *Pl. del Diamant* Ⓜ *L3 Fontana.*

Plaça Rovira i Trias. This charming little square and the story of Antoni Rovira i Trias shed much light on the true nature of Barcelona's eternal struggle with Madrid and Spanish central authority. Take a careful look at the map of Barcelona positioned at the feet of the bronze effigy of the architect and urban planners near the center of the square and you will see a vision of what the city might have looked like if Madrid's (and the Spanish army's) candidate for the design of the Eixample in 1860, Ildefons Cerdà, had not been imposed over the plan devised by Rovira i Trias, initial and legitimate winner of the open competition for the commission. Rovira i Trias's plan shows an astral design radiating out from a central Eixample square that military minds saw as avenues of approach; Cerdà's design, on the other hand, made the Diagonal into a natural barrier. ✉ *Pl. Rovira i Trias, Gràcia* Ⓜ *L3 Lesseps, L4 Joanic.*

UPPER BARCELONA: SARRIÀ AND PEDRALBES

Sightseeing
★★★
Nightlife
★★
Dining
★★★★
Lodging
★★★
Shopping
★★★

Sarrià was originally a country village, overlooking Barcelona from the foothills of the Collserola. Eventually absorbed by the westward-expanding city, the village, 15 minutes by FGC commuter train from Plaça de Catalunya, has become a unique neighborhood with at least four distinct populations: the old-timers, who speak only Catalan among themselves, and talk of "going down to Barcelona" to shop; writers, artists and designers, and people in publishing and advertising, drawn here in the '70s and '80s by the creative vibe; young wealthy starter families, who largely support Sarrià's gourmet shops and upscale restaurants; and a cadre of expats, who prize the neighborhood for its proximity to the international schools. Sarrià and environs, in fact, have perhaps more schools than any single postal code in Europe, many of them occupying what were once the palatial Moderniste summer homes of the city's financial and industrial moguls.

Did we mention gourmet shops? J. V. Foix, the famous Catalan poet, was a native son of Sarrià; his father founded what is arguably the best patisserie in Barcelona, and his descendants still run the quintessential Sarrià family business. On Sunday, barcelonins come to the village from all over town; Sunday just wouldn't be Sunday without a cake from Foix to take to grandma's. Cross Avinguda Foix from Sarrià and you're in Pedralbes—the wealthiest residential neighborhood in the city. (Fútbol superstar Leo Messi has his multimillion-euro home here, and the exclusive Real Club de Tenis de Barcelona is close by.) The centerpiece of this district is the 14th-century Monestir (Monastery) de Pedralbes; other points of interest include Gaudí's Pavellons de la Finca Güell on Avinguda de Pedralbes, and the gardens of the Palau Reial de Pedralbes, a 20-minute walk downhill from the monastery. The Futbol Club at Barcelona's Camp Nou stadium and the museum are another 20 minutes' walk, down below the Diagonal.

Getting Oriented

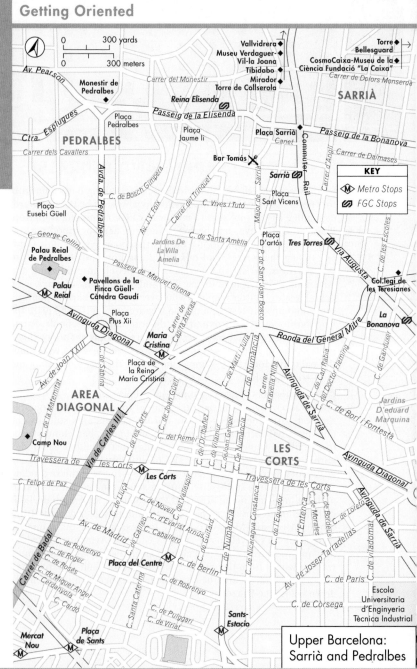

0 300 yards
0 300 meters

Av. Pearson

Monestir de Pedralbes

Carrer del Monestir

Vallvidrera ◆
Museu Verdaguer- ◆
Vil·la Joana
Tibidabo ◆
Mirador ◆
Torre de Collserola

Torre ◆
Bellesguard
CosmoCaixa-Museu de la ◆
Ciència Fundació "La Caixa"

Carrer de Dolors Monserdà

SARRIÀ

Reina Elisenda

Passeig de la Elisenda

Ctra. Esplugues

Plaça Pedralbes

PEDRALBES

Carrer dels Cavallers

Plaça Jaume Ii

Plaça Sarrià
Canet

Passeig de la Bonanova

Commuter Rail

Carrer d'Anglí

Carrer de Dalmases

Bar Tomás ✕

C. de Bosch Gimpera

Avda. de Pedralbes

C. de Trinquet

Major de Sarrià

Sarrià 🚇

Plaça Eusebi Güell

Av. J.V. Foix

C. Vives i Tutó

Plaça Sant Vicens

C. de Santa Amèlia

C. George Collins

Palau Reial de Pedralbes

Jardins De La Villa Amelia

Plaça D'artós

Tres Torres 🚇

Via Augusta

C. de les Escotes

Palau Reial 🚇

Pavellons de la Finca Güell-Càtedra Gaudí

Passeig de Manuel Girona

Carrer de Sant Joan Bosco

Col·legi de les Teresianes

Plaça Pius Xii

Maria Cristina 🚇

Avinguda Diagonal

Av. de Joan XXIII

C. de Sabina

Carrer de Capità Arenas

Ronda del General Mitre

La Bonanova

C. de Ganduxer

Plaça de la Reina María Cristina

AREA DIAGONAL

C. de la Maternitat

C. de Martí i Julià

Carrer Caravella Niña

Avinguda de Sarrià

C. de Can Rabia
C. del Doctor Fleming

C. de Bori i Fontestà

Jardins D'eduard Marquina

Camp Nou

C. de les Corts

C. de Joan Güell

C. del Rémei

C. del Dr. Ibañez

C. de Vilamur

C. de Numancia

Avinguda Diagonal

Travessera de les Corts

LES CORTS

Avinguda de Sarrià

C. Felipe de Paz

Les Corts 🚇

Travessera de les Corts

C. de Lluça

C. de Novell

C. del Vallespir

C. de Nicaragua

C. de Constança

C. de l'Equador

C. d'Entença

C. de Morales

C. de Bordeus

C. de Loreto

C. de viladomat

Av. de Madrid

C. de Galileo

C. d'Evarist Arnús

C. Caballero

C. de Guitard

C. de Numancia

Av. de Josep Tarradellas

C. de Paris

Escola Universitaria d'Enginyeria Tècnica Industrial

Carrer de Badal

C. de Robrenyo
C. de Roger
C. de Roses
C. de Miquel Angel
C. Cerdanyola
C. Cardó

Plaça del Centre 🚇

C. de Berlin

C. de Robrenyo

C. de Córsega

C. Santa Caterina

C. de Puiggari
C. de Viriat

Sants-Estacio 🚇

Mercat Nou 🚇

Plaça de Sants 🚇

Upper Barcelona: Sarrià and Pedralbes

KEY
🚇 Metro Stops
🚇 FGC Stops

2

TIMING

An exploration of Sarrià and Pedralbes is a three- to four-hour jaunt, including at least an hour in the monastery. Count four or five with lunch included. Plan to visit the monastery in the morning. Bar Tomás serves its famous potatoes with *allioli* (spicy garlic mayonnaise) 1–4 pm and 7–10 pm, another key timing consideration, while the Foix de Sarrià pastry emporium *(see Sarrià)* is open until 9 pm.

GETTING HERE

Sarrià is best reached on the FGC (Ferrocarril de la Generalitat de Catalunya) line, which is integrated with the city metro system, though a cut above. From Plaça de Catalunya, all the FGC trains (except those bound for Tibidabo) stop at Sarrià; only local trains branch off from there to the terminus at Reina Elisenda. The trip uptown takes about 15 minutes. By bus, you can take the V7, which runs from Plaça d'Espanya to Sarrià, or the No. 64, which takes a somewhat roundabout route from Barceloneta to Pedralbes, with a stop at Plaça Sarrià.

QUICK BITES

Bar Tomás. On the corner of Mayor de Sarrià and Carrer Jaume Piquet, Bar Tomás is a Barcelona institution, home of the finest *patatas bravas* (fried potatoes) in town—a cynosure so prosperous it can afford to shut for the night at 10 pm. Order the famous *doble mixta* of potatoes with *allioli* and hot sauce, and a draft beer (ask for a *caña*) to sluice them down. ⊠ *Major de Sarrià 49, Sarrià* ☎ *93/203–1077* ☉ *Closed Sun.* Ⓜ *Sarrià (FCG).*

TOP ATTRACTIONS

Monestir de Pedralbes

Plaça de Sarrià

Torre Bellesguard

TOP EXPERIENCES

Browsing through the Sarrià market

Stocking up on calories at Pasteleria Foix

Hiking up to the Torre de Bellesguard

Meditating in the cloister of the Pedralbes Monastery

Scarfing patatas allioli at Bar Tomás

Wandering the village streets

WHERE TO EAT (CH. 3)

A Contraluz

Bar Tomás

Dole Café

Fishhh!

Freixa Tradició

Tram-Tram

Vivanda

AREA SHOPS (CH. 7)

Big Sur La Cave

JC Apotecari

TOP ATTRACTIONS

FAMILY **Camp Nou.** If you're in Barcelona from September to June you can wit-
Fodor'sChoice ness the celebrated FC Barcelona play soccer (preferably against Real
★ Madrid) at Barcelona's gigantic stadium—a quintessential Barcelona
experience. Just walking down to the field from the Diagonal alongside
100,000 fans hushed in electric anticipation is unforgettable. Games
are normally played Saturday night at 9 pm or Sunday afternoon at
5 pm, though there may be international Champions League games
on Tuesday or Wednesday evening as well. A huge renovation project
approved in 2014 for Camp Nou is still in the works, slated to give the
stadium a roof, increase the seating capacity from 99,000 to 105,000,
and create a "quality gastronomic space" in the first tier for tapas and
desserts, with a bird's-eye view of the pitch. Can't conjure up game
tickets? You can still take the guided tour of the grounds, club facilities,
and the FC Barcelona museum—one of the city's most visited tourist
attractions. ⊠ *Arístides Maillol 12–18, Les Cortes* ☎ *902/189900 club
office and museum* ⊕ *www.fcbarcelona.cat* ✏ *Tour of museum, field,
and sports complex €25 online, €26.50 at box office* Ⓜ *L5 Collblanc,
L3 Palau Reial/Les Corts.*

OFF THE **CosmoCaixa–Museu de la Ciència Fundació "La Caixa".** Young scientific
BEATEN minds work overtime in this interactive science museum, just below
PATH Tibidabo. Among the many displays designed for children seven and
up are the Geological Wall, a history of rocks and rock formations; the
digital Planetarium; and the Underwater Forest, showcasing a slice of
the Amazonian rain forest in a large greenhouse. ⊠ *Carrer Isaac New-
ton 26, Sant Gervasi* ☎ *93/212–6050* ⊕ *obrasociallacaixa.org/es/cien-
cia/cosmocaixa/el-museo* ✏ *€4 (plus €4 per interactive activity inside);
accompanied children under 16 free* ☉ *Closed Mon.* Ⓜ *FGC line L7 to
Av. de Tibidabo and Tramvía Blau.*

Fodor'sChoice **Monestir de Pedralbes.** This marvel of a monastery, named for its original
★ white stones (*pedres albes*), is really a convent, founded in 1326 for
the Franciscan order of Poor Clares by Reina (Queen) Elisenda. The
three-story Gothic cloister, one of the finest in Europe, surrounds a
lush garden; the occasional evening concert of medieval music here is
an unforgettable experience. The day cells, where the nuns spend their
mornings praying, sewing, and studying, circle the arcaded courtyard.
The queen's own cell, the Capella de Sant Miquel, just to the right of the
entrance, has murals painted in 1346 by Catalan master Ferrer Bassa.
Look for the letters spelling out "*Joan no m'oblides*" ("John, do not
forget me") scratched between the figures of St. Francis and St. Clare
(with book and quill), written by a brokenhearted novice. Farther along,
inscriptions over the tombs of nuns who died here can be seen through
the paving grates. The nuns' upstairs dormitory contains the convent's
treasures: paintings, liturgical objects, and seven centuries of artistic and
cultural patrimony. Temporary exhibits are displayed in this space. The
refectory where the Poor Clares dined in silence has a pulpit used for
readings, while wall inscriptions exhort "*Silentium*" ("Silence"), "*Audi
tacens*" ("Listening makes you wise"), and "*Considera morientem*"
("Consider, we are dying"). Notice the fading mural in the corner, and

the paving tiles broken by heavy cannon positioned here during the 1809 Napoleonic occupation. ✉ *Baixada del Monestir 9, Pedralbes* ☎ *93/256–3434* ⊕ *monestirpedralbes.bcn.cat/en* 💶*€5; free Sun. after 3 pm, and 1st Sun. of every month* ⊘ *Closed Mon.* ☞ *The €7 multiticket to Museu d'Història de la Ciutat includes free admission to Monestir* Ⓜ *Reina Elisenda (FGC).*

Pavellons de la Finca Güell–Càtedra Gaudí. Work on the Finca began in 1883 as an extension of Count Eusebi Güell's family estate. Gaudí, the count's architect of choice, was commissioned to do the gardens and the two entrance pavillions (1884–87); the rest of the project was never finished. The Pavellons (pavillions) now belong to the University of Barcelona; the one on the right houses the Càtedra Gaudí, a Gaudí library and study center. The fierce wrought-iron dragon gate is Gaudí's reference to the Garden of the Hesperides, as described by national poet Jacint Verdaguer's epic poem *L'Atlàntida* (1877)—the *Iliad* of Catalonia's historic-mythic origins. The property is open for guided tours in English on weekends at 10:15, 11:15, and 3. Admission is limited to 25 visitors: call ahead, or book on the Ruta del Modernisme website. The Ruta is a walking tour covering 120 masterworks of the Moderniste period, including those by Gaudí, Domènech i Montaner, and Puig i Cadafalch. Pick up a guide— which includes a map, suggested short and longer itineraries, and a book of discount vouchers for admission to many of the sites—here at the Pavellons. ✉ *Av. Pedralbes 7, Pedralbes* ☎ *93/317–7652, 93/256–2504 guided tours* ⊕ *www.rutadelmodernisme.com* 💶*€5 (50% discount with Ruta del Modernisme packet)* Ⓜ *L3 Palau Reial.*

Sarrià. The village of Sarrià was originally a cluster of farms and country houses overlooking Barcelona from the hills. Once dismissively described as nothing but "winds, brooks, and convents," this quiet enclave is now a prime residential neighborhood at the upper edge of the city. Start an exploration at the square—the locus, at various times, of antique and bric-a-brac markets, book fairs, artisanal food and wine fairs, *sardana* dances (Sunday morning), concerts, and Christmas pageants. The 10th-century Romanesque **Church of Sant Vicenç** dominates the square; the bell tower, illuminated on weekend nights, is truly impressive. Across Passeig de la Reina Elisenda from the church (50 yards to the left) is the 100-year-old Moderniste **Mercat de Sarrià.**

From the square, cut through the Placeta del Roser to the left of the church to the elegant **Town Hall** (1896) in the Plaça de la Vila; note the buxom bronze sculpture of **Pomona,** goddess of fruit, by famed Sarrià sculptor Josep Clarà (1878–1958). Follow the tiny Carrer dels Paletes, to the left of the Town Hall (the saint enshrined in the niche is Sant Antoni, patron saint of *paletes,* or bricklayers), and right on Major de Sarrià, the High Street of the village. For lunch, try Casa Raphael, on the right as you walk down—in business (and virtually unchanged) since 1873. Farther on, turn left into **Carrer Canet.** The two-story row houses on the right were first built for workers on the village estates, now converted to other uses (including a preschool); these, and the houses opposite at Nos. 15, 21, and 23, are among the few remaining original village homes in Sarrià. Turn right at the first corner on Carrer Cornet i Mas and walk two blocks down to Carrer Jaume Piquet.

A quiet space for reflection: the courtyard of the Monestir de Pedralbes

On the left is No. 30, Barcelona's most perfect small-format **Modern-iste house,** thought to be the work of architect Domènech i Montaner, complete with faux-medieval upper windows, wrought-iron grillwork, floral and fruited ornamentation, and organically curved and carved wooden doors either by or inspired by Gaudí himself. The next stop down Cornet i Mas is Sarrià's prettiest square, **Plaça Sant Vicens,** a leafy space ringed by old Sarrià houses and centered on a statue of Sarrià's patron St. Vicenç, portrayed (as always) beside the millstone used to sink him to the bottom of the Mediterranean after he was martyred in Valencia in AD 302. **Can Pau,** the café on the lower corner with Carrer Mañé i Flaquer, is the local hangout, once a haven for authors Gabriel García Marquez and Mario Vargas Llosa, who lived in Sarrià in the late 1960s and early 1970s.

Other Sarrià landmarks to look for include the two **Foix** pastry shops, one at Plaça Sarrià 9–10 and the other at Major de Sarrià 57, above Bar Tomás. The late J.V. Foix (1893–1987), son of the shop's founder, was one of the great Catalan poets of the 20th century, a key player in keeping the Catalan language alive during the 40-year Franco regime. The shop on Major de Sarrià has a bronze plaque identifying the house as the poet's birthplace and inscribed with one of his most memorable verses, translated as, "Every love is latent in the other love / every language is the juice of a common tongue / every country touches the fatherland of all / every faith will be the lifeblood of a higher faith." ⊠ *Sarrià* Ⓜ *Sarrià (FGC Line L6).*

Fodor'sChoice
★ **Torre Bellesguard.** For an extraordinary Gaudí experience, climb up above Plaça de la Bonanova to this private residence built between 1900 and 1909 over the ruins of the summer palace of the last of the

sovereign count-kings of the Catalan-Aragonese realm, Martí I l'Humà (Martin I the Humane), whose reign ended in 1410. In homage to this medieval history, Gaudí endowed the house with a tower, gargoyles, and crenellated battlements; the rest—the catenary arches, the trencadís in the facade, the stained-glass windows—are pure Art Nouveau. Look for the red and gold Catalan *senyera* (banner) on the tower, topped by the four-armed Greek cross Gaudí often used. Over the front door is the inscription *"Sens pecat fou concebuda"* ("Without sin was she conceived"), referring to the Immaculate Conception of the Virgin Mary; on either side of the front door are benches with trencadís of playful fish bearing the crimson *quatre barres* (four bars) of the Catalan flag as well as the Corona d'Aragó (Crown of Aragón). Still a private home and long closed to visitors, the Torre Bellesguard is now accessible to small groups. ■TIP➔ Reservations required for the highly recommended guided tour (reserva@bellesguardgaudi.com). ✉ *Calle Bellesguard 16–20, Sant Gervasi* ☎ *93/250–4093* ⊕ *www.bellesguardgaudi. com* 🔊 *Full guided tour €16; self-guided tour of house and grounds €9 (with audio guide)* ⊘ *Closed Mon.* Ⓜ *Av. Tibidabo (FGC).*

OFF THE
BEATEN
PATH

Vallvidrera. This perched village is a quiet respite from Barcelona's headlong race. Oddly, there's nothing exclusive or upmarket—for now—about Vallvidrera, as most well-off barcelonins prefer to be closer to the center. From **Plaça Pep Ventura,** in front of the Moderniste funicular station, there are superb views over the Vallvidrera houses and the Montserrat. Vallvidrera can be reached from the Peu Funicular train stop and the Vallvidrera funicular, by road, or on foot from Tibidabo or Vil·la Joana. The cozy Can Trampa at the center of town in Plaça de Vallvidrera, and Can Martí down below are fine spots for a meal. ✉ *Vallvidrera* Ⓜ *Peu Funicular (FGC).*

WORTH NOTING

Col·legi de les Teresianes. Built in 1889 for the Reverend Mothers of St. Theresa, when Gaudí was still occasionally using straight lines, the upper floors of this former operating school are reminiscent of those in Berenguer's apartment at Carrer de l'Or 44, with its steep peaks and verticality. Hired to take over for another architect, Gaudí found his freedom of movement somewhat limited in this project. The dominant theme here is the architect's use of steep, narrow catenary arches and Mudejar exposed-brick pillars. The most striking effects are on the second floor, where two rows of a dozen catenary arches run the width of the building, each of them unique; as Gaudí explained, no two things in nature are identical. The brick columns are crowned with T-shaped brick capitals (for St. Theresa). Look down at the marble doorstep for the inscription by mystic writer and poet Santa Teresa de Avila (1515–82), the much-quoted "todo se pasa" (all things pass). The Col·legi is a private secondary school, and normally not open to visitors, but the sisters may organize guided group visits on request. ✉ *Ganduxer 85, Sant Gervasi* ☎ *93/212–3354* ⊕ *ganduxer.escolateresiana.com* Ⓜ *La Bonanova, Les Tres Torres (FGC).*

Museu Verdaguer–Vil·la Joana. Catalonian poet Jacint Verdaguer died in this house in 1902. The story of Verdaguer's reinvention of Catalan nationalism in the late 19th century, and his ultimate death in disgrace, defrocked and impoverished, is a fascinating saga. Considered the national poet of Catalonia and the most revered and beloved voice of the Catalan "Renaixença" of the 19th century, Verdaguer—universally known as *Mossèn Cinto* (Mossèn is Catalan for priest; Cinto is from Jacinto, Spanish for Jacint)—finally succumbed to tuberculosis and a general collapse triggered by economic, existential, and doctrinal religious troubles. Priest, poet, mystic, student, hiker, and lover of the Pyrenees, he was seen as a virtual saint, and wrote works of great religious and patriotic fervor such as *Idilis* and *Cants mistichs,* as well his famous long masterpiece, *Canigó* (1886). In *La Atlàntida* (1877), eventually to become a Manuel de Falla opera-oratorio, he wrote about prehistoric myths of the Iberian Peninsula and the Pyrenees. Verdaguer's death provoked massive mourning. His popularity was so enormous that violently anticlerical Barcelona anarchists in mid-uprising ceased fighting and stormed the churches to ring the bells on hearing the news of his death. The funeral was one of the most heavily attended events in Barcelona history, comparable only to Gaudí's in spontaneity and emotion.

Lines from his patriotic poem *Enyorança* (*Yearning*) are slowly and sonorously recited at Vil·la Joana every June 10 on the anniversary of his death. ✉ *Vil.la Joana, Ctra. de l'Església 104, Vallvidrera* ☎ *93/256–2122* ⊕ *www.museuhistoria.bcn.cat/es/muhba-villa-joana* ✒ *Free* Ⓜ *Baixador de Vallvidrera (FGC).*

Palau Reial de Pedralbes (*Royal Palace of Pedralbes*). Built in the 1920s as the palatial estate of Count Eusebi Güell—one of Gaudí's most important patrons—this mansion was transformed into a royal palace by architect Eusebi Bona i Puig and completed in 1929. King Alfonso XIII, grandfather of Spanish king Juan Carlos I, visited the palace in the mid-1920s before its completion. In 1931, during the Second Spanish Republic, the palace became the property of the municipal government, and it was converted to a decorative arts museum in 1932. (The museum is now part of the Disseny Hub complex in Plaça de les Glòries Catalanes.) In 1936 the rambling, elegant country-manor-house palace was used as the official residence of Manuel Azaña, last president of the Spanish Republic. The gardens and grounds are open to the public; the buildings are not. ✉ *Av. Diagonal 686, Pedralbes* Ⓜ *L3 Palau Reial.*

OFF THE BEATEN PATH

Tibidabo. One of Barcelona's two promontories, this hill bears a distinctive name, generally translated as "To Thee I Will Give." It refers to the Catalan legend that this was the spot from which Satan tempted Christ with all the riches of the earth below (namely, Barcelona). On a clear day, the views from this 1,789-foot peak are legendary. Tibidabo's skyline is marked by a neo-Gothic church, the work of Enric Sagnier in 1902, and—off to one side, near the village of Vallvidrera—the 854-foot communications tower, the **Torre de Collserola,** designed by Sir Norman Foster. If you're with kids, take the San Francisco–style Tramvía Blau (Blue Trolley) from Plaça

Kennedy to the overlook at the top, and transfer to the funicular to the 100-year-old **amusement park** at the summit. ⊠ *Pl. Tibidabo 3–4, Tibidabo* ☎ *93/211–7942* ⊕ *www.tibidabo.cat* ⊡ *Amusement park €28.50 (includes all rides and shows)* ⊘ *Closed Mon. and Tues.* Ⓜ *FGC L7 Tibidabo, then Tramvía Blau.*

OFF THE BEATEN PATH

Mirador Torre de Collserola. The Collserola communications tower was designed by Norman Foster for the 1992 Olympics; an industrial spike on an otherwise pristine wooded skyline, it was not universally admired. A vertigo-inducing elevator ride takes you to the observation deck. Take the FGC S1, S2, or S5 line to Peu del Funicular, then the funicular up to Vallvidrera; from the village of Vallvidrera it's a pleasant walk to the tower. ⊠ *Ctra. de Vallvidrera al Tibidabo s/n, Tibidabo* ☎ *93/211–7942* ⊕ *www.torredecollserola.com* ⊡ *€5.60* Ⓜ *Peu del Funicular (FGC).*

The L7 trains on the FGC (Ferrocarrils de la Generalitat de Catalunya, a separate system from the city-administered Metro) run from Plaça Catalunya to the Avinguda Tibidabo station in Plaça Kennedy, at the top of Carrer de Balmes. The first building on the right as you start up Avinguda del Tibidabo is known as La Rotonda, notable for its Art Nouveau ceramic ornamentation on the upper part of the facade. The Tramvía Blau (Blue Trolley) sets out from just above La Rotonda and, passing the imposing white **Casa Roviralta–El Frare Blanc,** drops you at Plaça del Doctor Andreu, where the funicular climbs up to the heights of **Tibidabo.** Plaça del Doctor Andreu has several restaurants, the best of which is La Venta. From Tibidabo the road to the **Torre de Collserola** continues another 2 km (1 mile) over to **Vallvidrera,** where there are several good restaurants (such as Can Trampa in Plaça de Vallvidrera). From Vallvidrera, return to Barcelona via the funicular or on foot. The other way to approach is via the Baixador de Vallvidrera stop on the FGC Generalitat railway line to San Cugat, Sabadell, or Terrassa. A five-minute walk up to the **Museu Verdaguer** at Vil·la Joana will put you on well-marked trails through the Parc de Collserola. There are also trail markings to Vil·la Joana from the Torre de Collserola. The Barcelona train from the Baixador de Vallvidrera will drop you back in Plaça de Catalunya in 20 minutes.

DID YOU KNOW?

The Museu Nacional d'Art de Catalunya embraces art from multiple mediums, including drawings, engravings, sculpture, paintings, photography, coinage, and objets d'art from the Romanesque era to the 20th century.

MONTJUÏC

Sightseeing	A bit remote f
★★★★★	more than jus
Nightlife	Museu Nacio
★★★	Pavilion, the
Dining	and auditoriu
★★★	factory) are a
Lodging	Museu Nacio
---	sidered the wo
Shopping	restoration fro
★★★	with their orig

collection of
Gothic art. Ot
stadium, the F
within Montj

TOP ATTRACTIONS

FAMILY **CaixaForum** (C
Fodor's Choice terpiece, origi
★ (architect of C
Quadras) is a
events, and w
leisure listings
lays on a whol
for kids. The c
liant example
ditional (even
by Japanese a
Jordi. ⊠ *Av. F*
⊕ *www.obras*

Fodor's Choice **Fundació Joan**
★ Miró to his na
modern and cc
views north c
and collaborat
added by Sert i

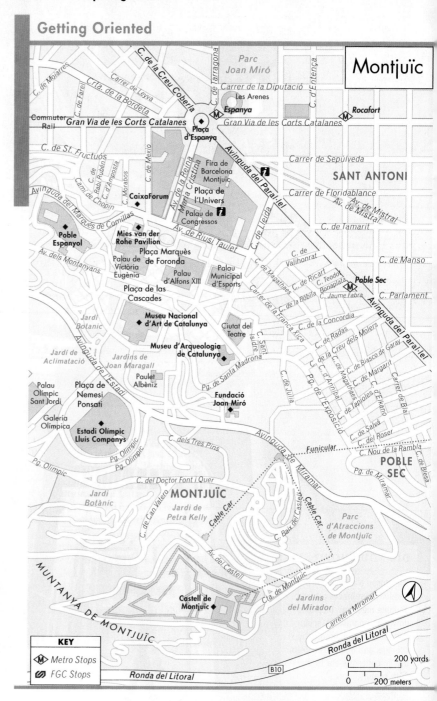

Getting Oriented

Montjuïc

Parc Joan Miró
C. de Tarragona
C. de la Creu Coberta
C. de Moiares
Carrer de Leiva
Crta. de la Bordeta
C. de Farell
Carrer de la Diputació
Les Arenes
Espanya Ⓜ
C. d'Entença
Rocafort Ⓜ
Commuter Rail
Gran Via de les Corts Catalanes
Gran Via de les Corts Catalanes
Plaça d'Espanya
C. de St. Fructuós
C. de Mèxic
Carrer de Sepúlveda
SANT ANTONI
C. de Fadi Rubert
Cami de Chopin
C. d'Amposta
C. Morabos
Fira de Barcelona Montjuïc
Carrer de Floridablance
Av. de Mistral
Avinguda del Marquès de Comillas
CaixaForum
Plaça de l'Univers
Palau de Congressos
C. de Tamarit
Av. dels Montanyans
Poble Espanyol
Mies van der Rohe Pavilion
Plaça Marquès de Foronda
Av. de Riusi Taulet
C. de Manso
Palau de Victòria Eugènia
Palau d'Alfons XIII
Palau Municipal d'Esports
C. de Valihonrat
C. de Ricart
C. Teodot
Poble Sec Ⓜ
C. de Manso
Plaça de las Cascades
Carrer de la França Xica
C. Jaume Fabra
C. Parlament
Jardí Botànic
Museu Nacional d'Art de Catalunya
Ciutat del Teatre
C. de la Concordia
C. de Radas
Jardí de Aclimatació
Jardins de Joan Maragall
Museu d'Arqueologia de Catalunya
C. de Sant Isidre
Pg. de Santa Madrona
C. de la Creu dels Molers
C. de Biasco de Garay
Paulet Albèniz
C. de Margarit
Palau Olímpic Sant Jordi
Plaça de Nemesi Ponsatí
Fundació Joan Miró
C. de Jula
de Tapioles
C'Elkano
Carrer de Blai
Galeria Olímpica
Estadi Olímpic Lluís Companys
C. dels Tres Pins
C. de Salvá
C. del Roser
Pg. Olímpic
Funicular
C. Nou de la Rambla
POBLE SEC
Pg. Olímpic
Avinguda de Miramar
Pg. de Miramar
C. del Doctor Font i Quer
Jardí Botànic
MONTJUÏC
Jardí de Petra Kelly
C. de Can Valero
Cable Car
Cable Car
Parc d'Atraccions de Montjuïc
Av. del Castell
C. Baix del Castell
MUNTANYA DE MONTJUÏC
Cta. de Montjuïc
Castell de Montjuïc
Jardins del Mirador
Carretera Miramart
Ronda del Litoral
B10
Ronda del Litoral

KEY
Ⓜ *Metro Stops*
◎ *FGC Stops*

0		200 yards
0		200 meters

TIMING

With unhurried visits to the Miró Foundation and any or all of the Museu Nacional d'Art de Catalunya collections in the Palau Nacional, this is a four- to five-hour excursion, if not a full day. Have lunch afterward in the Poble Espanyol, just up from Mies van der Rohe's Barcelona Pavilion or in the cafeteria-restaurant at the Fundació Miró.

GETTING HERE

The most dramatic approach to Montjuïc is the cross-harbor cable car (Transbordador Aeri) from Barceloneta or from the mid-station in the port. You can also take a taxi or Bus No. 61 (or walk) from Plaça d'Espanya; yet another option is the funicular from the Paral·lel (Paral·lel metro stop, L3). The Telefèric de Montjuïc from the funicular stop to the Castell de Montjuïc is the final leg to the top.

Architect Arata Isozaki designed the futuristic Palau Sant Jordi Sports Palace.

style, filled with Mediterranean light and humor, seems a perfect match for its surroundings, and the exhibits and retrospectives that open here tend to be progressive and provocative—look for Alexander Calder's fountain of moving mercury. Miró himself rests in the cemetery on Montjuïc's southern slopes. ⊠ *Av. Miramar 71–75, Parc de Montjuïc, Montjuïc* 🕾 *93/443–9470* ⊕ *www.fmirobcn.org* 🖃 *€12* ⊙ *Closed Mon.* Ⓜ *L1/L3 Pl. Espanya; L3 Paral.lel, then Funicular de Montjuic.*

Mies van der Rohe Pavilion. One of the masterpieces of the Bauhaus School, the legendary Pavelló Mies van der Rohe—the German contribution to the 1929 International Exhibition, reassembled between 1983 and 1986—remains a stunning "less is more" study in interlocking planes of white marble, green onyx, and glass. In effect, it is Barcelona's aesthetic antonym (in company with Richard Meier's Museu d'Art Contemporani and Rafael Moneo's Auditori) to the flamboyant Art Nouveau—the city's signature Modernisme—of Gaudí and his contemporaries. Note the mirror play of the black carpet inside the pavilion with the reflecting pool outside, or the iconic Barcelona chair designed by Ludwig Mies van der Rohe (1886–1969); reproductions have graced modern interiors around the world for decades. ⊠ *Av. Francesc Ferrer i Guàrdia 7, Montjuïc* 🕾 *93/423–4016, 93/215–1011* ⊕ *www.miesbcn.com* 🖃 *€5 (20% off with Barcelona and Bus Turistic cards)* Ⓜ *L1/L3 Pl. Espanya.*

Fodor'sChoice ★ **Museu Nacional d'Art de Catalunya** (*Catalonian National Museum of Art, MNAC*). Housed in the imposingly domed, towered, frescoed, and columned **Palau Nacional,** built in 1929 as the centerpiece of the International Exposition, this superb museum was renovated in 1995 by Gae Aulenti, architect of the Musée d'Orsay in Paris. In 2004 the museum's three holdings (Romanesque, Gothic, and the Cambó Collection—an eclectic trove, including a Goya, donated by Francesc Cambó) were joined by the 19th- and 20th-century collection of Catalan impressionist and Moderniste painters. Also now on display is the Thyssen-Bornemisza collection of early masters, with works by Zurbarán, Rubens, Tintoretto, Velázquez, and others. Pride of place goes to the Romanesque exhibition, the world's finest collection of Romanesque frescoes, altarpieces, and wood carvings, most of them rescued from chapels in the Pyrenees during the 1920s. The central hall of the museum, with its enormous pillared and frescoed cupola, is stunning. ⊠ *Palau Nacional, Parc de Montjuic s/n, Montjuïc* ☎ *93/622–0360* ⊕ *www.mnac.cat* ✉ *€12 (valid for day of purchase and 1 other day in same month; free Sat. after 3 pm and 1st Sun. of month); additional charges for access to special temporary exhibitions; access to rooftop panorama and bar €2* ☉ *Closed Mon.* Ⓜ *L1/L3 Pl. Espanya.*

WORTH NOTING

Castell de Montjuïc. Built in 1640 by rebels against Felipe IV, the castle has had a dark history as a symbol of Barcelona's military domination by foreign powers, usually the Spanish army. The fortress was stormed several times, most famously in 1705 by Lord Peterborough for Archduke Carlos of Austria. In 1808, during the Peninsular War, it was seized by the French under General Dufresne. Later, during an 1842 civil disturbance, Barcelona was bombed from its heights by a Spanish artillery battery. After the 1936–39 civil war, the castle was used as a dungeon for political prisoners. Lluís Companys, president of the Generalitat de Catalunya during the civil war, was executed by firing squad here on October 14, 1940. In 2007 the fortress was formally ceded back to Barcelona. The present uses of the space include a Interpretation Center for Peace, a Space for Historical Memory, and a Montjuïc Interpretation Center, along with cultural and educational events and activities. A popular weekend park and picnic area, the moat contains attractive gardens, with one side given over to an archery range, and the various terraces have panoramic views over the city and out to sea. From July through the first week of August on Mondays, Wednesdays, and Fridays from 8:30 pm the castle hosts the Sala Montjuic Open Air Cinema of subtitled classic films (⊕ *www.salamontjuic.org*), with live music concerts before the showings. ⊠ *Ctra. de Montjuïc 66, Montjuïc* ☎ *93/256–4440, 93/302–3553 for Sala Montjuic* ⊕ *www.bcn.cat/castelldemontjuic* ✉ *€5 (free Sun. from 3 pm); Sala Montjuic tickets €6.50* Ⓜ *L2/L3 Paral.lel and Funicular.*

Estadi Olímpic Lluís Companys (*Olympic Stadium*). Open for visitors, the Olympic Stadium was originally built for the International Exhibition of 1929, with the idea that Barcelona would then host the 1936 Olympics (ultimately staged in Hitler's Berlin). After failing twice to win the nomination, the city celebrated the attainment of its long-cherished goal by renovating the semi-derelict stadium—preserving the original facade and shell—in time for 1992, providing seating for 70,000. The nearby **Museu Olímpic i de l'Esport,** a museum about the Olympic movement in Barcelona, shows audiovisual replays from the 1992 Olympics, and provides interactive simulations for visitors to experience the training and competition of Olympic athletes. An information center traces the history of the modern Olympics from Athens in 1896 to the present. Next door and just downhill stands the futuristic **Palau Sant Jordi Sports Palace,** designed by the noted Japanese architect Arata Isozaki. ⊠ *Av. de l'Estadi s/n, Montjuïc* ☎ *93/426–2089 Estadi Olímpic, 93/292–5379 Museu Olímpica* ⊕ *www.fundaciobarcelonaolimpica.es* ⊠ *Free* ⊗ *Museum closed Mon.* Ⓜ *L1/L3 Espanya.*

Museu d'Arqueologia de Catalunya. Just downhill to the right of the Palau Nacional, the Museum of Archaeology holds important finds from the Greek ruins at Empúries, on the Costa Brava. These are shown alongside fascinating objects from, and explanations of, megalithic Spain. ⊠ *Passeig Santa Madrona 39–41, Montjuïc* ☎ *93/423–2149* ⊕ *www. mac.cat/eng* ⊠ *€4.50; last Tues. of month; free Oct.–June* ⊗ *Closed Mon.* Ⓜ *L1/L3 Pl. Espanya.*

Plaça d'Espanya. This busy circle is a good place to avoid, but sooner or later you'll probably need to cross it to go to the convention center or to the Palau Nacional. It's dominated by the so-called Venetian Towers (they're actually Tuscan) built in 1927 as the grand entrance to the 1929 International Exposition. The towers flank the lower end of the Avinguda Maria Cristina (the buildings on both sides are important venues for the trade fairs and industrial expositions that regularly descend on Barcelona); at the far end is the Font Màgica (the Magic Fountain, which has a spectacular nighttime display of lights and music) below the National Museum of Catalan Art in the Palau Nacional on Montjuic. The fountain is the work of Josep Maria Jujol, the Gaudí collaborator who designed the curvy and colorful benches in Park Güell. The sculptures are by Miquel Blay, one of the master artists and craftsmen who put together the Palau de la Música. To the right of the Towers, the neo-Mudejar bullring, Les Arenes, is now a multilevel shopping mall. On the corner of Carrer Llançà, just down to the right looking at the bullring, you can just get a glimpse of the huge polychromatic butterfly atop the Art Nouveau building known popularly as the "Casa de la Papallona" (House of the Butterfly). From the plaza, you can take the metro or Bus 38 back to the Plaça de Catalunya. ⊠ *Pl. Espanya, Sants* Ⓜ *L1/L3 Pl. Espanya.*

FAMILY
Fodor'sChoice
★

Poble Espanyol (*Spanish Village*). Created for the 1929 International Exhibition, the Spanish Village is a sort of open-air architectural museum, with faithful replicas to scale of building styles, from an Aragonese Gothic-Mudejar bell tower to the tower walls of Avila, drawn from all over Spain; the ground-floor spaces are devoted to boutiques, cafés and restaurants, workshops, and studios. The liveliest time to come is at night, and a reservation at one of the half dozen restaurants gets you in for free, as does the purchase of a ticket for either of the two discos or the Tablao del Carmen flamenco club. ⊠ *Av. Francesc Ferrer i Guàrdia 13, Montjuïc* ☎ *93/508–6300* ⊕ *www.poble-espanyol.com* ⊠ *€14 (€12.60 online); after 8 pm €7 (€6.30 online)* Ⓜ *L1/L3 Pl. Espanya.*

WHERE TO EAT

TAPAS, PINTXOS, MONTADITOS, AND OTHER BITE-SIZE FOOD

Barcelona arrived late on the tapas scene, which originated in Andalusia and flourished in the Basque Country, but Catalan restaurateurs eventually embraced tapas with abandon.

Tapas (small snacks or appetizers), got their moniker from the Spanish verb *tapar*, meaning "to cover"; they were originally pieces of ham or cheese laid across glasses of wine to keep flies out and stagecoach drivers sober.

The term now covers a wide variety of snacks, from individual bites on toothpicks to steaming pots of stick-to-your-ribs creations served in small portions.

A Seville-style evening of weaving from one tapas bar to the next, known as a *tapeo*, is difficult in Barcelona; while there are excellent spots, they're spread out widely across the city. Instead, pick one spot and work your way through the menu. Be sure to ask your server for a wine to match.

A BRIEF HISTORY

Tapas owes much to the Moorish presence on the Iberian Peninsula. The Moorish taste for small and varied delicacies has become Spain's best-known culinary innovation. Spanish king Alfonso X (1221–84) took small morsels with wine on his doctor's advice and so enjoyed the cure that he made it a regular practice in his court. Miguel de Cervantes, in his universal classic, *Don Quixote*, refers to tapas as *llamativos* (attention-getters), for their stimulating appetite-enhancing properties.

TAPAS 101

Belly up to the bar, order a drink, and dig in. You'll receive a plate for staging your tapas and collecting your toothpicks, which is sometimes how the bartender tallies up your bill. If you're sitting at a table, the waiter will keep track of the dishes you've ordered and bring them to you in rapid succession.

The term *tapas* covers various forms of nibbling. *Tentempiés* are "keep you on your feet" snacks. *Pintxos* are bite-size offerings on toothpicks; *banderillas* are wrapped in colorful paper resembling the batons used in bullfights. *Montaditos* are canapés, delicacies "mounted" on toast; *raciones* (rations) are hot tapas served in small casseroles.

A few tapas to try: *calamares* (fried cuttlefish, often mistaken for onion rings), *pulpo a feira* (aka *pulpo gallego*, octopus on slices of potato), *chipirones* (baby cuttlefish), *chistorra* (fried spicy Basque sausage), *champiñones* (mushrooms), *setas* (wild mushrooms), *gambas al ajillo* (shrimp cooked in parsley, oil, and garlic), *langostinos* (jumbo shrimp or prawns), *patatas bravas* (potatoes in spicy sauce), *pimientos de Padrón* (peppers from the Galician town of Padrón), and *almendras* (almonds fried and sprinkled with salt).

Some of the tastiest tapas often sound unappealing, so be bold and

take chances. *Caracoles* (snails) are usually served in a rich, meaty sauce, best mopped up with crusty bread after you've tackled the snails with a toothpick.

Many skeptics have been won over by *callos* (tripe), a hearty dish served in a spicy tomato sauce. *Morro* (pork rinds) is the perfect snack to enjoy with cold beer, as is *oreja* (fried pig's ear). *Anchoas* (salt-cured anchovies) are good, but even those who dislike them may enjoy *boquerones en vinagre* (anchovies marinated in vinegar and oil).

Updated by Steve Tallantyre

Barcelona's restaurant scene is an ongoing adventure. Between avant-garde culinary innovation and the more rustic dishes of traditional Catalan fare, there is a fleet of brilliant classical chefs producing some of Europe's finest Mediterranean cuisine.

Catalans are legendary lovers of fish, vegetables, rabbit, duck, lamb, game, and natural ingredients from the Pyrenees or the Mediterranean. The *mar i muntanya* (literally, "sea and mountain"—that is, surf and turf) is a standard. Combining salty and sweet tastes—a Moorish legacy—is another common theme.

The Mediterranean diet—based on olive oil, seafood, fibrous vegetables, onions, garlic, and red wine—is at home in Barcelona, embellished by Catalonia's four basic sauces: *allioli* (whipped garlic and olive oil), *romesco* (almonds, nyora peppers, hazelnuts, tomato, garlic, and olive oil), *sofregit* (fried onion, tomato, and garlic), and *samfaina* (a ratatouille-like vegetable mixture).

Typical entrées include *faves a la catalana* (a broad-bean stew), *arròs caldós* (a rice dish more typical of Catalonia than paella, often made with lobster), and *espinacas a la catalana* (spinach cooked with oil, garlic, pine nuts, raisins, and cured ham). Toasted bread is often doused with olive oil and rubbed with squeezed tomato to make *pa amb tomaquet*—delicious on its own or as a side order.

Beware of the advice of hotel concierges and taxi drivers, who have been known to falsely warn that the place you are going is either closed or no good anymore, and to instead recommend places where they get kickbacks.

Aside from restaurants, Barcelona is brimming with bars and cafés, the latter of which can serve as an outdoor meeting spot or a place to socialize and enjoy a cocktail. Be advised that the sidewalk cafés along La Rambla are noisy, dusty, overpriced, and exposed to pickpockets.

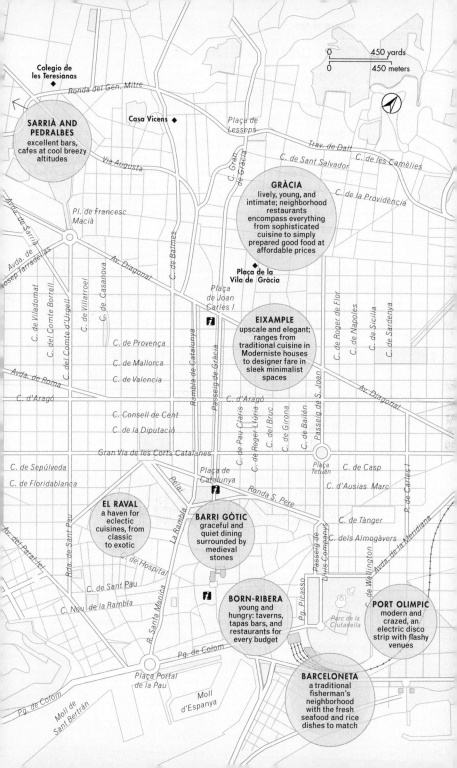

BARCELONA DINING PLANNER

DINING PLANNER

EATING-OUT STRATEGY

The selection here represents the best this city has to offer—from tapas bars to haute cuisine.

HOURS

Barcelona dines late. Lunch is served from 2 to 4 pm and dinner from 9 to 11 pm. Arrive a half hour early if you want to secure a table, but the liveliness of each place picks up later in the evening. The city is slowly adapting to the eating timetables of tourists, and a number of restaurants now offer all-day and late-night hours. Satiate cravings between meals in the city's numerous cafés and tapas bars.

PRICES

Barcelona is no longer a bargain. Though low-end fixed-price lunch menus can be found for as little as €10, most good restaurants cost closer to €40 or €50 for a full meal when ordering à la carte. For serious evening dining, plan on spending €55–€80 (or more) per person.

■ TIP→ Barcelona restaurants, even many of the pricey establishments, offer a daily lunchtime menu (menú del día) consisting of two courses plus wine, coffee, or dessert.

WHAT IT COSTS IN EUROS				
	$	$$	$$$	$$$$
Restaurants	under €15	€15–€22	€23–€29	over €29

Prices in the restaurant reviews are the average cost of a main course at dinner or, if dinner is not served, at lunch.

TIPPING AND TAXES

Tipping, though common (and appreciated), is not required; the gratuity is included in the check. If you do tip as an extra courtesy, anywhere from 5% to 10% is perfectly acceptable.

The 10% Value-Added Tax (IVA) will not appear on the menu, but is tacked on to the final tally on your check.

RESERVATIONS

Nearly all of Barcelona's best restaurants require reservations. As the city has grown in popularity, more and more receptionists are able to take your reservations in English. Your hotel concierge will also be happy to call and reserve you a table.

USING THE MAPS

Throughout the chapter, you'll see mapping symbols and coordinates (✢ F:2) at the end of the reviews that correspond to the atlas at the end of this chapter. The letter and number after the symbol indicate the property's coordinates on the map grid.

RESTAURANT REVIEWS

Restaurants are listed alphabetically within neighborhoods. Reviews have been shortened. For full information, visit Fodors.com.

CIUTAT VELLA (OLD CITY)

Ciutat Vella includes La Rambla, Barri Gòtic, Born-Ribera, and El Raval districts between Plaça de Catalunya and the port. Chic new restaurants and cafés seem to open daily in Barcelona's Ciutat Vella, but classic, family-owned eateries still offer generations of accumulated culinary expertise.

BARRI GÒTIC

$$ CATALAN 🍴 **Agut.** Wainscoting and 1950s canvases are the background for the mostly Catalan crowd in this homey restaurant in the lower reaches of the Barri Gòtic. Agut was founded in 1924, and its popularity has never waned—after all, hearty Catalan fare at a fantastic value is always in demand. **Known for:** must-try civet of wild boar; local wines; local favorite. [$] *Average main: €15* ✉ *Gignàs 16, Barri Gòtic* ☎ *93/315–1709* 🌐 *www.restaurantagut.com* 🕒 *Closed Sun. and Mon. and 2 wks in Aug.* [M] *Jaume I* ✥ *I:13.*

$$ TAPAS FAMILY 🍴 **Bobo Pulpín.** A family-friendly restaurant looking onto the back of the cathedral with food that's fit for the choosiest of grown-ups. Look past the stuffed toys and cartoon menus and you'll find traditional tapas, creative octopus dishes, and lighter plates full of dense flavors. **Known for:** child-friendly atmosphere; superior tapas. [$] *Average main: €17* ✉ *Freneria 5, Barri Gòtic* ☎ *93/639–3213* 🌐 *bobopulpin.com* [M] *Jaume I* ✥ *I:12.*

$$$$ CATALAN 🍴 **Caelis.** Newly relocated to the Hotel OhLa Barcelona near the Palau de la Música Catalana, Caelis keeps its starred, fine-dining style and adds the pizzazz of open-kitchen show cooking. The two tasting menus (€87 and €132) change regularly and you can pick a course from them as an à la carte alternative. **Known for:** refined fine dining; open kitchen. [$] *Average main: €42* ✉ *Laietana, 49, Barri Gòtic* ☎ *93/510–1205* 🌐 *www.caelis.com* 🕒 *Closed Sun. and Mon.* [M] *Urquinaona* ✥ *I:12.*

$$ CATALAN 🍴 **Cafè de l'Acadèmia.** With wicker chairs, stone walls, and classical music, this place is sophisticated-rustic; contemporary Mediterranean cuisine specialties such as *timbal d'escalibada amb formatge de cabra* (roast vegetable salad with goat cheese) make it more than just a café. Politicians and functionaries from the nearby Generalitat frequent this dining room, which is always boiling with life. **Known for:** lively terrace; great set lunch. [$] *Average main: €16* ✉ *Lledó 1, Barri Gòtic* ☎ *93/319–8253* 🕒 *Closed weekends and 2 wks in Aug.* [M] *Jaume I* ✥ *I:13.*

$ ECLECTIC 🍴 **Cuines Santa Caterina.** A lovingly restored market designed by the late Enric Miralles and completed by his widow Benedetta Tagliabue provides a spectacular setting for one of the city's most original dining operations. Under the undulating wooden superstructure of the market, the breakfast and tapas bar offers a variety of culinary specialties. **Known for:** open all day; vegetarian options; Mediterranean fare. [$] *Average main: €14* ✉ *Av. Francesc Cambó 16, Barri Gòtic* ☎ *93/268–9918* 🌐 *www.grupotragaluz.com* [M] *Urquinaona, Jaume I* ✥ *J:12.*

CLOSE UP

A Primer on Barcelona's Cuisine

Menus in Catalan are as musical as they are aromatic, with rare ingredients such as *salicornia* (seawort, or sea asparagus) with *bacalao* (cod), or fragrant wild mushrooms such as *rossinyols* (chanterelles) and *moixernons* (St. George's mushroom) accompanying dishes like *mandonguilles amb sepia* (meatballs with cuttlefish).

Four sauces grace the Catalan table: *sofregit* (fried onion, tomato, and garlic—a base for nearly everything); *samfaina* (a ratatouille-like sofregit with eggplant and sweet red peppers); *picada* (garlic, almonds, bread crumbs, olive oil, pine nuts, parsley, saffron, or chocolate); and *allioli* (pounded garlic and virgin olive oil).

The three *e*'s deserve a place in any Catalan culinary anthology: *escalibada* (roasted red peppers, eggplants, and tomatoes served in garlic and olive oil); *esqueixada* (shredded salt-cod salad served raw with onions, peppers, olives, beans, olive oil, and vinegar); and *escudella* (a winter stew of meats and vegetables with noodles and beans).

Universal specialties are *pa amb tomaquet* (toasted bread with squeezed tomato and olive oil), *espinaques a la catalana* (spinach cooked with raisins, garlic, and pine nuts), and *botifarra amb mongetes* (pork sausage with white beans). The *mar i muntanya* (Catalan "surf

'n' turf") has been a standard since Roman times. Rice dishes are simply called *arròs*, and range from standard seafood paella to the *arròs a banda* (paella with shelled prawns, shrimp, and mussels), to *arròs negre* (paella cooked in cuttlefish ink) or *arròs caldós* (a brothy risotto-like dish often made with lobster). *Fideuà* is a paella made of vermicelli noodles, not rice.

Fresh fish such as *llobarro* (sea bass, *lubina* in Spanish) or *dorada* (gilthead bream) cooked *a la sal* (in a shell of salt) are standards, as are grilled *llenguado* (sole) and *rodaballo* (turbot). Duck, goose, chicken, and rabbit frequent Catalan menus, as do *cabrit* (kid or baby goat), *xai* (lamb), *porc* (pork), *vedella* (young beef), and *bou* (mature beef). Finally come the two Catalan classic desserts, *mel i mató* (honey and fresh cream cheese) and *crema catalana* (a crème brûlée–like custard with a caramelized glaze).

A typical session *à table* in Barcelona might begin with *pica-pica* (hors d'oeuvres), a variety of delicacies such as *jamón ibérico de bellota* (acorn-fed ham), *xipirones* (baby squid), *pimientos de Padrón* (green peppers, some spicy), or *bunyols de bacallà* (cod fritters or croquettes), and pa amb tomaquet. From here you can order a starter such as *canelones* (cannelloni) or you can go straight to your main course.

$$

BASQUE

✕ **Irati Taverna Basca.** There's only one drawback to this lively Basque bar between Plaça del Pi and La Rambla: it's narrow at the street end, and harder to squeeze into than the Barcelona metro at rush hour. Skip the tapas on the bar and opt for the plates brought out piping-hot from the kitchen. **Known for:** quick bites; Basque specialities; txakoli wine. $ *Average main:* €17 ⊠ *Cardenal Casañas 17, Barri Gòtic* ☎ *93/302–3084* ⊕ *www.iratitavernabasca.com* Ⓜ *Liceu* ✛ *H:12.*

$$$$ ✕ **Koy Shunka.** Two blocks away from their mothership Shunka, part-
JAPANESE ners Hideki Matsuhisa and Xu Changchao have done it again. This
time, with more space to work with, the Japanese-Chinese team of
master chefs has organized a tribute to Asian fusion cooking based
on products from the Catalan larder. **Known for:** inventive fusion
cuisine; contemporary atmosphere; scrumptious cerdo ibérico. $ *Av-
erage main: €30* ✉ *Copons 7, Barri Gòtic* ☎ *93/412–7939* ⊕ *www.
koyshunka.com* ☉ *Closed Mon. and 3 wks in Aug. No dinner Sun.*
Ⓜ *Urquinaona* ✛ *I:12.*

$ ✕ **La Castanya.**"The Chestnut" turns out inventive, slow-food tapas in
TAPAS an eclectic, bohemian setting. Italian chef Nico brings his fine-dining
FAMILY experience to bear on bite-sized dishes including osso-bucco croquettes,
oysters, trout tataki, and a hispano-Italian salmorejo-mozzarella salad
collision. **Known for:** exceptional burgers and sandwiches; Italian-Span-
ish tapas; late hours. $ *Average main: €8* ✉ *Escudellers 30, Barri Gòtic*
☎ *93/667–1617* ⊕ *barnawood.com/la-castanya* Ⓜ *Drassanes* ✛ *H:13.*

$ ✕ **La Cereria.** At the corner of Baixada de Sant Miquel and Passatge
VEGETARIAN de Crèdit, this humble terrace and musical instrument store/café has
charm to spare. The tables in the Passatge itself are shady and breezy in
summer, and the vegetarian and vegan cuisine is organic and creative.
Known for: creative vegetarian and vegan cuisine; tasty escalivada;
next to birthplace of Catalan painter Joan Miró. $ *Average main: €10*
✉ *Baixada de Sant Miquel 3–5, Barri Gòtic* ☎ *93/301–8510* ☉ *Closed
Sun. and Mon.* Ⓜ *Liceu* ✛ *H:13.*

$ ✕ **La Palma.** Behind the Plaça Sant Jaume's *ajuntament* (city hall),
CAFÉ toward the post office, sits this cozy and ancient café. An old favorite of
early-20th-century artists ranging from Salvador Dalí to Pablo Picasso,
it has marble tables, wine barrels, sausages hanging from the ceiling,
and newspapers to pore over. **Known for:** local wines; historic setting.
$ *Average main: €10* ✉ *Palma Sant Just 7, Barri Gòtic* ☎ *93/315–0656*
⊕ *www.bodegalapalma.com* ▭ *No credit cards* ☉ *Closed Sun. No lunch
in Aug.* Ⓜ *Jaume I* ✛ *I:13.*

$$ ✕ **La Plassohla.** A trendy international crowd packs this place, sam-
TAPAS pling tapas such as free-range eggs cooked at low temperature with
mushrooms, and charcoal-grilled fresh mussels with tomato sauce.
The stylish, high-ceilinged space keeps noise levels under control, and
huge windows allow both natural light and views of passing street life.
Known for: sophisticated atmosphere; open late; cheap fixed lunch.
$ *Average main: €20* ✉ *Via Laietana 49, Barri Gòtic* ☎ *93/341–5050*
⊕ *www.ohlabarcelona.com* Ⓜ *Urquinaona* ✛ *I:12.*

$$$$ ✕ **Mercer.** The Mercer hotel's beautiful, historical restaurant has been a
CATALAN revolving door for chefs in recent years, but Harry Wieding has stuck
his foot in to hold it closed with an ingredient-led menu based on
Catalan classics. Don't miss the smokey grilled mussels, which won
him the Catalan Chef of the Year award. **Known for:** beautiful his-
toric architecture; organic garden-fresh produce; award-winning grilled
mussels. $ *Average main: €30* ✉ *Lledó 7, Barri Gòtic* ✛ *Entrance is
through lobby of the Mercer hotel* ☎ *93/310–7480* ⊕ *www.mercerbar-
celona.com/en/restaurants/mercer-restaurant* ☉ *Closed Sun. and Mon.*
Ⓜ *Jaume I* ✛ *I:13.*

$$ CATALAN 🍴 **Pla.** Filled with couples night after night, this combination music, drinking, and dining place is candlelit and sleekly designed in glass over ancient stone, brick, and wood. The cuisine is light and contemporary, featuring inventive salads and fresh seafood, as well as options for vegetarians and vegans. **Known for:** romantic ambience; extensive wine list. [$] *Average main: €20* ✉ *Bellafila 5, Barri Gòtic* ☎ *93/412–6552* 🌐 *www.restaurantpla.cat* ⏲ *No lunch* [M] *Jaume I* ✥ *I:13.*

BORN-RIBERA

$$ TAPAS 🍴 **Cal Pep.** A two-minute walk east of Santa Maria del Mar, Cal Pep has been in a permanent feeding frenzy for more than 30 years, intensified even further by the hordes of tourists who now flock here. Pep serves a selection of tapas, cooked and served hot over the counter. **Known for:** excellent fish fry; delicious potato omelet; lively counter scene. [$] *Average main: €20* ✉ *Pl. de les Olles 8, Born-Ribera* ☎ *93/310–7961* 🌐 *www.calpep.com* ⏲ *Closed Sun. and 3 wks in Aug. No lunch Mon.* [M] *Jaume I, Barceloneta* ✥ *J:13.*

$$ ECLECTIC 🍴 **El Foro.** Painting and photographic exhibits line the walls of this large and lively Born restaurant, and the menu is dominated by meat cooked over coals, pizzas, and salads. Flamenco and jazz performances downstairs are a good post-dinner diversion. **Known for:** Argentine meat; live jazz. [$] *Average main: €18* ✉ *Princesa 53, Born-Ribera* ☎ *93/310–1020* 🌐 *www.restauranteelforo.com* ⏲ *Closed Mon.* [M] *Jaume I* ✥ *J:13.*

$$$$ SEAFOOD 🍴 **El Passadís d'en Pep.** Hidden away at the end of a narrow unmarked passageway off the Pla del Palau, near the Santa Maria del Mar church, this restaurant is a favorite with well-heeled and well-fed gourmands who tuck in their napkins before devouring some of the city's best traditional seafood dishes. Sit down and waiters will begin serve delicious starters of whatever's freshest that day in the market in rapid-fire succession. **Known for:** fresh seafood; starters served in rapid-fire succession; no menu. [$] *Average main: €30* ✉ *Pl. del Palau 2, Born-Ribera* ☎ *93/310–1021* 🌐 *www.passadis.com* ⏲ *Closed Sun. and 3 wks in Aug.* [M] *Jaume I* ✥ *J:13.*

$ TAPAS 🍴 **El Xampanyet.** Just down the street from the Museu Picasso, dangling *botas* (leather wineskins) announce one of Barcelona's liveliest and most visually appealing taverns, with marble-top tables and walls decorated with colorful ceramic tiles; it's usually packed to the rafters with a rollicking mob of local and out-of-town celebrants. Avoid the treacle house sparkler—go for draft beer, real cava, or wine—but don't miss the *pa amb tomàquet* (toasted bread with squeezed tomato and olive oil) or the Iberian ham. **Known for:** perfect Iberian ham; mouthwatering pa amb tomàquet; real cava. [$] *Average main: €10* ✉ *Montcada 22, Born-Ribera* ☎ *93/319–7003* 💳 *No credit cards* ⏲ *Closed Mon., Easter wk, and Aug. No dinner Sun.* [M] *Jaume I* ✥ *J:13.*

$$$ BASQUE 🍴 **Euskal Etxea.** An elbow-shaped, pine-paneled space, this spot (one of the Sagardi group of Basque restaurants) is one of the better grazing destinations in the Barri Gòtic, with a colorful array of tapas and canapés on the bar, ranging from the olive-pepper-anchovy on a toothpick to chunks of tortilla. Other good bets include the *pimientos de piquillo* (red piquillo peppers) stuffed with codfish paste. **Known for:** Basque

Barcelona's Sweet Tooth

For a long time, desserts were the Achilles heel of the Barcelona culinary scene. Diners groaning in anticipation after devouring their lovingly prepared starters and entrées often experienced disappointment when the final course arrived at the table—straight from the local supermarket's deep freeze. Occasionally, the waiter delivered a good, homemade *crema catalana* (crème brûlée), but the odds of a truly memorable ending to one's meal weren't favorable. To find Barcelona's sweet spot, you needed to skip the *postres* and head to the local *pastiseria.*

These neighborhood bakeries have always supplied Catalans with a cornucopia of seasonal treats. Some of the most beloved delectables include *xuixos* (pastries stuffed with, yes, crema catalana) and *pastissets de cabell d'àngel* (half-moon pastries). *Coques* are flatbreads, usually enjoyed around Easter, Christmas, or on saints' days. They're often topped with pine nuts and candied fruit, or even some delicious sweet-and-savory combinations, such

as pork crackling and sugar. *Panellets* are another local favorite, worth seeking out in autumn: balls of baked marzipan and pine nuts served with a sweet wine.

More acclaimed establishments have raised the bar for Barcelona desserts, and local chefs are applying the lessons learned in prestigious local cooking schools. One of them, the dazzlingly innovative school-restaurant Espai Sucre (Sugar Space), specializes in all things sweet.

For the best treats in town, try the chocolate. Oriol Balaguer sells pure black gold at his two shops, which look more like exquisite jewelry stores than food retailers. Often rated among the world's top chocolatiers, he competes with Enric Rovira for the crown of Catalonia's best. Another contender for top haute confectioner is Cacao Sampaka, founded by Quim Capdevila. Travelers with children should consider a trip to the Museu de la Xocolata (Chocolate Museum) in El Born, where they can enjoy some finger-licking fun in the workshops, and shop for delicious sweets in the museum shop.

pintxos; art gallery on-site; excellent Euskal Txerria confit. $ *Average main: €23* ⊠ *Placeta de Montcada 1–3, Born-Ribera* ☎ *93/310–2185,* ⊕ *www.gruposagardi.com* Ⓜ *Jaume I* ✛ *J:13.*

$ ✕ **La Báscula de la Cerería.** On one of the Born area's most picturesque
VEGETARIAN   streets, you'll find this cozy vegetarian and vegan café. The building was actually the main candy factory in 19th- and early-20th-century Barcelona. **Known for:** homemade cakes; sustainable and organic ingredients; daily specials. $ *Average main: €9* ⊠ *Carrer del Flassaders 30 bis, Born-Ribera* ☎ *93/319–9866* ▭ *No credit cards* ◷ *No dinner Sun.* Ⓜ *Jaume I* ✛ *J:13.*

$$ ✕ **La Habana Vieja.** If you have an itch for a taste of Old Havana—
CUBAN   *ropa vieja* (shredded beef) or *moros y cristianos* (black beans and rice) with *mojitos* (a cocktail of rum, mint, and sugar), or a round of *plátanos a puñetazos* (punched plantains)—this is your Barcelona refuge. The upstairs tables overlooking the bar are cozy little crow's

nests, and the neighborhood is filled with quirky dives and saloons for pre- and post-dinner carousing. **Known for:** Cuban specialities; post-dinner hot spot. [$] *Average main: €16* ✉ *Banys Vells 2, Born-Ribera* ☎ *93/268–2504* 🌐 *www.habanavieja.es* 🕑 *No lunch Mon. No dinner Sun.* [M] *Jaume I* ✣ *J:13.*

$ ITALIAN 🍴 **Le Cucine Mandarosso.** This no-frills, big-flavor southern-Italian restaurant near the Via Laietana is a favorite with locals. Like Naples itself, it's cheap, charming, and over-full, with a generous €11 lunch menu featuring authentic ingredients from the in-store deli. **Known for:** reservations not accepted; long wait times; great homemade pastas. [$] *Average main: €8* ✉ *Verdaguer i Callís 4, Born-Ribera* ☎ *93/269–0780* 🌐 *www.lecucinemandarosso.com* [M] *Urquinaona* ✣ *I:12.*

$$ TAPAS 🍴 **Llamber.** It may look like one of the stylish, tourist-trap tapas restaurants that have sprung up recently, but Llamber's culinary pedigree sets it apart from the competition; chef Francisco Heras earned his chops in Spain's top restaurants. This dapper, friendly space attracts a mixed crowd with its excellent wine list and well-crafted tapas based on classic Catalan and Asturian recipes. **Known for:** well-crafted tapas; traditional Catalan and Asturian specialities; delectable eggplant with honey. [$] *Average main: €16* ✉ *Fusina 5, Born-Ribera* ☎ *93/319–6250* 🌐 *www.llamber.com* [M] *Jaume 1* ✣ *J:13.*

$$ ECLECTIC 🍴 **Mercat Princesa.** The ancient exposed-brick walls and cozy nooks of this compact tapas market are home to 17 different food stands. Located one street behind Carrer Montcada and the Picasso Museum, it's a unique space that offers a round-the-world snack selection including Basque pintxos, sushi, gourmet fried eggs, and pizza. **Known for:** off the beaten path; live music or DJ on Thursdays; beer and wine tastings. [$] *Average main: €17* ✉ *Flassaders 21, Born-Ribera* ☎ *93/268–1518* 🌐 *www.mercatprincesa.com* 💳 *No credit cards* [M] *Jaume I* ✣ *J:13.*

$$$ BASQUE 🍴 **Sagardi.** An attractive wood-and-stone cider-house replica, Sagardi piles the counter with a dazzling variety of cold tapas; even better, though, are the hot offerings straight from the kitchen. The restaurant in back serves Basque delicacies like veal sweetbreads with artichokes and *txuletas de buey* (beef steaks) grilled over coals. **Known for:** multiple locations, all equally good; veal sweetbreads; charcoal grill. [$] *Average main: €24* ✉ *Argenteria 62, Born-Ribera* ☎ *93/319–9993* 🌐 *www.gruposagardi.com* [M] *Jaume I* ✣ *I:13.*

LA RAMBLA

$ CAFÉ 🍴 **Café de l'Opera.** Directly across from the Liceu opera house, this high-ceiling Art Nouveau café has welcomed operagoers and performers for more than 100 years. It's a central point on the Rambla tourist traffic pattern, so locals are increasingly hard to find, but the Café has hung onto its atmosphere of faded glory nonetheless. **Known for:** Art Nouveau decor; historical location. [$] *Average main: €14* ✉ *La Rambla 74, La Rambla* ☎ *93/317–7585* 🌐 *www.cafeoperabcn.com* [M] *Liceu* ✣ *H:12.*

$ CAFÉ 🍴 **Café Viena.** There are seven Viena cafés in Catalonia, but this particular branch is always packed with international travelers trying what Mark Bittman of the *New York Times* once consecrated as "the best sandwich in the world." One wonders if it was the only one he'd ever eaten. **Known for:** quick bites; ham sandwich. [$] *Average main: €12* ✉ *La Rambla 115, La Rambla* ☎ *93/317–1492* 🌐 *www.viena.es* [M] *Catalunya* ✥ *H:11.*

$ CAFÉ 🍴 **Café Zurich.** This traditional café at the top of La Rambla and directly astride the main metro and transport hub remains the city's prime meeting point. Forget the food and enjoy a beer or coffee at a table on the terrace, perhaps the best spot in the city to observe street life. **Known for:** people-watching; sunny terrace; watch for pickpockets. [$] *Average main: €5* ✉ *Pl. de Catalunya 1, La Rambla* ☎ *93/317–9153* [M] *Catalunya* ✥ *H:11.*

3

$ CATALAN 🍴 **Can Culleretes.** Just off La Rambla in the Barri Gòtic, this family-run restaurant founded in 1786 displays tradition in both decor and culinary offerings. Generations of the Manubens and Agut families have kept this unpretentious spot—Barcelona's oldest restaurant, listed in the *Guinness Book of Records*—popular for more than two centuries. **Known for:** Barcelona's oldest restaurant; traditional Catalan cuisine; large portions. [$] *Average main: €14* ✉ *Quintana 5, La Rambla* ☎ *93/317–3022* 🌐 *www.culleretes.com* 🕒 *Closed Mon. and mid-July–1st wk of Aug. No dinner Sun.* [M] *Liceu* ✥ *H:13.*

EL RAVAL

$ ISRAELI 🍴 **A Tu Bola.** Fresh, falafel-like balls of meat, fish, and vegetables in unique, mouthwatering combinations are prepared with laser-sharp focus by Israeli chef Shira. Everything from the *harissa* (spicy chili paste) to the *hummus* is made by hand, elevating the standard far beyond that of typical street-food in the surrounding Raval. **Known for:** quality street food; quick snacks; amazing chocolate ball dessert. [$] *Average main: €12* ✉ *Hospital 78, El Raval* ☎ *93/315–3244* 🌐 *www.atubolarest.com* 🕒 *Closed Tues.* [M] *Liceu* ✥ *G:12.*

$$ TAPAS 🍴 **Bar Cañete.** A superb tapas and *platillos* (small plates) emporium, this spot is just around the corner from the Liceu Opera House. The long bar overlooking the burners and part of the kitchen leads down to the 20-seat communal tasting table at the end of the room. **Known for:** Spanish ham specialists; superb tapas; secreto ibérico. [$] *Average main: €20* ✉ *Unió 17, El Raval* ☎ *93/270–3458* 🌐 *www.barcanete.com/en* 💳 *No credit cards* 🕒 *Closed Sun.* [M] *Liceu* ✥ *G:13.*

$ CATALAN 🍴 **Ca l'Estevet.** Ca l'Estevet has been serving up old-school Catalan cuisine to local and loyal customers since 1940 (and under a different name for 50 years before that). The practice has been made perfect; tuck into the likes of grilled botifarra sausages or roasted kid. **Known for:** Catalan specialities; large portions of escudella i carn d'olla (meat stew). [$] *Average main: €14* ✉ *Valldonzella 46, El Raval* ☎ *93/302–4186* 🌐 *www.restaurantestevet.com* 🕒 *No dinner Sun.* [M] *Universitat* ✥ *G:11.*

$$$ CATALAN Fodor's Choice ★ 🍴 **Ca l'Isidre.** A throwback to an age before foams and food science took over the gastronomic world, this restaurant has elevated simplicity to the level of the spectacular since the early 1970s. Isidre and Montserrat share their encyclopedic knowledge of local cuisine with guests, while their daughter Núria cooks traditional Catalan dishes. **Known for:** once frequented by Miró and Dalí; locally sourced produce; art collection. [$] *Average main: €29* ✉ *Les Flors 12, El Raval* ☎ *93/441–1139* 🌐 *www.calisidre.com* 🕒 *Closed Sun. and 1st 2 wks of Aug.* [M] *Paral.lel* ✥ *F:13.*

Café Zurich has been a popular meeting spot since the 1920s.

$$ **Cera 23.** Top pick among a crop of new restaurants putting the razzle
SPANISH back into the run-down Raval, Cera 23 offers a winning combination of
great service and robust cooking in a fun, friendly setting. Stand at the
bar and enjoy a blackberry mojito while you wait for your table. **Known
for:** volcano black rice; open kitchen viewable to diners; exceptional
service. *$ Average main: €16 ⊠ Cera 23, El Raval* ☎ *93/442–0808*
⊕ *www.cera23.com* ☾ *No lunch Tues. and Wed.* Ⓜ *Sant Antoni* ✛ *F:12.*

$$$ **Dos Palillos.** After 10 years as the chief cook and favored disciple of
ECLECTIC pioneering chef Ferran Adrià, Albert Raurich opened this Asian-fusion
restaurant—and he's since garnered a Michelin star. Past the typical
Spanish bar in the front room, the Japanese dining room inside is a canvas of rich black surfaces bordered with red chairs. **Known for:** creative
pan-Asian cooking; gin- and chocolate-filled donuts; interesting wine
pairings. *$ Average main: €29 ⊠ Elisabets 9, El Raval* ☎ *93/304–0513*
⊕ *www.dospalillos.com* ☾ *Closed Sun. and Mon. and mid-Aug.–Sept.
1. No lunch Tues. and Wed.* Ⓜ *Catalunya, Universitat* ✛ *H:11.*

$$ **Dos Pebrots.** Albert Raurich of Dos Palillos has transformed his favor-
MEDITERRANEAN ite neighborhood haunt into a retro cutting-edge tapas bar that explores
FAMILY the history of Mediterranean cuisine. Everything from the Roman con-
Fodor's Choice diment *garum* to 10th-century Xarab fruit salad gets reinvented in a
★ contemporary context. **Known for:** historical-themed tapas; unique
dishes like pigs' nipples; restored original exterior. *$ Average main:
€20 ⊠ Doctor Dou 19, El Raval* ☎ *93/853–9598* ⊕ *www.dospebrots.
com* Ⓜ *Catalunya* ✛ *H:11.*

$ **En Ville.** With pan-Mediterranean cuisine and reasonable prices,
BISTRO this attractive bistro 100 yards west of the Rambla in the MACBA
section of El Raval is a keeper. The inexpensive lunch menu attracts

in-the-know locals, and à la carte choices like scallops with pea foam are tempting and economical. **Known for:** value lunch menu; romantic setting; gluten-free cuisine. $ *Average main: €14* ⊠ *Doctor Dou 14, El Raval* 🕾 *93/302–8467* ⊕ *www.envillebarcelona.es/en* ⊗ *No dinner Sun. Closed Aug. 10–17* Ⓜ *Catalunya, Liceu, Universitat* ✢ *H:11.*

$$ ✕ **Fonda España.** The sumptuous glory of this restored late-19th-century

CATALAN Art Nouveau dining room now has food to match, courtesy of superstar chef Martín Berasategui. Avoid the overelaborate "gastronomic voyage" tasting menu and feast à la carte on updated period dishes such as "the mermaids"—a smooth cod pil-pil (a Basque sauce)—and pigeon with a liver paté heart. **Known for:** Art Nouveau decor; satisfying traditional dishes; excellent set lunches. $ *Average main: €20* ⊠ *Sant Pau 9, El Raval* 🕾 *93/550–0000* ⊕ *www.hotelespanya.com* ⊗ *No dinner Sun.* Ⓜ *Liceu* ✢ *H:13.*

$$ ✕ **4amb5 Mujades.** A mujada is an archaic unit of field measurement

CATALAN in Catalonia, and vegetables—but not vegetarianism—are the focus here. Impeccable, seasonal, homegrown produce stars in root, leaf, flower, and fruit dishes that relegate meat to a supporting role. **Known for:** creative vegetable dishes; homegrown produce. $ *Average main: €18* ⊠ *Rambla de Raval 45, El Raval* 🕾 *93/681–5093* ⊕ *suculent.com/en/4amb5* ⊗ *Closed Tues.* Ⓜ *Liceu* ✢ *G:13.*

$ ✕ **Opera Samfaina.** This gastronomic fantasyland below the Liceu opera

CATALAN house should be terrible but it smashes straight through kitsch and into

FAMILY pure fun. A multisensory mash-up of movie, food, wine, and mind-

Fodor's Choice bending design from the multi-starred Roca brothers, it merges tapas

★ bar with total madness to create a unique take on Catalan food traditions. **Known for:** watch a movie while you eat; multiple tapas bars; excellent local wines. $ *Average main: €13* ⊠ *La Rambla 51, El Raval* 🕾 *93/481–7871* ⊕ *www.operasamfaina.com* Ⓜ *Liceu* ✢ *H:13.*

$$ ✕ **Suculent.** This is a strong contender for the crown of Barcelona's best

CATALAN bistro. Up-and-coming young chef Antonio Romero is working with

Fodor's Choice established megastar Carles Abellan to turn out tapas and dishes that

★ have roots in rustic classics but reach high modern standards of execution. **Known for:** delicious bread for dipping; must-try steak tartare on marrow bone. $ *Average main: €20* ⊠ *Rambla del Raval 43, El Raval* 🕾 *93/443–6579* ⊕ *www.suculent.com* ⊗ *Closed Mon. and Tues.* Ⓜ *Liceu* ✢ *G:12.*

POBLE SEC

$$$ ✕ **espai Kru.** What happens when one of Barcelona's most venerable

ECLECTIC seafood restaurants joins the creative cooking revolution? The answers

Fodor's Choice can be found at espai Kru, upstairs from the eye-wateringly expensive

★ Rías de Galicia, where the finest ingredients from the deep are given a more modestly priced makeover in contemporary surroundings. **Known for:** fresh seafood; oyster bar; light-as-air lobster sandwiches. $ *Average main: €28* ⊠ *Lleida 7, Poble Sec* 🕾 *93/424–8152* ⊕ *www.espaikru.com* ⊗ *Closed Mon. No dinner Sun.* Ⓜ *Pl. Espanya/Poble Sec* ✢ *E:11.*

$$ ✕ **Quimet i Quimet.** A foodie haunt, this tiny place is hugely popular with

TAPAS locals and in-the-know visitors alike. If you show up too late, you might not be able to get in—come before 1:30 pm and 7:30 pm, however,

and you might snag a stand-up table. **Known for:** local wines; family-run; intimate space (long wait times). $ *Average main: €15* ⊠ *Poeta Cabanyes 25, Poble Sec* ☎ *93/442–3142* ⊙ *Closed Sun. and Aug. No dinner Sat.* Ⓜ *Paral.lel* ⊹ *E:13.*

$$$$

TAPAS

✕**Tickets.** Ferran and Albert Adrià of former "World's Best Restaurant" elBulli fame are the ringleaders behind this circus-themed big top of creative tapas. Tickets offers tapas twists you've never dreamed of, like strawberry-bearing trees (complete with pruning scissors) with pistachio acorns, and a round-the-world ride of oysters. **Known for:** off-the-wall creativity; online reservations only; enthusiastic and knowledgeable waitstaff. $ *Average main: €30* ⊠ *Av. Paral.lel 164, Poble Sec* ⊕ *www.ticketsbar.es/en* ⊙ *Closed Mon. No lunch Tues.–Fri.* Ⓜ *Poble Sec* ⊹ *E:11.*

BARCELONETA AND THE PORT OLÍMPIC

Barceloneta and the Port Olímpic (Olympic Port) have little in common beyond their seaside location. Port Olímpic offers a somewhat massive-scaled and modern environment with a crazed disco strip, while Barceloneta has retained its traditional character as a blue-collar neighborhood, even if few fishermen live here now. Traditional family restaurants and tourist traps can look similar from the street; a telltale sign of unreliable establishments is the presence of hard-selling waiters outside, aggressively courting passing customers.

$$

MEDITERRANEAN

✕**Agua.** Hit Agua's terrace on warm summer nights and sunny winter days, or just catch rays inside the immense bay windows. Either way you'll have a prime spot for beachside people-watching. **Known for:** fresh seafood; must reserve in advance; popular tourist spot. $ *Average main: €20* ⊠ *Passeig Marítim de la Barceloneta 30, Marina Village, Port Olímpic* ☎ *93/225–1272* ⊕ *www.grupotragaluz.com* Ⓜ *Ciutadella–Vila Olímpica* ⊹ *L:15.*

$$$$

TAPAS

✕**Arola.** Top-class tapas on a terrace are surprisingly hard to find, which is why sophisticated snack-seekers head for the eponymous restaurant of Michelin-starred chef Sergi Arola in the Hotel Arts. DJs provide a chilled-out evening atmosphere where diners can sip cocktails and enjoy views of Frank Gehry's Mediterranean-facing *Fish* statue. **Known for:** signature patatas bravas; novel presentation of dishes; superior quality. $ *Average main: €30* ⊠ *Marina 19–21, Port Olímpic* ⊹ *Entrance is via lift near street-level entrance to Hotel Arts* ☎ *93/483–8090* ⊕ *www.hotelartsbarcelona.com* ⊙ *Closed Tues.* Ⓜ *Ciutadella/Vila Olimpica* ⊹ *L:15.*

$$$

SEAFOOD

✕**Barceloneta.** This restaurant in an enormous riverboat-like building at the end of the yacht marina in Barceloneta is definitely geared up for high-volume business. The food is delicious, the service impeccable, and the hundreds of fellow diners make the place feel like a cheerful New Year's Eve celebration. **Known for:** lively spot; excellent salads, rice, and fish dishes; free valet parking. $ *Average main: €27* ⊠ *L'Escar 22, Barceloneta* ☎ *93/221–2111* ⊕ *www.restaurantbarceloneta.com* Ⓜ *Barceloneta* ⊹ *I:15.*

$$ ✕ **Barraca.** Sea views and superior seafood dishes have elevated this breezy faux beach shack to a top-tier restaurant in this former fishermen's district. Star chef Xavier Pellicer drops by regularly to check that the paella, chili shellfish, and spicy signature *patatas bravas* (potatoes) remain up to scratch. **Known for:** organic wines on the terrace; top-notch paella; all-day kitchen. Ⓢ*Average main: €20* ⊠ *Passeig Marítim Barceloneta 1, Barceloneta* ☎ *93/224–1253* ⊕ *www.tribuwoki.com* Ⓜ *Barceloneta* ✣ *J:15.*

SEAFOOD
Fodor's Choice
★

$$ ✕ **Bestial.** Sea views from a multilevel terrace are Bestial's most obvious attraction, but its luxury location beneath Frank Gehry's *Fish* statue is in no way diminished by the food. On the menu, spicy clams and seasonal soups lead up to a star dish of roasted wild fish on a bed of waxy potatoes. **Known for:** beachfront terrace; fresh seafood; pre-club crowd. Ⓢ *Average main: €18* ⊠ *Ramon Trias Fargas 2–4, Port Olímpic* ☎ *93/224–0407* ⊕ *www.grupotragaluz.com* Ⓜ *Ciutadella-Vila Olímpica* ✣ *L:15.*

MEDITERRANEAN

$$$ ✕ **Bravo 24.** The gleaming glass walls of the ultramodern Hotel W are an unlikely place to find some of Barcelona's most traditional dishes, but celebrity chef Carles Abellan has playfully crafted an old-fashioned menu that gives hipness a history lesson. The decked terrace, complete with sun-loungers, is prime spot on sunny days. **Known for:** delicious stew recipe dating to 1728; dishes come with a history lesson; Barcelona's best chicken croquettes. Ⓢ *Average main: €29* ⊠ *Pl. Rosa dels Vents 1, Barceloneta* ✣ *The restaurant is reached by stairs or elevator from hotel lobby* ☎ *93/295–2686* ⊕ *www.w-barcelona.com* Ⓜ *Barceloneta* ✣ *H:16.*

CATALAN

$$$ ✕ **Can Majó.** One of Barcelona's best-known seafood restaurants sits by the beach in Barceloneta and specializes in such house favorites as *caldero de bogavante* (a cross between paella and lobster bouillabaisse) and *suquet* (fish stewed in its own juices), but the full range of typical Spanish rice and seafood dishes are also available. Can Majó doesn't consistently reach the standards that once made it famous, but the cooking is still a notch above most of the touristy haunts nearby. **Known for:** terrace overlooking the Mediterranean; Spanish rice and fish dishes. Ⓢ *Average main: €26* ⊠ *Almirall Aixada 23, Barceloneta* ☎ *93/221–5455* ⊕ *www. canmajo.es* ⊘ *Closed Mon. No dinner Sun.* Ⓜ *Barceloneta* ✣ *J:15.*

SEAFOOD
FAMILY

$$$ ✕ **Can Solé.** With no sea views or touts outside to draw in diners, Can Solé has to rely on its reputation as one of Barceloneta's best options for seafood for more than 100 years. Faded photos of half-forgotten local celebrities line its walls but there's nothing out-of-date about the food. **Known for:** open kitchen; fresh fish daily; traditional Spanish rice dishes. Ⓢ *Average main: €28* ⊠ *Sant Carles 4, Barceloneta* ☎ *93/221– 5012* ⊕ *restaurantcansole.com* ⊘ *Closed Mon. and 2 wks in Aug. No dinner Sun.* Ⓜ *Barceloneta* ✣ *I:15.*

SEAFOOD
Fodor's Choice
★

$$$ ✕ **1881 Per Sagardi.** Views of yachts sailing out into the glittering Mediterranean sea and the aroma of a wood-fired grill that turns out classic Basque cuisine are a compelling combination here. The Sagardi group's most stylish establishment is perched atop a handsomely renovated former warehouse, which now houses the Catalan History Museum. **Known for:** pleasant terrace; all-day kitchen; sea views. Ⓢ *Average main: €24* ⊠ *Pl. de Pau Vila 3, Barceloneta* ☎ *93/221–0050* ⊕ *www. gruposagardi.com* Ⓜ *Barceloneta* ✣ *J:14.*

BASQUE

3

$$ CATALAN FAMILY

🍴 **El Nou Ramonet.** This spin-off restaurant has finally stepped out of Can Ramonet's shadow thanks to the input of Manairó's chef Jordi Herrera. He's built on the Barceloneta blueprint of classic tapas and added his signature creativity to dishes such as fresh sardines blowtorched tableside and garlicky salt-cod fritters, served in a jaunty, nautical environment. **Known for:** good value set lunch; creative twists on traditional tapas and seafood. [$] *Average main: €20* ✉ *Carbonell 5, Barceloneta* ☎ *93/268–3313* 🌐 *www.grupramonet.com* [M] *Barceloneta* ✥ *J:14.*

LA BARCELONETA, LAND OF PAELLA

Paella is Valencian, not Catalan, but Sunday paella in La Barceloneta is a classic Barcelona family outing. *Paella marinera* is a seafood rice boiled in fish stock and seasoned with clams, mussels, prawns, and jumbo shrimp, while the more traditional paella valenciana omits seafood but includes chicken, rice, and snails. *Arròs negre* (black rice) is rice cooked in squid ink, and *arròs caldòs* is a soupier dish that often includes lobster. *Fideuá* is made with vermicelli noodles mixed with the standard ingredients. Paella is for a minimum of two diners—it's usually enough for three.

$$ TAPAS Fodor's Choice ★

🍴 **El Vaso de Oro.** A favorite with gourmands, this often overcrowded little counter serves some of the best beer and tapas in town. The house-brewed artisanal draught beer—named after the Fort family who own and run the bar—is drawn and served with loving care by veteran epauletted waiters who have it down to a fine art. **Known for:** old-school service; stand-up dining; beef fillet is a favorite. [$] *Average main: €15* ✉ *Balboa 6, Barceloneta* ☎ *93/319–3098* 🌐 *www.vasodeoro.com* ⏲ *Closed 1st 3 wks of Sept.* [M] *Barceloneta* ✥ *J:14.*

$$$$ CATALAN

🍴 **Enoteca.** Located in the Hotel Arts, Enoteca is the Barcelona outlet for the talents of five-Michelin star chef Paco Pérez, two of which he has earned here. His creative and technically accomplished cooking uses peerless Mediterranean and Pyrenean products, transforming them into astonishing dishes that are both surprising and satisfying. **Known for:** superstar chef; extensive wine list; tasting menu with Quentin Tarantino–inspired dishes. [$] *Average main: €40* ✉ *Hotel Arts, Marina 19, Port Olímpic* ☎ *93/483–8108* 🌐 *www.enotecapacoperez.com* ⏲ *Closed Sun.* [M] *Ciutadella–Vila Olímpica* ✥ *L:15.*

$ VEGETARIAN

🍴 **Green Spot.** To call somewhere one of Barcelona's best vegan and vegetarian restaurants can be to damn it with faint praise—this is very much a city of omnivores. But Green Spot's pale oak paneling elegantly frames an open kitchen and airy dining room serving fun, fresh fusion food that everyone will like. **Known for:** delicious black pizza with activated charcoal; craft beer. [$] *Average main: €14* ✉ *Reina Cristina 12, Barceloneta* ✥ *Main door is in pedestrianized Porxos de Xifré between Passeig Colom and Port Vell* ☎ *93/802–5565* 🌐 *www.encompaniadelobos.com* [M] *Barceloneta* ✥ *J:14.*

$ TAPAS Fodor's Choice ★

🍴 **La Cova Fumada.** There's no glitz, no glamour, and not even a sign on the wall, but the battered wooden doors of this old, family-owned tavern hide a tapas bar to be treasured. Loyal customers queue for the market-fresh seafood, served hot from the furiously busy kitchen.

Known for: impromptu live music; the original "bomba" fried potato croquette. $ *Average main: €10* ✉ *Del Baluard 56, in corner of Barceloneta's main market square, Barceloneta* ☎ *93/221–4061* ⊗ *Closed Sun. No dinner Mon.–Wed. and Sat.* Ⓜ *Barceloneta* ✚ *J:15.*

$$ ✕ **La Mar Salada.** This restaurant stands out on a street of seafood specialists by offering creative twists on classic dishes at rock-bottom prices. Traditional favorites such as paella, black rice, and fideuà (a paella-like pasta dish) are reinvigorated, and freshness is assured as ingredients come directly from the lonja fish quay across the street, a lively auction where Barcelona's small fishing fleet sells its wares. **Known for:** fresh in-season ingredients; excellent value seafood; creative desserts. $ *Average main: €20* ✉ *Passeig Joan de Borbó 58, Barceloneta* ☎ *93/221–2127* ⊕ *www.lamarsalada.cat* ⊗ *Closed Tues.* Ⓜ *Barceloneta* ✚ *I:15.*

SEAFOOD
Fodor's Choice
★

$$ ✕ **Pez Vela.** The quality of beach-side dining in Barcelona has surged in recent years, and this pseudo- *chiringuito* (beach bar) beneath the towering W Hotel is as good a place as any to combine paella with a perfect view of the sea. Rice dishes are better than at many better-known seafood specialists. **Known for:** Galician-style octopus; zingy lemon pie. $ *Average main: €20* ✉ *Passeig del Mare Nostrum 19–21, Barceloneta* ☎ *93/221–6317* ⊕ *www.grupotragaluz.com* Ⓜ *Barceloneta* ✚ *H:16.*

SPANISH
FAMILY

EIXAMPLE

The sprawling blocks of the Eixample contain Barcelona's finest selection of restaurants, from upscale and elegant traditional cuisine in Moderniste houses to high-concept fare in sleek minimalist-experimental spaces. Many chefs with experience in multi-star kitchens have started their own businesses here, leading to the so-called "bistronomic" movement of tiny restaurants offering limited menus of humble ingredients cooked to exacting standards. These stellar experiences at budget prices are as close as you can still get to a bargain in Barcelona.

$$$$ ✕ **Angle.** ABaC may hog the spotlight, but chef Jordi Cruz's second restaurant, the relatively humble Angle, is an oft-overlooked star in its own right. Eschewing the gonzo creativity of the mother ship, it instead focuses on a greatest hits menu of Cruz's dishes that have proven their appeal over the years. **Known for:** value fixed lunch; Bloody Mary appetizer; celebrity chef. $ *Average main: €75* ✉ *Aragó 214, Eixample* ☎ *93/216–7777* ⊕ *www.anglebarcelona.com* Ⓜ *Universitat* ✚ *H:9.*

CATALAN

$ ✕ **Au Port de la Lune.** The stereotypical decor of this French bistro (think Serge Gainsbourg photos) verges on parody, but the authentic food is no joke. "There's no ketchup. There's no Coca-Cola. And there never will be," reads Guy Monrepos's sign that sets the tone for a no-compromise showcase of Gallic gastronomy. **Known for:** classic French bistro food; no substitutions; outrageously boozy sorbet. $ *Average main: €12* ✉ *Pau Claris 103, Eixample* ☎ *93/412–2224* ⊕ *www.auportdelalune.net* ⊗ *No dinner Sun. No early breakfast weekends* Ⓜ *Passeig de Gràcia* ✚ *I:10.*

FRENCH
Fodor's Choice
★

$$$
CATALAN

✕ **Bar Mut.** Just above Diagonal, this elegant retro space serves first-rate products ranging from wild sea bass to the best Ibérico hams. Crowded, noisy, chaotic, delicious—it's everything a great tapas bar or restaurant should be. **Known for:** upmarket tapas; great wine list; snacks at nearby spin-off Entrepanes Diaz. $ *Average main: €28* ☒ *Pau Claris 192, Eixample* ☎ *93/217–4338* ⊕ *www.barmut.com* Ⓜ *Diagonal* ✛ *I:8.*

$
CAFÉ

✕ **Bar Paris.** Always a popular place to hang out and watch barcelonins kill some time, this lively café has hosted everyone from local poets to King Felipe. The tapas are nothing special but the sandwiches are excellent and the beer is cold. **Known for:** open every day of the year; superior sandwiches. $ *Average main: €9* ☒ *París 187, Eixample* ☎ *93/209–8530* ▭ *No credit cards* Ⓜ *Diagonal* ✛ *G:7.*

$$$
TAPAS
Fodor'sChoice
★

✕ **Bardeni.** This "meat bar" doesn't take reservations; instead they offer a walk-in-and-graze tapas menu of items like steak tartare and aged filet mignon. Former Catalan Chef of the Year Dani Lechuga throws in the occasional fine-dining dish to lighten things up. **Known for:** mouthwatering steak tartare; great aged filet mignon; award-winning chef. $ *Average main: €23* ☒ *València 454, Eixample* ☎ *93/232–5811* ⊕ *www.bardeni.es* ☽ *Closed Sun. and Mon.* Ⓜ *Sagrada Família* ✛ *L:9.*

$
CATALAN

✕ **Blau BCN.** Despite its name, there's nothing about Marc Roca's restaurant that will give you the blues; its stylish interior featuring black-and-white photos sets an elegant stage for jazzed-up versions of rustic Catalan dishes that attract discerning local diners. Slow-cooked beef cheeks, a salad of tomatoes picked the same day, and wild mushroom–studded cannelloni all impress, but the menu is ruled by a mighty alpha-cheesecake that combines an iron fist of Roquefort in a velvet Brie glove. **Known for:** delightful wild mushroom–studded cannelloni; tasty slow-cooked beef cheeks; killer cheesecake. $ *Average main: €14* ☒ *Londres 89, Eixample* ☎ *93/419–3032* ⊕ *blaubcn.com* ☽ *Closed Sun.* Ⓜ *Hospital Clínic* ✛ *G:7.*

$$$
MEDITERRANEAN

✕ **Boca Grande.** This three-floor design triumph by Spain's hottest interior decorator, Lázaro Rosa Violán, makes up for in sheer panache what it lacks in consistency. Don't plan on a quick visit: the fresh seafood and rice dishes on offer here can take a while to reach your table. **Known for:** innovative interior design; glamorous terrace. $ *Average main: €28* ☒ *Passatge de la Concepció 12, Eixample* ☎ *93/467–5149* ⊕ *www.bocagrande.cat* Ⓜ *Diagonal* ✛ *I:8.*

$$$$
CATALAN

✕ **Casa Calvet.** It's hard to pass up the opportunity to break bread in a Gaudí-designed building. Completed in 1900, the Art Nouveau Casa Calvet includes a graceful dining room decorated with looping parabolic door handles, polychrome stained glass, etched glass, and wood carved in floral and organic motifs. **Known for:** intimate setting; seasonal local dishes; elegant interior. $ *Average main: €31* ☒ *Casp 48, Eixample* ☎ *93/412–4012* ⊕ *www.casacalvet.es* ☽ *Closed Sun.* Ⓜ *Urquinaona* ✛ *J:11.*

$$$
TAPAS

✕ **Casa Lucio.** With fresh ingredients and original dishes flowing from the kitchen, this intimate and expensive dazzler two blocks south of the Mercat de Sant Antoni is well worth tracking down if you're not on a budget. Lucio's wife, chef Maribel, is relentlessly inventive. **Known for:** splurge-worthy; no menu (take the chef's recommendations); excellent black beans and sausage. $ *Average main: €25*

CLOSE UP

Dining with Children?

Barceloneta's beachfront paella specialists are great favorites for Sunday lunches, with children free to get up and run, skate, cycle, or generally race up and down the boardwalk while their parents linger over brandies and coffee. **Els Pescadors** (✉ *Pl. de Prim 1, Port Olímpic, Poblenou* ☎ *93/225–2018*), a seafood restaurant, has a lovely terrace opening onto a little square that is handy for children letting off steam.

The miniature scale and finger-food aspect of tapas usually appeals, and children will happily munch on a variety of commonly found dishes, including croquettes, cured meats, toasted almonds, and fried squid rings.

Every café, bar, and terrace in town can whip up sandwiches on the go, served on fresh bread—an inexpensive and respectable snack—or the Catalan staple pa amb tomaquet. And for dessert, Barcelona's ubiquitous ice-cream parlors and vendors are another favorite. Try **Cremeria Toscana** (✉ *Carrer Muntaner 161 or Carrer Princesa 26*) for some of the city's best *gelat.*

3

✉ *Viladomat 59, Eixample* ☎ *93/424–4401* 🕒 *Closed Sun. and Mon.* [M] *Sant Antoni, Poble Sec* ✥ *E:11.*

$$ TAPAS FAMILY 🍴 **Cervecería Catalana.** A bright and booming tapas bar with a few tables outside, this spot is always packed for a reason: good food at reasonable prices. Try the small *solomillos* (filets mignons), mini-morsels that will take the edge off your carnivorous appetite without undue damage to your wallet, or the jumbo shrimp brochettes. **Known for:** affordable tapas; perfect jumbo shrimp brochettes; lively atmosphere. [$] *Average main: €16* ✉ *Mallorca 236, Eixample* ☎ *93/216–0368* [M] *Diagonal, Provença (FGC)* ✥ *H:8.*

$$$$ CATALAN Fodor's Choice ★ 🍴 **Cinc Sentits.** Obsessively local, scrupulously sourced, and masterfully cooked, the dishes of Catalan-Canadian chef Jordi Artal put the spotlight on the region's finest ingredients in an intimate, sophisticated setting. It's hard to believe that this starred restaurant is Jordi's first-ever, but there's no arguing with the evidence of your *cinc sentits* (five senses). **Known for:** Michelin-starred cuisine; cutting-edge techniques; tasting menu only. [$] *Average main: €100* ✉ *Aribau 58, Eixample* ☎ *93/323–9490* 🌐 *www.cincsentits.com* 🕒 *Closed Sun. and Mon.* [M] *Provença* ✥ *G:9.*

$$ TAPAS 🍴 **Ciudad Condal.** At the bottom of Ramba Catalunya, this scaled-up tapas bar draws a throng of mostly international clients and has tables outside on the sidewalk virtually year-round. The *solomillo* (miniature beef fillet) is a winner here, as is the *broqueta d'escamarlans* (brochette of jumbo shrimp). **Known for:** long wait times; great location; reliable quality. [$] *Average main: €18* ✉ *Rambla de Catalunya 18, Eixample* ☎ *93/318–1997* [M] *Passeig de Gràcia, Catalunya* ✥ *H:10.*

$$$$ ECLECTIC Fodor's Choice ★ 🍴 **Disfrutar.** Three former head chefs from the now-closed "World's Best Restaurant" elBulli have combined their considerable talents to create this roller-coaster ride of culinary fun. Sun streams into the gorgeous interior through skylights, spotlighting a tasting menu of dazzling inventiveness and good taste. **Known for:** otherwordly desserts; tasting

menus only; excellent beetroot meringues. $ *Average main: €110* ⊠ *De Villarroel 163, Eixample* ☎ *93/348–6896* ⊕ *en.disfrutarbarcelona.com* ⊙ *Closed Sun. and Mon.* Ⓜ *Hospital Clínic* ⊹ *F:8.*

$$ CATALAN ✕ **Embat.** An *embat* is a puff of wind in Catalan, and this little bistro is a breath of fresh air in the swashbuckling Eixample. The highly affordable market cuisine is always impeccably fresh and freshly conceived, from flavorful brunches to a bargain lunch selection and a more elaborate evening menu. **Known for:** modern unfussy fare; stylish interior; palatable cod. $ *Average main: €16* ⊠ *Mallorca 304, Eixample* ☎ *93/458–0855* ⊙ *Closed Sun. No dinner Mon.–Wed.* Ⓜ *Verdaguer* ⊹ *J:8.*

$$ SPANISH ✕ **Etapes.** By concentrating on sophisticated execution rather than groundbreaking creativity, the family-run Etapes provides a reliably satisfying dining experience that suits a wide range of palates. Take a seat on the pleasant terrace or in the narrow, cave-like interior and enjoy elegant interpretations of classic Catalan dishes. **Known for:** delectable roast suckling pig with calçot; homemade desserts by the co-owners' grandmother. $ *Average main: €20* ⊠ *Enric Granados 10, Eixample* ☎ *93/323–6914* ⊕ *www.restaurantetapes.com* ⊙ *No lunch weekends* Ⓜ *Universitat* ⊹ *H:9.*

$$$ BASQUE ✕ **Gorría.** Named for founder Fermín Gorría, this is quite simply the best straightforward Basque-Navarran cooking in Barcelona. Everything from the stewed *pochas* (white beans) to the heroic *chuletón* (steak) is as clear and pure in flavor as the Navarran Pyrenees. **Known for:** classic Basque cuisine; excellent wine pairings. $ *Average main: €26* ⊠ *Diputació 421, Eixample* ☎ *93/245–1164* ⊕ *www.restaurantegorria.com* ⊙ *Closed Sun. and Aug. No dinner Mon.* Ⓜ *Monumental* ⊹ *L:10.*

$$ CATALAN **Fodor's**Choice ★ ✕ **Gresca.** Chef/owner Rafa Peña applies the skills he honed in the world's most celebrated kitchens in this phenomenally good value restaurant and its adjacent wine/tapas bar. He cranks out inventive dishes based on humble ingredients to a fervently loyal customer base of local foodies. **Known for:** tapas of the day; adjacent wine/tapas bar; great affordable cuisine. $ *Average main: €20* ⊠ *Provença 230, Eixample* ☎ *93/451–6193* ⊕ *www.gresca.net* ⊙ *Closed Sun. and last wk in Aug.– 1st wk in Sept.* Ⓜ *Provença (FGC)* ⊹ *H:8.*

$$ BASQUE ✕ **Igueldo.** Basque dishes are competently updated and delivered with a dash of style at this smart, white-walled Eixample establishment. A fiery grill turns out excellent regional meat specialties, but don't overlook fish dishes such as baby squid with cured ham and caramelized onions. **Known for:** Basque cuisine; excellent service; great wine pairings. $ *Average main: €20* ⊠ *Rosselló 186, Eixample* ☎ *93/452–2555* ⊕ *www.restauranteigueldo.com* ⊙ *Closed Sun.* Ⓜ *Diagonal* ⊹ *H:8.*

$ TAPAS ✕ **La Bodegueta.** If you can find this dive (literally: it's a short drop below sidewalk level), you'll encounter a warm and cluttered space with a dozen small tables and a few spots at the marble counter. Try the excellent pa amb tomàquet and Manchego cheese, Iberian cured ham, or *tortilla de patatas* (potato and onion omelet). **Known for:** traditional tapas; hard-to-spot dive. $ *Average main: €10* ⊠ *Rambla de Catalunya 100, Eixample* ☎ *93/215–4894* ⊕ *www.labodegueta.cat* ⊙ *No breakfast or lunch Sun.* Ⓜ *Provença* ⊹ *H:8.*

$ **✕ La Falconera.** This down-home family restaurant in the upmarket
CATALAN Eixample eschews fads and trendiness for flavor. Tuck into nose-to-tail tapas, hearty stews, traditional *mar i muntanya* (surf and turf) dishes, and an untraditional but outstanding Olivier salad. **Known for:** robust market cuisine; friendly atmosphere; outdoor seating. $ *Average main: €9* ✉ *Enric Granados 58, Eixample* ☎ *608/804923* ☾ *Closed Sun.* Ⓜ *Provença/Diagonal* ✛ *H:8.*

$ **✕ La Flauta.** The name of this boisterous restaurant refers to the staple
TAPAS flutelike loaves of slipper bread used for sandwiches here. There is also an infinite number of tapas and small portions of everything from wild mushrooms in season to wild asparagus or *xipirones* (baby cuttlefish) served in this tightly packed space. **Known for:** infinite tapas list; wonderful flautas (thin sandwiches); delicious in-season vegetables. $ *Average main: €14* ✉ *Aribau 23, Eixample* ☎ *93/323–7038* ☾ *Closed Sun. and Aug.* Ⓜ *Diagonal* ✛ *G:10.*

$ **✕ La Pastisseria Barcelona.** This stylish *pastisseria* looks more like a
BAKERY designer jewelry store than a bakery. Rows of world-class cakes and
Fodor'sChoice pastries gleam temptingly in glass cases, ready to be taken away or
★ enjoyed in-store with coffee or a glass of cava. **Known for:** award-winning cakes; handmade delicacies; high-quality ingredients. $ *Average main: €10* ✉ *Aragó 228, Eixample* ☎ *93/451–8401* ⊕ *www.lapastisseriabarcelona.com* ☾ *Closed Sun. evening* Ⓜ *Passeig de Gràcia* ✛ *H:9.*

$$$$ **✕ Lasarte.** Martin Berasategui, one of San Sebastián's fleet of master
BASQUE chefs, placed his Barcelona kitchen in the capable hands of Paolo
Fodor'sChoice Casagrande in 2006 and was recently rewarded with three Michelin
★ stars. Expect an eclectic selection of Basque, Mediterranean, and off-the-map creations, a hefty bill, and fierce perfectionism apparent in every dish. **Known for:** Barcelona's only three-Michelin-star restaurant; magnificent tasting menu; heavenly grilled pigeon. $ *Average main: €50* ✉ *Mallorca 259, Eixample* ☎ *93/445–3242* ⊕ *www.restaurantlasarte. com* ☾ *Closed Sun. and Mon. and 3 wks in Aug.* Ⓜ *Diagonal, Passeig de Gràcia, Provença (FGC)* ✛ *I:8.*

$$$ **✕ La Taverna Del Clínic.** The Simoes brothers have earned a solid reputa-
SPANISH tion with discerning and deep-pocketed locals for serving creative and contemporary tapas. Their bar spills out onto a sunny street-side terrace where customers can enjoy truffle cannelloni and an award-winning variation on patatas bravas, paired with selections from the excellent wine list. **Known for:** contemporary tapas; award-winning patatas bravas. $ *Average main: €28* ✉ *Roselló 155, Eixample* ☎ *93/410–4221* ⊕ *www.latavernadelclinic.com* ▭ *No credit cards* ☾ *Closed Sun.* Ⓜ *Hospital Clinic* ✛ *G:8.*

$$$ **✕ La Yaya Amelia.** Just two blocks uphill from Gaudí's Sagrada Famí-
CATALAN lia church, this kitchen serves lovingly prepared and clued-in dishes ranging from warm goat-cheese salad to foie (duck or goose liver) to *chuletón de buey a la sal* (beef cooked in salt). Decidedly old-school, the interior is largely unchanged since the restaurant opened in 1976. **Known for:** old-fashioned charm; great value; medley of Basque and Catalan cuisine. $ *Average main: €24* ✉ *Sardenya 364, Eixample* ☎ *93/456–4573* Ⓜ *Sagrada Família* ✛ *L:7.*

$$
CATALAN

✕ **L'Olivé.** Streamlined but traditional Catalan cooking means this busy and attractive spot is always packed. The crowd may be boisterous, but the dining room is seriously elegant, with crisp white tablecloths, leather chairs, and a loft-like wall of windows. **Known for:** traditional Catalan cuisine; always packed; best pa amb tomàquet in town. $ *Average main: €22* ✉ *Balmes 47, Eixample* ☎ *93/452–1990* ⊕ *www.restaurantlolive.com* Ⓜ *Universitat, Passeig de Gràcia* ✛ *H:9.*

$$$
CATALAN
Fodor's Choice
★

✕ **Manairó.** A *manairó* is a mysterious Pyrenean elf, and Jordi Herrera may be the culinary version. His ingenious meat-cooking methods—such as filet mignon *al faquir* (heated from within on red-hot spikes) or blowtorched on a homemade centrifuge—may seem eccentric but produce diabolically good results. **Known for:** innovative contemporary cuisine; delicious meat dishes. $ *Average main: €28* ✉ *Diputació 424, Eixample* ☎ *93/231–0057* ⊕ *www.jordiherrera.es/manairo* ☉ *Closed Sun. and 1st wk of Jan.* Ⓜ *Monumental* ✛ *M:10.*

$$$$
CATALAN
Fodor's Choice
★

✕ **Moments.** Inside the ultrasleek Hotel Mandarin Oriental Barcelona, this restaurant continues the glamour with mod white chairs and glinting goldleaf on the ceiling. The food by Raül Balam and his mother—the seven-Michelín-starred Carme Ruscalleda—lives up to its stellar pedigree, with original preparations that draw on deep wells of Catalan culinary traditions. **Known for:** chef's table; elaborate tasting menus; outstanding wine list. $ *Average main: €55* ✉ *Passeig de Gràcia 38–40, Eixample* ☎ *93/151–8888* ⊕ *www.mandarinoriental.com* ☉ *Closed Sun., Mon., 2 wks in Jan, 1 wk in Aug, and 1 wk in Sept.* Ⓜ *Passeig de Gràcia* ✛ *I:10.*

$$$
CATALAN
FAMILY
Fodor's Choice
★

✕ **Mont Bar.** Mont Bar's cramped interior belies the size of the flavors delivered from its kitchen. Star-quality morsels such as a sea cucumber carbonara and mochis stuffed with Mallorcan sobrassada are complemented by an immense wine list. **Known for:** upmarket bistro atmosphere; friendly service; mix of fine-dining dishes and bar-room snacks. $ *Average main: €23* ✉ *Diputació 220, Eixample* ☎ *93/323–9590* ⊕ *www.montbar.com* Ⓜ *Universitat* ✛ *G:10.*

$$
MEDITERRANEAN

✕ **Mordisco.** The columns and skylights of this former high-class jewelers now frame a Mediterranean restaurant that emphasizes wholesome and flavorsome fare. Market-fresh produce is available to buy in the deli-like entrance, and makes its way into dishes such as artichoke hearts and hot veal carpaccios that come sizzling from the charcoal grill. **Known for:** enclosed patio; late-night cocktails at upstairs bar Thursday–Sunday. $ *Average main: €16* ✉ *Passatge de la Concepció 10, Eixample* ☎ *93/487–9656* ⊕ *www.grupotragaluz.com* Ⓜ *Diagonal* ✛ *I:8.*

$$
TAPAS

✕ **Paco Meralgo.** The name, a pun on *para comer algo* ("to eat something" with an Andalusian accent), may be only marginally amusing, but the tapas here are no joke at all, from the classical *calamares fritos* (fried cuttlefish rings) to the *pimientos de Padrón* (green peppers, some fiery, from the Galician town of Padrón). Whether *à table*, at the counter, or in the private dining room upstairs, this modern space does traditional tapas that reliably hit the spot. **Known for:** traditional tapas; excellent wine list. $ *Average main: €18* ✉ *Muntaner 171, Eixample* ☎ *93/430–9027* ⊕ *www.restaurantpacomeralgo.com* Ⓜ *Hospital Clínic, Provença (FGC)* ✛ *G:7.*

Continued on page 156

Vineyard in Rioja.

THE WINES OF SPAIN

After years of being in the shadows of other European wines, Spanish wines are finally gunning for the spotlight—and what has taken place is nothing short of a revolution. The wines of Spain, like its cuisine, are currently experiencing a firecracker explosion of both quality and variety that has brought a new level of interest, awareness, and recognition throughout the world, propelling them to superstar status. A generation of young, ambitious winemakers has jolted dormant areas awake and even the most established regions have undergone makeovers in order to compete in the global market. And it's paid off: 2016 figures show Spain as the world's biggest wine producer by land area, surpassing France and Italy.

THE ROAD TO GREAT WINE

Frank Gehry designed the visitor center for the Marqués de Riscal winery in Rioja.

Spain has a long wine history dating back to the time when the Phoenicians introduced viticulture, over 3,000 years ago. Some of the country's wines achieved fame in Roman times, and the Visigoths enacted early wine laws. But in the regions under Muslim rule, winemaking slowed down for centuries. Starting in the 16th century, wine trade expanded along with the Spanish Empire, and by the 18th and 19th centuries the Sherry region *bodegas* (wineries) were already established.

In the middle of the 19th century, seeds of change blossomed throughout the Spanish wine industry. In 1846, the estate that was to become Vega Sicilia, Spain's most revered winery, was set up in Castile. Three years later the famous Tío Pepe brand was established to produce the excellent dry fino wines. Marqués de Murrieta and the Marqués de Riscal wineries opened in the 1860s creating the modern Rioja region and clearing the way for many centenary wineries. *Cava*—Spain's white or pink sparkling wine—was created the following decade in Catalonia.

After this flurry of activity, Spanish wines languished for almost a century. Vines were hit hard by phylloxera, and then a civil war and a long dictatorship left the country stagnant and isolated. Just 30 short years ago, Spain's wines were split between the same dominant trio of Sherry, Rioja, and cava, and loads of cheap, watered-down wines made by local cooperatives with little gumption to improve and even less expertise.

Starting in the 1970s, however, a wave of innovation crashed through Rioja and emergent regions like Ribera del Duero and Penedés. In the 1990s, it turned into a revolution that spread all over the landscape—and is still going strong. Today, Spain is the largest wine producer in the world in terms of land area and volume. Europe's debt crisis means domestic wine consumption is down and vintners are doubling their effort to appeal to export markets.

SPANISH WINE CATEGORIES BY AGE

A unique feature of Spanish wines is their indication of aging process on wine labels. DO wines (see "A *Vino* Primer" on following page) show this on mandatory back panels. Aging requirements are longer for reds, but also apply to white, rosé, and sparkling wines. For reds, the rules are as follows:

Vino Joven
A young wine that may or may not have spent some time aging in oak barrels before it was bottled. Some winemakers have begun to shun traditional regulations to produce cutting-edge wines in this category. An elevated price distinguishes the ambitious new reds from the easy-drinking *jóvenes*.

Crianza
A wine aged for at least 24 months, six of which are in barrels (12 in Rioja, Ribera del Duero, and Navarra). A great bargain in top vintages from the most reliable wineries and regions.

Reserva
A wine aged for a minimum of 36 months, at least 12 of which are in oak.

Gran Reserva
Traditionally the top of the Spanish wine hierarchy, and the pride of the historic Rioja wineries. A red wine aged for at least 24 months in oak, followed by 36 months in the bottle before release.

Joven or Cosecha	Crianza	Reserva	Gran Reserva
Minimum Aging Period in Months	24	36	48	60

READING LABELS LIKE A PRO

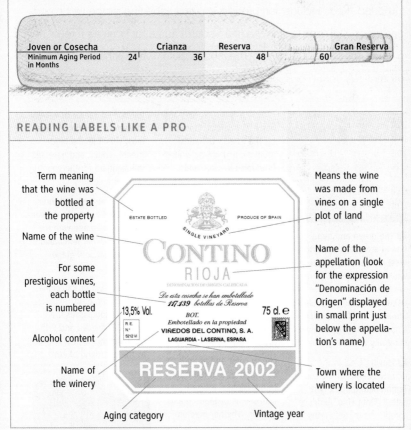

Term meaning that the wine was bottled at the property

ESTATE BOTTLED

PRODUCE OF SPAIN

Means the wine was made from vines on a single plot of land

Name of the wine

SINGLE VINEYARD

CONTINO

RIOJA

DENOMINACIÓN DE ORIGEN CALIFICADA

De esta cosecha se han embotellado 117.139 *botellas de Reserva*

Name of the appellation (look for the expression "Denominación de Origen" displayed in small print just below the appellation's name)

For some prestigious wines, each bottle is numbered

13,5% Vol.

BOT.
Embotellado en la propiedad
VIÑEDOS DEL CONTINO, S. A.
LAGUARDIA - LASERNA, ESPAÑA

75 cl. ℮

R.E.
N.°
5212 VI

Alcohol content

Name of the winery

RESERVA 2002

Town where the winery is located

Aging category

Vintage year

A *VINO* PRIMER

Spain offers a daunting assortment of wine styles, regions, and varietals. But don't worry: a few pointers will help you understand unfamiliar names and terms. Most of Spain's quality wines come from designated regions called *Denominaciones de Origen* (Appellations of Origin), often abbreviated as DO. Spain has more than 69 of these areas, which are tightly regulated to protect the integrity and characteristics of the wines produced there. Beyond international varieties like Cabernet Sauvignon and Chardonnay, the country is home to several high-quality varietals, both indigenous and imported. Reds include Tempranillo, an early-ripening grape that blends and ages well, and Garnacha (the Spanish name for France's Grenache), a spicy, full-bodied red wine. The most popular white wines are the light, aromatic Albariño or Ruedas, and the full-bodied Verdejo.

Rioja wines

GENTES DE FORASTI
RIOJA
DENOMINACIÓN DE ORIGEN CALIFICADA

❶ The green and more humid areas of the Northwest deliver crisp, floral white albariños in Galicia's Rías Biaxas. In the Bierzo DO, the Mencía grape distills the essence of the schist slopes, where it grows into minerally infused red wines.

❷ Moving east, in the iron-rich riverbanks of the Duero, Tempranillo grapes, here called "Tinto Fino," produce complex and age-worthy Ribera del Duero reds and hefty Toro wines. Close by, the Rueda DO adds aromatic and grassy whites from local Verdejo and adopted Sauvignon Blanc.

❸ The Rioja region is a winemaker's paradise. Here a mild, nearly perfect vine-growing climate marries limestone and clay soils with Tempranillo, Spain's most noble grape, to deliver wines that possess the two main features of every great region: personality and quality. Tempranillo-based Riojas evolve from a young cherry color and aromas of strawberries and red fruits, to a brick hue, infused with scents of tobacco and leather. Whether medium or full-bodied, tannic or velvety, these reds are some of the most versatile and food-friendly wines, and have set the standard for the country for over a century.

Nearby, Navarra and three small DO's in Aragón deliver great wines made with the local Garnacha, Tempranillo, and international grape varieties.

❹ Southwest of Barcelona is the region of Catalonia, which encompasses the areas of Penedès and Priorat. Catalonia is best known as the heartland of *cava*,

Chardonnay vines in Navarra.

Grapes harvested for Sherry

the typically dry, sparkling wine made from three indigenous Spanish varietals: Parellada, Xarel-lo, and Macabeo. The climatically varied Penedès—just an hour south of Barcelona—produces full-bodied reds like Garnacha on coastal plains, and cool-climate varietals like Riesling and Sauvignon Blanc in the mountains. Priorat is a region that has emerged into the international spotlight during the past decade, as innovative winemakers have transformed winemaking practices there. Now, traditional grapes like Garnacha and Cariñena are blended with Cabernet Sauvignon and Syrah to produce rich, concentrated reds with powerful tannins.

❺ The region of Valencia is south of Catalonia on the Mediterranean coast. The wines of this area have improved markedly in recent years, with red wines from Jumilla and other appellations finding their way onto the international market. Tempranillo and Monastrell (France's Mourvèdre) are the most common reds. A local specialty of the area is Moscatel de Valencia, a highly aromatic sweet white wine.

❻ In the central plateau south of Madrid, rapid investment, modernization, and replanting is resulting in medium bodied, easy drinking, and fairly priced wines made with Tempranillo (here called

"Cencíbel"), Cabernet, Syrah, and even Petit Verdot, that are opening the doors to more ambitious endeavors.

❼ In sun-drenched Andalusia, where the white albariza limestone soils reflect the powerful sunlight while trapping the scant humidity, the fortified Jerez (Sherry) and Montilla emerge. In all their different incarnations, from dry finos, Manzanillas, amontillados, palo cortados, and olorosos, to sweet creams and Pedro Ximénez, they are the most original wines of Spain.

JUST OFF THE VINE: NEW WINE DEVELOPMENTS

Beyond Tempranillo: The current wine revolution has recovered many native varieties. Albariño, Godello, and Verdejo among the whites, and Callet, Cariñena, Garnacha, Graciano, Mandó, Manto Negro, Mencía, and Monastrell among the reds, are gaining momentum and will likely become more recognized.

Cult Wines: For most of the past century, Vega Sicilia Unico was the only true cult wine from Spain. The current explosion has greatly expanded the roster: L'Ermita, Pingus, Clos Erasmus, Artadi, Cirsion, Terreus, and Termanthia are the leading names in a list that grows every year.

Vinos de Pagos: *Pago*, a word meaning plot or vineyard, is the legal term chosen to create Spain's equivalent of a *Grand Cru* hierarchy, by protecting quality oriented wine producers that make wine from their own estates.

V.O.S. and V.O.R.S: Sherry's most dramatic change in over a century is the creation of the "Very Old Sherry" designation for wines over 20 years of age, and the addition of "Rare" for those over 30, to easier distinguish the best, oldest, and most complex wines.

Petit Verdot: Winemakers in Spain are discovering that Petit Verdot, the "little green" grape of Bordeaux, ripens much easier in warmer climates than in its birthplace. This is contributing to the rise of Petit Verdot in red blends, and even to the production of single varietal wines.

Innovative New Blends: A few wine regions have strict regulations concerning the varieties used in their wines, but most allow for experimentation. All over the country, *bodegas* are crafting wines with creative blends that involve local varieties, Tempranillo, and famous international grapes.

Andalusia's New Wines: For centuries, scorching southern Andalusia has offered world-class Sherry and Montilla wines. Now trailblazing winemakers are making serious inroads in the production of quality white, red, and new dessert wines, something deemed impossible a few years back.

Island Wines: In both the Balearic and Canary Islands the strong tourist industry helped to revive local winemaking. Although hard to find, the best Callet and Manto Negro based red wines of Majorca, and the sweet *malvasías* of Lanzarote will reward the adventurous drinker.

SPAIN'S SUPERSTAR WINEMAKERS

Mariano García   Peter Sisseck   Alvaro Palacios   Josep Lluís Pérez

The current wine revolution has made superstars out of a group of dynamic, innovative, and visionary winemakers. Here are some of the top names:

Mariano García. His 30 years as winemaker of Vega Sicilia made him a legend. Now García displays his deft touch in the Ribera del Duero and Bierzo through his four wineries: Aalto, Mauro, San Román, and Paixar.

Peter Sisseck. A Dane educated in Bordeaux, Sisseck found his calling in the old Ribera del Duero vineyards, where he crafted Pingus, Spain's most coveted cult wine.

Alvaro Palacios. In Priorat, Palacios created L'Ermita, a Garnacha wine that is one of Spain's most remarkable bottlings. Palacios also is a champion of the Bierzo region, where he produces wines from the ancient Mencía varietal, known for their vibrant berry flavors and stony minerality.

Josep Lluís Pérez. From his base in Priorat and through his work as a winemaker, researcher, teacher, and consultant, Pérez (along with his daughter Sara Pérez) has become the main driving force in shaping the modern Mediterranean wines of Spain.

MATCHMAKING KNOW-HOW

A pairing of wine with *jamón* and Spanish olives.

Spain has a great array of regional products and cuisines, and its avant-garde chefs are culinary world leaders. As a general rule, you should match local food with local wines—but Spanish wines can be matched very well with some of the most unexpected dishes.

Albariños and the white wines of Galicia are ideal partners for seafood and fish. Dry sherries complement Serrano and Iberico hams, *lomo, chorizo,* and *salchichón* (white dry saugage), as well as olives and nuts. Pale, light, and dry finos and Manzanillas are the perfect aperitif wines, and the ideal companion for fried fish. Fuller bodied amontillados, palo cortados, and olorosos go well with hearty soups. Ribera del Duero reds are the perfect match for the outstanding local lamb. Try Priorat and other Mediterranean reds with strong cheeses and barbecue meats. Traditional Rioja harmonizes well with fowl and game. But also take an adventure off the beaten path: manzanilla and fino are great with sushi and sashimi; Rioja *reserva* fit tuna steaks; and cream sherry will not be out of place with chocolate. *¡Salud!*

$
TAPAS
✕ **Piratas.** Named for Roman Polanski's film of the same name, this extraordinary little spot just a block away from the Auditori de Barcelona and the new Encants market is an excellent choice for a pre- or post-concert taste of chef Lluís Ortega's improvisational cuisine, all prepared behind the bar on a single salamander. Hams, potatoes, foies, caviars, olives, anchovies, and tuna, as well as carefully selected wines and cavas, flow freely here. **Known for:** cozy space; superb cheeses; reservations essential. $ *Average main: €14* ✉ *Ausiàs Marc 157, Eixample* ☎ *93/245–7642* 🕙 *Closed weekends and Aug.* Ⓜ *Marina* ⊹ *L:11.*

$$$
CATALAN
✕ **Restaurant Gaig.** With a refined interpretation of traditional cuisine, this cozy split-level restaurant has made a name for itself in Barcelona's ever-changing dining scene. As passions have cooled for molecular gastronomy, Carles Gaig and a growing number of top chefs have returned to simpler and more affordable models. **Known for:** classic Catalan cuisine; stylish interior; glazed veal sweetbreads. $ *Average main: €29* ✉ *Còrsega 200, Eixample* ☎ *93/453–2020,* ⊕ *www.restaurantgaig.com* 🕙 *Closed Mon. and 2 wks in Aug. No dinner Sun.* Ⓜ *Hospital Clínic, Provença (FGC)* ⊹ *G:8.*

$$$
CATALAN
Fodor's Choice
★
✕ **Roca Moo.** In any space as stylish as Roca Moo, located in the Hotel Omm, there's a real risk of the food playing second fiddle to the surroundings. Fortunately, the spotlight is fixed firmly on dishes designed by the Roca brothers, whose Celler de Can Roca restaurant has been rated as the world's best. **Known for:** fashionable haunt; Joan Roca tasting menu; sublime ice cream. $ *Average main: €29* ✉ *Hotel Omm, Roselló 265, Eixample* ☎ *93/445–4000* ⊕ *www.hotelomm.com* 🕙 *Closed Sun. and Mon., 2 wks in Jan., and 3 wks in Aug.* Ⓜ *Diagonal* ⊹ *I:8.*

$$
MEDITERRANEAN
✕ **Sense Pressa.** *Sense pressa* means "without hurry" or "no rush" in Catalan, and if you can score one of the coveted half-dozen tables here at the corner of Carrer Córsega, you will want to linger as long as possible to enjoy this miniscule winner. *Risotto de ceps* (wild mushroom risotto), *garbanzos con espardenyes y huevos fritos* (chickpeas with sea cucumbers and fried eggs), or filet mignon of Girona beef cooked to perfection are all good choices. **Known for:** intimate tavern atmosphere; fresh local produce; toothsome risotto de ceps. $ *Average main: €22* ✉ *Enric Granados 96, Eixample* ☎ *93/218–1544* ⊕ *www.sensepressarestaurant.com* 🕙 *Closed Sun. and 2 wks in Aug. No dinner Mon.* Ⓜ *Diagonal* ⊹ *G:8.*

$$
CATALAN
Fodor's Choice
★
✕ **Sergi de Meià.** Sergi takes sourcing seriously, serving only ingredients foraged, caught, reared, or grown by people he knows personally. The result is a menu full of wild game, free-range and organic meat, seasonal vegetables, and sustainable fish, raised a notch by the skilled chef. **Known for:** family-run; breakfast and brunch; always packed. $ *Average main: €15* ✉ *Arribau 106, Eixample* ☎ *93/125–5710* ⊕ *www.restaurantsergidemeia.cat* 🕙 *Closed Sun. and Mon.* Ⓜ *Universitat* ⊹ *G:8.*

$$
BASQUE
✕ **Taktika Berri.** Specializing in San Sebastián's favorite dishes, this Basque restaurant has only one drawback: a table is hard to score unless you call weeks in advance (an idea to consider before you travel). Your backup plan? The tapas served over the first-come, first-served bar. **Known for:** Basque pintxos; convivial tavern atmosphere; hospitable service. $ *Average main: €20* ✉ *València 169, Eixample* ☎ *93/453–4759* 🕙 *Closed Sun. No dinner Sat.* Ⓜ *Hospital Clinic, Provença (FGC)* ⊹ *G:9.*

$$ ✕ **Tapas 24.** The tapas emporium of celebrity chef Carles Abellán shows
TAPAS us how much he admires traditional Catalan and Spanish bar food, from
patatas bravas to *croquetas de pollo rostido* (roast chicken croquettes).
The counter and terrace are constantly crowded, but the slightly pricey
food is worth elbowing your way through the crowd for. **Known for:**
traditional tapas with a twist; all-day kitchen. $ *Average main: €20*
✉ *Diputació 269, Eixample* ☎ *93/488–0977* ⊕ *www.carlesabellan.com/
mis-restaurantes/tapas-24* Ⓜ *Passeig de Gràcia* ✚ *I:10.*

$$$ ✕ **Tragaluz.** *Tragaluz* means "skylight" (the sliding roof opens to the
MEDITERRANEAN stars in good weather) and this is an excellent choice if you're still on
a design high from shopping on Passeig de Gràcia or visiting Gaudí's
Pedrera. The Mediterranean cuisine is traditional yet light and will
please most palates, and is a popular lunch spot. **Known for:** open-
air dining; coffee or post-dinner drink upstairs; entrance is through
Japanese tavern. $ *Average main: €27* ✉ *Passatge de la Concepció 5,
Eixample* ☎ *93/487–0621* ⊕ *grupotragaluz.com* Ⓜ *Diagonal* ✚ *I:8.*

$ ✕ **Woki Organic Market.** Just off Plaça de Catalunya, this combination
ECLECTIC eco-market and restaurant serves organic ingredients prepared via healthy
techniques and traditions. But the real secret ingredient is star chef Xavier
Pellicer, who oversees the group's restaurants. **Known for:** great vegetarian and vegan dishes; sustainable food and decor; pastas made with
pure flour. $ *Average main: €12* ✉ *Ronda Universitat 20, Eixample*
☎ *93/302–5206* ⊕ *www.tribuwoki.com* Ⓜ *Catalunya* ✚ *H:10.*

$$$$ ✕ **Xerta.** The restaurant of the new Ohla Eixample hotel won a Michelin
CATALAN star in its first year. Much of Xerta's menu is the expected swanky fine-
dining fare but it stands out for its unique produce from the deltas and
rivers of the Terres de l'Ebre region, such as sweet miniature *canyuts*
(razor clams). **Known for:** produce from Terres de l'Ebre region; outstanding seafood and rice dishes. $ *Average main: €30* ✉ *Corsega 289,
Eixample* ☎ *93/737–9080* ⊕ *www.xertarestaurant.com* ✺ *Closed Sun.
and Mon.* Ⓜ *Provença* ✚ *H:8.*

GRÀCIA

This lively and intimate neighborhood is home to many of Barcelona's
artists, musicians, and actors. The bohemian atmosphere is reflected in
an eclectic collection of restaurants encompassing everything from street
food and affordable ethnic cuisine to thoroughly sophisticated dining.

$$$$ ✕ **Hofmann.** The late Mey Hofmann, German-born and Catalonia-
MEDITERRANEAN trained, was revered for decades for her creative Mediterranean and
international cuisine based on carefully selected raw materials prepared
with unrelenting quality. Her team carries on her legacy at her locale, a
graceful designer space with a glassed-in kitchen as center stage. **Known
for:** sardine tartare; foie gras in puff pastry; prawn risotto. $ *Average
main: €33* ✉ *La Granada del Penedès 14–16, Gràcia* ☎ *93/218–7165*
⊕ *www.hofmann-bcn.com* ✺ *Closed weekends and Aug.* Ⓜ *Gràcia,
Diagonal* ✚ *H:6.*

$$$ ✕ **Ipar-Txoko.** This excellent Basque enclave has managed to stay under
BASQUE the radar, possibly because it doesn't look like much from outside.
Once seated in the wood-beam dining room, you'll find flawlessly pre-
pared San Sebastián specialties such as a magnificent *txuleta de buey*

Barcelona's Must-Eat

Top priorities for a trip to Barcelona might just read: see great art and architecture, enjoy the nightlife, eat ham. In all seriousness, you shouldn't pass up the opportunity to eat Spain's exquisite artisanal ham—known in Catalan as *pernil* and in Spanish as *jamón*—made from acorn-fed native black pigs whose meat is salt-cured and then air-dried for two to four years. The best kind, *jamón ibérico de bellota*, comes from carefully managed and exercised pigs fed only acorns. This lengthy process results in a silky, slightly sweet and nutty meat that is contradictorily both light and intensely rich.

You can casually approach the quest for this delicacy at nearly any bar or restaurant across Barcelona, feasting on different qualities of hams, including jamón ibérico's lesser but still stellar cousin, *jamón serrano*.

Catalonia's love affair with cured pork isn't restricted to jamón. Sausages and other pork derivatives, known as *embutits* (*embutidos* in Spanish), are equally common sandwich-fillers, and are regularly served as starters in even high-end restaurants. For an authentic experience, try some with a cold glass of vermut and a side of potato chips, ideally as a light snack on a terrace before a full lunch.

Chorizo is, of course, the best-known and most ubiquitous sausage in Spain. Pork and paprika are the two key ingredients, but styles and quality vary widely, ranging from cheap, mass-produced batons for stews to handmade *chorizo ibérico*, best savored in wafer-thin slices.

Local Catalan favorites include the chewy but tasty *llonganissa* (cured sausages), and *fuet*. The latter can be almost too tough to eat or wonderfully delicious, depending on the quality, so don't rush to judgment after your first experience. *Bull* (pronounced, more or less, "boo-eey") comes in *blanc* (white) and *negre* (black) varieties—the latter is made with blood. Served cold in thin slices, bull is often served with salads.

Botifarra sausages are important components of Catalan cuisine. Most are served hot, typically with *mongetes* (white haricot beans), but cold *botifarra blanc* and negre are also common. A third variety, *botifarra d'ou*, includes eggs and has an unusual yellow hue. For a truly Catalan taste experience, look for *botifarra dolça*—this decidedly odd dessert sausage incorporates lemon and sugar.

---

or *besugo a la donostiarra* (sea bream with crispy garlic). **Known for:** chef announces daily changing menu; Basque specialties. $ *Average main: €24* ✉ *Mozart 22, Gràcia* ☎ *93/218–1954* ⊕ *www.ipartxoko.es* ☉ *Closed Sun. and Aug. No dinner Mon.* Ⓜ *Gràcia, Diagonal* ✛ *I:7.*

$

MEDITERRANEAN

✕ **La Panxa del Bisbe.** "The Bishop's Belly" achieves a rare feat: putting modern international twists on Mediterranean cuisine without ruining it. La Panxa is off the beaten path and thrives on a steady stream of repeat customers, who file into its bare-brick dining room for tapas and small dishes such as veal cheeks with beetroot gnocchi. **Known for:** good stop on way back from Parc Güell; value set lunch. $ *Average main: €14* ✉ *Torrent de les Flors 158, Gràcia* ☎ *93/213–7049* ☉ *Closed Sun. and Mon.* Ⓜ *Lesseps or Joanic* ✛ *K:5.*

$$
SPANISH
✕ **L'Arrosseria Xàtiva.** This rustic dining room in Gràcia, a spin-off from the original in Les Corts, evokes the rice paddies and lowlands of Valencia. Low lighting imparts a warm glow over exposed brick walls, wood-beam ceilings, and bentwood chairs, and it's a great spot to savor some of Barcelona's finest paellas and rice dishes. **Known for:** traditional paella; lovingly prepared food. $ *Average main: €22* ✉ *Torrent d'en Vidalet 26, Gràcia* ☎ *93/284–8502* ⊕ *www.arrosseri-axativa.com* Ⓜ *Joanic* ✛ *J:6.*

$$
CATALAN
✕ **Roig Robí.** Rattan chairs and a garden terrace characterize this polished dining spot in the bottom corner of Gràcia just above the Diagonal (near Vía Augusta). Rustic and relaxed, Roig Robí (ruby red in Catalan, as in the color of certain wines) maintains a high level of culinary excellence. **Known for:** top-notch guinea-fowl canelón; seasonal specials; helmed by excellent chef Mercé Navarro. $ *Average main: €21* ✉ *Sèneca 20, Gràcia* ☎ *93/218–9222* ⊕ *www.roigrobi.com* ☾ *Closed Sun. and 2 wks in Aug. No lunch Sat.* Ⓜ *Diagonal, Gràcia (FGC)* ✛ *I:7.*

> ### CALÇOTS FROM HEAVEN
>
> Since the late 19th century, *calçots*, long-stemmed, twice-planted white onions cooked over grapevine clippings, have provided a favorite early-spring outing from Barcelona. Restaurants now serve calçots in the Collserola hills or on the beaches of Gavá and Casteldefells from November to April. Some in-town restaurants also serve calçots, always consumed with romescu sauce and accompanied by lamb chops, botifarra sausage, and copious quantities of young red wine poured from a long-spouted *porró* held overhead. Wear dark (and preferably expandable) clothing.

POBLENOU

East of the Eixample and extending to the sea just beyond Port Olímpic, this formerly rough-around-the-edges neighborhood with a historical heart has lately seen an influx of edgy art studios, design shops, and even a few hip restaurants—many of these spaces are installed in converted warehouses and industrial concerns.

$$$
SEAFOOD
FAMILY
✕ **Els Pescadors.** Northeast of the Port Olímpic, in the interesting Poblenou neighborhood, this handsome late-19th-century dining room has a lovely terrace on a little square shaded by immense ficus trees. Kids can play safely in the traffic-free square while their parents feast on well-prepared seafood specialties such as paella, fresh fish, *fideuà* (a paella-like noodle dish), and the succulent *suquet.* **Known for:** village-square atmosphere; standard-setting rice and fish dishes. $ *Average main: €29* ✉ *Pl. de Prim 1, Sant Martí* ☎ *93/225–2018* ⊕ *www.elspescadors.com* Ⓜ *Poblenou* ✛ *L:15.*

$$
TAPAS
✕ **Els Tres Porquets.** Somewhat off the beaten path (though just a 15-minute stroll from the Auditori and the Teatre Nacional de Catalunya), Els Tres Porquets (The Three Little Pigs) packs in foodies and bon vivants with a wide range of small dishes. The interesting wine list includes lesser-known but noteworthy selections from Spain and around the world. **Known for:** Iberian specialties; delicious cheeses. $ *Average main: €16* ✉ *Rambla del Poblenou 165, Poblenou* ☎ *93/300–8750* ⊕ *www.elstresporquets.es* ☾ *Closed Sun.* Ⓜ *Glòries, Clot* ✛ *L:12.*

SARRIÀ, PEDRALBES, AND SANT GERVASI

Take an excursion to the upper reaches of town for an excellent selection of bars, cafés, and restaurants, along with cool summer evening breezes and a sense of well-heeled village life in Sarrià.

$$
CATALAN

✗ A Contraluz. A stylish covered terrace in the leafy upper-Barcelona neighborhood of Tres Torres, A Contraluz, so named for its translucent ceiling, has a strenuously varied market-based menu ranging from game in season, such as *rable de liebre* (stewed hare) with chutney, to the more northern *pochas con almejas* (beans with clams). All dishes are prepared with care and talent, and the lunch menu is a relative bargain. **Known for:** stylish dining room with a retractable roof; bargain lunch menu; excellent stewed hare. $ *Average main: €16* ⊠ *Milanesat 19, Tres Torres* ☎ *93/203–0658* ⊕ *acontraluz.com* ♥ *Closed 2 wks in Aug. No dinner Sun.* Ⓜ *Les Tres Torres* ✛ *E:3.*

$
TAPAS

✗ Bambarol. This unpretentious restaurant isn't what you might expect from chef-owners Ferran Maicas and Albert Ferrer, considering that they have worked in some of Spain's most famous kitchens. The decor is simple, the names of dishes straightforward, and the cooking style entirely absent of palate-twisting molecular gastronomy. **Known for:** wonderful scallops; off-menu croquetas; friendly service. $ *Average main: €14* ⊠ *Santaló 21, Sant Gervasi* ☎ *93/250–7074* ⊕ *bambarol.cat* ♥ *Closed Sun. and Mon.* Ⓜ *Gràcia, Muntaner (FGC)* ✛ *G:6.*

$
TAPAS

✗ Bar Tomás. Famous for its *patatas bravas amb allioli* (potatoes with fiery hot sauce and allioli, an emulsion of crushed garlic and olive oil), accompanied by freezing mugs of San Miguel beer, this old-fashioned Sarrià classic is worth seeking out as a contrast to the bland designer tapas bars that are ubiquitous in Barcelona. You'll have to elbow your way to a tiny table and shout to be heard over the hubbub, but you'll get an authentic taste of local bar life. **Known for:** excellent patatas bravas; traditional tavern atmosphere; San Miguel beer in frozen mugs. $ *Average main: €9* ⊠ *Major de Sarrià 49, Sarrià* ☎ *93/203–1077* ⊕ *www. eltomasdesarria.com* ▭ *No credit cards* ♥ *Closed Sun.* Ⓜ *Sarrià* ✛ *D:2.*

$$$
MEDITERRANEAN
Fodor'sChoice
★

✗ Céleri. When a fine dining chef with as many Michelin stars on his resume as Xavier Pellicer decided that what he really wanted to do was cook vegetables, even the jamón-loving locals formed lines outside to try the result. Unsurprisingly, his light, healthy dishes based around seasonal organic produce are an utter delight. **Known for:** starred vegetable-centric cuisine; open kitchen; natural wines. $ *Average main: €24* ⊠ *Passatge Marimón 5, Sant Gervasi* ☎ *93/252–9594* ⊕ *www. tribuwoki.com* ♥ *Closed Sun.* Ⓜ *Diagonal/FGC Provença* ✛ *G:6.*

$$
MEDITERRANEAN
Fodor'sChoice
★

✗ Coure. *Cuina d'autor* is Catalan for creative or original cooking, and that is exactly what you get in this smart subterranean space on the intimate and restaurant-centric Passatge Marimón, just above the Diagonal thoroughfare. The upstairs bar gets busy with a post-work crowd of food-loving locals, but downstairs is a cool, minimalist restaurant. **Known for:** interesting wine list; great local fish; seasonal mushrooms. $ *Average main: €22* ⊠ *Passatge Marimón 20, Sant Gervasi* ☎ *93/200–7532* ⊕ *www.restaurantcoure.es* ♥ *Closed Sun. and Mon. and Aug. 1–21* Ⓜ *Diagonal* ✛ *G:6.*

CLOSE UP

Ground Rules for Coffee

Coffee culture in Barcelona continues to focus on simplicity, in defiance of the near-infinite choices offered by certain barista-fronted international chains now moving into the city. A normal espresso, black coffee, is simply *un cafè*—a *café solo* in the rest of Spain. Add some extra water and it's a *cafè Americá.* In summer add ice for a *cafè amb gel,* and in winter add a dash of rum or brandy to make a *cigaló* (*carajillo* in Spanish). A *tallat,* from the Catalan verb *tallar* (to cut), is coffee with just a little milk (*café cortado* in Spanish), while *cafè amb llet* is Catalan for café con leche, or coffee mixed more evenly with milk. That's about as far as coffee menus stretch, but if you really want to see the waiter's eyes glaze over, order a *café descafeinado de maquina con leche desnatada natural* (decaffeinated coffee made in the espresso machine with skim milk applied at room temperature).

Finally, a word of warning to those who prefer their java to go: coffee is still, for the most part, a sit-down or belly-up-to-the-bar affair; take time to stop and smell the fresh roast.

$ CAFÉ 🍴 **Dole Café.** Little more than a slender slot on the corner of Capità Arenas and Manuel de Falla, this famous upper Barcelona café is absolutely vital to the Sarrià and Capità Arenas neighborhoods. Sandwiches and pastries here are uncannily well made and tasty. **Known for:** top-notch sandwiches and pastries; popeye sandwich is a favorite; often packed. [$] *Average main: €10* ✉ *Manuel de Falla 16–18, Sarrià* ☎ *93/204–1120* 🌐 *www.dolecafe.com* 💳 *No credit cards* 🕒 *Closed Sun.* [M] *Metro: Maria Cristina, FGC: Sarrià* ✥ *C:3.*

$$ CATALAN 🍴 **El Mató de Pedralbes.** Named for the *mató* (cottage cheese) traditionally prepared by the Clarist nuns across the street in the Monestir de Pedralbes, this is a great choice for lunch after exploring the monastery. It also has one of the most authentically Catalan menus around at a fairly reasonable price, given its posh Pedralbes environs. **Known for:** lunch is a great value; authentic Catalan cuisine; post-monastery lunch. [$] *Average main: €18* ✉ *Bisbe Català 10, Pedralbes* ☎ *93/204–9212* 🌐 *matodepedralbes.es* 🕒 *No dinner Sun.* [M] *Reina Elisenda* ✥ *B:1.*

$$ SEAFOOD 🍴 **Fishhh!** Housed inside the L'Illa Diagonal shopping mall, you can combine retail therapy with a seafood feast at Fishhh!, a first-rate oyster bar and fish restaurant. Owner Lluís de Buen' is long a major seafood supplier of Barcelona's top restaurants (check out his seafood-central command post off the back left corner of the Boqueria market) and his staff have put together a lively and popular dining space that exudes Boqueria market-style excitement in the midst of a busy shopping venue. **Known for:** oysters and champagne; seafood specialities; king crab served tableside. [$] *Average main: €21* ✉ *Av. Diagonal 557, Sant Gervasi, Les Corts* ☎ *93/444–1139* 🌐 *fishhh.net* 🕒 *Closed Sun.* [M] *Les Corts* ✥ *D:5.*

$$ CATALAN Fodor's Choice ★ 🍴 **Freixa Tradició.** When culinary techno-wizard Ramón Freixa turned the family restaurant back over to his father, Josep Maria Freixa, there was some speculation about the menu's headlong rush into the past. Now that the results are in, Barcelona food cognoscenti come

in droves for the authentic Catalan fare. **Known for:** Josep Maria's homemade bread; old-school charm in a modern setting; tasty creamy rice with cuttlefish. *[$] Average main: €21 ✉ Sant Elies 22, Sant Gervasi ☎ 93/209–7559 🌐 www.freixatradicio.com ⏲ Closed Mon. and Aug. No dinner Sun. [M] Sant Gervasi (FGC) ✥ G:5.*

$$ SEAFOOD 🍴 **Gouthier.** This Paris-style oyster bar spills out onto a pretty square in the former village of Sarrià. Pristine oysters of all kinds are shucked and served fresh alongside rye bread and creamy pats of French butter. **Known for:** supplies oysters to leading restaurants; quiet location; pleasant terrace. *[$] Average main: €16 ✉ Mañé i Flaquer 8, Sarrià ✥ Located on the Pl. Vicenç de Sarrià ☎ 93/205–9969 🌐 www.gouthier.es ⏲ Closed Mon. [M] Sarrià ✥ D:2.*

$$$ CATALAN Fodor's Choice ★ 🍴 **Hisop.** The minimalist interior design of Oriol Ivern's small restaurant is undistinguished, but his cooking has won him a well-deserved Michelin star. This is budget-conscious fine dining that avoids exotic ingredients but lifts local dishes to exciting new heights. **Known for:** great value Michelin-starred cuisine; minimalist interior; delicious cod with morel sauce. *[$] Average main: €25 ✉ Passatge de Marimon 9, Sant Gervasi ☎ 93/241–3233 🌐 www.hisop.com ⏲ Closed Sun. and 1st wk of Jan. No lunch Sat. [M] Diagonal ✥ G:6.*

$$ CATALAN 🍴 **Silvestre.** A graceful and easygoing mainstay in Barcelona's culinary landscape, this restaurant serves modern market cuisine to discerning diners. Look for fresh produce lovingly prepared in dishes such as tuna tartare, noodles and shrimp, or wood pigeon with duck liver. **Known for:** semisecret wine list; cozy setting. *[$] Average main: €22 ✉ Santaló 101, Sant Gervasi ☎ 93/241–4031 🌐 www.restaurante-silvestre.com ⏲ Closed Sun. and 3 wks in Aug. No lunch Sat. [M] Muntaner ✥ G:5.*

$$$ CATALAN Fodor's Choice ★ 🍴 **Tram-Tram.** At the end of the old tram line above the village of Sarrià, this restaurant offers one of Barcelona's finest culinary stops, with Isidre Soler and his wife, Reyes, at the helm. Perfectly sized portions and an airy white space within this traditional Sarrià house add to the experience. **Known for:** menú de degustació; pleasant interior garden patio; refined Catalan cuisine. *[$] Average main: €24 ✉ Major de Sarrià 121, Sarrià ☎ 93/204–8518 🌐 tram-tram.com ⏲ Closed Sun. and Mon. and 2 wks in Aug. No dinner Tues. [M] Sarrià ✥ D:1.*

$$$$ CATALAN Fodor's Choice ★ 🍴 **Via Veneto.** Open since 1967, this family-owned temple of fine Catalan dining offers a contemporary menu punctuated by old-school classics. Service from the veteran waiters is impeccable, and diners can safely place themselves in the hands of the expert sommelier to guide them through a daunting 10,000-strong wine list. **Known for:** favorite of Salvador Dalí; incredible roast duck; smoking room for postprandial cigars. *[$] Average main: €38 ✉ Ganduxer 10, Sant Gervasi ☎ 93/200–7244 🌐 www.viaveneto.es ⏲ Closed Sun., Aug., and first 2 wks of Sept. No lunch Sat. [M] La Bonanova (FGC), Maria Cristina ✥ E:5.*

$$ MEDITERRANEAN 🍴 **Vivanda.** Just above Plaça de Sarrià, Vivanda produces traditional Catalan miniatures *para picar* (small morsels), *platillos* (little dishes), and half rations of fish and meat listed as platillos *de pescado* and platillos *de carne,* thanks to a redesigned menu by star chef Jordi Vilà. The *coca de pa de vidre con tomate* (a delicate shell of bread

with tomato and olive oil) and the *presa de ibérico* (fillet of Iberian pig) are both exquisite. **Known for:** exquisite coca de pa de vidre con tomate; delicious presa de ibérico; dine in lush garden. [$] *Average main: €18* ✉ *Major de Sarrià 134, Sarrià* ☎ *93/203–1918* 🌐 *www.vivanda.cat* 🕒 *Closed Mon. No dinner Sun.* [M] *Reina Elisenda, Sarrià (FGC)* ✥ *D:1.*

TIBIDABO

From the Latin *tibi dabo* ("I will give to you"), the name of this mountain overlooking the city reflects the splendor of its views—the "kingdoms of the world" offered to Jesus by the devil, according to local legend. Restaurants here now offer some of Barcelona's best cuisine, often at prices as high as the mountain itself.

$$$$ CATALAN

🍴 **ABaC.** Jordi Cruz is a culinary phenomenon in Spain. The only choice here is between the two tasting menus; you can trust this chef to give you the best he has; the hyper-creative sampling varies wildly from season to season, but no expense or effort is ever spared. **Known for:** celebrity chef; two Michelin stars; creative in-season dishes. [$] *Average main: €140* ✉ *Av. del Tibidabo 1–7, Tibidabo* ☎ *93/319–6600* 🌐 *www.abacbarcelona.com* [M] *Tibidabo* ✥ *H:2.*

$$ SPANISH FAMILY Fodor's Choice ★

🍴 **El Asador de Aranda.** It's a hike to get to this immense palace above the Avenida Tibidabo metro station—but it's worth it. The kitchen, featuring a vast, wood-fired clay oven, specializes in Castilian cooking, with *cordero lechal* (roast suckling lamb), *morcilla* (black sausage), and pimientos de piquillo as star players. **Known for:** Art Nouveau setting; excellent roasted lamb; spectacular city views from terrace. [$] *Average main: €22* ✉ *Av. del Tibidabo 31, Tibidabo* ☎ *93/417–0115* 🌐 *www.asadordearanda.com* 🕒 *No dinner Sun.* [M] *Tibidabo (FGC)* ✥ *H:1.*

OUTSKIRTS OF BARCELONA

With the many fine in-town dining options available in Barcelona, any out-of-town recommendations must logically rank somewhere in the uppermost stratosphere of gastronomic excellence. These three, all rated among the top five or six establishments below the Pyrenees, undoubtedly do.

$$ CATALAN FAMILY

🍴 **Cal Xim.** This ordinary-looking village restaurant is the preferred dining place for many winemakers in the Penedès region, less than a one-hour drive from Barcelona. The traditional Catalan cuisine here is as good as anywhere, with a vast wood grill adding a smoky touch to dishes such as *escalivada* (grilled vegetables) with romesco sauce. **Known for:** note-perfect crema catalana; sensational faux burger of pig's trotter. [$] *Average main: €16* ✉ *Pl. Subirats 5, Sant Pau d'Ordal* ☎ *93/899–3020* 🌐 *www.calxim.com* 🕒 *No dinner Sun.* ✥ *F:10.*

$$$$ CATALAN Fodor's Choice ★

🍴 **El Celler de Can Roca.** Diners who can plan far enough ahead to deal with the waiting list for tables at this three-Michelin-star (and multiple-time winner of *Restaurant* magazine's World's Best Restaurant crown) are rewarded with an all-encompassing feast for the senses. Fine dining doesn't get any better than this. **Known for:** one of the world's greatest restaurants; outstanding wine list; dazzling creativity and perfectionism. [$] *Average main: €180* ✉ *Can Sunyer 48, Girona* ☎ *97/222–2157* 🌐 *www.cellercanroca.com* ⏲ *Closed Sun. and Mon. No lunch Tues. Closed Dec. 23–Jan. 18, Apr. 9–17, and Aug. 20–28* ✣ *L:15.*

$$$$ CATALAN 🍴 **Hispania.** This famous pilgrimage—one of the best restaurants in Catalonia for the last 50 years—is 39 km (24 miles) up the beach north of Barcelona. Sisters Francisca and Dolores Reixach continue to turn out the same line of classical Catalan cuisine that, despite the name Hispania, has characterized this spot from the start. **Known for:** classic Catalan cuisine; ultrafresh local seafood. [$] *Average main: €35* ✉ *Ctra. Real 54, Ctra. N II, 2 km (1 mile) south of Arenys de Mar, Arenys de Mar* ☎ *93/791–0457* 🌐 *www.restauranthispania.com* ⏲ *Closed Tues., 2 wks in Feb., and 2 wks in Oct. No dinner Sun.* ✣ *L:15.*

$$$$ CATALAN 🍴 **Sant Pau.** One of the best restaurants below the Pyrenees, this Sant Pol de Mar treasure is a scenic 40-minute train ride along the beach from Barcelona (take Calella-bound train from the RENFE station on the Plaça Catalunya). Chef Carme Ruscalleda is a household name in Spain, with seven Michelin stars to her credit, and this is the main stage for her talents. **Known for:** three-Michelin-starred cuisine; scenic train ride along the beach; perfect place to spend Sant Jordi. [$] *Average main: €49* ✉ *Carrer Nou 10, Sant Pol de Mar* ☎ *93/760–0662* 🌐 *www.ruscalleda.cat* ⏲ *Closed Sun. and Mon., 3 wks in May, and 3 wks in Nov. No lunch Thurs.* ✣ *L:15.*

WHERE TO EAT AND STAY IN BARCELONA

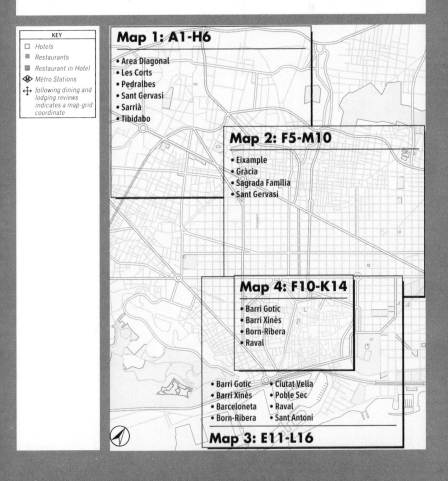

KEY

☐ Hotels
■ Restaurants
■ Restaurant in Hotel
◈ Métro Stations
✛ following dining and lodging reviews indicates a map-grid coordinate

Map 1: A1-H6

- Area Diagonal
- Les Corts
- Pedralbes
- Sant Gervasi
- Sarrià
- Tibidabo

Map 2: F5-M10

- Eixample
- Gràcia
- Sagrada Família
- Sant Gervasi

Map 4: F10-K14

- Barri Gotic
- Barri Xinès
- Born-Ribera
- Raval

- Barri Gotic
- Barri Xinès
- Barceloneta
- Born-Ribera

- Ciutat Vella
- Poble Sec
- Raval
- Sant Antoni

Map 3: E11-L16

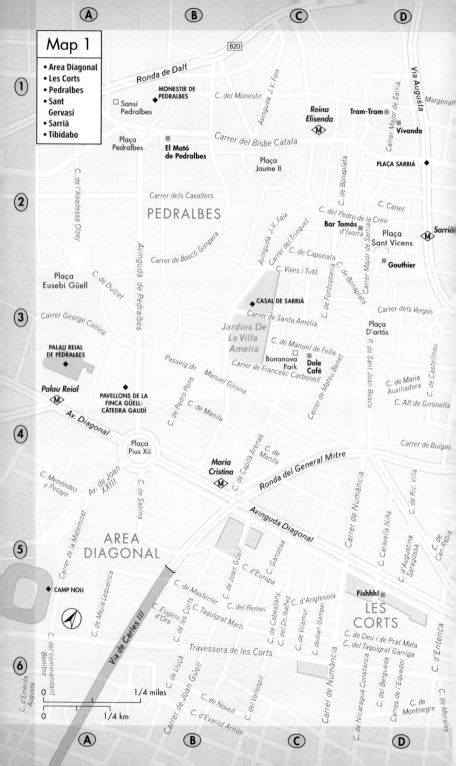

E   F   G   H

Gran Hotel la Florida

El Asador de Aranda

C. del Cister

C. dels Quatre Camins

Carrer dels Planella

Carrer de Jesús i Maria

TIBIDABO

1

C. de Sant Joan de la Salle

ABaC

Passeig de Sant Gervasi

Avinguda del Tibidabo

C. d'Angli

C. de Pomaret

C. d'Iradier

C. de les Escoles Pies

C. de Dolors Monserdà

C. de l'Esperança

SARRIÀ

Passeig de la Bonanova

Vilana Hotel

2

Carrer de Dalmases

Carrer de l'Emancipacio

Carrer de Bigai

Carrer de Mao

C. de Sant Gervasi de Cassoles

C. de Teodora Lamadrid

Carre de Balmes

Carrer de Bertran

Carrer d'Angli

Carrer de Pau Alcover

C. de Calatrava

Carrer de les Escoles Pies

Carrer de Mandri

Carrer de la Ciutat de Balaguer

C. del Camp

C. de Muntaner

Carrer del Champ

Carrer del Doctor Carulla

C. de Ganduxer

Primero Primera

Tres Torres

Carrer dels Vergos

M

A Contraluz

C. del Milanesat

Carrer de Carrenca

Carrer d'Alacant

C. de la Nena Casas

C. de Sant Marius

C. d'Arimon

3

Via Augusta

C. del Doctor Roux

C. d'Angel Guimera

COL.LEGI DE LES TERESIANES

Ronda del General Mitre

Carrer de Modolell

Carrer de Copèrnic

C. de Freixa

Carrer de Vallmayor

C. de Láz Cárdenas

La Bonanova

M

Carrer de Rasel

Via Augusta

Carrer de Copèrnic

C. de Sant Hermeneglid

C. de la Gleva

C. del Francolf

4

C. de les Tres Torres

Carrer de Ganduxer

Carrer de la Reina Victòria

C. de Castelló

Carrer de Descartes

Freixa Tradició

C. de Sant Elies

Carrer de Brusi

C. de Guillem Tell

C. del Doctor Fleming

C. de Jac Benavente

C. de Santa Fe de Nou Mèxic

C. dels Vafero

C. de Johann Seb Bach

Silvestre

C. del Rector Ubach

SANT GERVASI

C. de Saragossa

5

Carrer de Borí i Fontestà

C. de Francesc Pérez Cabrero

C. de Josep Bertrand

Jardins D'eduard Marquina

C. de Ferran Aguilló

C. d'Amigo

C. de Calaf

C. de Sant Eusebi

Carrer de Balmes

C. de Lincoln

Avinguda de Sarrià

Via Veneto

C. de Beethoven

Av. de Pau Casals

C. dels Madrazo

C. de Tavern

Carrer d'Aribau

C. d'Oliana

C. d'Alfons XII

C. de la Forja

C. de la Forja

Hotel Gran Derby Suite 4*

Carrer de Loreto

Avinguda Diagonal

C. de Calvet

C. Sagués

C. de l'Avenir

C. de Santaló

C. de Marià Cubi

C. Camp d'en Vidal

Carrer de Muntaner

C. de Moliner

C. de Marià Cubi

C. de Regàs

6

C. de Bordeus

C. Rita Bonnat

Bambarol

Travessera de Gràcia

Coure   Hisop

Céleri

Hofmann

C. J. Romea

C. St. Gabriel

C. de Buenos Aires

E   F   G   H

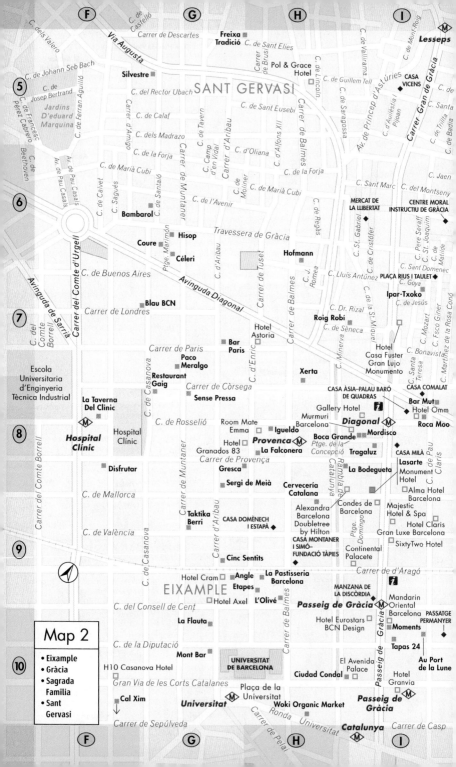

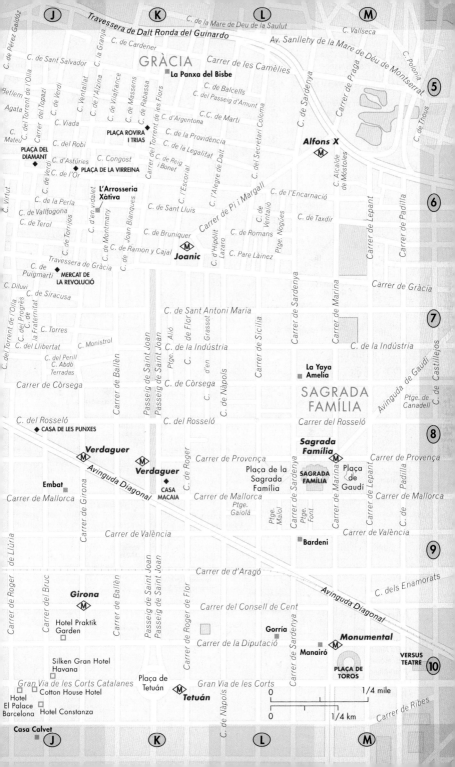

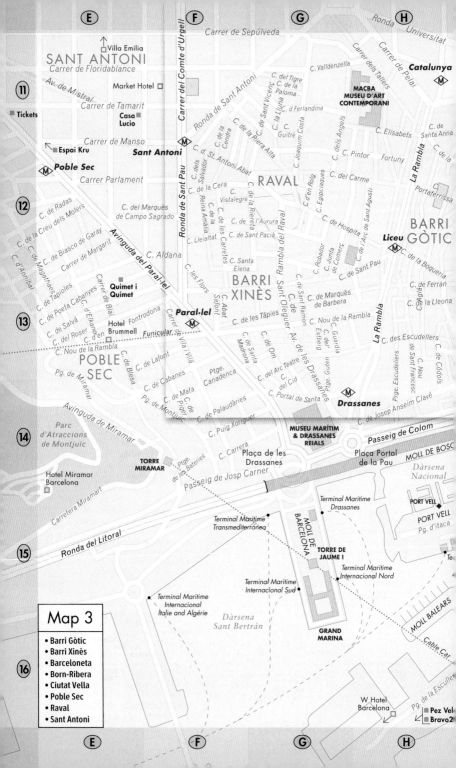

E F G H

SANT ANTONI
↑ Villa Emilia
Carrer de Floridablance

Carrer de Sepúlveda

Ronda Universitat

Catalunya Ⓜ

Carrer dels Tallers

Carrer de Petal

C. Valldenzella

(11)

Av. de Mistral

■ Market Hotel □

**MACBA
MUSEU D'ART
CONTEMPORANI**

C. del Tigre

C. de la Paloma

C. de la Lluna

C. de St. Vicenç

C. d Ferlandina

C. del
Santa Anna

La Rambla

C. de

■ Tickets

Carrer de Tamarit

Casa ■
Lucio

Ronda de Sant Antoni

C. de la Cendra

C. de la Riera Alta

C. de Joaquím Costa

C. dels Angels

C. Elisabets

Carrer de Manso

Ⓜ **Sant Antoni**

C. d. St. Antoni Abat

C. dels Salvador

C. de la Riereta

C. d'en Roig

C. Pintor Fortuny

Portaferrissa

■ Espai Kru

Ⓜ **Poble Sec**

Carrer Parlament

Ronda de Sant Pau

C. de la Cera

C. Vistalegre

C. de l'Aurora

C. del Carme

RAVAL

C. Egipciaques

C. de Hospita

C. de l'Arc de Sant Agustí

BARRI GÒTIC

(12)

C. de Radas

C. de la Creu dels Molers

C. del Marquès de Campo Sagrado

C. de la Reina Amália

C. Lleialtat

C. de les Carretes

C. de Sant Pacià

Rambla del Raval

C. Robador

C. Junta de Comerç

C. de Sant Pau

Liceu Ⓜ

C. de la Boqueria

C. de Ferran

C. d'Annibal

C. de Magalhaes

C. de Biasco de Garay

Carrer de Margarit

Avinguda del Paral·lel

C. Aldana

C. les Flors

C. Santa Elena

C. Abat Safont

BARRI XINÈS

Sant Oleguer

C. de Sant Ramon

C. de Sant Pau

La Rambla

C. de la Lleona

C. de Tàpioles

C. de Poeta Cabanyes

C. de Blai

Quimet i ■ Quimet

C. de les Tàpies

C. Nou de la Rambla

C. des Escudellers

C. Nou de Sant Francesc

C. de Còdols

(13)

C. de Salvà

C. del Roser

C. d'Elkano

Hotel Fontrodona Brummell

Paral·lel Ⓜ

Carrer de Vila i Vilá

C. de Santa Madrona

C. de Om

Av. de les Drassanes

C. de Sant Ramon

C. del Esborg

Ptge. Escudellers

Ptge. de Sant Francesc

C. Nou de la Rambla

POBLE SEC

C. d'en

Funicular de

C. de Blesa

C. de Lafont

Ptge. Canadenca

C. de l'Arc Teatre

C. de la Guardia

C. del Cid

C. del Guten

Pg. de Miramar

C. de Cabanes

C. de Mata

C. de Piquer

C. del Portal de Santa

Drassanes Ⓜ

Avinguda de Miramar

Pg. de Montjuïc

C. de Palaudàries

C. de Josep Anseim Clavé

(14)

Parc d'Atraccions de Montjuïc

C. Puig Xoriguer

MUSEU MARÍTIM & DRASSANES REIALS

Passeig de Colom

TORRE MIRAMAR

Ptge. de les Bateríes

C. Carrera

Plaça de les Drassanes

Plaça Portal de la Pau

MOLL DE BOSC

Hotel Miramar Barcelona

Passeig de Josp Carner

Dàrsena Nacional

PORT VELL □

PORT VELL

Carretera Miramart

Terminal Marítime Drassanes

Pg. d'itaca

Terminal Marítime Transmediterrània

MOLL DE BARCELONA

(15)

Ronda del Litoral

TORRE DE JAUME I

Terminal Marítime Internacional Nord

Te

Terminal Marítime Internacional Sud

MOLL BALEARS

Cable Car

Terminal Marítime Internacional Ítalie and Algérie

Dàrsena Sant Bertrán

GRAND MARINA

Pg. de la Esculle

(16)

W Hotel Barcelona

■ **Pez Vel**
■ **Bravo2**

E F G H

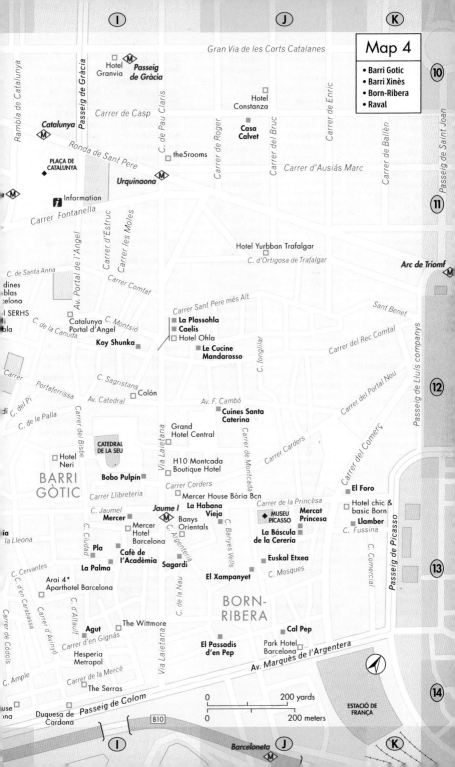

Restaurants

1881 Per Sagardi J:14
4amb5 Mujades G:13
ABaC H:2
A Contraluz E:3
Adarra J:6
Agua L:15
Agut I:13
Angle H:9
Arola L:15
A Tu Bola G:12
Au Port de la Lune I:10
Bambarol G:6
Bar Cañete G:13
Bar Mut I:8
Bar Paris G:7
Bar Tomás D:2
Barceloneta I:15
Bardini L:9
Barraca J:15
Bestial L:15
Blau BCN G:7
Bobo Pulpín I:13
Boca Grande I:8
Bravo 24 H:16
Ca l'Estevet G:11
Ca l'Isidre F:13
Caelis I:12
Café de l'Acadèmia I:13
Café de l'Opera H:12
Café Viena H:11
Café Zurich H:11
Cal Pep J:13
Cal Xim F:10
Can Culleretes H:13
Can Majó J:15
Can Solé I:15
Casa Calvet J:11
Casa Lucio E:11
Céleri G:6
Cera 23 F:12
Cerveseria Catalana H:8
Cinc Sentits G:9
Ciudad Condal H:10
Coure G:6
Cuines Santa Caterina J:12
Disfrutar F:8
Dole Café C:3
Dos Palillos H:11
Dos Pebrots H:11

El Asador de Aranda H:1
El Celler de Can Roca L:15
El Foro J:13
El Mató de Pedralbes B:1
El Nou Ramonet J:14
El Passadís d'en Pep J:13
El Vaso de Oro J:14
El Xampanyet J:13
Els Pescadors L:15
Els Tres Porquets L:12
Embat J:8
En Ville H:11
Enoteca L:15
espai Kru E:11
Etapes H:9
Euskal Etxea J:13
Fishhh! D:5
Fonda España H:13
Freixa Tradició G:5
Gorría L:10
Gouthier D:2
Green Spot J:14
Gresca H:8
Hisop G:6
Hispania L:15
Hofmann H:6
Iguelda H:8
Ipar-Txoko I:7
Irati Taverna Basca H:12
Koy Shunka I:12
L'Arrosseria Xàtiva J:6
La Báscula de la Cereria J:13
La Bodegueta H:8
La Castanya H:13
La Cereria H:13
La Cova Fumada J:15
La Falconera H:8
La Flauta G:10
La Habana Vieja J:13
La Mar Salada L:15
La Palma I:13
La Panxa del Bisbe K:5
La Pastisseria Barcelona H:9
La Plassohla I:12
La Taverna Del Clínic G:8
La Yaya Amelia L:7
Lasarte I:8
Le Cucine Mandarosso I:12

Llamber J:13
L'Olivé H:9
Manairó M:10
Mercat Princesa J:13
Mercer I:13
Moments I:10
Mont Bar G:10
Mordisco I:8
Paco Meralgo G:7
Pez Vela H:16
Piratas L:11
Pla I:13
Opera Samfaina H:13
Quimet i Quimet E:13
Restaurant Gaig G:8
Roca Moo I:8
Roig Robí I:7
Sagardi I:13
Sant Pau L:15
Sense Pressa G:8
Sergi de Meià G:8
Silvestre G:5
Suculent G:12
Taktika Berri G:9
Tapas 24 I:10
Tickets E:11
Tragaluz I:8
Tram-Tram D:1
Via Veneto E:5
Vivanda D:1
Woki Organic Market H:10
Xerta H:8

Hotels

Alexandra Barcelona Doubletree by Hilton I:8
Alma Hotel Barcelona I:8
Arai 4* Aparthotel Barcelona I:13
Bagués H:12
Banys Orientals I:13
Barceló Raval G:12
Bonanova Park C:3
Casa Camper Barcelona H:11
Catalunya Portal d'Angel I:12
Citadines Ramblas Barcelona H:12
Colón I:12
Condes de Barcelona I:9
Continental Palacete I:10
Cotton House Hotel J:10
Duquesa de Cardona I:14
El Avenida Palace I:10
el Jardí H:12
Gallery Hotel I:8
Gran Hotel la Florida H:1
Grand Hotel Central I:12
Grupotel Gravina H:11
H10 Montcada Boutique Hotel I:12
H1898 H:12
Hotel 54 Barcelona I:15
Hotel Arts Barcelona L:15
Hotel Astoria H:7
Hotel Axel G:9
Hotel Brummell E:13
Hotel Casa Fuster Gran Lujo Monumento I:7
Hotel chic&basic Born J:13
Hotel Claris Grand Luxe Barcelona I:8
Hotel Constanza J:10
Hotel Cram G:9
Hotel DO Plaça Reial H:13
Hotel El Palace Barcelona J:10
Hotel España H:13
Hotel Eurostars BCN Design I:10

Hotel Gran Derby Suite 4* E:6
Hotel Granvia I:10
Hotel Granados 83 H:8
Hotel Grums F:14
Hotel H10 Casanova F:10
Hotel Jazz H:10
Market Hotel F:11
Hotel Midmost H:11
Hotel Miramar Barcelona E:14
Hotel Neri I:12
Hotel Ohla I:12
Hotel Omm I:8
Hotel Praktik Garden J:10
Hotel Pulitzer H:11
Hotel Regina H:11
Hotel SERHS Rivoli Rambla H:12
Hotel Yurbban Trafalger J:11
Jardí H:12
Le Méridien Barcelona H:12
Majestic Hotel & Spa I:9
Mandarin Oriental Barcelona I:10
Meliá Barcelona Sky L:12
Mercer Hotel Barcelona I:13
Mercer House Bòria Bcn I:12
Mesón Castilla H:11
Monument Hotel I:8
Murmuri Barcelona H:8
Park Hotel Barcelona J:13
Pol & Grace Hotel F:8
Primero Primera E:3
Room Mate Emma H:8
Sansi Pedralbes A:1
Sant Agustí H:12
Silken Gran Hotel Havana J:10
SixtyTwo Hotel I:9
Soho House Barcelona H:14
the5rooms I:11
The Serras I:14
The Wittmore I:13
Vilana Hotel F:2
Villa Emilia E:11
W Barcelona H:16

WHERE TO STAY

Updated by
Jared Lubarsky

Barcelona's hotel trade may be centuries removed from Miguel de Cervantes's 17th-century description of it as a fountain of courtesy and a shelter for strangers, but in the 400 years or so since *Don Quixote* was written, the city continues to pamper and impress visitors.

Barcelona's pre-Olympics hotel surge in the early 1990s was matched only by its post-Olympics hotel surge in the early 2000s. The city is the premier tourist destination in Spain, and the major cruise port in the Mediterranean. "Starchitects" like Ricardo Bofill and Rafael Moneo have changed the skyline with skyscraper hotels of eye-popping luxury; the real heroes of this story, however, are the architect-designer teams that take one after another of the city's historic properties and restore them with an astonishing tour de force of taste. Hotel restaurants, too—from the Arts' Enoteca to the Mandarin's Moments—are among the superstar attractions in the city's gastronomic scene.

Hotels in the Barri Gòtic and along La Rambla now compete with the newer lodgings in the Eixample, or west along Diagonal; waterfront monoliths like the W Barcelona, removed from the bustle of midtown, set the standard for upscale hospitality. Many Eixample hotels occupy restored late 19th- or early 20th-century town houses. Billets like the Claris, the Majestic Hotel & Spa, the Monument, the Hotel Neri, and the Colón mix style and luxury with a sense of place.

Small hotels in the Ciutat Vella, such as the Sant Agustí, Hotel Market, or Hotel Chic & Basic Born are considerably less expensive and—in the accommodations you'll find listed here—at no substantial sacrifice of comfort and convenience. Wherever you choose to stay, you'll never be far from anything you'll want to see and do in this hospitable city.

WHERE TO STAY?

	Neighborhood Vibe	Pros	Cons
Barri Gòtic and Born-Ribera	With lamps glowing in the corners of Roman and Gothic areas, this is a romantic part of town. The Picasso Museum and Santa Maria del Mar basilica are nearby.	The architecture of the Barri Gòtic is a great repository of the city's past. Plaça Sant Jaume, the cathedral, Plaça del Rei, and the Born-Ribera district are among the main reasons to visit the city.	It's easy to lose yourself in this labyrinth of narrow cobblestone streets. The Barri Gòtic can also be noisy, with echoes reverberating around this ancient sound chamber.
El Raval	El Raval has always been a rough-and-tumble part of town, but the nightlife is exciting and the diversity of the neighborhood is exemplary. Bonus: it's just steps from the Boqueria market.	For the closest thing to Marrakesh in Barcelona, El Raval has a buzz all its own. A contemporary art museum, the medieval hospital, and the Mercat de Sant Antoni offer plenty to explore.	El Raval can seem dangerous, and demands street-sense, especially at night. Certain pockets of the neighborhood are the haunts of prostitutes, drug dealers, and other seamy characters.
La Rambla	Constantly bustling, La Rambla is a virtual anthology of Barcelona street life, shared equally by visitors, hucksters, café hoppers, and local residents.	Boqueria market, flower stalls, the Liceu opera house, and Plaça Reial are all quintessential Barcelona sites.	The crowds can be overwhelming, especially if FC Barcelona wins a championship match and the entire city descends on La Rambla to celebrate.
Barceloneta and Port Olímpic	At one time the fishermen's quarter, Barceloneta retains its informal and working-class ambience, with sidewalk restaurants lining Passeig Joan de Borbó.	Near the beach, this part of town has a laid-back feel. Barceloneta is where to go for the best casual seafood restaurants in town.	Barceloneta offers few accommodations beyond the W Hotel; Port Olímpic's monolithic Hotel Arts is a bit isolated from the rest of town.
Eixample	Gaudí masterpieces Casa Milà and Casa Battló are here, on the Passeig de Gràcia; this Moderniste quarter boasts many of the city's top-tier hotels and restaurants. And then there's the shopping...	Art Nouveau architecture is everywhere in the Eixample, constantly rewarding to the eye. Gaudí's yet-unfinished masterpiece La Sagrada Família is within walking distance.	Too few buildings here have street numbers; for a neighborhood that was supposed to be structured as a grid, the Eixample can be difficult to navigate.
Pedralbes, Sarrià, and Upper Barcelona	Upper Barcelona is leafy and residential, and the air is always a little cooler and cleaner. Pedralbes is Barcelona's wealthiest residential quarter; Sarrià is the rustic little village next door.	A 15-minute train ride connects Sarrià with the middle of the Eixample and La Rambla.	Staying in upper Barcelona involves a 15-minute trip, at least, to the most important attractions. Traveling to and from here after midnight on weeknights will require a taxi.

4

BARCELONA LODGING PLANNER

LODGING PLANNER

RESERVATIONS

Because of the annual summer onslaught of millions of tourists, you'll want to reserve well in advance from early April to late October. Note that high-season rates (May and June for most hotels, rather than July and August) prevail also during the week before Easter, during local fiestas, and for events like the Mobile World Congress in February, the Formula 1 Grand Prix races in May, and for the at-home *classico* confrontation between FC Barcelona and Real Madrid. When reserving, specify whether you prefer two beds or one double bed. Although single rooms (*habitacións sencillas*) are usually available, they are often on the small side, and you might prefer to pay a bit extra for single occupancy in a double room (*habitación doble uso individual*).

FACILITIES

Hotel entrances are marked with a plaque bearing the letter H and the number of stars. The letter R (standing for *residencia*) after the letter H indicates an establishment with no meal service. The designations *fonda* (F), *pensión* (P), and *hostal* (Hs) indicate budget accommodations— although a Spanish *hostal* (hostel) can often be just as well appointed and comfortable as a hotel.

Hotel ratings used by the Turisme de Barcelona are expressed in stars, with five stars as the highest category. The rating system, however, is essentially based on a checklist of facilities (pool, restaurant, concierge, etc.) more than an evaluation of quality; a hotel can lack one or more of the amenities on the list and still be a better choice than one in the next highest category.

PRICES

Barcelona's finer hotels are as expensive as those of any other major city—but rates can vary as widely (and mysteriously) as airline tickets. Prices are generally lower from November through March, when hotels have more availability, except when there are huge conventions in town or other special events.

WHAT IT COSTS IN EUROS			
$	$$	$$$	$$$$
Hotels	under €125	€125–€174	€175–€225	over €225

Prices are for two people in a standard double room in high season.

HOTEL REVIEWS

Listed alphabetically within neighborhoods. Use the coordinate (✦ B:2) at the end of each review to locate a property on the corresponding map. For expanded reviews, visit Fodors.com.

CIUTAT VELLA (OLD CITY)

The Ciutat Vella includes La Rambla, Barri Gòtic, Born-Ribera, and El Raval districts between Plaça de Catalunya and the port.

BARRI GÒTIC

$$$$
HOTEL
FAMILY
Fodor's Choice
★

Arai 4* Aparthotel Barcelona (*Arai-Palau Dels Quatre Rius Monument*). You couldn't ask for a better location from which to explore Barcelona's Barri Gòtic—or for a bivouac more elegant—than one of the Aparthotel suites in this stunning restoration. **Pros:** warm and attentive service; double showerheads; picnic box breakfast (€15.40) delivered to your room. **Cons:** somewhat seedy area; on busy street; rooms on the top floor lack historic charm. $ *Rooms from: €370* ✉ *Avinyó 30, Barri Gòtic* ☎ *93/320–3950* ⊕ *www.hotelarai.com* ⇌ *31 rooms* ⦾ *No meals* Ⓜ *L3 Liceu* ✣ *I:13.*

$$$
HOTEL

Catalunya Portal d'Angel. Converted in 1998 from a historic stately home dating back to 1825, the Catalunya Portal d'Angel beckons with its neoclassic facade and original grand marble staircase. **Pros:** pet-friendly; includes walking tours of the Old City and the Eixample; pleasant breakfast pavilion in the garden. **Cons:** small rooms; faces busy pedestrian mall; lighting needs improvement. $ *Rooms from: €200* ✉ *Av. Portal d'Angel 17, Barri Gòtic* ☎ *93/318–4141* ⊕ *www. hoteles-catalonia.com* ⊟ *No credit cards* ⇌ *82 rooms, 1 suite* ⦾ *No meals* Ⓜ *Pl. Catalunya* ✣ *I:12.*

$$$
HOTEL

Colón. Around since 1951, the quiet and conservative Colón feels like it's been around forever, and is reasonably priced for the location: near the Catedral de la Seu which is spectacular when illuminated at night. **Pros:** central location; some rooms have balconies overlooking square; new rooftop terrace with heated Jacuzzi. **Cons:** can feel a bit stodgy; no pets; narrow bathrooms. $ *Rooms from: €220* ✉ *Av. Catedral 7, Barri Gòtic* ☎ *93/301–1404* ⊕ *www.hotelcolon.es* ⇌ *136 rooms, 5 suites* ⦾ *No meals* Ⓜ *L4 Jaume I* ✣ *I:12.*

$
HOTEL
FAMILY
Fodor's Choice
★

el Jardí. Facing charming Plaça del Pi and Plaça Sant Josep Oriol, in a pair of conjoined buildings that date to 1860, this family-friendly little budget hotel couldn't be better situated for exploring La Rambla and the Barri Gòtic. **Pros:** central location; friendly English-speaking staff; breakfast free if you book online through the hotel's own website. **Cons:** no room service; no pool, gym, or spa; no place for suitcases in small rooms. $ *Rooms from: €100* ✉ *Pl. Sant Josep Oriol 1, Barri Gòtic* ☎ *93/301–5900* ⊕ *www.eljardi-barcelona.com* ⇌ *40 rooms* ⦾ *No meals* Ⓜ *L3 Liceu, L4 Jaume I, Catalunya* ✣ *H:12.*

$$$$
HOTEL
FAMILY

Grand Hotel Central. At the edge of the Gothic Quarter, very near the Barcelona cathedral, this fashionable midtown hotel is popular with business and pleasure travelers alike, with contemporary decor and upscale amenities. **Pros:** excellent location between the Gothic Quarter and the Born; infinity pool with city views; Mediterranean City Bar and Restaurant on-site. **Cons:** no pets; busy thoroughfare outside; pricey breakfast. $ *Rooms from: €300* ✉ *Via Laietana 30, Barri Gòtic* ☎ *93/295–7900* ⊕ *www.grandhotelcentral.com* ⇌ *147 rooms* ⦾ *No meals* Ⓜ *L4 Jaume I* ✣ *I:12.*

4

$$$$ HOTEL Fodor's Choice ★ 🏨 **Hotel Neri.** Just steps from the cathedral, in the heart of the city's old Jewish Quarter, this elegant, upscale, boutique hotel, part of the prestigious Relais & Chateaux hotel group, marries ancient and avant-garde designs. **Pros:** central location (close to Barri Gòtic); barbecue and occasional live music on the rooftop terrace; 24-hour room service. **Cons:** noisy on summer nights and school days; pets allowed only in deluxe rooms with terraces; pricy surcharge; lighting over beds could improve. [$] *Rooms from: €350* ✉ *Carrer Sant Sever 5, Barri Gòtic* ☎ *93/304–0655* 🌐 *www.hotelneri.com/en* 🛏 *22 rooms* 🍴 *No meals* [M] *L3 Liceu, L4 Jaume I* ✥ *I:12.*

$$$$ HOTEL 🏨 **Hotel Ohla.** One of Barcelona's top design hotels (also with incredible food), the Ohla's neoclassical exterior (not counting the playful eyeballs stuck to the facade) belies its avant-garde interior, full of witty, design-conscious touches. **Pros:** steps from Palau de la Música Catalana; remarkable restaurant La Plassohla on-site; high-end wines at Vistro 49. **Cons:** adjacent to noisy Via Laietana; no pets; uncomfortable furniture in lobby. [$] *Rooms from: €324* ✉ *Via Laietana 49, Barri Gòtic* ☎ *93/341–5050* 🌐 *www.ohlabarcelona.com* 💳 *No credit cards* 🛏 *74 rooms* 🍴 *Breakfast* [M] *L4 Urquinaona* ✥ *I:12.*

$$$$ HOTEL 🏨 **Mercer Hotel Barcelona.** On a narrow side street near Plaça Sant Jaume, this romantic boutique hotel, a medieval town house, is among the latest examples of Barcelona's signature genius for the redesign and rebirth of historical properties. **Pros:** minutes from the Old City; comfortable rooftop terrace with a plunge pool and (in season) a bar-café; breakfast in glassed-in patio. **Cons:** very pricey; no gym or spa; expensive breakfast. [$] *Rooms from: €480* ✉ *Carrer dels Lledó 5, Barri Gòtic* ☎ *93/310–7480* 🌐 *www.mercerhoteles.com* 🛏 *28 rooms* 🍴 *No meals* [M] *L4 Jaume I* ✥ *I:13.*

$$$ HOTEL FAMILY 🏨 **Mercer House Bòria Bcn.** Blink and you miss it: on a small side street between the Santa Caterina market and the Picasso Museum, this boutique hotel (just six rooms and five suites) announces itself with no more than a name etched in the glass on its discreet front door. **Pros:** walking distance to great attractions; pleasant rooftop terrace and solarium; en suite kitchens in suites and lofts. **Cons:** no restaurant or bar; no room service; no pool. [$] *Rooms from: €179* ✉ *Carrer de la Bòria 24–26, Barri Gòtic* ☎ *93/295–5893* 🌐 *www.boriabcn.com* 🛏 *6 double rooms, 5 suites* 🍴 *No meals* [M] *L4 Jaume I* ✥ *I:12.*

BORN-RIBERA

$$ HOTEL 🏨 **Banys Orientals.** Despite its name, the "Oriental Baths" has no spa, but it does have chic high-contrast design, with dark stained wood and crisp white bedding, and is reasonably priced for the location. **Pros:** Rituals toiletries; tasteful design; steps from the port, Picasso Museum, and the Born area. **Cons:** rooms are on the small side; no room service; no terrace. [$] *Rooms from: €125* ✉ *Argenteria 37, Born-Ribera* ☎ *93/268–8460* 🌐 *www.hotelbanysorientals.com* 🛏 *43 rooms* 🍴 *No meals* [M] *L4 Jaume I* ✥ *I:13.*

$$ HOTEL 🏨 **Hotel chic&basic Born.** The lobby of this hip little boutique hotel in the Born with its leather sofa and banquettes might remind you of a Starbucks, but the rooms tell a different story: opening in 2006, the concept for chic&basic was whimsical, edgy accommodations at affordable prices

(most budget billets in Barcelona at the time were probably best avoided), and designer Xavier Claramunt rose to the occasion. **Pros:** near upbeat Born-Ribera scene; bicycle rentals for guests; remote lets you change color of lights in room. **Cons:** no room service or minibars; no children under 12; clothing storage limited, on open racks. [$] *Rooms from: €129* ✉ *Carrer Princesa 50, Born-Ribera* ☎ *93/295–4650* 🌐 *www.chicandbasic.com* 🛏 *31 rooms* 🍴 *No meals* [M] *L4 Jaume I* ✥ *J:13.*

$$$ HOTEL 🏨 **H10 Montcada Boutique Hotel.** A short walk from the attractions of the Gothic Quarter and the Born-Ribera district, the Montcada is one of the 50 properties in the sleek H10 chain and a good choice for comfort and convenience. **Pros:** astounding rooftop deck with Jacuzzi; great location; pleasant breakfast room. **Cons:** wardrobes a tight fit by the bed; bed lighting could improve; no pets. [$] *Rooms from: €209* ✉ *Via Laietana 24, Born-Ribera* ☎ *93/268–8570* 🌐 *www.h10hotels.com* 🛏 *80 rooms* 🍴 *No meals* [M] *Jaume I* ✥ *I:12.*

$$$ HOTEL Fodor's Choice ★ 🏨 **Hotel Yurbban Trafalgar.** Guests and locals alike have been raving about the rooftop terrace at the Yurbban Trafalgar since it opened late in 2014, and with good reason: the panoramic view is hands-down one of the best in the city at this hip yet sophisticated hotel. **Pros:** free cheese and wine tasting nightly (8–9 pm); bicycles free for guests; minutes from Palau de la Música. **Cons:** small rooms; room service ends at 11 pm; small shower stalls. [$] *Rooms from: €180* ✉ *Carrer Trafalgar 30, Born-Ribera* ☎ *93/268–0727* 🌐 *www.yurbban.com/en* 🛏 *56 rooms* 🍴 *No meals* [M] *L1/L3 Urquinaona* ✥ *J:11.*

$$$ HOTEL 🏨 **Park Hotel Barcelona.** Well situated for exploring the Born-Ribera district, Barceloneta, and the port—and in a neighborhood blessed with wine and tapas bars—this mid-priced hotel has basic rooms with espresso-color wood floors and comfortable (if generic) furnishings. **Pros:** good location; decently sized pool on rooftop terrace; room service noon to midnight. **Cons:** rooms fairly small; no pool, gym, or spa; soundproofing between rooms could improve. [$] *Rooms from: €220* ✉ *Av. Marquès de l'Argentera 11, Born-Ribera* ☎ *93/319–6000* 🌐 *www.parkhotelbarcelona.com* 🛏 *91 rooms* 🍴 *No meals* [M] *L4 Barceloneta* ✥ *J:13.*

$$$$ HOTEL Fodor's Choice ★ 🏨 **The Wittmore.** Opened in 2016, the Wittmore is the adults-only romantic hideaway *par excellence*, tucked away in a tiny cul-de-sac in the maze of streets just north of the marina, a short walk to the Plaça Colón. **Pros:** rooms include robes and slippers; cocktail bar with fireplace; plunge pool and bar on rooftop terrace. **Cons:** no spa or gym; budget-busting rates. [$] *Rooms from: €350* ✉ *Riudares 7, Born-Ribera* ☎ *93/550–0885* 🌐 *www.thewittmore.com* 🛏 *21 rooms* 🍴 *No meals* [M] *L3 Drassanes* ✥ *I:13.*

EL RAVAL

$$$ HOTEL 🏨 **Barceló Raval.** With an edgy contemporary design, reasonable rates, and location in one of Barcelona's most colorful neighborhoods, Barceló Raval is a welcome addition to the city's hotel scene. **Pros:** 10 minutes from La Rambla; 360-degree vistas from rooftop terrace; DJ during Sunday brunch. **Cons:** Rambla del Raval a bit dicey at night; mood lighting not to everyone's taste; pool on terrace is very small. [$] *Rooms from: €200* ✉ *Rambla del Raval 17–21, El Raval* ☎ *93/320–1490* 🌐 *www.barcelo.com/en-us/hotels/spain/barcelona/barcelo-raval* 🛏 *186 rooms* 🍴 *No meals* [M] *L3 Liceu* ✥ *G:12.*

$$$
HOTEL
FAMILY
Fodor's Choice
★

⛨ **Casa Camper Barcelona.** A marriage between the Camper footwear empire and the Vinçon design store produced this 21st-century hotel halfway between La Rambla and the MACBA (Museum of Contemporary Art), with a focus on sustainability (think solar panels and water recycling) and a unique "one big family" feel. **Pros:** great buffet breakfast with dishes cooked to order; just steps from MACBA and the Boqueria; hip, friendly staff. **Cons:** expensive; extra per person charge for children over three years old; no in-room minibar. ⓢ *Rooms from: €220* ⊠ *Carrer Elisabets 11, El Raval* ☎ *93/342–6280* ⊕ *www.casacamper.com* ↘ *40 rooms* ⓘⓄⓘ *Breakfast* Ⓜ *Catalunya, L3 Liceu* ✢ *H:11.*

$$$$
HOTEL
Fodor's Choice
★

⛨ **Hotel España.** This recently renovated Art Nouveau gem is the second oldest (after the nearby Sant Agustí) and among the best of Barcelona's smaller hotels. **Pros:** near Liceu opera house and La Rambla; alabaster fireplace in the bar lounge; lavish breakfast buffet. **Cons:** lower rooms facing Carrer Sant Pau get some street noise; bed lighting could be improved; no views. ⓢ *Rooms from: €290* ⊠ *Carrer Sant Pau 9–11, El Raval* ☎ *93/550–0000* ⊕ *www.hotelespanya.com* ↘ *83 rooms* ⓘⓄⓘ *No meals* Ⓜ *L4 Liceu* ✢ *H:13.*

$$
HOTEL

⛨ **Hotel Midmost.** New management took over this handsome Moderniste property (formerly the Inglaterra) in 2016 and gave it an extensive makeover; rooms feature parquet floors, white walls, and touches of Mediterranean blue; amenities include robes and slippers. **Pros:** near El Raval, the Rambla, and the MACBA; superior doubles have private terrace; small "Wellness" room for massages and treatments. **Cons:** noisy avenue in front of hotel; tiny lobby; small rooms, but good value for price. ⓢ *Rooms from: €139* ⊠ *Carrer Pelai 14, El Raval* ☎ *93/505–1100* ⊕ *www.hotelmidmost.com* ↘ *56 rooms* ⓘⓄⓘ *No meals* Ⓜ *L1/L3 Catalunya, L1/L2 Universitat, FGC Catalunya* ✢ *H:11.*

$
HOTEL

⛨ **Market Hotel.** Wallet-friendly and design conscious, this boutique hotel is named for the Mercat de Sant Antoni a block away, one of Barcelona's best bargains and walking distance from all of El Raval and the Gothic Quarter sites and attractions. **Pros:** excellent value Catalan cuisine at on-site restaurant; friendly staff; great showers. **Cons:** standard rooms on lower floors are a little cramped; soundproofing needs upgrade. ⓢ *Rooms from: €100* ⊠ *Carrer del Comte Borrell 68, El Raval* ☎ *93/325–1205* ⊕ *www.andilanahotels.com/en/hotels/hotel-market* ↘ *68 rooms* ⓘⓄⓘ *No meals* Ⓜ *L2 Sant Antoni, L1 Urgell* ✢ *F:11.*

$$
HOTEL
FAMILY
Fodor's Choice
★

⛨ **Mesón Castilla.** A few steps down Carrer Tallers from the top of La Rambla, on a short side street, there's almost nothing Barcelona about the Mesón Castilla, which feels like a well-appointed country hotel or a parador in Castile or La Mancha: classically Spanish, with mosaic tile floors and sconces, painted coffered ceilings and coats of arms, rooms with antique carved headboards and painted wooden armoires. **Pros:** close to medieval Barcelona and the Eixample; spotlessly kept; lush patio for dining in warm weather. **Cons:** no terrace, pool, or spa; no laundry or room service; bathrooms a bit cramped. ⓢ *Rooms from: €130* ⊠ *Carrer Valldonzella 5, El Raval* ☎ *93/318–2182* ⊕ *www.atiramhotels.com* ↘ *57 rooms* ⓘⓄⓘ *No meals* Ⓜ *Catalunya, L1/L2 Universitat* ✢ *H:11.*

$$ HOTEL FAMILY 🏨 **Sant Agustí.** In a leafy square just off La Rambla, the Sant Agustí bills itself as the oldest billet in Barcelona—built in the 1720s for the library of the adjacent convent and reborn as a hotel in 1840. **Pros:** steps from the Boqueria market, La Rambla, and the Liceu opera house; intimate breakfast room; very good value for price. **Cons:** Plaça Sant Agusti can be a homeless hangout; not enough closet space; safe boxes too small for laptops. [$] *Rooms from: €150* ✉ *Pl. Sant Agustí 3, El Raval* ☎ *93/318–1658* 🌐 *www.hotelsa.com* 🛏 *80 rooms* 🍴 *Breakfast* [M] *L3 Liceu* ✣ *H:12.*

LA RAMBLA

$$$$ HOTEL 🏨 **Bagués.** The luxury of the Eixample has worked is way down to La Rambla, as this boutique gem (formerly the shop and atelier of the well-known Art Nouveau jeweler of the same name) bears ample witness. **Pros:** steps from the opera house; view of the cathedral and port from the rooftop terrace; free entrance to the Egyptian Museum of Barcelona. **Cons:** rooms a bit small for the price. [$] *Rooms from: €291* ✉ *La Rambla 105, La Rambla* ☎ *93/343–5000* 🌐 *www.hotelbagues.com* 🛏 *28 rooms, 3 suites* 🍴 *No meals* [M] *Pl. Catalunya, L3 Liceu* ✣ *H:12.*

$$$$ HOTEL FAMILY 🏨 **Citadines Ramblas Barcelona.** Located in two buildings at the upper end of La Rambla, Citadines is an excellent choice for families, groups of friends, or long-term visitors; the accommodations consist of apartments with sitting rooms and one-room studios with kitchenettes and small dining areas. **Pros:** central location; spacious rooms; pet-friendly. **Cons:** basic amenities; no pool; rooms only cleaned during six-night stays (and only once). [$] *Rooms from: €280* ✉ *La Rambla 122, La Rambla* ☎ *93/270–1111* 🌐 *www.citadines.com* 🛏 *115 studios, 16 apartments* 🍴 *No meals* [M] *Catalunya* ✣ *H:12.*

$$$ HOTEL Fodor's Choice ★ 🏨 **Duquesa de Cardona.** A refurbished 17th-century town house, built when the Passeig de Colom in front was lined with the summer homes of the nobility, this hotel on the waterfront is a 5-minute walk from everything in the Barri Gòtic and Barceloneta, and no more than a 30-minute walk to the Eixample. **Pros:** 24-hour room service; menu of fragrances to order for your room; glass of cava on check-in. **Cons:** rooms on the small side; no spa; no parking. [$] *Rooms from: €185* ✉ *Passeig de Colom 12, Port Olímpic* ☎ *93/268–9090* 🌐 *www.hduquesadecardona.com* 🛏 *63 rooms* 🍴 *No meals* [M] *L4 Barceloneta, L3 Drassanes* ✣ *I:14.*

$ HOTEL 🏨 **Grupotel Gravina.** On a side street near the Plaça de Catalunya and just five minutes from the MACBA and the Raval, this modern hotel offers comfort and prime location at a very affordable price. **Pros:** great location; room with private terrace for extra €30; friendly, competent staff. **Cons:** rooms are a bit small; generic furniture. [$] *Rooms from: €120* ✉ *Gravina 12, La Rambla* ☎ *93/301–6868* 🌐 *www.grupotelgravina.com* 🛏 *84 rooms* 🍴 *No meals* [M] *Catalunya, L1/L2 Universitat* ✣ *H:11.*

$$$$ 🏨 **H1898.** Overlooking La Rambla, this imposing mansion (once the
HOTEL   headquarters of the Compañiá General de Tabacos de Filipinas),
Fodor'sChoice   couldn't be better located—especially for opera fans, with the Liceu
★   just around the corner. **Pros:** impeccable service; ideal location for
exploring the Barri Gòtic; great hangout the Library lounge. **Cons:**
subway rumble discernible in lower rooms on the Rambla side; no
pets. $ *Rooms from: €238* ⊠ *La Rambla 109, La Rambla* 🕾 *93/552–
9552* ⊕ *www.hotel1898.com* ⊅ *169 rooms* ⏀*No meals* Ⓜ *Catalunya,
Liceu* ✛ *H:12.*

$$$$ 🏨 **Hotel DO Plaça Reial.** Just at the entrance to the neoclassical Plaça
HOTEL   Reial, this 2012 addition to Barcelona's growing collection of boutique
hotels—with its with three restaurants, La Terraza (under the arcades
on the square), El Terrat, and La Cuina (downstairs under graceful brick
vaulting)—is a find for foodies and lovers of tasteful design. **Pros:** walking distance from old city center; helpful multilingual staff; 24-hour
room service. **Cons:** neighborhood can be rowdy at night. $ *Rooms
from: €340* ⊠ *Pl. Reial 1, La Rambla* 🕾 *93/481–3666* ⊕ *www.hotel-
doreial.com* ☉ *La Terrassa open daily 9 am–1 am Apr.–Oct., 12:30–
midnight Nov.–Jan.; El Terrat open mid-May–mid-Oct. 7 pm–1 am; La
Cuina open for special occasions with advance booking* ⊅ *15 rooms,
3 suites* ⏀*Breakfast* Ⓜ *L3 Liceu* ✛ *H:13.*

$$$ 🏨 **Hotel SERHS Rivoli Rambla.** Behind this traditional upper-Rambla
HOTEL   facade lies a surprisingly whimsical interior with marble floors and art-
work by well-known Barcelona artist Perico Pastor in the lobby. **Pros:**
ideal location; room 601 is the best in the house; good views from the
rooftop terrace. **Cons:** service inconsistent; no pool or spa; two-night
minimum stay for online bookings. $ *Rooms from: €205* ⊠ *La Rambla
128, La Rambla* 🕾 *93/481–7676* ⊕ *www.hotelserhsrivolirambla.com*
⊅ *126 rooms* ⏀*No meals* Ⓜ *Catalunya, L3 Liceu* ✛ *H:12.*

$$$$ 🏨 **Le Méridien Barcelona.** There's no dearth of hotels along La Rambla in
HOTEL   the heart of the city, but few rival the upscale Le Méridien, popular with
Fodor'sChoice   businesspeople and visiting celebrities alike for its suites overlooking the
★   promenade and cozy amenities. **Pros:** central location; soaker tubs in
rooms; Mediterranean suites have large private terraces. **Cons:** no pool;
rooms small for the price; €60-per-day surcharge for pets. $ *Rooms
from: €293* ⊠ *La Rambla 111, La Rambla* 🕾 *93/318–6200* ⊕ *www.
lemeridien.com/barcelona* ⊅ *231 rooms* ⏀*No meals* Ⓜ *Catalunya L3
Liceu* ✛ *H:12.*

$$$$ 🏨 **The Serras.** Opened in 2015, Picasso had his first studio here (on the
HOTEL   sixth floor) when the building was all walk-up flats; today, designer
Eva Martinez has found ingenious tasteful ways to make the best of the
space and its limits: a small lobby with a comfortable sofa suite leads
back to the long narrow El Informal, the hotel's excellent restaurant
presided over by award-winning young chef Marc Gascons; a mez-
zanine hosts the 24-hour lounge bar and a small gym. **Pros:** romantic
"El Sueño" rooftop terrace with DJ on weekends; fun in-room ameni-
ties like yoga mats; excellent restaurant El Formal. **Cons:** no sauna
or spa; hard on the budget. $ *Rooms from: €350* ⊠ *Passeig Colom
9* 🕾 *93/169–1868* ⊕ *www.hoteltheserrasbarcelona.com* ⊅ *28 rooms*
⏀*Breakfast* Ⓜ *L4 Barceloneta* ✛ *I:14.*

BARCELONETA, PORT OLÍMPIC, AND FÒRUM

$$ HOTEL **Hotel 54 Barceloneta.** Just a few minutes' walk from the beach, this 2007 addition to the Barcelona hotel scene has much to offer in location, comfort, and economy. **Pros:** rooftop terrace with great views of the marina and the Old Port; competent multilingual staff; pleasant rustic breakfast room. **Cons:** noisy around the clock on Passeig Joan de Borbó; bathrooms lack space and privacy. [$] *Rooms from: €150* ✉ *Passeig Joan de Borbó 54, Barceloneta* ☎ *93/225–0054* 🌐 *www.hotel54barceloneta.es* *28 rooms* 🍴 *No meals* [M] *L4 Barceloneta* ✣ *I:15.*

$$$$ HOTEL Fodor's Choice ★ **Hotel Arts Barcelona.** This luxurious Ritz-Carlton-owned, 44-story skyscraper overlooks Barcelona from the Port Olímpic, providing stunning views of the Mediterranean, the city, the Sagrada Família, and the mountains beyond. **Pros:** excellent tapas restaurant on-site; fine art throughout hotel; free cava served on club floors daily. **Cons:** a 20-minute hike or more from central Barcelona; very pricey; €150 surcharge for pets. [$] *Rooms from: €425* ✉ *Carrer de la Marina 19–21, Port Olímpic* ☎ *93/221–1000* 🌐 *www.hotelartsbarcelona.com* *455 rooms, 28 penthouse apartments* 🍴 *No meals* [M] *L4 Ciutadella–Vila Olímpica* ✣ *L:15.*

$$$$ HOTEL **Soho House Barcelona.** Not a hotel in the usual sense, Soho House is one of a group of private members' clubs for people professionally involved in one way or another in the arts; the concept originated in London in 1995 and now involves facilities worldwide. **Pros:** vibrant atmosphere; "Sunday Feast" brunch in the glassed-in atrium restaurant; well located for exploring the port, Barceloneta, and the Born-Ribera quarter. **Cons:** hard on the budget; some lounge areas and facilities are members-only; feels a bit exclusive. [$] *Rooms from: €340* ✉ *Plaça del Duc de Medinaceli 4, Port Olímpic* ☎ *93/220–4600* 🌐 *www.sohohouse.com* *57 rooms* 🍴 *No meals* [M] *L4 Barceloneta, L3 Drassanes* ✣ *H:14.*

$$$$ HOTEL Fodor's Choice ★ **W Barcelona.** This towering sail-shaped monolith dominates the skyline on the Barcelona waterfront; architect Ricardo Bofill's W, now part of the Marriott International chain, is a stunner inside and out, from the six-story atrium lobby with black ceramic tile floors, suspended basket chairs, and glitter walls, to the adjacent bar-lounge with direct access to the "Attitudes" lounge deck, chill-out divans, and pool. **Pros:** unrivaled views; excellent restaurants on-site; transfer service to/from airport and cruise dock. **Cons:** extra amenities can get pricey; far from public transportation (20-minute hike). [$] *Rooms from: €280* ✉ *Pl. de la Rosa del Vents 1, Moll de Llevant, Barceloneta* ☎ *93/295–2800* 🌐 *www.w-barcelona.com* *473 rooms* 🍴 *No meals* [M] *L4 Barceloneta* ✣ *H:16.*

EIXAMPLE

$$$ HOTEL **Alexandra Barcelona Doubletree by Hilton.** Compared with the pure mid-Eixample Moderniste buildings around it, the facade of the Alexandra can feel a bit featureless; the best of the hotel lies within this dependable lodging option (part of the Hilton group). **Pros:** excellent location; great steak restaurant Solomillo on-site; pool open daily 10 am–8 pm.

Lodging Alternatives

APARTMENT RENTALS

If you want a home base that's roomy enough for a family and comes with cooking facilities, consider an aparthotel or an apartment rental. These can save you money, especially if you're traveling with a group. Aparthotels, not always in the most convenient locations, offer furnished flats with kitchen units, on-site staff, and services such as daily cleaning; apartments are more often private properties listed for rent through agencies, many of them quoting prices per person/per night. Rentals are normally for two-night minimums; there are usually substantial discounts for early bookings and longer stays. Prices range from €90 to €300 per day depending on the quality of the accommodations and the season, but perfectly acceptable lodging for four can be found for under €150 per night. Apartment accommodations can be arranged through any of the agencies listed *below*.

LOCAL APARTMENT AGENCIES

AB Apartment Barcelona. ✉ *Gran Vía 558, bajos, Eixample* ☎ *93/481–3577* ⊕ *www.apartmentbarcelona.com* Ⓜ *L1 Universitat, Urgell.*

Aparthotel Bertran. ✉ *Carrer Bertran 150, Sant Gervasi* ☎ *93/212–7550* ⊕ *www.aparthotelbertran.com* ⤴ *31 rooms, 5 apartments* ⊙ *No meals* Ⓜ *Tibidabo (FGC), L3 Vallcarca.*

Aparthotel Bonanova. ✉ *Carrer Bisbe Sivilla 7, Sant Gervasi* ☎ *93/253–1563* ⊕ *www.bonanova-suite.com* ⤴ *22 apartments, 1 suite* Ⓜ *El Putxet (FGC).*

Aparthotel Nàpols. ✉ *Carrer Nàpols 116, Eixample* ☎ *93/246–4573*

⊕ *www.abapart.com* ⤴ *33 apartments* Ⓜ *L2 Tetuan, Monumental; L1 Arc de Triomf.*

Barcelona Apartment. ✉ *Eixample* ☎ *93/451–0402 reservations* ⊕ *www.barcelona-apartment.com.*

Barcelona for Rent. ✉ *Carrer Bailén 120, Eixample* ☎ *93/458–6340* ⊕ *www.barcelonaforrent.com* Ⓜ *L4/L5 Verdaguer.*

Barceloneta Suites. ✉ *Carrer Grau i Torras 17, Barceloneta* ☎ *93/221–4225* ⊕ *www.barcelonetasuites.com* ⤴ *16 suites* Ⓜ *L4 Barceloneta.*

Friendly Rentals. ✉ *Carrer Trafalgar 42, Eixample* ☎ *93/268–8051* ⊕ *www.friendlyrentals.com* Ⓜ *L1/L4 Urquinaona.*

Gobcn Apartments. ✉ *Av. Paral.lel 91, Poble Sec* ☎ *93/278–1156* ⊕ *www.gobcn.com* Ⓜ *Paral.lel, Poble Sec.*

Oh-Barcelona. ✉ *Eixample* ☎ *93/467–3779* ⊕ *www.oh-barcelona.com.*

Only-Apartments. ✉ *Edifici Colón 15F, Av. de les Drassanes 6, La Rambla* ☎ *93/301–7678* ⊕ *www.only-apartments.com* Ⓜ *L3 Drassanes.*

HOME EXCHANGES

You can also swap houses by joining a home-exchange organization, which will send you its updated listings of available exchanges for a year and will include your own listing in at least one of them. It's up to you to make specific arrangements. Home-exchange directories sometimes list rentals as well as exchanges.

Cons: no connecting rooms; rooms are narrow; black corridor walls on guest room floors can be overpowering. [$] *Rooms from: €220* ✉ *Carrer Mallorca 251, Eixample* ☎ *93/467–7166* 🌐 *www.hotel-alexandra.com* 🛏 *118 rooms* 🍴 *No meals* [M] *Provença (FGC)* ⊕ *I:8.*

$$$$ HOTEL Fodor's Choice ★ 🏨 **Alma Hotel Barcelona.** Only the facade is left to recall the Moderniste origins of the building; the inside spaces were completely redesigned in 2011, and the Alma emerged as Barcelona's sleekest mid-Eixample hotel. **Pros:** British afternoon tea served daily (open to the public); gorgeous garden with sushi bar; complementary minibar. **Cons:** budget-stretching room rates; pricey buffet breakfast. [$] *Rooms from: €300* ✉ *Carrer Mallorca 271, Eixample* ☎ *93/216–4490* 🌐 *www.almahotels.com* 🛏 *72 rooms* 🍴 *No meals* [M] *L3/L5 Diagonal, L4 Girona, FGC Provença* ⊕ *I:8.*

$$ HOTEL 🏨 **Condes de Barcelona.** One of Barcelona's most popular hotels, the Condes de Barcelona is perfectly placed for exploring the sights (and shops) of the city's most fashionable quarter, and—for the privileged location—offers exceptional value. **Pros:** elegant building with subdued contemporary furnishings; prime spot in the middle of the Eixample; excellent value. **Cons:** no spa; €45 surcharge for pets. [$] *Rooms from: €149* ✉ *Passeig de Gràcia 73, Eixample* ☎ *93/467–4780* 🌐 *www.condesdebarcelona.com* 🛏 *126 rooms* 🍴 *No meals* [M] *L3/L5 Diagonal, Provença (FGC)* ⊕ *I:9.*

$$ HOTEL FAMILY Fodor's Choice ★ 🏨 **Continental Palacete.** This former palatial family home, or *palacete,* provides a splendid drawing room, a location nearly dead-center for Barcelona's main attractions, views over leafy Rambla de Catalunya, and a 24-hour free buffet. **Pros:** ornate design; attentive staff; ideal location. **Cons:** room decor is relentlessly pink and overdraped; bathrooms are a bit cramped. [$] *Rooms from: €158* ✉ *Rambla de Calatunya 30, at Diputació, Eixample* ☎ *93/445–7657* 🌐 *www.hotelcontinental.com* 🛏 *22 rooms* 🍴 *Breakfast* [M] *L2/L3/L4 Passeig de Gràcia, Plaça Catalunya* ⊕ *I:9.*

$$$$ HOTEL Fodor's Choice ★ 🏨 **Cotton House Hotel.** First a sumptuous family home, this 1879 property was bought in 1961 by the city's Cotton Producers Guild for the headquarters of its Cotton Textile Foundation, in the well-padded, Old-Boys-Club style befitting a then-profitable industry, and became a hotel in 2015. **Pros:** spot-on professional, friendly service; restaurant Batuar (€23) open 7 am–midnight; huge terrace off the bar with original fountains. **Cons:** bed size leaves little room to maneuver in basic rooms; some rooms with vanities outside the shower room. [$] *Rooms from: €320* ✉ *Gran Vía de les Corts Catalanes 670* ☎ *93/450–5045* 🌐 *www.hotelcottonhouse.com* 🛏 *88 rooms* 🍴 *No meals* 💳 *No credit cards* [M] *L2/L3/L4 Passeig de Gràcia* ⊕ *J:10.*

$$$$ HOTEL 🏨 **El Avenida Palace.** A minute's walk from Plaça Catalunya and the Passeig de Gràcia, this 1952 hotel earns top marks for location—and for nostalgia. **Pros:** prime location; excellent soundproofing; "Beatles suite" (the band stayed here in 1965). **Cons:** not for fans of minimalism or cutting-edge design; service can be snooty; low ceilings on guest room floors. [$] *Rooms from: €250* ✉ *Gran Via 605–607, Eixample* ☎ *93/301–9600* 🌐 *www.avenidapalace.com* 🛏 *151 rooms* 🍴 *No meals* [M] *L2/L3/L4 Passeig de Gràcia, Pl. Catalunya* ⊕ *I:10.*

4

$$ ⬚ **Gallery Hotel.** In the upper part of the Eixample below the Diagonal, this
HOTEL   contemporary hotel offers impeccable service and a superb central location
for exploring, with the city's prime art-gallery district just a few blocks
away on Consell de Cent. **Pros:** two large rooftop terraces with year-round
pools; DJ or live music on summer weekends; recently renovated. **Cons:**
small closet space; rooftop deck does not offer great views. $\boxed{\$}$ *Rooms from:*
€165 ✉ *Rosellò 249, Eixample* ☎ *93/415–9911* ⊕ *www.galleryhotel.com*
↜ *105 rooms* †◎| *No meals* Ⓜ *L3/L5 Diagonal, Provença (FGC)* ✛ *I:8.*

$$ ⬚ **Hotel Astoria.** Three blocks west of Rambla Catalunya, near the upper
HOTEL   middle of the Eixample, this renovated classic property, part of the cutting-
edge Derby Hotels Collection group of brilliant artistic restorations, is
a trove for the budget-minded. **Pros:** prime location; excellent value for
price; free entrance to the Egyptian Museum of Barcelona. **Cons:** gym
has only three machines; rooms on lower floors on the street side can
be noisy; rooftop terrace pool is small. $\boxed{\$}$ *Rooms from: €140* ✉ *Carrer*
Paris 203, Eixample ☎ *93/209–8311* ⊕ *www.hotelastoria-barcelona.com*
↜ *117 rooms* †◎| *No meals* Ⓜ *Provença (FGC), L3/L5 Diagonal* ✛ *H:7.*

$$$ ⬚ **Hotel Axel.** In the heart of the more fashionable *Esquerra* (west or
HOTEL   "left" side) of the Eixample, this recently expanded and renovated hotel
caters primarily to gay travelers in an area dubbed by locals as the
"Gayxample." The spacious rooms are soundproof and well lighted,
with comfortable contemporary furniture and decor in white-on-white
punctuated by hints of black, red, and chrome; most have queen-size
beds. **Pros:** great location; exceptionally well-equipped gym; rooftop
deck with pool, bar, cascade, and Jacuzzi (April–October). **Cons:**
uninviting lobby; extra €2 charge for faster Wi-Fi; standard rooms
have limited storage space. $\boxed{\$}$ *Rooms from: €177* ✉ *Carrer Aribau 33,*
Eixample ☎ *93/323–9393* ⊕ *www.axelhotels.com* ↜ *96 rooms* †◎| *No*
meals Ⓜ *L1/L2 Universitat* ✛ *G:9.*

$$$$ ⬚ **Hotel Claris Grand Luxe Barcelona.** Acclaimed as one of Barcelona's best
HOTEL   hotels, the Claris is an icon of design, tradition, and connoisseurship.
Fodor'sChoice   **Pros:** first-rate restaurant La Terraza; Mayan Secret spa with temazcal
★   and pure chocolate skin treatment; limo to/from the airport or cruise
dock. **Cons:** basic ("Superior") rooms small for the price; rooftop ter-
race noise at night can reach down into sixth-floor rooms; capacity
bookings can sometimes overwhelm the staff. $\boxed{\$}$ *Rooms from: €350*
✉ *Carrer Pau Claris 150, Eixample* ☎ *93/487–6262* ⊕ *www.hotelclaris.*
com ↜ *124 rooms* †◎| *No meals* Ⓜ *L2/L3/L4 Passeig de Gràcia* ✛ *I:9.*

$$ ⬚ **Hotel Constanza.** A few minutes' walk from the heart of the city at
HOTEL   Plaça Catalunya, this moderately priced boutique hotel has guest rooms
restfully decorated in lush coffee and chocolate tones, offset with leather
and wood textures. **Pros:** excellent value for price; friendly, professional staff; good grazing at restaurant Bruc 33 Tapas. **Cons:** no views;
no room service. $\boxed{\$}$ *Rooms from: €174* ✉ *Carrer Bruc 33, Eixample*
☎ *93/270–1910* ⊕ *www.hotelconstanza.com* ↜ *46 rooms* †◎| *No meals*
Ⓜ *L1/L4 Urquinaona, L2/L3/L4 Pl. Catalunya* ✛ *J:10.*

$$ ⬚ **Hotel Cram.** A short walk from La Rambla, this Eixample design
HOTEL   hotel offers impeccable mid-city accommodations with cheerful avant-
Fodor'sChoice   garde decor and luxurious details. **Pros:** Jordi Cruz's Angle restaurant
★   on-site; great location; dolly slides under the bed for suitcase storage.

Cons: Aribau is a major uptown artery, noisy at all hours; rooms are a bit small, with quirky shapes; no gym or spa. $ *Rooms from: €140* ✉ *Carrer Aribau 54, Eixample* ☎ *93/216–7700* 🌐 *www.hotelcram.com* 🛏 *67 rooms* 🍴 *No meals* [M] *L1/L2 Universitat, Provença (FGC)* ✥ *G:9.*

$$$$ HOTEL Fodor's Choice ★ 🏨 **Hotel El Palace Barcelona.** Founded in 1919 by Caesar Ritz, the original Ritz (the grande dame of Barcelona hotels) was renamed in 2005, but kept its lavish Old European style intact, from the liveried doorman in top hat and tails to the lobby's ormolu clocks and massive crystal chandelier. **Pros:** equidistant from Barri Gòtic and central Eixample; Bar 19/Nineteen features live jazz and more; Mayan-style sauna in the award-winning Spa. **Cons:** €30-per-night surcharge for small pets; painfully pricey. $ *Rooms from: €500* ✉ *Gran Vía de les Corts Catalanes 668, Eixample* ☎ *93/510–1130* 🌐 *www.hotelpalacebarcelona.com* 🛏 *108 rooms* 🍴 *No meals* [M] *L2/L3/L4 Passeig de Gràcia* ✥ *J:10.*

$$$ HOTEL 🏨 **Hotel Eurostars BCN Design.** This quirky property is what happens when design is allowed to triumph over tradition. **Pros:** friendly, helpful staff; good breakfast; in-room massage service; room service 24 hours; free late check-out to 1 pm. **Cons:** wardrobes have no drawers; washbasins and toiletry shelves poorly placed; no pets; no pool. $ *Rooms from: €220* ✉ *Passeig de Gràcia 29–31, Eixample* ☎ *93/344–4555* 🌐 *www.eurostarsbcndesign.com/en* 🛏 *70 rooms* 🍴 *No meals* [M] *Passeig de Gràcia* ✥ *I:10.*

$$$ HOTEL 🏨 **Hotel Gran Derby Suite 4*.** Clubby and comfortable, this Eixample hotel, made up entirely of suites and duplexes with living rooms, is ideal for groups and families. **Pros:** rooms and suites are spacious and tastefully hip; on a quiet side street; free entrance to the Egypian Museum of Barcelona. **Cons:** far from the city's main attractions. $ *Rooms from: €190* ✉ *Carrer Loreto 28, Eixample* ☎ *93/445–2544* 🌐 *www.hotelgranderby.com* 🛏 *43 suites* 🍴 *No meals* [M] *T1/T2/T3 Tram, L5 Hospital Clinic* ✥ *E:6.*

$$$ HOTEL Fodor's Choice ★ 🏨 **Hotel Granados 83.** Designed in the style of a New York City loft and seated on a tree-shaded street in the heart of the Eixample, this hotel blends exposed brick, steel, and glass with Greek and Italian marble and Indonesian tamarind wood to achieve downtown cool. **Pros:** luxurious duplexes with private terraces and semiprivate pools; wide variety of good casual restaurants nearby; free entrance to the Egypian Museum of Barcelona. **Cons:** rooftop terrace pool quite small; standard rooms need more storage space. $ *Rooms from: €190* ✉ *Carrer Enric Granados 83, Eixample* ☎ *93/492–9670* 🌐 *www.hotelgranados83.com* 🛏 *84 rooms* 🍴 *No meals* [M] *Provença (FGC)* ✥ *H:8.*

$$ HOTEL Fodor's Choice ★ 🏨 **Hotel Granvía.** A 19th-century palatial home (built for the owner of the Bank of Barcelona), the Granvía opened as a hotel in 1935, and reopened in 2013 after a lengthy renovation, with its original features still intact: an art deco cupola in the entrance, coffered ceilings, pillared arches, and a marble grand staircase. **Pros:** historical setting; pleasant terrace; British-style high tea served in the salon daily 5–7 pm. **Cons:** no pool, gym, or spa; most standard rooms have twin beds yoked together rather than doubles; bathrooms a bit cramped; few amenities. $ *Rooms from: €170* ✉ *Gran Vía de les Corts Catalanes 642, Eixample* ☎ *93/318–1900* 🌐 *www.hotelgranvia.com* 🛏 *58 rooms* 🍴 *Breakfast* [M] *L2/L3/L4 Passeig de Gràcia* ✥ *I:10.*

4

$$ ⊡ **Hotel H10 Casanova.** A chic postmodern addition to Barcelona's lodg-
HOTEL ing options is hidden behind this traditional facade, a 15-minute walk
FAMILY from the top of La Rambla; public spaces have a nightclub feel, with
leather chairs, pillar candles, and backlit neon-green plexiglass panels
at reception and the bar. **Pros:** good combination of comfort and style;
hotel has its own parking; bicycles for guests to rent. **Cons:** must walk
through busy artery to get to Plaça Catalunya; room lighting could be
better; breakfasts must be booked in advance for the duration of your
stay. $ *Rooms from: €149* ⊠ *Gran Via de les Corts Catalanes 559,
Eixample* 🕾 *93/396–4800* ⊕ *www.h10hotels.com* ⌨ *124 rooms* ⦿ *No
meals* Ⓜ *L1 Urgell, L2 Universitat* ✛ *F:10.*

$$ ⊡ **Hotel Jazz.** Bright colors, clean lines and contemporary artwork give
HOTEL this hotel (dead center in the heart of Barcelona) a hip, fashionable feel.
Pros: elevators work only on room keys, for added security; central
location; rooftop bar serves pizza and tapas. **Cons:** no pets; a bit pricey.
$ *Rooms from: €170* ⊠ *Carrer Pelai 3, Eixample* 🕾 *93/552–9696*
⊕ *www.hoteljazz.com* ⌨ *108 rooms* ⦿ *No meals* Ⓜ *L1/L2 Universitat, Catalunya* ✛ *H:10.*

$$$$ ⊡ **Hotel Omm.** The lobby of this postmodern architectural stunner tells
HOTEL you what to expect throughout: perfect comfort, cutting-edge design, and
FAMILY meticulous attention to every detail. **Pros:** perfect location for the upper
Fodor's Choice Eixample; fireplace in lounge; superb spa. **Cons:** small plunge pools; res-
★ taurant is pricey and a little precious; parking is expensive. $ *Rooms
from: €315* ⊠ *Rosselló 265, Eixample* 🕾 *93/444000* ⊕ *www.hotelomm.
com* ⌨ *91 rooms* ⦿ *No meals* Ⓜ *L3/L5 Diagonal, Provença (FGC)* ✛ *I:8.*

$$ ⊡ **Hotel Praktik Garden.** If you've ever dreamed about running away
HOTEL with the circus, this quirky little boutique hotel, where the walls are
covered with gaily colored circus posters, is just for you. **Pros:** free
coffee service in the garden; close to Passeig de Gràcia; pleasant ter-
race/lounge. **Cons:** pipe racks instead of closets; minimal amenities; no
breakfast room. $ *Rooms from: €145* ⊠ *Carrer Diputacio 325, Eix-
ample* 🕾 *93/467–5279* ⊕ *www.hotelpraktikgarden.com* ⌨ *59 rooms*
⦿ *No meals* Ⓜ *L4 Girona* ✛ *J:10.*

$$$ ⊡ **Hotel Pulitzer.** Built squarely over the metro's central hub and within
HOTEL walking distance of everything in town, this breezy clubhouse-hotel
could not be better situated. **Pros:** rooftop terrace has live music or
DJ on weekends; bicycle rentals for guests; breakfast room bright and
cheery. **Cons:** narrow standard rooms; no pool or gym (but privileges at
nearby fitness center); pricey surcharge for pets (dogs only). $ *Rooms
from: €180* ⊠ *Bergara 8, Eixample* 🕾 *93/481–6767* ⊕ *www.hotelpulit-
zer.es* ⌨ *91 rooms* ⦿ *No meals* Ⓜ *Catalunya* ✛ *H:11.*

$$$ ⊡ **Hotel Regina.** What it lacks in bells and whistles, this family-friendly
HOTEL little hotel makes up for in its unparalleled location—on a side street
FAMILY just steps from Plaça Catalunya—and its relaxed contemporary feel.
Pros: just steps from Plaça Catalunya; charming breakfast room has
excellent buffet; live sessions in the piano bar Tuesdays at 9 pm. **Cons:**
no pool or gym (but privileges at nearby fitness center); bathrooms in
some superior rooms are really small; no pets. $ *Rooms from: €180*
⊠ *Calle Bergara 4, Eixample* 🕾 *93/301–3232* ⊕ *www.reginahotel.com/
en* ▭ *No credit cards* ⌨ *99 rooms* ⦿ *No meals* Ⓜ *Catalunya* ✛ *H:11.*

$$$$ HOTEL FAMILY Fodor's Choice ★ **Majestic Hotel & Spa.** With an unbeatable location on Barcelona's most stylish boulevard, steps from Gaudí's La Pedrera and a stone's throw from the area's swankiest shops, this hotel is a near-perfect place to stay. **Pros:** rooftop terrace with views of the Mediterranean, Montjuïc, and the Sagrada Família; 24-hour room service; art (including Miró prints) from owner's private collection. **Cons:** some standard rooms a bit small for the price; no pets; very pricey buffet breakfast. [$] *Rooms from: €289* ✉ *Passeig de Gràcia 68, Eixample* ☎ *93/488–1717* 🌐 *www.hotelmajestic.es* 🛏 *275 rooms* 🍴 *No meals* [M] *L2/L3/L4 Passeig de Gràcia, Provença (FGC)* ✥ *I:9.*

$$$$ HOTEL FAMILY **Mandarin Oriental Barcelona.** A carpeted ramp leading from the elegant Passeig de Gràcia (flanked by Tiffany and Brioni boutiques) lends this hotel the air of a privileged—and pricey—inner sanctum. **Pros:** central location; babysitters and parties for the kids, on request; Mimosa interior garden great for drinks. **Cons:** rooms relatively small for a 5-star accommodation; Wi-Fi free in rooms only if booked online; lighting a bit dim. [$] *Rooms from: €625* ✉ *Passeig de Gràcia 38–40, Eixample* ☎ *93/151–8888* 🌐 *www.mandarinoriental.com/barcelona* 🛏 *120 rooms* 🍴 *No meals* [M] *L2/L3/L4 Passeig de Gràcia, L3/L5 Diagonal, Provença (FGC)* ✥ *I:10.*

4

$$ HOTEL **Meliá Barcelona Sky.** At a bit of a remove from the major tourist attractions, east along Diagonal from Plaça de les Glòries, the Meliá hotel group's Barcelona Sky gets much of its business from professional and trade conference organizers, but wins high marks as well from recreational visitors for its luxurious appointments and lively design. **Pros:** handy to Sagrada Família, beach, and Poble Nou nightlife scene; great views from rooftop deck; 24-hour free drinks and snacks on terrace. **Cons:** inconvenient to Eixample and Gothic Quarter; high-rise glass-and-concrete slab architecture; "open concept" bedroom/bathroom layout lacks privacy. [$] *Rooms from: €160* ✉ *Carrer Pere IV 272–286, Eixample* ☎ *902/144440* 🌐 *www.melia.com* 🛏 *258 rooms* 🍴 *No meals* [M] *L4 Poble Nou* ✥ *L:12.*

$$$$ HOTEL Fodor's Choice ★ **Monument Hotel.** Originally the home of Enric Battló, a brother of the textile magnate who commissioned Gaudí to redesign the Moderniste masterpiece Casa Battló, and a minute's walk away on the Passeig de Gràcia, the historic 1898 building that houses the Monument went through several incarnations before architect Oscar Tusquets and his project team transformed it into the elegant upmarket hotel it is today. **Pros:** helpful, professional multilingual staff; ideal mid-Eixample location; under-floor heating in the bathrooms. **Cons:** hard on the budget; most "junior suites" are in effect large doubles with seating areas; pricey American breakfast. [$] *Rooms from: €300* ✉ *Passeig de Gràcia 73, Eixample* ☎ *93/548–2000* 🌐 *www.monument-hotel.com* 🛏 *158 rooms* 🍴 *No meals* [M] *L3/L5 Diagonal, Provença (FGC)* ✥ *I:8.*

$$$ HOTEL FAMILY Fodor's Choice ★ **Murmuri Barcelona.** British designer Kelly Hoppen took this 19th-century town house on La Rambla de Catalunya and transformed it in 2008 into a chic, intimate urban retreat. **Pros:** private terraces in Privilege doubles; strategic Eixample location; exclusive rooftop terrace open year-round. **Cons:** no pool, gym, or spa (though guest privileges at the nearby affiliated Majestic hotel); no pets, except in the apartments;

Design doubles a bit small. [$] *Rooms from: €185* ✉ *Rambla de Catalunya 104, Eixample* ☎ *93/550–0600* 🌐 *www.murmuri.com* 💳 *No credit cards* 🛏 *53 rooms, 5 apartments* 🍴 *No meals* [M] *L3/L5 Diagonal, Provença (FGC)* ✥ *H:8.*

$$ HOTEL 🏨 **Room Mate Emma.** While the hotel's slogan, "Do You Want To Sleep With Me?" is a bit gimmicky, the Emma itself is a comfortable, centrally positioned billet at an affordable price. **Pros:** pivotal location; futuristic design; bike rentals for guests at €10/four hours, €15 full day. **Cons:** rooms on lower floors can be noisy; no pool, spa, or gym; no room service. [$] *Rooms from: €150* ✉ *Carrer Rosselló 205, Eixample* ☎ *93/238–5606* 🌐 *www.room-matehotels.com* 🛏 *56 rooms* 🍴 *No meals* [M] *Provença (FGC)* ✥ *H:8.*

$$$ HOTEL 🏨 **Silken Gran Hotel Havana.** Popular with cruise ship passengers who extend their vacations to savor the city, the Havana is about equidistant from the Moderniste sights of the Eixample and the Gothic Quarter. **Pros:** bright, lively public spaces; helpful, English-speaking staff; in-room massage service. **Cons:** on a major crosstown artery, where traffic is heavy night and day; not well situated for views; room service shuts down at 10:30 pm. [$] *Rooms from: €180* ✉ *Gran Via 647, Eixample* ☎ *93/341–7000* 🌐 *www.granhotelhavana.com* 🛏 *145 rooms* 🍴 *No meals* [M] *L2/L3/L4 Passeig de Gràcia, L4 Girona, L2 Tetuan* ✥ *J:10.*

$$$$ HOTEL 🏨 **SixtyTwo Hotel.** Across from Gaudí's Casa Batlló and just down Passeig de Gràcia from his Casa Milà (La Pedrera), this sleek boutique hotel, which opened in 2009, is surrounded by Barcelona's top shopping addresses and leading restaurants. **Pros:** ideal location; free coffee, tea, and snacks in the lounge, 24/7; complementary cava every evening at 6. **Cons:** some rooms a bit small; no pool, gym, or spa; room service ends at 10 pm. [$] *Rooms from: €250* ✉ *Passeig de Gràcia 62, Eixample* ☎ *93/272–4180* 🌐 *www.sixtytwohotel.com* 🛏 *44 rooms* 🍴 *No meals* [M] *L2/L3/L4 Passeig de Gràcia* ✥ *I:9.*

$$ B&B/INN FAMILY 🏨 **the5rooms.** This charming little boutique B&B in the heart of the city has been expanded into a complex of nine spacious guest rooms and three suites, with two full residential apartments next door. **Pros:** a sense of home away from home; comfortable contemporary design; honesty bar in the common area. **Cons:** no bar or restaurant; Pau Claris a busy and noisy artery; no reception after 9 pm. [$] *Rooms from: €155* ✉ *Carrer Pau Claris 72, Eixample* ☎ *93/342–7880* 🌐 *www.the5rooms.com* 🛏 *12 rooms, 2 apartments* 🍴 *Breakfast* [M] *L1/L4 Urquinaona, L2/L3/L4 Passeig de Gràcia* ✥ *I:11.*

$$ HOTEL 🏨 **Villa Emilia.** The stylish, comfortable Villa Emilia is a bit removed from the tourist attractions of the Eixample and the Old City, but a mere five minutes' walk to the Fira de Barcelona exposition grounds, Las Arenas shopping center, and the airport shuttle bus stop in Plaça Espanya. **Pros:** excellent wines at on-site bistro; barbecue and drinks on the opulent rooftop terrace (May–October). **Cons:** no pool; staff struggles a bit in English; no gym or spa. [$] *Rooms from: €170* ✉ *Carrer Calàbria 115–117, Eixample* ☎ *93/252–5285* 🌐 *www.hotelvillaemilia.com* 🛏 *53 rooms* 🍴 *No meals* [M] *L1 Rocafort* ✥ *E:11.*

POBLE SEC/MONTJUÏC

$$$ ⊡ **Hotel Brummell.** Opened in 2015, the Brummell is among the more
HOTEL recent of the stylish new ventures now starting to give the once-scruffy
neighborhood of Poble Sec a different buzz. **Pros:** young, friendly inter-
national staff; smart TVs; excellent brunch. **Cons:** no room service; stor-
age is limited; vending machines in lieu of in-room minibars. $ *Rooms
from: €180* ✉ *Nou de la Rambla 174, Poble Sec* ☎ *93/125–8622* ⊕ *www.
hotelbrummell.com* ⬳ *20 rooms* ¶◎¶ *No meals* Ⓜ *L3 Para.lel* ✚ *E:13.*

$$$ ⊡ **Hotel Grums.** Tucked off on a side street in Poble Sec, on the far side
HOTEL of El Raval, this pleasant little boutique hotel lies within easy walking
FAMILY distance to the port and La Rambla—an especially convenient bivouac
for cruise ship visitors, and with easy access to the museums and gardens of Montjuic. **Pros:** quiet location; good for families; each room
has its own character. **Cons:** bed lighting could be better; far from the
attractions of the Eixample; charge for the spa. $ *Rooms from: €177*
✉ *Carrer Palaudaries 26, Poble Sec* ☎ *93/442066* ⊕ *www.hotelgrums-
barcelona.com* ⬳ *78 rooms* ¶◎¶ *No meals* Ⓜ *L2/L3 Paral.lel* ✚ *F:14.*

$$$ ⊡ **Hotel Miramar Barcelona.** Only the facade remains of this imposing
HOTEL "palace," built in 1929 for Barcelona's second Universal Expositionas
FAMILY and later acquired by a TV network as its studio headquarters, then
Fodor'sChoice abandoned from 1983 until 2006, when it was gutted and transformed
★ by architect Oscar Tusquets into an elegant, romantic hillside resort.
Pros: complimentary glass of cava on check-in; easy access to beach
and Barceloneta by cable car; parking free if booked online (otherwise
€12 outside, €18 inside). **Cons:** no shuttle service; pricey breakfast.
$ *Rooms from: €220* ✉ *Plaza Carlos Ibáñez 3, Montjuïc* ☎ *93/281–
1600* ⊕ *www.hotelmiramarbarcelona.com* ⬳ *66 doubles, 8 suites*
¶◎¶ *No meals* Ⓜ *L3 Drassanes* ✚ *E:14.*

GRÀCIA

$$$$ ⊡ **Hotel Casa Fuster Gran Lujo Monumento.** This hotel offers one of two
HOTEL chances (the other is the Hotel España) to stay in an Art Nouveau build-
Fodor'sChoice ing designed by Lluís Domènech i Montaner, architect of the sumptuous
★ Palau de la Música Catalana. **Pros:** well situated for exploring both
Gràcia and the Eixample; ample rooms; luxury-level amenities. **Cons:**
rooms facing Passeig de Gràcia could use better soundproofing; no
pets; service can be a bit stiff. $ *Rooms from: €271* ✉ *Passeig de Grà-
cia 132, Gràcia* ☎ *93/255–3000* ⊕ *www.hotelscenter.com/casafuster*
⬳ *105 rooms* ¶◎¶ *No meals* Ⓜ *L3/L5 Diagonal* ✚ *I:7.*

$$ ⊡ **Pol & Grace Hotel.** Renovated and reopened in 2015 under new own-
HOTEL ership—the hip young enthusiastic pair renamed the hotel after them-
selves—the Pol & Grace is strategically located for exploring Gràcia, a
short walk to Gaudí's Casa Vicens, and well connected by FGC train to
the head of the Rambla. **Pros:** fun and laid-back atmosphere; children
under 10 stay free; book exchange and DVD collection in the lobby.
Cons: no restaurant on-site; building of no particular architectural interest; no gym or pool. $ *Rooms from: €130* ✉ *Guillem Tell 49, Gràcia*
☎ *93/415–4000* ⊕ *www.polgracehotel.es* ⬳ *64 rooms* ¶◎¶ *No meals*
Ⓜ *Sant Gervasi, Pl. Molina (FGC)* ✚ *H:5.*

SARRIÀ, SANT GERVASI, PUTXET, AND PEDRALBES

$$ HOTEL FAMILY 🏨 **Bonanova Park.** In upper Barcelona near Sarrià, this no-frills hotel offers an escape from busy downtown at a moderate cost. **Pros:** close to great restaurants and metro stops; bargain breakfast; short walk to the Camp Nou stadium. **Cons:** soundproofing and bed lighting could be improved; no pool or spa; reception service can be hit-or-miss. [$] *Rooms from: €125* ✉ *Carrer Capità Arenas 51, Sarrià* ☎ *93/204–0900* 🌐 *www.hotelbonanovapark.com* 🛏 *63 rooms* 🍴 *No meals* [M] *Sarrià (FGC), L3 Maria Cristina* ✣ *C:3.*

$$$ HOTEL FAMILY Fodor's Choice ★ 🏨 **Primero Primera.** The Perez family converted their apartment building on a leafy side street in the quiet, upscale, residential neighborhood of Tres Torres and opened it as an exquisitely designed, homey boutique hotel in 2011. **Pros:** retro-modern ambience; 24-hour free snack bar; electric bicycle rentals for guests. **Cons:** bit of a distance from downtown. [$] *Rooms from: €205* ✉ *Doctor Carulla 25–29, Sant Gervasi* ☎ *93/417–5600* 🌐 *www.primeroprimera.com* 💳 *No credit cards* 🛏 *30 rooms* 🍴 *Breakfast* [M] *Tres Torres (FGC)* ✣ *E:3.*

$$ HOTEL 🏨 **Sansi Pedralbes.** A contemporary polished-marble-and-black-glass box, with Japanese overtones, a stone's throw from the gardens of the Monestir de Pedralbes, this hotel may be a bit removed from the action downtown, but there's a stop on the Bus Turistic just across the street, and the views up into the Collserola Hills above Barcelona are splendid. **Pros:** small and intimate; close to Carretera de les Aigües, Barcelona's best running track; quiet area near the Güell Pavilions. **Cons:** the nearest subway stations are 15–20 minutes away on foot; no pets; pricey breakfast. [$] *Rooms from: €150* ✉ *Av. Pearson 1–3, Pedralbes* ☎ *93/206–3880* 🌐 *www.sansihotels.com* 🛏 *60 rooms* 🍴 *No meals* [M] *Reina Elisenda (FGC), L3 Maria Cristina* ✣ *A:1.*

$ HOTEL 🏨 **Vilana Hotel.** In an upscale residential neighborhood above Passeig de la Bonanova, this boutique accommodation can ease some of the budgetary strains of coming to a prime tourist destination. **Pros:** quiet surroundings; large, sunlit rooms; pleasant, attentive English-speaking staff. **Cons:** 30 minutes to center of town; no pool or spa; room service closes at 10:30. [$] *Rooms from: €99* ✉ *Vilana 7, Sant Gervasi* ☎ *93/434–0363* 🌐 *www.vilanahotel.com* 🛏 *22 rooms* 🍴 *No meals* [M] *Sarrià (FGC)* ✣ *F:2.*

TIBIDABO

$$$$ HOTEL FAMILY 🏨 **Gran Hotel la Florida.** Two qualities set this luxurious mountaintop retreat apart: its peace and privacy, and its stunning panoramic view. **Pros:** first-rate spa, fitness center, and sauna; friendly and attentive front staff; decor by celebrity designers. **Cons:** pricey food and beverage add-ons; pets accepted with an €80 surcharge. [$] *Rooms from: €280* ✉ *Ctra. Vallvidrera al Tibidabo 83–93, Tibidabo* ☎ *93/259–3000* 🌐 *www.hotel-laflorida.com* 🛏 *70 rooms* 🍴 *No meals* [M] *Tibidabo (FGC)* ✣ *H:1.*

5

NIGHTLIFE AND
PERFORMING ARTS

NIGHTS OF WINE AND REVELRY

Wine-tasting (with cava-sipping on the side) has proliferated in Barcelona over the last decade. With light tapas for accompaniment, nomadic tippling is an unbeatable way to begin an evening.

A typical night out in Barcelona has several stages. Discos and music bars don't jump to life until after midnight, so the early part of the evening is a culinary and oenological prologue. The city is well equipped with opportunities to take advantage of this warm-up time; wine bars, specializing in light fare and new and interesting vintages, have become a popular part of Barcelona's nocturnal routine. Whether in Sarrià, the Eixample, or the Ciutat Vella, there are countless taverns to choose from. Wine served by the glass is usually chalked up on a blackboard, and selections change frequently. Walking between stops is important for the longevity of your nightlife plans; covering a couple of miles with short hops between *copas* is essential and will keep you clearheaded enough to last through the wee hours.

A GOOD WINE BAR CRAWL

Start at **Paco Meralgo** (⊠ *Muntaner 171* ☎ *93/309027*), a tapas bar with creative fare and a good selection of wines by the glass. Next, head to **Cellarer** (⊠ *Mallorca 211* ☎ *93/451–7233*), where you can ask one of the sommeliers for suggestions. Afterwards head east to **La Bodegueta Provença** (⊠ *Provença 245* ☎ *93/487–5221*), where an interesting selection of wines is detailed on the chalkboard. Nearby is the original **La Bodegueta** (⊠ *Rambla de Catalunya 100* ☎ *93/215–4894*), a charming dive—literally. **Monvínic** (⊠ *Diputació 249* ☎ *93/272–6187*) is the biggest and smartest of the bunch.

SIPS TO SAMPLE

When you're eyeballing the wine list, keep a look out for these copas.

GRANS MURALLES

This Torres single-vineyard red wine will cost you well over $100 a bottle, so this is one to look for sold by the glass at La Vinya del Senyor and Vinoteca Torres. Made with ancient, pre-Phylloxera grapes (monastrell, garnacha tinto, carró, samsó, and cariñena), some of which are now extinct, this vineyard tucked in under the medieval walls of the Cistercian monastery of Poblet is a taste of history: dense, complex, peppery, tannic, and fruity.

JUVÉ I CAMPS RESERVA DE LA FAMILIA

A Barcelona favorite, this mid-range cava made with the standard Penedès grape varieties of macabeu (40%), parellada (40%), and xarel·lo (20%) grapes is a tawny gold hue with feisty bubbles and a tart apple and citrus flavor. Crisp and fresh on the palate, the finish is balanced and clean as a whistle.

KRIPTA GRAN RESERVA

Agustí Torrelló, one of the fathers of Catalonia's cava, created this excellent gran reserva in homage to the Mediterranean wine-making tradition. The bottle is shaped like an amphora, requiring the use of an ice bucket à table. Made from old vines and aged for five years, the wine is a straw-color gold, intensely bubbly, and superbly crisp and refreshing. Complex on the palate, tastes range from chocolate to butter, with a solid mineral base.

TORRE LA MOREIRA

This full-bodied and acidic albariño from northwestern Spain's Rías Baixas wine region is a refreshing and fully satisfying accompaniment for seafood tapas at Cal Pep or Botafumeiro.

PAIR THAT WITH...

Start light with a few of Catalonia's own Arbequina olives. *Boquerones* (small, fresh, pickled, white anchovies) are another excellent and refreshing morsel to pair with an albariño or a flute of cava. A *ración* (portion) of regular anchovies will also pair nicely. Beyond those preliminaries, *pimientos de Padrón*, lovely deep green peppers from the Galician village of Padrón, are always great additions, as are *croquetas* (croquettes), small breaded fritters with a minced-meat filling of ham or chicken. La Barceloneta has its own mega-croquetas called *bombas*—round, slightly larger-than-golf-ball-size fritters filled with mashed potato and ham. *Chipirones* (baby octopi), cooked to a dry crisp, are delicious with white wines and cavas, while, as wines turn darker, a plate of *jamón ibérico de bellota* might be the perfect closer, unless a *ración de albóndigas* (serving of meatballs) or a sizzling *chistorra* (spicy sausage) proves irresistible.

Updated
by Steve
Tallantyre

Once the sun goes down, Barcelona streets are filled with carousers out to play, often late into the night. Many an evening begins with a cultural fix: the latest art gallery openings, theater performances, concerts at the cabaret-inspired Milano Cocktail Bar, or opera at the 19th-century Liceu. After midnight, rub elbows with locals at Rubi Bar, a cozy hidden tavern nestled among the posh lounges that pepper Ciutat Vella's labyrinthine streets, or try one of the organic wine bars of El Born and Gràcia. Be sure to stop by Poble Sec's Casa Martino, a rising star among the growing selection of evening *vermuterias* (vermouth bars).

In the urban-hip Eixample district, mixologists whip up classic cocktails with a twist at the ritzy Solange. Poblenou—a neighborhood that has remained defiantly unchanged for years—has experienced something of a renaissance with haunts like the retro Balius Bar, where gin and tonics are served with a jazz chaser. After 2 am, explore the city's incandescent club life, from the moody dance halls of La Rambla's hell-raising Plaça Reial, to a selection of glamorous seaside venues in Port Olímpic. Whatever you choose, one thing is clear: Barcelona never surrenders to the night.

NIGHTLIFE AND PERFORMING ARTS PLANNER

HOURS
Evening concerts, plays, and dance performances in Barcelona usually start around 9 pm. On weekends, drinks are enjoyed with light bites and often extend past dinnertime, which is at a stomach-churning 10 pm. Then, sometime after 1 or 2 am, the *real* nightlife kicks in.

SCORING TICKETS

Tickets for performances are available either at the theater (ticket offices generally open only in the evenings) or online: Ticketea (⊕ *www.telentrada.com*) and Ticketmaster (⊕ *www.ticketmaster.es*)—both have English-language options. After ordering your seats and giving credit-card information, pick up tickets at the door of the venue or print them out in advance. Ticketmaster uses the ATMs of local bank La Caixa, which print the tickets for you. If you want to do things the old-fashioned way, FNAC on Plaça de Catalunya has an office on the ground floor that sells tickets to many pop and rock performances.

TOP FIVE NIGHTLIFE EXPERIENCES

Musical performances at stunning venues; Palau de la Música Catalana and Liceu, among others

Wednesday eve jazz sessions at the chichi Banker Bar at the Mandarin Oriental

Sunday night indie film viewing at CinesVerdi (or nearby annexe Verdi Park) in bohemian Gràcia

Dancing till the wee hours at the upscale seaside clubs of Port Olímpic

Witnessing sensational beachfront views at the Eclipse Bar on the 26th floor of the ultraluxe W Barcelona

WHAT TO WEAR

The dress code in Barcelona is eclectic but casual. Although there are rarely hard-and-fast rules at elegant restaurants or concert venues, tourists in shorts, tank tops, and baseball caps will feel out of place. Discos are a different story: uptown or at the seaside venues, autocratic bouncers may inspect aspiring clients carefully—the better you dress, the higher your chance of getting in. The Liceu Opera House often has black-tie evening galas; the Palau de la Música Catalana and the Auditori are less formal than the Liceu, but upscale dress is still expected.

WHERE TO GET INFORMATION

To find out what's on (in Spanish or Catalan), check *"Ocio y cultura"* listings in Barcelona's leading daily newspapers online versions: *La Vanguardia*, ⊕ *www.lavanguardia.com*) and *El Periódico* (⊕ *www. elperiodico.com*) or the weekly English-language edition of *TimeOut*, (⊕ *www.timeout.com/barcelona*). *Le Cool* (⊕ *barcelona.lecool.com*) offers a curated list of events and activities online (available in English). *Barcelona Metropolitan* magazine updates their online "what's on" section regularly, and features a monthly print version, available for free in English-language bookstores and hotel lobbies (⊕ *www. barcelona-metropolitan.com*). Barcelona city hall's culture website (⊕ *barcelonacultura.bcn.cat*) also publishes an English edition of listings and highlights. A nose and ear to the ground is the best way to find out about rock and pop gigs—look out for posters and flyers as you explore the city.

YEARLY FESTIVALS

Barcelona Acció Musical (BAM). Held over a week toward late September, this musical celebration forms part of the lively La Mercé festival, an annual event honoring Our Lady of Mercy, Barcelona's patron saint. BAM showcases emerging talent (both national and international) in

Vermouth: A Classic Comeback

After decades of irrelevance and disfavor, vermouth (*vermut* in Spanish), the inexpensive aperitif made from sweet or dry wine, herbs, seeds, botanicals, and caramelized sugar, has reemerged with a vengeance. Vermouth was once the drink of choice for the local working class, whose consumption was relegated to the dusty backrooms of tiny neighborhood bodegas on Sunday. Today, the syrupy, tawny-color drink is imbibed in venues throughout Barcelona that resemble the original 19th-century *vermuterias*. It's often served with traditional anchovy tapas, accompanied by soda (*sifón*) for DIY dilution, and garnished with olives or orange wedges. Both strong and cheap, vermouth is having a cultural resurgence, and is available most days of the week all over the city, from retro family-owned establishments, to sleek, modern hotel bars and hipster cocktail lounges (*coctelerias*). Granted, vermouth is not for everyone. Some believe this spirit has no place but in a stirred martini or tangy Negroni, but if you're willing to experiment, it'll be easy to find during your stay in Barcelona. Vintage in look and flavor, cozy venues like La Confiteria, Casa Martino, and Cellar Cal Marino remain loyal to the classics, while relative newcomers Balius Bar, Senyor Vermut, and Jonny Aldana offer an innovative mix of past and present. Morro Fi brings vermouth into the 21st century with a collection of colorful mixes and their very own blend, while Bodegas 1900 pays a contemporary tribute to this tasty aperitif by pairing it with gourmet tapas in a stylish venue dedicated to all things vermouth.

dance, rock, pop, and electronic genres; acts perform in parks, squares, and venues around the city. ☎ *010 Barcelona information: daily 24 hrs (local call)* ⊕ *www.barcelona.cat/bam.*

Festival Ciutat Flamenco. Held annually in May, this lively festival, co-organized by the Taller de Músics (Musicians' Workshop) and the Mercat de les Flors, offers visitors a chance to experience authentic flamenco instrumental, song, and dance performances by both local and international artists. ⊠ *Mercat de les Flors, Carrer de Lleida 59, Poble Sec* ☎ *93/329–5667 Taller de Músics, 93/256–2600 Mercat de les Flors* ⊕ *www.ciutatflamenco.com* Ⓜ *Poble Sec, Plaça Espanya.*

Fodor'sChoice ★ **Grec** (*Festival del Grec*). Barcelona's monthlong summer arts festival (late June–July) features acts from the world of dance, performance art, music, and theater. Performances take place in such historic venues as Mercat de les Flors and the Teatre Grec on Montjuic—an open-air theater built for the 1929 Barcelona International Exposition, which gives the festival its name and serves as the main venue. ⊠ *Barcelona* ☎ *93/316–1000* ⊕ *lameva.barcelona.cat/grec.*

Guitar Bcn. Held between mid-February and late July, this annual festival features concerts in the Palau de la Música Catalana and other venues by master guitarists of all musical genres and styles. Folk, jazz, classical, and flamenco are all well represented. ☎ *93/481–7040* ⊕ *www.guitarbcn.com.*

International Jazz Festival. One of Europe's oldest jazz festivals, this festive gathering takes place from late September to early December, with concerts all around the city in illustrious venues like the Palau de la Musica, L'Auditori, and smoky side street bars such as the Harlem Jazz Club. Highlights include vocal and instrumental jazz renditions from around the globe. ☎ *93/481–7040* ⊕ *www.barce-lonajazzfestival.com.*

Primavera Sound. From its modest beginnings at the architectural miniature museum Poble Espanyol, this event has evolved into one of the biggest and most exciting music festivals in Spain, attracting more than 100,000 visitors each year. Concerts are organized in small venues around the city during the weeks leading up to the event, but the main stint takes place over four days in late May or early June at the Parc del Fòrum. Everybody who's anybody, from Nine Inch Nails to The National, has played here, and you can rest assured that whoever is doing the big summer festival circuit will pass through Primavera. Festival tickets can be bought online. ⊠ *Parc del Fòrum, Poblenou* ⊕ *www. primaverasound.com* Ⓜ *El Maresme Fòrum.*

Sónar. For more than a decade, Sónar has grown from a niche festival for electronic and dance music fans to one of Barcelona's largest and most celebrated happenings. Over three days in mid-June, thousands descend upon the city, turning Plaça Espanya—the site of the festival's principal venues—into a huge rave. The celebration is divided into "Day" and "Night" activities. Sónar by Day sees sets by international DJs, record fairs, and digital art exhibits at the Fira Montjuic. Sónar by Night takes place in the Fira Gran Via Hospitalet for acts on the forefront of the dance music scene like Skrillex, Die Antwoord, and The Chemical Brothers. It's best to purchase tickets early via the festival website. ⊕ *www.sonar.es.*

NIGHTLIFE

Barcelona nights are long and as wild as you want. Most of the best clubs don't even open until after midnight, but cafés and music bars serve as recruiting venues for the night's mission. The typical progression begins with drinks, tapas and dinner, a jazz or flamenco concert around 11 pm, then a pub or a music bar or two, and then— if the body can keep up with the spirit—dancing. Late-night bars and early-morning cafés provide an all-important break to refresh and refuel.

New wine bars, cafés, music bars, and tiny live-music clubs are constantly scraping plaster from 500-year-old brick walls to expose medieval structural elements that offer striking backdrops for postmodern people and conversations. The most common closing time for Barcelona's nocturnal bars is 3 am, while clubs are open until 5 am.

BARRI GÒTIC AND LA RAMBLA

Medieval Barri Gòtic is a wanderer's paradise filled with ancient winding streets, majestic squares, and myriad period-perfect wine bars and dimly lighted pubs found in the hidden corners of labyrinthine alleyways. The adjoining La Rambla, the liveliest pedestrian promenade in the city, bustles with a dizzying array of tourist-baiting shops, eateries, and arched paths to Plaça Reial's euphoric nightlife scene. Casual and unpretentious, the scene erupts nightly with a parade of rambunctious crowds of expats, curious interlopers, and assorted celebrations.

BARS

Bar Pastis. On a tiny street off the bottom of La Rambla, this dusty hole-in-the-wall is a city treasure. For six decades, Bar Pastis has provided patrons with a nostalgic, elbow-to-elbow glimpse at bohemian back-alley Paris circa the 1940s. The nicotine-stained walls, grimy shelves filled with ancient bottles, and the faded portraits of long-ago performers are all genuine. The bar holds acoustic gigs nightly for a hard-to-beat €2 per concert (generally starting around 10 pm) featuring tango, flamenco, soft jazz, blues, or anything that fits the bar's speakeasy groove. ⊠ *Santa Mònica 4, La Rambla* 🕾 *93/318–7980,* ⊕ *www.barpastis.es* Ⓜ *Drassanes.*

Boadas. Barcelona's oldest cocktail bar opened its doors in 1933 and quickly gained a reputation as the only place to enjoy a genuine mojito. The faithful—who still include a few of the city's luminaries—have been flocking ever since, despite the bar's decidedly lackluster decor. The space has the look and feel of an old-fashioned private club and is still the spot where old-school barmen in dapper duds mixing drinks the way tradition dictates. ⊠ *Tallers 1, La Rambla* 🕾 *93/318–9592* ⊕ *boadascocktails.com* Ⓜ *Catalunya.*

El Paraigua. This eatery's stunning Modernist facade—intricately carved wood, an exquisite vintage register, and other delicate reminders of its former incarnation as a turn-of-the-20th-century umbrella shop—is usually enough to lure newcomers inside for a closer look. But for fiesta-loving night owls, the real attraction is downstairs in the arched, exposed-brick cocktail club, a former convent basement offering first-rate cocktails and weekend jazz concerts in a note-perfect setting. ⊠ *Carrer del Pas de l'Ensenyança 2, Barri Gòtic* 🕾 *93/317–1479* ⊕ *www.elparaigua.com* Ⓜ *Jaume I.*

Harlem Jazz Club. Located on a rare tree-lined street in Barri Gòtic, this club attracts patrons of all ages and musical tastes. Listen to live Cuban salsa, swing, and reggae while enjoying killer cocktails in a relaxed and friendly atmosphere. Most concerts start at 10 pm and finish around 1 am, and many linger until closing time. ⊠ *Comtessa de Sobradiel 8, Barri Gòtic* 🕾 *93/310–0755* ⊕ *www.harlemjazzclub.es* Ⓜ *Jaume I, Liceu.*

Jamboree-Jazz and Dance-Club. This legendary nightspot has hosted some the world's most influential jazz musicians since its opening in 1960. Decades later, the club continues to offer two nightly shows and remains a notable haven for new generations of jazz and blues aficionados. After the last performance, the spot transforms into a late-night dance club playing soul, hip-hop, and R&B. ⊠ *Pl. Reial 17, La Rambla* 🕾 *93/319–1789* ⊕ *www.masimas.com/en/jamboree* Ⓜ *Liceu.*

La Vinateria del Call. Located in the heart of Barcelona's former Jewish Quarter, this rustic charmer serves a wide variety of hearty national wines paired with regional cheeses, meats, and tapas. Popular with wine-loving romantics for its antique carved-wood furnishings and candlelit setting, the venue also attracts visitors and regulars looking for a respite from the area's chaotic pace. ✉ *Sant Domènec del Call 9, Barri Gòtic* ☎ 93/302–6092 ⊕ *www.lavinateriadelcall.com* Ⓜ *Liceu, Jaume I.*

Marula Café. After six years in the business, Marula Café has remained steadfast in its ambitious quest to keep Barcelona grooving with funk and all its sister sounds. No electronic music will enter this slick, red-curtained venue with back-lighted glass walls: once past the bouncer, it's just funk, disco, and Latin spiced up with Afro-funk licks. The crowd is a mix of funk-loving locals who come to dance and foreigners who've stumbled in from the tourist circuit off Plaça Reial. There is also a regular line up of DJ sessions and concerts. Check out the regularly updated website. ✉ *Escudellers 49, Barri Gòtic* ☎ 93/318–7690 ⊕ *www.marulacafe.com/bcn* Ⓜ *Liceu, Drassanes.*

Milk. Resembling a prim parlor lounge with touches of kitsch, this cozy bar bistro with plush sofas, gilded mirrors, handmade knickknacks, and tastefully worn tapestry wallpaper has been a favorite hangout for young expats for more than a decade. Offering a perfect setup for cocktails and conversation until 2 am, Milk serves the usual classics (as well as beer and wine) with a dab of personality—the Michelada, for one, is a dramatic alternative Bloody Mary reserved for the strongest constitutions: Corona beer mixed with hot sauce, Worcestershire, and tomato juice. ✉ *Gignas 21, Barri Gòtic* ☎ 93/268–0922 ⊕ *www.milk-barcelona.com* Ⓜ *Jaume I.*

Fodor's Choice ★ Ocaña. Located in a trio of ancient mansions on buzzy Plaça Reial's southern flank, this venue is dedicated to Jose Peréz Ocaña, a cross-dressing artist and proud bohemian, and a dominating figure of Barcelona's decadent post-Franco explosion of alternative culture. With an adjoining Mexican restaurant, as well as a sizable café bar, club, and cocktail lounge, Ocaña also has the fiercest drag queen hostesses on the square. The showstopping interior was conceived as an homage to the establishment's namesake, via a *mise en scene* of decaying period elegance scattered with head-turning pop art. Open in the afternoon during the summer and on weekends (it opens at 5 pm during the week the rest of the year) it's a wonderful place for people-watching on the terrace, followed by dinner in one of two distinctive spaces and cocktails at the Moorish-chic Apotheke bar (closed Sunday and Monday) downstairs. ✉ *Pl. Reial 13–15, Barri Gòtic* ☎ 93/676–4814 ⊕ *www.ocana.cat* Ⓜ *Drassanes.*

Sidecar Factory Club. A mainstay of the decadent nightlife centered on Plaça Reial, this long-running music club has never fallen out of fashion—in fact, it attracts new fans just as the old ones bow out. With a firm focus showcasing up-and-coming indie talent, the venue offers a way to discover new favorites in moody neon red surroundings. ✉ *Pl. Reial 7, Barri Gòtic* ☎ 93/302–1586 ⊕ *www.sidecarfactoryclub.com* Ⓜ *Drassanes.*

Sor Rita. Beyond kitschy, this wacky joint is inspired by the "anything goes" antiestablishment spirit of director Pedro Almodóvar's most memorable characters. The decor is an mishmash of pop culture quirk: stilettos stuck on the ceiling, a wall of framed retro icons, a Barbie-head lamp, and other off-the-wall treasures. For the open-minded, several nights a week are dedicated to the pursuit of mindless mischief; Mondays are for spicy cocktails and tarot readings; Tuesdays mean all-you-can-eat salads and beer; Thursdays are host to karaoke stylings of iconic cheeseball (mostly Spanish) songs. Meanwhile, any night of the week, patrons—mostly locals—get in the mood by wearing one of several wigs available at the bar. Though anyone is welcome, it's recommended to leave the day's stress at the door. ⊠ *Mercé 27, Barri Gòtic* ☎ *93/176–6266* ⊕ *www.sorritabar.es* Ⓜ *Jaume I.*

BORN-RIBERA

La Ribera, considered one of Barcelona's most posh areas during medieval times, is still home to some of the city's loveliest ancient architecture. It exudes a tranquil yet distinctive vibe, the very same atmosphere found in the select number of bars, galleries, and eateries sprinkled between patches of greenery and arched stone passageways. El Born, the most voguish part of this district, provides a more eclectic collection of bars and lounge spots specializing in everything from craft beer to organic wines.

BARS

Ale and Hop. Ale and Hop leads the pack in the latest craft beer bar invasion to hit the city. A slick microbrewery with exposed brick walls, monochrome wallpaper, and indie beats, Ale and Hop serves artisan brews on tap or directly from the bottle. A slew of eco-wines and vegetarian snacks provide a health-conscious change of pace. ⊠ *Carrer de les Basses de Sant Pere 10* ☎ *93/126–9094* ⊕ *www.aleandhop.com* Ⓜ *Arc de Triomf.*

Bar Brutal. Whimsically fashionable with its red tabletops, arched ceiling, and lacquered bar counter, Bar Brutal (and its adjoining bodega Can Cisa) is revered for its dedication to sustainability. The bar's entire stock of wines (300 and counting) is organically produced and served straight from the barrel, without a lick of artificial additives to spoil the natural flavors. Focusing primarily on regional wines, the savvy staff is always game to suggest new vintages or the perfect food pairing. ⊠ *Barra de Ferro 1* ☎ *93/295–4797* ⊕ *www.cancisa.cat* Ⓜ *Jaume I.*

Cocktail Bar Juanra Falces. Elegant and discreet best describes this spot reminiscent of a Manhattan speakeasy circa 1920. The tiny cocktail bar, a local favorite since the '80s, accommodates up to 60 patrons in a wood-paneled interior, with a varnished dark-wood bar highlighted by two tiers of backlit cocktail bottles and a playful pop art illustration. Dapper barmen and soothing jazz music complete the mood. Sample expertly prepared concoctions including the signature gimlet and a choice selection of martinis. ⊠ *Rec 24, Born-Ribera* ☎ *93/310–1027* Ⓜ *Jaume I.*

La Vinya del Senyor. Ambitiously named "The Lord's Vineyard," this romantic wine bar directly across from the entrance to the emblematic church of Santa Maria del Mar is etched into the ground floor of an ancient building. Featuring an extensive wine list and bite-size edibles, ardent aficionados order by the bottle and favor tables found up a rickety ladder on the pint-size mezzanine or, when the weather cooperates, outside on the people-watching terrace. ⊠ *Pl. de Santa Maria 5, Born-Ribera* ☏ *93/310–3379* Ⓜ *Jaume I.*

Paspartu. Dark and inviting with just a smidgen of whimsy (check out the pop art posters and wooden crate stools), Paspartu boasts 25 gin flavors and the unspoken invitation to settle in and try each one—what else could comfy pillows, nonintrusive music, and bite-size nibbles mean? And if gin is not your bag, don't fret: the chummy bar staff is always ready to suggest the perfect combo to enhance your favorite spirit. This is a perfect unwinding spot for the young of body and at heart. ⊠ *Carrer de les Basses de Sant Pere 12* ☏ *93/310–3379* Ⓜ *Arc de Triomf.*

Fodor'sChoice
★ **Rubi Bar.** The whimsical apothecary-like spirits cabinet, exposed-stone wall, and dramatic red lighting will be the first things to catch your eye at this cozy hidden gem, tucked away in the maze-like backstreets of El Born. However, it's the friendly service, relaxed atmosphere, and inventive selection of cocktails—most notably a choice of home-brewed flavored gins tantalizingly displayed on the bar shelves in hand-labeled bottles—that brings patrons back time and again. Add to the mix an eclectic playlist of funk, soul, rock, and pop classics, tasty snacks, and inexpensive mojitos that attracts locals, expats, and the curious, ages 25–50 and beyond. ⊠ *Banys Vells 6, Born-Ribera* ☏ *671/441888* Ⓜ *Jaume I.*

EL RAVAL

El Raval has slowly evolved from a forgotten, seedy no-man's-land into one of the choicest districts to enjoy provocative modern art and a pulsating, boho-glam party scene. Though not for everyone's taste, hippy students, tattooed misfits, artists, and more recently trend-seeking nomads routinely bar crawl up and down a stretch of nightlife-friendly streets (Joaquin Costa is one) featuring a wide assortment of divey dens, music bars, pubs, and funky coctelerias

BARS

Ambar. Right off the tree-lined Rambla del Raval, the clientele at this popular watering hole is as colorful as the snazzy, red-quilted bar and moody green-blue lighting: expat students and pierced young artists rub shoulders with visiting rabble-rousers warming up for a wild night out. With its basic menu of classic cocktails and long drinks, the main attraction is arguably the space itself. The dim interior is spacious, strewn with a calculated mix of modern and retro; shabby sofas and antique lamps are in perfect harmony with the contempo floor-to-ceiling windows, artless frames, and slick metallic stools. ⊠ *Sant Pau 77, El Raval.*

Casa Almirall. The twisted wooden fronds framing the bar's mirror, an 1888 vintage bar-top iron statue of a muse, and Art Nouveau touches such as curvy door handles make this one of the most authentic bars in Barcelona. It's also the second oldest, dating to 1860. (The oldest is the Marsella, another Raval favorite.) It's a good spot for evening drinks after hitting the nearby MACBA (Museu d'Art Contemporani de Barcelona) or for a prelunch *vermut* (vermouth) on weekends. ✉ *Joaquín Costa 33, El Raval* ☎ *93/318–9917* ⊕ *www.casaalmirall.com/en* Ⓜ *Universitat.*

La Confitería. Located in a former pastry shop, this vintage bar has retained so much of the 19th-century Modernist facade and interior touches (onetime cake display cases are now filled with period memorabilia) that visitors undoubtedly experience the sensation of time standing still. Divided into two equally inviting spaces and opened unconventionally late for a bar (3 am), the front is usually packed with regulars, while the granite-and-metal tables in the back are popular with couples and small groups of friends enjoying a few beers or a bottle of cava. Sunday afternoons features live music during the traditional vermouth hour (1–2 pm). ✉ *Sant Pau 128, El Raval* ☎ *93/140–5435* Ⓜ *Paral.lel.*

Manchester. There's no doubt about what the name of this laid-back Raval hangout pays tribute to: that of the early Haçienda years and the Manchester scene, of Joy Division and Happy Mondays and the Stone Roses, when rock and dance music shook an entire country. The sheer number of people (both locals and foreigners) crowding around the wood tables and dancing in the spaces in between suggest that a tribute is welcome. ✉ *Valldonzella 40, El Raval* ☎ *62/773–3081* Ⓜ *Catalunya.*

Marsella. Inaugurated in 1820, this historic venue, a favored haunt for artistic notables such as Gaudí, Picasso, and Hemingway, has remained remarkably unchanged since its celebrated heyday. The chipped paint on the walls and ceiling, cracked marble tables, and elaborate spiderwebs on chandeliers and bottles all add to the charm, but the main reason patrons linger is one special shot: Marsella is one of few establishments serving homemade absinthe (*absenta* in Spanish), a potent aniseed-flavored spirit meant to be savored and rumored to enhance productivity. ✉ *Sant Pau 65, El Raval* ☎ *93/442–7263* Ⓜ *Liceu.*

BARCELONA JAZZ

Barcelona has loved jazz ever since Sam Wooding and his Chocolate Kiddies triumphed here in 1929. Jack Hilton's visits in the early 1930s paved the way for Benny Carter and the Hot Club of Barcelona in 1935 and 1936. In the early years of the post–Spanish civil war Franco dictatorship, jazz was viewed as a dangerous influence from beyond, but by 1969 Duke Ellington's Sacred Concerts smuggled jazz into town under the protective umbrella of the same Catholic Church whose conservative elements cautioned the Franco regime against the perils of this "degenerate music."

Negroni. This cocktail bar is for no-nonsense sophisticates of all ages: pared down to mostly black decor and a shiny varnished bar. What sets Negroni apart and keeps it popular even a decade after its inception is the talented barmen's dedication to the art of cocktail creation; no menus, just reveal your favorite spirit and have a little trust. ⊠ *Joaquin Costa 46, El Raval* ⊕ *www.negronicocktailbar.com* Ⓜ *Universitat.*

33/45. From the street, this indie-cool hipster haven seems too brightly lighted for gritty-glam Raval. But upon closer inspection, a copious, cushy area with oversize pillows; ratty, mismatched sofas; and a cocktail menu available day and night make it tempting enough to linger. Featuring weekly live music sessions and occasional pop-up expositions, it's the establishment's chill vibe and eclectic selection of flavored gins, tequila blends, and imported beer that attract a steady flow of lounge lizards. ⊠ *Joaquin Costa 4, El Raval* ☎ *93/187–4138* ⊕ *www.3345. struments.com* Ⓜ *Sant Antoni.*

Ultramarinos Hendricks. Gintonic (in Spanish it's all one word), the cocktail of choice for many a hip barcelonin, is the undisputed star of this retro-fabulous neighborhood bar. Old-school aficionados favor the saucy collection of signature Hendricks blends, but for those with more curious palettes, more than 175 international gins are flavored, perfumed, and/or mixed into no less than 25 killer concoctions. Beyond the gin, a varied selection of spirits and cocktails are on offer and a rotating lineup of local DJs keep the joint jumping by playing everything from classic jazz to the more obscure (Latin Tropical Disco anyone?). ⊠ *Carrer de Sant Pau 126, El Raval* ☎ *653/582424* ⟳ *Mon.–Sat. 8:30 pm–3 am* Ⓜ *Parallel.*

MUSIC CLUBS: JAZZ AND BLUES

Jazz Sí Club. Run by the Barcelona contemporary music school next door, this workshop and (during the day) café is a forum for musicians, teachers, and fans to listen and debate their art. There is jazz on Monday; pop, blues, and rock jam sessions on Tuesday; jazz Wednesday; Cuban salsa on Thursday; flamenco on Friday; and rock and pop on weekends. The small cover charge (€5–€10, depending on which night you visit) includes a drink; Wednesdays have no cover charge. Gigs start between 6:30 and 8:45 pm. ⊠ *Requesens 2, El Raval* ☎ *93/329–0020* ⊕ *www.tallerdemusics.com* Ⓜ *Sant Antoni.*

BARCELONETA AND PORT OLÍMPIC

Once a dingy industrial port, the stretch of seaside between Port Vell and Port Olímpic was dramatically beautified for the 1992 Summer Olympics. Today, the scenic area is bursting with Barceloneta's trendy *chiringuitos* (beach shacks), laid-back bars, and terraced seafood restaurants. In sharp contrast, Port Olímpic's posh nightclub scene caters to the city's fashionable glitterati, aged 21 and over. Both areas are just a short walking distance from each other, so whatever mood strikes you, dress accordingly.

BARS

FodorsChoice ★ **Eclipse Bar.** The sensational shoreline views from the 26th floor of the seaside W Hotel are undoubtedly a major part of Eclipse's attraction. Add to the mix an ultraslick interior design, an impressive roster of international DJs spinning themed parties every day of the week, and deluxe cocktails decadently paired with sushi, and it's of little wonder that this is a favorite spot for glitterati to be seen and heard. ⊠ *Pl. de la Rosa dels Vents 1, Barceloneta* ☎ *93/295–2800* ⊕ *www.eclipse-barcelona.com* Ⓜ *Drassanes.*

CASINOS

Gran Casino de Barcelona. Situated on the shore underneath the Hotel Arts, Barcelona's modern casino has everything from slot machines to roulette, plus restaurants, a bar, and a dance club. The casino regularly hosts Texas Hold'em poker tournaments, which add an air of Vegas-style excitement. ⊠ *Marina 19–21, Port Olímpic* ☎ *900/354354* ⊕ *www.casino-barcelona.com/en* Ⓜ *Ciutadella–Vila Olímpica.*

DANCE CLUBS

CDLC. Among the glitziest of Barcelona's waterfront clubs, the Carpe Diem Lounge Club embraces all the clichés of Ibizan over-the-top decor. The music is electronic; cocktails are exotic—and pricey. If there are celebrities in town, sooner or later they show up here. ⊠ *Passeig Marítim 32, Marina Beach, Port Olímpic* ☎ *932/240470, 647/779999 VIP services* ⊕ *www.cdlcbarcelona.com* Ⓜ *Ciutadella–Vila Olímpica.*

Opium Mar. Bordering on ostentatious, this cavernous nightspot, open until 6 am, is where most die-hard revelers end up after neighboring clubs have called it a night. Opium, flashy in every sense of the word, is a maze of split-level dance areas, pristine white lounge seating awash with dramatic pinkish-blue lighting, and scantily-clad go-go dancers at every turn. All this excess culminates in the quasi-pretentious VIP area that offers patrons a privileged 360-degree view of the action. A strict door policy means style-conscious divas and debonair gents abound. ⊠ *Passeig Marítim 34, Port Olímpic* ☎ *655/576998* ⊕ *www.opiummar. com* Ⓜ *Ciutadella | Vila Olímpica.*

Pacha. Celebrated cherry-logoed nightlife brand Pacha is back in Barcelona after a multiyear absence. This latest reincarnation boasts an envied beachfront spot and a pricey restaurant catering mostly to summer tourists familiar with the name. After the sun goes down, however, the glitzy, floor-to-ceiling white interior transforms into a pulsating Ibiza-style showcase for local and international house and electronic acts as well as the spot for regularly changing weekday parties for the city's large community of Erasmus and under-25 partygoers. ⊠ *Passeig Marítim 38, Port Olímpic* ☎ *648/815985* ⊕ *www.pachabarcelona.es* Ⓜ *Ciutadella | Vila Olímpica.*

Shôko. With tony design touches and Eastern fusion cuisine, Shôko brings its own particular brand of cool to the Barcelona seaside. Located just below Frank Gehry's famous fish sculpture, the swanky restaurant and lounge morphs into a party paradise featuring theme nights with international DJs ready to spin until dawn. ⊠ *Passeig Marítim de la Barceloneta 36, Port Olímpic* ☎ *93/225–9200* ⊕ *www.shoko.biz/en* Ⓜ *Ciutadella | Vila Olímpica.*

EIXAMPLE

Home to a magnificent array of Modernist architectural wonders, including Gaudí masterpieces Casa Mila, Casa Batllo, and La Sagrada Família, Barcelona's modish L'Eixample district is at once the largest and most diverse nightlife destination in town. With truly something for all tastes, on any given night you can find expat students blowing off steam at themed pubs and dance clubs catering to their likes, the LGBTQ community partying in the fashionable area affectionately known as "Gaixample," and the posh set rushing from high-end restaurants and chandeliered hotel bars to find a place at VIP tables in the city's swankiest clubs and lounges.

BARS

Fodor's Choice ★ **Banker's Bar.** With allusions to its past life as a bank (like the safety deposit boxes on the wall), the swank cocktail bar of the 5* Mandarin Oriental Hotel lounge is perfect for an opulent night out. DJs play relaxing jazz, swing, and blues tunes on weekends. Wednesday night is reserved for live musical performances. Oversize brown leather chairs and taupe-color detailing surround the black lacquer bar manned by barmaids dressed in matching Asian-inspired qipaos serving fare from a biannually changing "East meets West" menu that includes classic cocktail favorites alongside signature creations paired with light, bicontinental bites. ⊠ *Hotel Mandarin Oriental, Passeig de Gràcia 38–40, Eixample* ☎ *93/151–8782* ⊕ *www.mandarinoriental.es* Ⓜ *Passeig de Gràcia.*

Fodor's Choice ★ **Dry Martini Bar.** An homage to the traditional English martini bar of decades past, this stately spot is paradise for cocktail aficionados seeking the most expertly mixed drinks in town (martinis even have their own prep section). From the wood-paneled fixtures of the mirrored bar featuring a vintage brass register, to the knowledgeable barmen dressed in impeccable white coats and ties, to the wall of vintage spirit bottles overlooking plush and regal turquoise and red leather seating, each detail aims to transport the loyal clientele back to an era of inspired excellence. ⊠ *Aribau 162, Eixample* ☎ *93/205–8070* ⊕ *www.drymartiniorg.com* Ⓜ *Provença.*

La Vinoteca Torres. Ideally located on Barcelona's exclusive shopping avenue, Passeig de Gràcia, the acclaimed Torres wine dynasty offers an ample selection of their international wines and spirits to accompany delectable Mediterranean fish or meat dishes such as the signature oxtail in Sangre de Toro red wine sauce. The dark, ultramodern space is adorned with walls of stacked wine bottles and strategic lighting illuminates the natural wood tables. For an extra-special treat, book the private back room that seats up to 14. When the weather is nice, stop by for a quick glass of wine and tapas on the parasol-covered terrace. ⊠ *Passeig de Gràcia 78, Eixample* ☎ *93/272–6625* ⊕ *www.lavinotecatorres.com* Ⓜ *Passeig de Gràcia, Diagonal.*

Les Gens que J'aime. Bohemia meets the Moulin Rouge at this intimate, below-street-level bordello-inspired pub with turn-of-the-20th-century memorabilia, including fringed lampshades, faded period portraits, stacked blue light chandelier, and comfy wicker sofas cushioned with lush red velvet. First opened in 1967, this jazz-playing dark and dusty spot offers attentive yet laid-back service, allowing guests to linger for a cocktail (whiskey sours are popular), a telling tarot card reading, or a romantic tête-à-tête by Tiffany lamplight. ✉ *València 286, bajos, Eixample* ☎ *93/215–6879* ⊕ *www.lesgensquejaime.com* Ⓜ *Passeig de Gràcia.*

Milano. For more than a decade, this "secret" basement bar, located in an area otherwise dominated by student pubs and tourist traps, has a rotating lineup of international acts including blues, soul, jazz, flamenco, swing, and pop. Resembling a 1940s cabaret, you'll find paneled oak, a brass bar, spotlit photo prints of previous acts, and red banquette-style seating alongside matching armchairs and tables. The stage is complete with moody lighting and a curtain backdrop. Open from noon for tapas lunch with cocktails (classic and creative), shows run nightly at 9 pm and 11 pm. ✉ *Ronda Universitat 35, Eixample* ☎ *93/112–7150* ⊕ *www.camparimilano.com/en* Ⓜ *Catalunya, Universitat.*

Fodor'sChoice ★ **Monvínic.** Conceptualized to celebrate wine culture at its finest, this spectacular space, aptly called "Wineworld" in Catalan, features a ritzy wine bar complete with tablet wine lists, a cavernous culinary space, a reference library, a vertical garden, and the pièce de résistance: a vast cellar housing a mind-blowing 3,500 vintages from around the world. Small plates of regional jamón and inventive riffs on classical Catalan cuisine complement the vino. Wine tastings, both traditional and creative, are held regularly for groups or individuals looking to become oenophiles. ✉ *Diputació 249, Eixample* ☎ *93/272–6187* ⊕ *www.monvinic.com* Ⓜ *Passeig de Gràcia.*

Morro Fi. Tiny and unpretentious yet decidedly on trend, this untraditional vermuteria is reintroducing classic vermouth to the masses. Opened by a trio of vermouth aficionados, Morro Fi (loosely translates as "refined palate") was originally a foodie blog that morphed into a bar determined to educate visitors about enjoying vermouth (they even produce their own brand) with select tapas. The result? Locals and the odd expat routinely spilling out into the streets, drink in hand while indie music blares. ✉ *Consell de Cent 171, Eixample* ⊕ *www.morrofi.cat* Ⓜ *Urgell.*

Senyor Vermut. This snazzy, high-ceilinged vermuteria has guests lining up to sample a generous selection of more than 40 vermuts served with traditional tapas. From bitter to earthy or aged in a barrel, this classic aperitif is clearly the star attraction despite other offerings including wine, beer, juices, and hot beverages. Located on a quiet corner free of the tourist-baiting menus that abound in the neighborhood, Senyor Vermut serves its legion of loyal customers an uninterrupted array of food and drink daily, either inside, or outside on the year-round terrace. ✉ *Carrer de Provença 85, Eixample* ☎ *93/532–8865* ☞ *Closed Mon.* Ⓜ *Entença.*

Fodor'sChoice ★ **Solange Cocktails and Luxury Spirits.** The latest venture from the Pernia brothers—the trio whose Tandem Cocktail Bar (Aribau 86) pioneered Barcelona's emerging cocktail scene back in the '80s—is a sleek, golden-hued, luxurious lounge space aptly named after Solange Dimitrios, 007's original Bond girl. Smartly dressed barmen cater to well-heeled 30-plus professionals at the stunning long bar or on posh lounge divans so extravagant in look and feel that one expects the debonair spy to walk in at any moment. The homage continues with signature cocktails that reference Bond films, characters, and even a "secret mission" concoction for the more daring. ⊠ *Carrer Aribau 143, Eixample* ☎ *93/164–3625* ⊕ *www.solangecocktail.com* ⌁ *Mon.–Sun. 6 pm–2:30 pm* Ⓜ *Hospital Clínic, Diagonal.*

DANCE CLUBS

Antilla Salsa Barcelona (*Antilla Salsa Barcelona*). You'll find this exuberant Caribbean spot sizzling with salsa, son cubano, and merengue from the moment you step in the door. From 10 to 11 on Wednesdays, enthusiastic dance instructors teach bachata for free. After that, the dancing begins and the dancers rarely stop to draw breath. This self-proclaimed "Caribbean cultural center" cranks out every variation of salsa ever invented. There are regular live concerts, and on Friday and Saturday, the mic gives way to animated Latin DJs. ⊠ *Aragó 141, Eixample* ☎ *93/451–4564* ⊕ *www.antillasalsa.com* Ⓜ *Urgell, Hospital Clínic.*

Bikini Barcelona. This sleek megaclub, which was reborn as part of L'Illa shopping center, boasts the best sound system in Barcelona. A smaller sala puts on concerts of emerging and cult artists—the Nigerian singer-songwriter Asa, local soulsters The Pepper Pots, and Gil Scott-Heron in one of his final performances are just some of the noteworthy events here. When gigs finish around midnight, the walls roll back and the space ingeniously turns into a sweaty nightclub. ⊠ *Diagonal 547, Eixample* ☎ *93/322–0800* ⊕ *www.bikinibcn.com* Ⓜ *Maria Cristina.*

Boyberry. This gay hub combines a wide range of resources, from films and darkrooms to Internet connections, and a lounge. ⊠ *Calàbria 96, Eixample* ☎ *93/426–2312* ⊕ *www.boyberry.com* Ⓜ *Rocafort.*

City Hall. Nightly parties starring electro house music and guest DJs from neighboring clubs guarantee dancing till you drop at this raging mid-city favorite, set in a gorgeously revamped turn-of-the-20th-century theater. ⊠ *Rambla Catalunya 2–4, Eixample* ☎ *93/233–3333* ⊕ *cityhallbarcelona.com* Ⓜ *Catalunya.*

Luz de Gas. Luz de Gas has events every night of the week, from live performances (mostly world music and Latin) to wild late-night dancing (expect soul and standards). ⊠ *Muntaner 246, Eixample* ☎ *93/209–7711* ⊕ *www.luzdegas.com* Ⓜ *Muntaner, Diagonal.*

Otto Zutz. Just off Vía Augusta above Diagonal, this nightclub and disco (dating back to 1985) is a perennial Barcelona favorite that keeps attracting a glitzy mix of Barcelona movers and shakers, models, ex-models, wannabe models, and the hoping-to-get-lucky mob that predictably follows this sort of pulchritude. Hip-hop, house, and Latin make up the standard sound track on the dance floor, with more mellow notes upstairs and in the coveted Altos Club Privé (or "VIP section," to you and me). ⊠ *Lincoln 15, Eixample* ☎ *93/238–0722 office* ⊕ *www.ottozutz.com* Ⓜ *Sant Gervasi, Gràcia.*

Punto BCN. A musical bar with billiards tables, this mid-Eixample hub is a clearinghouse for all persuasions and tastes, with women often outnumbering the men, pool tables or not. ⊠ *Carrer Muntaner 63–65, Eixample* ☎ *93/453–6123* Ⓜ *Universitat.*

Sala B. Music described as "humana" (suggesting no teeth-rattling techno) keeps Sala B filled with the mid-twenties and thirtysomething set until 5 in the morning on Friday and Saturday. Just above the Diagonal near Luz de Gas, this veteran nightspot is an offshoot of the parent club as evidenced by the shared website. Concerts and DJ music for dancing alternate at this comfortable club designed for semicivilized nightlife. ⊠ *Muntaner 244, Eixample* ☎ *93/209–7711* ⊕ *www.luzdegas.com* Ⓜ *Provença.*

The Sutton Club. If there's anywhere you should dress up to get past the door, it's here. If the international see-and-be-seen crowd converges around the seaside clubs below Hotel Arts, their local equivalent come to Sutton. The club is segregated into several bars and dancing areas, playing R&B, hip-hop, house, and the occasional live performance. Not as happening as in its mid-2000s heyday, it still merits a visit, if anything to enjoy the festive atmosphere. Sutton is like a Vegas club in Barcelona: it may not be classy, but it's always entertaining. ⊠ *Tuset 13, Eixample* ☎ *93/414–4217* ⊕ *www.thesuttonclub.com* Ⓜ *Diagonal.*

GRÀCIA

With a bohemian look and feel more akin to a small village than an urban landscape, Gràcia welcomes revelers of all stripes looking for easygoing pleasures. On any given night, hordes of visitors pour into the district's ancient squares to sample freshly made tapas paired with beer or wine. But for the slightly more adventurous, exploring the graffiti-filled, maze-like back alleyways and side streets usually provides ample rewards: gourmet eateries, upscale wine bars, and contempo coctelerias that coexist in perfect harmony with the neighborhood dives.

BARS

Fodor'sChoice ★ **Elephanta.** Elephanta is that rare neighborhood spot that offers a little something for everyone. Diminutive in size but huge in personality and warmth, patrons enjoy an extensive menu (printed on authentic vinyl covers) of quality gins and seasonal fruity cocktails in a dimly lighted retro space peppered with comfy mismatched furnishings and India-inspired decor. Music varies though the ambience is always chill; perfect for laptop lounging or hosted cultural screenings. ⊠ *Torrent d'en Vidalet 37, Gràcia* ☎ *93/237–6906* ⊕ *www.elephanta.cat* Ⓜ *Joanic.*

Ítaca. This contemporary cervecería resembles many of the cool offerings routinely sprouting up in Gràcia, one of the city's most popular neighborhoods. Patrons can top off drinks with self-service pours from local brewer Estrella Damm. Local craft favorites such as Brew Dog Punk IPA and classic cocktails are also on offer. Enjoy a drink with nachos, burgers, and tapas while listening to local tunes around the tiny, natural-wood bar. ⊠ *Santa Rosa 14, Gràcia* ☎ *93/013–1047* ⊕ *www.grupitaca.cat* Ⓜ *Fontana.*

L'Entresòl. Come for the laid-back vibe and retro furnishings, stay for the large selection of premium gin (35-plus and counting), and guest DJs playing the grooviest indie, funk, and soul on weekends. Perfect for pre-club gintonics with friends or dates. ⊠ *Carrer del Planeta 39, Gràcia* ☎ *685/533941* Ⓜ *Fontana.*

Fodor'sChoice
★
Old Fashioned. This small-but-swanky bar, reminiscent of a '50s-style gin joint—black and white with red quilted booths and framed prints—regularly draws in the crowds due in large part to entertaining master mixologists (nattily dressed in suspenders and ties) and their out-of-this-world experimental takes on cocktail classics. Try a Fashionista, the house special prepared with bourbon, sherry, and hazelnuts flambéed with a blowtorch, among other ingredients. Other playfully named concoctions include Anything Goes and Run to Your Mama. ⊠ *Carrer de Santa Teresa 1, Gràcia* ☎ *93/368–5277* Ⓜ *Diagonal.*

Fodor'sChoice
★
Viblioteca. Adding a little uptown pizzazz to boho-chic enclave Gràcia, this diminutive, minimalist white wine bar and eatery is the local "it" vintage. Wines sourced and served with engaging backstories can be sampled at the seven-seater bar or at a table, accompanied by a large assortment of cured meats, cheeses, and salads or with a few choice liquors. Advance booking is highly recommended. ⊠ *Vallfogona 12, Gràcia* ☎ *93/284–4202* ⊕ *www.viblioteca.com* Ⓜ *Fontana.*

POBLENOU

Once the city's central industrial hub, this area's contrasting faces—a quaint tree-lined rambla surrounded by vast warehouse spaces and ultramodern edifices—are the main reason for its recent metamorphosis into Barcelona's hippest enclave. Once-abandoned spaces have been renovated into chic artists' lofts and work spaces while vintage shops and nondescript restos are now enjoying new lives as retro-fab bars and lounges oozing with charm. Far enough from the hustle and bustle of the city's main attractions, locals in the know have turned Poblenou into paradise.

BARS

Fodor'sChoice
★
Balius Bar. Named after the historic hardware store that once stood here, Balius Bar's retro-chic decor, snazzy playlist (don't miss the live jazz sessions on Sundays), and puckish "no standing" policy attracts hepcats aged 30 and above looking to kick back with a good cocktail and a side of nostalgia. Afternoons are reserved for vermouth and all the fixings or a chilled cava cocktail paired with fresh, often eco-conscious, bites. In the evenings, creative cocktails are the main draw; try a Cusco Maki, a tangy mixture of pisco, elderflower, and red berries with a splash of lemon. If you're lucky you might also get a lindy lesson or two. ⊠ *Carrer de Pujades 196, Poblenou* ☎ *93/315–8650* ⊕ *baliusbar. com* Ⓜ *Poblenou.*

La Cervecita Nuestra de Cada Día. For craft beer lovers, this modern high-ceilinged bar and shop is must. Filled to the brim with more than 300 international craft brands (India Pale Ale is a favorite) plus several local artisan beers on tap, the venue solidifies its devotion to everything cerveza with organized tastings, parings, and courses. Claim your spot early as regulars routinely dominate the seating at the long bar or the cozy corner tables up front. ⊠ *Carrer de Llull 184, Poblenou* ☎ *93/486–9271* Ⓜ *Llacuna.*

Madam George Lounge Bar. Everything about this stylish bar is a happy contradiction: the chandeliered space with large gold-gilded mirrors and polished chocolate brown stools curiously complement the rickety antiques and quirky touches (check out the bathtub sofa in the back room). The eclectic song list (jazz, rock, pop, and everything in between) alternates along with a monthly lineup of DJs and drag queen bingo sessions. And then there's the drinks: cocktails run the full gamut from classic to creative (the piscopolitan, a perfect marriage of Peruvian pisco and the classic cosmo cocktail, is a triumph) and are enjoyed by locals and expats aged 25 to young-at-heart. ⊠ *Carrer de Pujades 179, Poblenou* ☎ *93/500–5151* ⊕ *www.madamegeorgebar. com* Ⓜ *Poble Nou.*

Megataverna L'Ovella Negra. The ultimate hangout for expat students and sports fanatics, this huge (41,500 square feet) former warehouse (a follow-up to the original, smaller L'Ovella Negra, C/Sitges 5) accommodates rambunctious groups in a cavernous space with high ceilings, sturdy wooden tables, and quirky decorative touches on a brick-wall interior. The space is a one-stop shop for foosball, billiards, eating, cheap drinks (5-liter pitchers of beer and sangria are the norm), big-screen TVs, and themed live music till 3 am on most weekends. ⊠ *Zamora 78, La Rambla* ☎ *93/309–5938* ⊕ *www.ovellanegrabcn. net* Ⓜ *Catalunya.*

MésDvi. The brainchild of two Catalan sommeliers, Mésdvi is a chic wine bar with a purpose: to educate visitors on the art of Spanish wines, with a particular focus on regional vintages. Shelves of up-to-the-moment wine bottles are the dominant decorative flourish/functional display. Depending on mood and company, there's plenty of seating options: a tasting table for serious aficionados, romantic tête-à-tête tables for a memorable night out, and a bar area for socializing. Sold by the bottle or by the glass, the regularly updated wine selections are paired with sample-size artisan tapas, cheese, and salads. ⊠ *Carrer de Marià Aguiló 123, Poblenou* ☎ *93/007–9151* ⊕ *www. mesdvi.cat* Ⓜ *Poble Nou.*

MUSIC CLUBS

Sala Razzmatazz. This mega industrial warehouse turned dance club and concert hall features five distinct clubs in one: Razz Club plays indie rock; The Loft and Lo·li·ta are all about techno and electronica; smaller more relaxed venues Pop Bar and Rex Bar focus on experimental electro pop and indie electro, respectively. Resident DJs play nightly though entrance tickets (including one drink) will set you back €10–€25 (cheaper if you buy online), depending on the live act selected. Despite a casual dress code and a party scene seldom pumping before 3 am, expect long lines to get in on the weekends. ⊠ *Almogàvers 122, Poblenou* ☎ *93/320–8200* ⊕ *www.salarazzmatazz.com* Ⓜ *Marina, Bogatell.*

POBLE SEC

Facing each other from opposite sides of the historic theater strip Avenida Paral·lel, the two contrasting areas, Poble Sec and Sant Antoni, are often overlooked by night birds. Sant Antoni's after-dark offerings may seem quiet in comparison to other iconic neighbors, but bars and bodegas here exude a genuine and welcoming quality only found in tourist-free zones. Poble Sec, on the other hand, is a stone's throw away from the huge L'Eixample district and routinely vies for a little attention with its eclectic collection of fashionable cafés, bars, and eateries.

BARS

Bodegas 1900. Celebrated chef Albert Adrià (Tickets, Avenida del Paral·lel 164, is just across the street) pays homage to time-honored traditional vermuterias by combining his creative culinary wizardry with conventional products, resulting in elevated versions of turn-of-the-20th-century dishes and drinks. Sleekly decorated in white and aged wood, this contemporary eatery resembles a dreamy but traditional vermouth bar with steep prices. ⊠ *Tamarit 91, Poble Sec* ☎ *93/325–2659* ⊕ *www.bodega1900.com* Ⓜ *Poble Sec.*

Casa Martino. This corner charmer, tiny and tasteful but with a modern edge, provides the perfect setting in which to sample authentic vermut (vermouth), particularly if you can bag a table on the terrace. Traditionally served in the afternoon with a splash of soda fizz, olives, and anchovies, Casa Martino elevates the time-honored aperitif ritual by adding gourmet tapas and toasts (with selections neatly hand-scrolled on a wall), mini art exhibitions, and a rule-breaking 11 pm closing time. ⊠ *Carrer de Manso 1, Poble Sec* ☎ *93/170–8096* ⊕ *www.casamartino.es* ⌖ *Tues.–Sat. noon–3 pm and 7 pm–11 pm, Sun. noon–4 pm* Ⓜ *Poble Sec.*

Cellar Cal Marino. Rustic and charming with an arched, brick-walled center, barrel tables, and rows of multicolor *sifón* fizzy water bottles, this homey venue serves wine by the glass or liter (for takeaway) from the wine cellar, artisan beers, and vermouth paired with homemade tapas. Tuesday through Friday the special is three drinks matched with three tapas, while Sunday is often dedicated to live jazz concerts and vermouth aperitifs. ⊠ *Margarit 54, Poble Sec* ☎ *93/329–4592* ⊕ *www.calmarino.com* Ⓜ *Poble Sec, Paral.lel.*

Domino Bar. On a quiet street, just steps from the buzzing Avenida Paral·lel, this little brick-walled bunker of inventive fruity concoctions effectively paired with artsy pizzas is a welcome sight. The space is diminutive but with just enough kitschy touches (domino seat cushions!) to give it oomph. Tunes range from jazz to soul to funky electronic, and the vibe transforms from tame to animated, attracting wandering souls in the mood for a chill night. ⊠ *Carrer de les Flors 16, Poble Sec* ☎ *696/461725* ⊕ *www.dominobar.com.*

Fodor'sChoice ★ **Jonny Aldana.** This cheery technicolor bar-resto, featuring a tiled facade and open-window bar with stools inside and out, is bursting with 1950s iconography and blackboards that demand your attention. Wines are sold by the glass, beer is served from the tap, but it's the superb vermouths and cocktails combined with vegan tapas that reel in patrons. Local DJs spin on certain nights. ⊠ *Carrer d'Aldana 9, Poble Sec* ☎ *93/174–2083* ⊕ *www.jonnyaldana.com* Ⓜ *Paral.lel.*

Rouge Bar. Rouge Bar has a bohemian vibe, complete with a selection of mismatched, threadbare furniture, posters of Impressionist paintings tacked to the wall, and the low light created by red pashmina shawls draped over lampshades. Here you'll find an excellent mixologist and tasteful lounge music playing in the background. ⊠ *Poeta Cabanyes 21, Poble Sec* ☎ *666/251556* ⊗ *Closed Wed. and Sun.* Ⓜ *Paral.lel.*

Fodor's Choice ★ **Xix Bar and Gin Corner.** The interior of this Alice in Wonderland–like venue of checkered half-walls, a marble bar, and contempo objets d'art rarely seen on ceilings, is the first clue that you've landed somewhere special. Beyond that, with 50-plus flavors of gins and infusions on offer—ranging from spicy ginger to tarty chocolate—an ultra-knowledgeable bar staff and a lounge-friendly 3 am curfew, Xix turns conventional cocktail drinkers into card-carrying gin lovers. ⊠ *Carrer de Rocafort 19, Poble Sec* ☎ *93/423–4314* ⊕ *www.xixbar.com* Ⓜ *Poble Sec.*

MUSIC CLUBS

Sala Apolo. Once part of the music-hall scene along the Paral·lel, these days the beats come from an eclectic and varied program of international and local acts. Salif Keïta, Kitty, Daisy and Lewis, and Sharon Jones and the Dap-Kings are just a few that have taken the stage in the past, though the offerings vary wildly from jazz and swing to flamenco and hard rock. After the last encore, Sala Apolo converts to a hugely popular dance club—the Nasty Monday and Crappy Tuesday nights are particularly sinful ways to start the week. ⊠ *Nou de la Rambla 113, Poble Sec* ☎ *93/441–4001* ⊕ *www.sala-apolo.com* Ⓜ *Paral.lel.*

PERFORMING ARTS

Countless concerts and performances can be found in Barcelona any night of the week. Consult local websites like TimeOut (⊕ *timeout. cat*), Guia del Ocio (⊕ *www.guiadelocio.com*), and Barcelona Cultura, (⊕ *lameva.barcelona.cat/barcelonacultura*) for a complete list, or keep your eyes peeled for flyers and posters in shops, bars, and cafés for the latest happenings.

ART GALLERIES

⇨ *For art-gallery shopping, see Chapter 7.*

Fodor's Choice ★ **CaixaForum.** The building itself, a restored textile factory, is well worth exploring (and is directly across from the Mies van der Rohe Pavillion on Montjuïc at the bottom of the steps up to the Palau Nacional). Temporary exhibits show the work of major artists from around the world, while the auditorium (and sometimes the outdoor area) hosts a regular program of world-music concerts, theater, and performance art. There are also regular workshops and special events for families. ⊠ *Av. Francesc Ferrer i Guàrdia 6–8, Montjuïc* ☎ *93/476–8600* ⊕ *obrasocial-lacaixa.org* Ⓜ *Espanya.*

Centre Cultural Metropolità Tecla Sala. Some of the most avant-garde exhibits and installations that come through Barcelona find their way to this cultural powerhouse, a 15-minute metro ride away in the suburb of Hospitalet de Llobregat. (Note that the Josep Tarradellas address is not the in-town Barcelona street that runs between Estació de Sants and Plaça Francesc Macià.) ✉ *Av. Josep Tarradellas 44, Hospitalet* ☎ *93/403–2620* ⊕ *www.teclasala.net* Ⓜ *La Torrasa.*

Col·legi Oficial d'Arquitectes de Catalunya. The architectural temporary exhibitions (see the website for details of the program) on the ground floor of the School of Architecture focus on urbanism and notable architects. The design and architecture bookshop in the basement is reason alone to visit. The stick figure frieze on the exterior of the building was designed by Picasso during his exile, and executed by the Norwegian artist Carl Nesjar in 1955. ✉ *Pl. Nova 5, Barri Gòtic* ☎ *93/301–5000* ⊕ *www.arquitectes.cat* Ⓜ *Liceu, Catalunya.*

Fundació Antoni Tàpies. This foundation created in 1984 by Catalonia's then-most important living artist continues to promote the work of important Catalan artists and writers, particularly that of the late Antoni Tàpies, whose passion for art and literature still echos in the halls of this enchanting Modernist building by esteemed architect Domènech i Montaner. It hosts thought-provoking temporary exhibitions, a comprehensive lecture series, and film screenings, and houses an excellent library specializing in contemporary art. ✉ *Aragó 255, Eixample* ☎ *93/487–0315* ⊕ *www.fundaciotapies.org* Ⓜ *Passeig de Gràcia.*

Fundació Miró. Occasionally used for outdoor concerts in the summer months, Joan Miró's sculpture garden at his foundation on Montjuïc hill is a surrealistic and enchanting place, and the permanent collection contains some of his most stunning paintings. What makes this foundation truly stand out though are the ambitious temporary exhibitions, often organized together with international museums, that can range from a showcase of leading mural artists to a masterpiece in the evolution of British art post–World War II. ✉ *Parc de Montjuïc, Montjuïc* ☎ *93/443–9470* ⊕ *www.fmirobcn.org.*

Palau de la Virreina. This beautiful edifice right on the bustling Rambla is an important Barcelona art hub, resource, and outpost of the Institut de Cultura, with photography on display at the Espai Xavier Miserachsm, temporary exhibits on the patio, and cultural events held regularly in the space. ✉ *La Rambla 99, La Rambla* ☎ *93/316–1000* ⊕ *ajuntament. barcelona.cat/lavirreina/en* Ⓜ *Catalunya, Liceu.*

CONCERTS

For details on concerts throughout the year, check city hall's culture website (⊕ *barcelonacultura.bcn.cat*), buy the handy *Guia del Ocio* (published every Thursday), pick up a free copy of *Time Out Barcelona*, or stop by any of the tourist information offices scattered throughout town. Listings are also found online at ⊕ *www.ticketmaster.es*, where you can buy *entradas* often more cheaply than at the box office.

Barts (Arts on Stage). This state-of-the-art theater right in the middle on the Avenida Paral·lel—remodeled from the old Artèria Music Hall—has wildly diverse programming, with everything from performance art to the latest indie bands, to musicals, magic shows, and cutting-edge theater. ⊠ *Paral.lel 62, Poble Sec* ☎ *93/324–8492* ⊕ *www.barts.cat* Ⓜ *Paral.lel.*

Fabra i Coats–Fàbrica de Creació. This self-proclaimed artist social club— remodeled from an old textile factory on the outer limits of the Poblenou district— is a great place for emerging young visual artists to find their footing. Part of the complex accommodates work spaces for resident artists and creatives; live performances and festivals are hosted here as well. ⊠ *Sant Adrià 20, Sant Andreu* ☎ *93/256–6150* ⊕ *fabraicoats. bcn.cat* Ⓜ *Sant Andreu.*

L'Auditori de Barcelona. Functional, sleek, and minimalist, the Rafael Moneo–designed Auditori has a full calendar of classical music performances—with regular forays into jazz, flamenco, and pop—near Plaça de les Glòries. Orchestras that perform here include the Orquestra Simfònica de Barcelona i Nacional de Catalunya (OBC) and the Orquestra Nacional de Cambra de Andorra. The excellent Museu de la Música is situated on the first floor. ⊠ *Lepant 150, Eixample* ☎ *93/247–9300* ⊕ *www.auditori.cat* Ⓜ *Marina, Monumental, Glòries.*

Fodor'sChoice **Palau de la Música Catalana.** Barcelona's most spectacular concert hall is
★ a Moderniste masterpiece, largely regarded as Domènech i Montaner's best work, just off the bustling Vía Laietana. Performances run year-round. While the focus is generally on classical (the Palau de la Música Catalana is the historic home of the Orfeó Català, or Catalan Choir), major music festivals—such as Barcelona's Jazz Festival and Sónar— also take place on Palau's magnificently ornate stage. An expansion of the original building by local architect Oscar Tusquets accommodates the Petit Palau, a smaller venue for recitals and children's shows. Tickets for most classical and family concerts can be bought at the box office, where you can also book a guided tour of the building. ⊠ *Carrer Palau de la Musica 4–6, Urquinaona* ☎ *93/295–7200, 902/442882 box office* ⊕ *www.palaumusica.cat* 🎫 *Guided tours €18* Ⓜ *Urquinaona.*

Palau Sant Jordi. Arata Isozaki's immense domed venue, built for the 1992 Olympic Games, has hosted superstar performers such as Bruce Springsteen and Beyoncé. Also presented are Disney specials, Cirque de Soleil, occasional operas, and other musical events. ⊠ *Palau Sant Jordi, Passeig Olímpic 5–7, Montjuïc* ☎ *93/426–2089* ⊕ *www.palausantjordi. cat/en* Ⓜ *Espanya.*

DANCE

Barcelona's dance scene has become more and more about flamenco, as this Andalusian art form has gained popularity in Catalonia over the last decade. Ballet troupes, both local and from abroad, perform at the Liceu Opera House regularly, while contemporary dance troupes such as those of Cesc Gelabert and Nacho Duato are often performing in a variety of theaters around town. Mercat de les Flors is the city's main dance center. Most venues that host dance primarily feature theater productions.

El Mercat de les Flors. An old flower market converted into a modern performance space, theater, and dance school, the Mercat de Les Flors forms part of the Institut de Teatre and is set on lovely, expansive grounds at the foot of verdant Montjuïc. Modern dance is the mercat's raison d'être, and it remains one of the few theaters in Spain that is exclusively dedicated to contemporary dance. The on-site café has a terrace out on the square, ideal for pre- or postperformance drinks. ✉ *Lleida 59, Poble Sec* ☎ *93/426–1875* ⊕ *www.mercatflors.org* Ⓜ *Poble Sec, Espanya.*

FLAMENCO

Barcelona's flamenco scene is surprisingly vibrant for a culture so far removed from Andalusia. Los Tarantos, in Plaça Reial, regularly stages authentic flamenco performances.

El Tablao de Carmen. Large tour groups come to this venerable flamenco dinner-theater venue in the Poble Espanyol named after, and dedicated to, the legendary dancer Carmen Amaya. Die-hard flamenco aficionados might dismiss the ensembles that perform here as a tad touristy, but the dancers, singers, and guitarists are pros. Visitors can enjoy one of the two nightly performances over a drink or over their choice of a full-course, prix-fixe meal. Reservations are recommended. Dinner shows are held daily at 6 pm and 8:30 pm. ✉ *Poble Espanyol, Av. Francesc Ferrer i Guàrdia 13, Montjuïc* ☎ *93/325–6895* ⊕ *www.tablaodecarmen. com* Ⓜ *Espanya.*

Los Tarantos. This small basement boîte spotlights some of Andalusia's best flamenco in 30-minute shows of dance, percussion, and song. At only €15 per ticket, these shows are a good intro to the art and feel much less touristy than most standard flamenco fare. Shows are daily at 7:30, 8:30, and 9:30 pm, with an additional 10:30 pm show June–September. ✉ *Pl. Reial 17, Barri Gòtic* ☎ *93/319–1789* ⊕ *www.masimas. com/en/tarantos* Ⓜ *Liceu.*

Palacio del Flamenco. This Eixample music hall showcases some of the city's best flamenco. Prices start at €45 for a drink and a show, up to €110. (Save money by purchasing tickets online in advance.) Late shows are slightly cheaper. ✉ *Balmes 139, Eixample* ☎ *93/218–7237* ⊕ *www. palaciodelflamenco.com* Ⓜ *Provença, Diagonal.*

FILM

Although most foreign films here are dubbed, Barcelona has an assortment of original-language cinemas; look for listings marked "VOS" (*versión original subtitulada*). Yelmo Cineplex Icària near the Vila Olímpica is the main movie mill, showing more than a dozen films at any given time, all in VOS and most in 3-D. Films in VOS are also shown at several other theaters.

Balmes Multicines. Barcelona's cine-aficionados praise this relatively new 12-screen complex which boasts one of the best sound systems in the city, and very comfortable seating designed to ensure no one's view is impeded. Screenings, which lean toward the latest Hollywood releases, are all in VOS. ⊠ *Balmes 422–424, Sarrià* ☎ *93/215–9570* ⊕ *www.grupbalana.com* Ⓜ *El Putxet.*

Cines Verdi. Gràcia's movie center, with bars and restaurants in the immediate vicinity, unfailingly screens recent releases (with a preference for serious-minded cinema) in their original-language versions. Sister cinema Verdi Park is just around the corner, and also shows films in VOS (original version with Spanish subs). ⊠ *Verdi 32, Gràcia* ☎ *93/238–7990* ⊕ *www.cines-verdi.com/barcelona* Ⓜ *Gràcia, Fontana.*

Filmoteca de Catalunya. The Filmoteca de Catalunya occupies a brutalist-style edifice designed by Josep Lluís Mateo. With plush seats, wide screens, and a state-of-the-art sound system, it's a film buff's paradise. Most movies are screened in VOS (though the original language is not always English) and are programmed in "cycles." The program is always serious and approached academically, whether the focus is musicals, film noir, or documentaries. The colorful café is a great spot for a vermut or some tapas, and has tables out on the square. ⊠ *Pl. de Salvador Seguí 1, El Raval* ☎ *93/567–1070* ⊕ *www.filmoteca.cat* Ⓜ *Paral.lel.*

Icaria Yelmo. On the lower level of a small neighborhood shopping mall, the Icaria Yelmo offers a solid mix of blockbusters, 3-D specials, and the latest releases in in their original language, though sometimes weeks after their general premieres. ⊠ *Salvador Espriu 61, Port Olímpic* ☎ *902/220922* ⊕ *www.yelmocines.es* Ⓜ *Ciutadella–Vila Olímpica.*

Renoir Floridablanca. A five-minute walk from the Plaça de la Universitat, this cinema is a good choice for current English-language features, primarily of the indie ilk. ⊠ *Floridablanca 135, El Raval* ☎ *93/228–9393* ⊕ *www.cinesrenoir.com* Ⓜ *Universitat, Sant Antoni.*

OPERA

Fodor'sChoice
★

Gran Teatre del Liceu. Barcelona's famous opera house on La Rambla—in all its gilt, stained-glass, and red-plush glory—runs a full season September–June, combining the Liceu's own chorus and orchestra with top-tier, invited soloists. In addition, touring dance companies—ballet, flamenco, and modern dance—appear here. The downstairs foyer often holds early-evening recitals, while the Petit Liceu program sees child-friendly opera adaptations (though not always held in the Liceu itself). The Espai Liceu in the opera house annex includes an excellent tapas bar/café and a gift shop for music-related DVDs, CDs, books, instruments, and knickknacks. A tiny 50-seat theater projecting fragments of operas and a video of the history of the Liceu can be viewed as part of a tour of the building (tickets available online or in the Espai Liceu). Seats for performances can be expensive and hard to get; reserve well in advance. ⊠ *La Rambla 51–59, La Rambla* ☎ *93/485–9900* ⊕ *www. liceubarcelona.cat* Ⓜ *Liceu.*

THEATER

Most plays here are performed in Catalan, though some—especially the more lighthearted shows—are performed in Spanish. Barcelona is well known for avant-garde theater and for troupes that specialize in mime, large-scale performance art, and special effects (La Fura dels Baus, Els Joglars, and Els Comediants are among the most famous). Musicals are also popular, with most big-name productions like *Mama Mía* and *The Sound of Music* regularly making it over from Madrid.

El Molino. For most of the 20th century, this venue was the most legendary of all the cabaret theaters on Avinguda Paral·lel. Modeled after Paris's Moulin Rouge, it closed in the late 1990s as the building was becoming dangerously run-down. After an ambitious refurbishment in 2010, El Molino reopened as one of the most stunning state-of-the-art cabaret theaters in Europe. The building now has five—instead of the original two—stories, with a bar and terrace on the third; the interior has been decked out with complex lighting systems that adapt to every change on the small stage. What has remained the same, however, is its essence—a contemporary version of burlesque, but bump-and-grind all the same. You can purchase tickets online, before performances (which start at 6:30 pm and 9:30 pm) or at the box office, Thursday–Saturday 5 pm–10 pm. ⊠ *Vilà i Vilà 99, Poble Sec* ☎ *93/205–5111* ⊕ *www. elmolinobcn.com* Ⓜ *Paral.lel.*

FAMILY **La Puntual** (*Putxinel·lis de Barcelona*). As one of the city's pioneering puppet (in Catalan, *putxinel·li*) theaters, this beloved venue features entertaining marionette, puppet, and shadow puppet performances. Private events for schools or birthday parties can be organized in Spanish, Catalan, and English. Weekend matinee performances are major kid magnets and tend to sell out fast, so arrive early or reserve a ticket in advance online. ⊠ *Allada Vermell 15, Born-Ribera* ☎ *639/305353* ⊕ *www.lapuntual.info* Ⓜ *Jaume I.*

Sala Beckett. Tucked away in upper Gràcia, Sala Beckett—and the Obrador Internacional de Dramatúrgia (International Drama Workshop)—provides two intimate stages for some of Barcelona's most interesting, experimental, and thoughtful theater events. A second and larger Sala Beckett is situated in Poblenou (C/Batusta 15). ⊠ *Alegre de Dalt 55, bis, Gràcia* ☎ *93/284–5312* ⊕ *www.salabeckett.cat* Ⓜ *Joanic.*

Teatre Apolo. This historic player in Barcelona's theater life stages musicals, comedies, and dramas. ⊠ *Av. del Paral.lel 59, El Raval* ☎ *93/299–7081* ⊕ *www.teatreapolo.com* Ⓜ *Paral.lel.*

Teatre Nacional de Catalunya. Near Glòries, the area with the highest concentration of development in recent years at the eastern end of the Diagonal, this grandiose glass-enclosed classical temple was designed by Ricardo Bofill, architect of Barcelona's airport. Programs cover everything from Shakespeare to avant-garde theater. Most productions, as the name suggests, are in Catalan but beautiful to witness all the same. ⊠ *Pl. de les Arts 1, Poblenou* ☎ *93/306–5700* ⊕ *www.tnc.cat* Ⓜ *Glóries, Monumental.*

Teatre Poliorama. Originally built as a cinema in the late 1890s, Teatre Polirama has also been immortalized in George Orwell's *Homage to Catalonia*, where the celebrated author describes it as the site of a shoot-out between opposing sides during the Spanish Civil War. In sharp contrast to its sinister past most of the productions offered focus on lighthearted comedy and musical plays in Spanish or Catalan, as well as flamenco and opera. ⊠ *Rambla del Estudis 115, La Rambla* ☎ *93/317–7599* ⊕ *www.teatrepoliorama.com* Ⓜ *Catalunya.*

Teatre Tívoli. One of the city's most beloved traditional theater and dance venues, the Tívoli has staged timeless classics and has hosted everyone from the Ballet Nacional de Cuba to flamenco and teeny-bopper treats. ⊠ *Casp 8, Eixample* ☎ *93/215–9570* ⊕ *www.grupbalana.com* Ⓜ *Catalunya.*

Teatre Victòria. This historic theater in the heart of Barcelona's show district features dramas, musicals, and dance productions, from ballet to Bollywood. ⊠ *Av. Paral.lel 67–69, Poble Sec* ☎ *93/324–9742* ⊕ *www.teatrevictoria.com* Ⓜ *Paral.lel.*

6

SPORTS AND
THE OUTDOORS

BARCELONA'S BEST BEACHES

It's an unusual combination in Europe: a major metropolis fully integrated with the sea. Barcelona's miles of beaches allow for its yin and yang of urban energy and laid-back beach vibe. When you're ready for a slower pace, seek out a sandy refuge.

Over the last decade, Barcelona's *platjas* (beaches) have been improved, now stretching some 4 km (2½ miles) from Barceloneta's Platja de Sant Sebastià at the southwestern end, northward via the Platjas de Sant Miquel, Barceloneta, Passeig Marítim, Port Olímpic, Nova Icària, Bogatell, Mar Bella (the last bit of which is a nudist enclave), and La Nova Mar Bella to Llevant. The Barceloneta beach is the most popular stretch, easily accessible by several bus lines, notably the No. 64, and by the L4 metro at Barceloneta or Ciutadella–Vila Olímpica. The best surfing is at the northeastern end of the Barceloneta beach, while the boardwalk offers miles of runway for walkers, cyclers, and joggers. Topless bathing is common on all beaches in and around Barcelona.

PLATJA DE LA BARCELONETA

Just to the left at the end of Passeig Joan de Borbó, this is the easiest beach to get to, hence the most crowded and the most fun from a people-watching standpoint. Along with swimming, there are windsurfing and kitesurfing rentals to be found just up behind the beach at the edge of La Barceloneta. Rebecca Horn's sculpture *L'Estel Ferit*, a rusting stack of cubes, expresses nostalgia for the beach-shack restaurants that lined the beach here until 1992. Surfers trying to catch a wave wait just off the breakwater in front of the excellent beachfront restaurant Agua.

PLATJA DE LA MAR BELLA

Closest to the Poblenou metro stop near the eastern end of the beaches, this is a thriving gay enclave and the unofficial nudist beach of Barcelona (but suited bathers are welcome, too). The water-sports center Base Nàutica de la Mar Bella rents equipment for sailing, surfing, and windsurfing. Outfitted with showers, safe drinking fountains, and a children's play area, La Mar Bella also has lifeguards who warn against swimming near the breakwater. The excellent Pescadors restaurant is just inland on Plaça Prim.

PLATJA DE LA NOVA ICÀRIA

One of Barcelona's most popular beaches, this strand is just east of Port Olímpic, with the full range of entertainment, restaurant, and refreshment venues close at hand. (Xiringuito Escribà, overlooking neighboring Bogatell beach, is one of the most popular restaurants on this stretch.) The beach is directly across from the area developed as the residential Vila Olímpica for the 1992 Games, an interesting housing project that has now become a popular residential neighborhood.

PLATJA DE SANT SEBASTIÀ

The landmark of Barceloneta's southwesternmost beach (at the end of Passeig Joan de Borbó) now is the ultramodern W Barcelona Hotel, but Sant Sebastià is in fact the oldest of the

city beaches, where 19th-century barcelonins cavorted in bloomers and bathing costumes. On the west end is the Club Natació de Barcelona, and there is a semiprivate feel that the beaches farther east seem to lack.

PLATJA DE GAVÀ-CASTELLDEFELS

South of Barcelona (take the 45-minute L94 bus from the Estació de SantsPlaça de Catalunya) is Gavà Mar, a popular outing for Barcelona families and beach partiers. Gavà Mar extends 4 km (2½ miles) south to join the beach at Castelldefels; returning to Barcelona from Castelldefels allows for a hike down the beach to seaside shacks and restaurants serving calçots and paella.

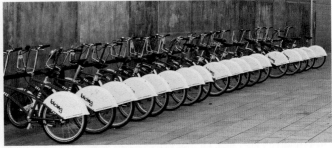

Updated by
Elizabeth
Prosser

"You've got to understand about us and Barça," said the barmaid at the little Catalan pub on the Costa Brava. "For all those years under Franco, Camp Nou (the Futbol Club Barcelona's 99,000-seat stadium) was the only place we could gather in numbers and shout out loud in our own language."

The FBC motto is "*Més que un club*" ("More than a club"); to its legion of fans, Barça is the symbol of their perennial itch for independence, the vessel for their pride in their decidedly un-Spanish Catalan identity. The way Barça plays the game embodies their sense of solidarity, their sense of style. Twice a year in La Liga (Spanish League) competition, they take on archrival Real Madrid; the matches—*los clasicos*—are showdowns no less political than they are athletic. When Barça loses (which isn't often these days), it's a national day of mourning.

In 2009 Barça claimed a historic Triple Crown, winning La Liga, the Spanish King's Cup, and the European Champions League. Even the British press wrote that this might have been the greatest soccer team of all time. Since then Barça has gone on to consolidate that claim, winning the 2011 European FIFA Club World Cup and the UEFA Super Cup with even more grace and authority than in 2009. In 2012–13, they topped La Liga again, though dropping away in the King's Cup and Champions League in the semifinals—only to come back stronger than ever, with an astonishing second Triple Crown in 2014–15.

Barcelona also boasts another first-division team, RCD (Reial Club Deportiu) Espanyol. Home for Espanyol is the 40,000-seat Estadi Cornellà-Prat, in the city's western suburb; tickets are easier to come by than for Barça matches, but the local fans are no less loyal.

If fútbol is not your spectator sport, Barcelona's Conde de Godó tournament brings the world's best tennis players here every April, while the Spanish Grand Prix at Mont Meló draws the top Formula One racing teams. Home court for the FC Barcelona basketball club, which has sent the likes of Pau and Marc Gasol to the NBA, is the Palau Blaugrana pavilion, next door to Camp Nou. As for keeping active yourself, there is diving, windsurfing, surfing, sailing, and water sports in Barceloneta, and all along the coast north and south of the city. Tennis and squash courts are available in various public and semiprivate clubs around town, and there are now nearly two dozen golf courses less than an hour away. Bicycle lanes run the length of Diagonal, and there are bike-rental agencies all over town.

BEACHES

See the illustrated feature for details on Barcelona's beaches.

BICYCLES

Exploring Barcelona on wheels, whether by bike or on skates, is a good way to see the city and to save on transport. Bicycle lanes run along most major arteries.

Barcelona By Bike. Gather at the meeting point next to the main entrance of the Barcelona Casino for a three-hour guided bike tour (€24 with a complimentary drink en route) of the Old City, Gaudí architecture, and the port. ⊠ *Calle Marina s/n, Port Olímpic* ☎ *671/307325* ⊕ *www.barcelonabybike.com* Ⓜ *Ciutadella/Vila Olímpica.*

Bike Tours Barcelona. This company offers a three-hour bike tour (in English) for €23, with a drink included. Just look for the guide with a bike and a blue flag at the northeast corner of the Casa de la Ciutat in Plaça Sant Jaume, outside the Tourist Information Office. Tours depart at 11 am daily; there is an additional tour at 4:30 pm Friday–Monday, April 1–September 15. The company will also organize private guided tours through the Barri Gòtic, parks, the Port Olímpic and Barceloneta, the Ruta Moderniste, and other itineraries on request. Touring on your own? The company also rents bikes by the hour or the day, at its shop in Carrer Esparteria. ⊠ *Carrer Esparteria 3, Barri Gòtic* ☎ *932/682105* ⊕ *www.biketoursbarcelona.com* Ⓜ *Jaume I.*

Classic Bikes. Just off pivotal Plaça de Catalunya, bicycles are available for rent here daily 9:30–8. The 24-hour rate is €15; take a bike in the morning and return it by closing time for €12; ride for two hours for €6, or four hours for €10. ⊠ *Calle Tallers 45, El Raval* ☎ *933/171970* ⊕ *www.barcelonarentbikes.com* Ⓜ *Catalunya.*

Fat Tire Bike Tours. Four-hour guided city tours with this company start in Plaça Sant Jaume daily at 11 am and 4 pm (from mid-October to mid-April, morning tours only), covering—with a lunch break—the usual suspects: the Barri Gòtic, Sagrada Familia, Ciutadella Park, the port, and Barceloneta. Reservations can be made on the website. ⊠ *Calle Marlet 4, Barri Gòtic* ☎ *933/429275* ⊕ *www.fattirebiketours.com/barcelona* ⊠ *€26* Ⓜ *Jaume I.*

Steel Donkey Bike Tours. Groups up to eight people can take four-hour "alternative" bike tours with this outfit on Tuesday, Friday, and Saturday mornings, meeting at the shop on Calle Ample at 10 am. The tours (€35, including bike and helmet rentals) are quirky, offering sights and experiences a bit off the beaten path from the standard itineraries. Call for reservations. ⊠ *Carrer de Cervantes 5, Barri Gòtic* ☎ *657/286854* ⊕ *www.steeldonkeybiketours.com* Ⓜ *Jaume I.*

GOLF

Weekday golf outings to one of the 22 golf courses within an hour of Barcelona are a good way to exercise and see the Catalonian countryside. Midweek greens fees range from €50 to €85; prices double on weekends. Midweek availability is excellent except during Easter vacation and August. Call ahead to confirm a tee time, and remember to bring proof of your USGA handicap or membership in a golf club or you may have trouble playing.

TOP 5 ACTIVITIES

■ Watching European Champion Futbol Club Barcelona play in Camp Nou

■ Playing the PGA Catalunya golf course in the Empordà

■ Scuba diving in the Isles Medes off the Costa Brava

■ Jogging the Carretera de les Aigües over Barcelona

■ Competing virtually in the event of your choice, at the "Open Camp Sportainment" theme park in the Olympic Stadium on Montjuic

Club de Golf de Sant Cugat. This hilly 18-hole course, in the upscale Barcelona satellite of Sant Cugat, is one of the oldest—and most challenging—in the area, and the nearest to the city. Laid out by renowned course architect Harry S. Holt, the fairways are relatively short for the most part, but bunkers and water hazards make for tricky play. Former world No. 1 Seve Ballesteros made his professional debut here in 1974. ⊠ *Calle Villa 79, Sant Cugat del Vallès* 🕾 *936/743908* ⊕ *www.golfsantcugat.cat* 🖅 *Oct.–May, €90 weekdays, €125 weekends; June, July, and Sept., €70 weekdays, €100 weekends; Aug. €45 every day* ⅄ *18 holes, 5050 yards, par 69* ☞ *Facilities: driving range, putting green, pitching area, golf carts, pull carts, rental clubs, pro shop, restaurant, bar.*

Club de Golf Terramar. This breezy seaside course has fine views of the Mediterranean from the early and final holes (the toughest to play), and lots of water hazards and woods to challenge your game. Essentially flat, it's an easy course to walk; book online 48 hours in advance for a course-savvy caddy to walk it with you. ⊠ *Ctra. del Golf s/n, Sitges* 🕾 *938/940580* ⊕ *www.golfterramar.com* 🖅 *Weekdays €169, weekends €95* ⅄ *18 holes, 5615 yards, par 71* ☞ *Facilities: driving range, putting green, pitching area, golf carts, pull carts, rental clubs, pro shop, lessons, restaurant, bar.*

Club de Golf Vallromanes. Thirty km (19 miles) north of Barcelona, between Masnou and Granollers, this challenging course designed by H. W. Hawtree in 1971 requires a handicap of 28 or less to play. Players have been known to weep over the fiendish water hazards, woods, and bunkers guarding the short par-3 12th hole. The club is closed Tuesday. ⊠ *Passeig de la Torre Tavernera s/n, Vallromanes* 🕾 *935/729064* ⊕ *www.clubdegolfvallromanes.com* 🖅 *Weekdays €85, weekends €105* ⅄ *18 holes, 6044 yards, par 72* ☞ *Facilities: driving range, putting green, pitching area, golf carts, pull carts, pro shop, golf academy, swimming pool, tennis, restaurant, bar.*

Real Club de Golf El Prat. Located roughly between the towns of Terrassa and Sabadell, about 30 km (19 miles) north of Barcelona, Real Club de Golf El Prat is a lovely but extremely difficult course—actually five 9-hole courses that can be combined in different ways—designed by Greg Norman. Long fairways (some 300 yards or more) favor the power hitters, but a range of highly technical holes, through pine forests, call for accuracy, strategy, and a command of all the clubs in your bag. ⊠ *Plans de Bonvilar 17, Terrassa* ☎ *937/281000* ⊕ *www.realclubdegolfelprat.com* ⧗ *July 15–Aug. 31, €70; otherwise Mon. €70, Tues. €100, Wed.–Fri. €114, weekends before 11:35 am €228, after 11:35 am €114* ⸸ *45 holes (up to 9 different courses), 6672 yards, par 72* ☞ *Facilities: driving range, putting green, pitching area, golf carts, pull carts, rental clubs, pro shop, lessons, restaurant, bar.*

GYMS AND SPAS

DiR. The DiR network has more than a dozen branches all over Barcelona. The minimum one-week membership costs €45 and includes fitness classes and the use of the sauna, steam room, swimming pool, and (at some branches) paddle tennis courts. Day passes cost €20 at the flagship facility just above Diagonal near Turo Park, where the palm-shaded lawns bracketing the Olympic-length indoor-outdoor pool are coveted summer chill-out spaces. ■TIP➔ Use prices as a guide. They are subject to change. ⊠ *DiR Diagonal, Carrer Ganduxer 25–27, Sant Gervasi* ☎ *932/022202* ⊕ *www.dir.cat* Ⓜ *La Bonanova (FCG).*

Seven DiR. Off Passeig de Gràcia near the hotel Condes de Barcelona, this center-city fitness club has a gym, sauna, indoor and outdoor pools (outdoors in summer only), and squash and paddle tennis courts. Nonmembers pay €15 from 7:15 am to 1 pm, €20 for a full-day pass. ■TIP➔ Use prices as a guide. They are subject to change. ⊠ *Passatge Domingo 7, Eixample* ☎ *932/152755* ⊕ *www.dir.cat* Ⓜ *Passeig de Gràcia, Provença (FGC).*

HIKING

The Collserola hills behind the city offer well-marked trails, fresh air, and lovely views. Take the San Cugat, Sabadell, or Terrassa FFCC train from Plaça de Catalunya and get off at Baixador de Vallvidrera; the information center, 10 minutes uphill next to Vil·la Joana (now the Jacint Verdaguer Museum), has maps of this mountain woodland just 20 minutes from downtown. The walk back into town can take two to five hours depending on your speed and the trails you choose. For longer treks, try the 15-km (9-mile) Sant Cugat–to–Barcelona hike, or take the train south to Sitges and make the three-day pilgrimage walk to the Monastery of Montserrat.

Centre Excursionista de Catalunya. The center has information on hiking throughout Catalunya and the Pyrenees, gives mountaineering and technical climbing courses, organizes excursions, and provides guides for groups. ⊠ *Carrer del Paradis 10, Barri Gòtic* ☎ *933/152311* ⊕ *www. cec.cat* Ⓜ *Jaume I.*

SAILING

On any day of the week in Barcelona you can see midday regattas taking place off the Barceloneta beaches or beyond the *rompeolas* (breakwater) on the far side of the port. Believe it or not, Olympic-level sailors are being trained for competition just a stone's throw (or two) from La Rambla.

Reial Club Marítim de Barcelona. Barcelona's most exclusive and prestigious yacht club can advise visitors on maritime matters, from where to charter yachts and sailboats to how to sign up for sailing programs. ⊠ *Moll d'Espanya s/n, Port Vell* ☎ *932/214859* ⊕ *www.maritimbarcelona.org* Ⓜ *L3 Drassanes.*

SCUBA DIVING

The Costa Brava's Illes Medes nature preserve offers some of the Mediterranean's finest diving adventures. Seven tiny islands off the coastal town of L'Estartit are home to some 1,400 species of flora and fauna in an underwater wonderland of tunnels and caves. Other diving sites include the Illes Formigues off the coast of Palamós, Els Ullastres off Llafranc, and the Balfegó tuna pens off l'Ametlla de Mar, south of Tarragona.

Aquàtica–Centro de Buceo. Aquàtica–Centro de Buceo teaches diving, rents equipment, and organizes outings to the Illes Medes. With top safety-code requirements and certified instructors and biologists directing the programs in English, French, Catalan, or Spanish, this is one of Estartit's best diving opportunities. Aquàtica operates year-round, but winter excursions are suitable only for PADI-certified experienced divers. ⊠ *Paratge Camp de l'Arbre s/n, L'Estartit* ☎ *972/750656, 609/311133* ⊕ *www.aquatica-sub.com/eng/home.*

Tuna Tours. The fisheries company Grup Balfegó catches young Atlantic bluefin tuna and raises them for sale 4 km (2½ miles) offshore from the port of l'Ametlla de Mar in Tarragona. From June through September, they offer daily snorkeling excursions by luxury catamaran from the port out to the pens where visitors can feed these 200-kilogram-plus creatures. The cost is €47 per person in summer high season, or €39 in September, with a meal of tuna sashimi. ⊠ *Port l'Ametlla de Mar* ☎ *977/047707* ⊕ *www.tuna-tour.com* Ⓜ *Lametla de Mar.*

SOCCER

Futbol Club Barcelona. Founded in 1899, FC Barcelona won its third European Championship in 2009, the Liga championship and its 27th Copa del Rey (King's Cup)—Spain's first-ever *triplete*—and again in 2015. Even more impressive was their razzle-dazzle style of soccer, rarely seen in the age of cynical defensive lockdowns and muscular British-style play. Barça, as the club is known, is Real Madrid's nemesis (and vice versa) and a sociological and historical phenomenon of deep significance in Catalonia. Ticket windows at Access 14 to the stadium are open Monday–Saturday and match-day Sunday 10–2 and 5–8; you can also buy tickets at Servicaixa ATMs at Caixa de Catalunya banks, through ticket agencies, at kiosks in the Plaça de Catalunya and on the Ramblas, or online. ⊠ *Camp Nou, Aristides Maillol 12, Les Corts* ☎ *934/963600, 902/189900* ⊕ *www.fcbarcelona.com* Ⓜ *Collblanc, Palau Reial.*

RCD Espanyol. Things improved for this soccer team when the club moved from a tiny stadium to a new state-of-the-art 40,500-seat home base in Cornellà. Espanyol still struggles to survive in the League First Division but has loyal fans. Purchase tickets at Servicaixa machines or online. Take the Metro Line 5 from Plaça Catalunya to Cornellà Centre or the FCG L8 suburban train from Plaça Espanya to Cornellà-Riera; the "Power8 Stadium" is a short walk from either. ⊠ *Estadi Cornellà-El Prat, Av. Baix Llobregat 100, Cornellà de Llobregat* ☎ *932/927700* ⊕ *www.rcdespanyol.com* Ⓜ *L5 Cornellà Centre; Cornellà-Riera (FGC).*

Spain Ticket Bureau. This company can score seats for Barça home games, as well as other sporting events, concerts, and musicals, in Barcelona and elsewhere in Spain. Booking ahead online is a good idea, especially for headliner events, but expect to pay a healthy premium. ⊠ *Rambla 54, Eixample* ☎ *934/618170 ticket purchases and pickups, 934/882266* ⊕ *www.spainticketbureau.com* Ⓜ *Liceu.*

SWIMMING

Club Natació Barcelona. Also known as Complex Esportiu Municipal Banys Sant Sebastià, this club in Barceloneta, just opposite the cable car terminal, has an indoor pool that overlooks the beach. It's open daily 7 am to 11 pm. A one-day pass for the use of the pool, gym, and other facilities costs €12.53. ⊠ *Passeig Joan de Borbó 93, Barceloneta* ☎ *932/214600* ⊕ *www.cnb.es* Ⓜ *L4 Barceloneta.*

Piscines Municipals Bernat Picornell. The daily fee at this swimming center with indoor and outdoor pools includes use of a sauna, gymnasium, and fitness equipment. The facility is open daily 7 am–midnight; pool hours vary with the season. ⊠ *Avda. del Estadi 30–38, Montjuïc* ☎ *934/234041* ⊕ *www.picornell.cat* Ⓜ *Plaça Espanya.*

TENNIS AND SQUASH

Centre Municipal de Tennis Vall d'Hebron. The Olympic tennis facilities here are open Monday–Friday 8 am–11 pm (Saturday 8–7 and Sunday 8–6). The Centre also boasts a fitness center and an outdoor pool. ⊠ *Passeig Vall d'Hebron 196, Vall d'Hebron* ☎ *934/276500* ⊕ *www. tennisvallhebron.cat* 🎾 *Clay courts €18/hr, hard courts €17/hr (lights €5)* Ⓜ *L3 Montbau.*

Complejo Deportivo Can Caralleu (*Can Caralleu Sports Complex*). Can Caralleu has hard surface tennis courts, a soccer pitch and running track, two pools, a fitness center, and a climbing wall. A one-day membership (€13.42) provides unlimited court time (as available), and the use of all other facilities. ✉ *Carrer dels Esports 2–8, Pedralbes* ☎ *932/037874* ⊕ *www.cemcancaralleu.cat* Ⓜ *Reina Elisenda (FGC).*

Trofeo Godó – Open Seat. Barcelona's main tennis tournament, held in late April, is a clay-court event long considered a French Open warm-up. For tickets to this event, consult with the Reial Club de Tenis de Barcelona or the tournament website beginning in late February. Tickets may also be obtained at ⊕ *www.servicaixa.com.* ✉ *Carrer de Bosch i Gimpera 21, Pedralbes* ☎ *902/044226* ⊕ *www.barcelonaopenbancsabadell.com* ✆ *Qualifying rounds from €7, semifinals and finals from €68.*

SHOPPING

Updated by
Malia Politzer

Characterized by originality and relative affordability, the shopping scene in Barcelona has become a jubilant fair of fashion, design, craft, and gourmet food. Different parts of town specialize in different goods, and you can explore parts of the city through shopping and browsing boutiques.

The Ciutat Vella, especially the Born-Ribera area, is rich in small-crafts shops, young designers, and an endless potpourri of artisans and merchants operating in restored medieval spaces that are often as dazzling as the wares on sale. Even the pharmacies and grocery stores of Barcelona are often sumptuous aesthetic feasts filled with charming details. Although the end of rent protection has seen many heritage establishments close, a new law will at least ensure that their unique architectural and decorative details will remain intact. Hat shop Barrets Obach and candlemakers Cereria Subirà are two old town traders who have remained charmingly unchanged over the decades.

Shopping for design objects and chic fashion in the Eixample is like buying art supplies at the Louvre: it's an Art Nouveau architecture theme park spinning off into dozens of sideshows—textiles, furnishings, curios, and knickknacks of every kind. Any specific shop or boutique will inevitably lead you past a dozen emporiums that you hadn't known were there. Original and surprising yet wearable clothing items are Barcelona's signature contribution to fashion. Rather than copying the runways, Barcelona designers are relentlessly daring and innovative, combining fine materials with masterful workmanship.

Browsing through shops in this unique metropolis feels more like museum-hopping than it does a shopping spree. Design shops like Doméstico and Jaime Beriestain delight the eye and stimulate the imagination, while the area around the Passeig del Born beckons young designers from across the globe. Passeig de Gràcia has joined the ranks of the Champs Elysées in Paris and Rome's Via Condotti as one of the great shopping avenues in the world, with the planet's fashion houses well represented, from Armani to Zara. Exploring Barcelona's antiques district along Carrer Banys Nous and Carrer de la Palla is always an adventure. The shops open daily around Santa

Maria del Mar in the Born-Ribera district range from Catalan and international design retailers to shoe and leather handbag designers, to T-shirt decorators and coffee emporiums. The megastores in Plaça de Catalunya, along Diagonal, and in L'Illa Diagonal farther west sell clothing, furniture, furs, books, music, and more. The village-like Sarrià and Gràcia are filled with intimate antique and clothing shops, with friendly boutique owners who add a personal touch.

SHOPPING PLANNER

BEST PURCHASES TO FIND IN SPAIN

Saffron: the lightest, most aromatic, and best-value buy left in all of Spain—available in any supermarket or grocery store

Rope-soled espadrilles from La Manual Alpargatera

Any items by legendary local designers Javier Mariscal or Miguel Milà

Ceramics from all over Spain at Art Escudellers

HOURS

Outside of the tourist areas, stores are generally open Monday–Saturday 9 am–2 pm, and 4:30–8 pm. Most stores are closed on Sundays except during the Christmas shopping period, and in July and August in the city center. Many stores in the Eixample, Barri Gòtic, and in the malls, such as L'Illa Diagonal, stay open through the lunch hour. Big department stores like El Corte Inglés and FNAC are open all day 9:30 am–9:30 pm. Designated pharmacies are open all night.

TAXES AND GUIDES

Food and basic necessities are taxed at the lowest rate, but most consumer goods are taxed at 21%. Non–EU citizens can request a Tax-Free Form on purchases of €90.16 and over in shops displaying the Tax-Free Shopping sticker. Refunds (either cash or credit) can be obtained at the airport. First get your forms stamped by the customs officer, then hand them to the refund counter in Terminal 1 or 2a (you can also mail them later). Remember that goods must be unused and unopened in order to get the refund. Global Blue Cheque users can also obtain a refund at the tourist office in Plaça de Catalunya, as well as the main office of Barcelona Turisme in the Eixample (Passatge de la Concepció 7–9, open 3–8), which can save you the stress of dealing with airport counters. For further information, plus tips on where to shop, check Turisme Barcelona's website (⊕ *www.barcelonashoppingline.com*).

BARRI GÒTIC

The Barri Gòtic was built on trade and cottage industries, and there are plenty of nimble fingers producing artisan goods in the old-world shops along its stone streets. Start at the cathedral and work your way outward.

ANTIQUES AND COLLECTIBLES

Antigüedades Fernández. Bric-a-brac is piled high in this workshop near the middle of this slender artery in the medieval Jewish Quarter. This master craftsman sells and restores antique furniture of all kinds. Stop by and stick your head in for the fragrance of the shellac and wood shavings and to take a look at one of the last simple carpentry and woodworking shops left in contemporary Barcelona. ⊠ *Carrer Sant Domènec del Call 3, Barri Gòtic* ☎ *93/301–0045, 617/532676* ⊕ *antiguedadesfernandez.blogspot.com.es* Ⓜ *Liceu, Jaume I.*

ART GALLERIES

Base Elements Urban Art Gallery. Robert Burt, a talented painter and restorer of found objects originally of California, founded this gallery in 2003 to provide a space where young street artists and graffiti-meisters could display their talents without risking jail time. The gallery serves a workshop and hangout for young artists, and paintings can be shipped all over the world. ⊠ *Palau 6, Barri Gòtic* ☎ *93/268–8312* ⊕ *www.baseelements.net* Ⓜ *Jaume I.*

Sala Parès. The dean of Barcelona's art galleries, this place opened in 1840 as an art-supplies shop; as a gallery, it dates to 1877 and has shown every Barcelona artist of note since then. Picasso and Miró exhibited their work here, as did Casas and Rossinyol before them. Nowadays, Catalan artists like Perico Pastor and Carlos Morago get pride of place. ⊠ *Petritxol 5, Barri Gòtic* ☎ *93/318–7020* ⊕ *www.sala-pares.com* ⊘ *Closed Mon. morning* Ⓜ *Liceu, Catalunya.*

BOOKS AND STATIONERY

Llibreria Quera. This is the bookstore to seek out if you're interested in the Pyrenees or in exploring any part of the Catalonian hinterlands. Maps, charts, and books detailing everything from Pyrenean ponds and lakes to Romanesque chapels are available in this diminutive giant of a resource. ⊠ *Petritxol 2, Barri Gòtic* ☎ *93/318–0743* ⊘ *Closed Sun. and Mon.* Ⓜ *Liceu.*

Papirvm. Exquisite hand-printed papers, marbleized blank books, and writing implements await you at this tiny, medieval-tone shop. ⊠ *Baixada de la Llibreteria 2, Barri Gòtic* ☎ *93/310–5242* ⊕ *www.papirumbcn.com* ⊘ *Closed Sun.* Ⓜ *Jaume I.*

CERAMICS AND GLASSWARE

Fodor's Choice ★ **Art Escudellers.** Ceramic pieces from all over Spain are on display at this large store across the street from the restaurant Los Caracoles; more than 140 different artisans are represented, with maps showing what part of Spain the work is from. Wine, cheese, and ham tastings are held downstairs, and you can even throw a pot yourself in the workshop. There are other branches of Art Escudellers in Carrers Montcada and Avinyó, both in old city. ⊠ *Escudellers 23–25, Barri Gòtic* ☎ *93/412–6801* ⊕ *www.artescudellers.com* Ⓜ *Liceu, Drassanes.*

Caixa de Fang. Glazed tiles, glass objects, and colorful sets of cups and saucers are on sale at this little shop just off Plaça Sant Jaume. Translatable as "Box of Mud" in Catalan, Caixa de Fang shows handmade earthenware cooking vessels from all over Spain, as well as boxwood and olive-wood kitchen utensils. ⊠ *Freneria 1, Barri Gòtic* ☏ *93/315–1704* Ⓜ *Jaume I.*

CLOTHING

Barrets Obach. This *sombrerería* (hat shop) is as much part of the Barri Gòtic's landscape as any of its medieval churches. Occupying a busy corner in El Call—the old Jewish district—curved glass windows displays the sort of hats, caps, and berets that have been dressing heads in Barcelona since 1924. Styles are classic and timeless, from traditional Basque berets to Stetsons and panamas. ⊠ *Call 2, Barri Gòtic* ☏ *93/318–4094* ⊕ *www.barretsobach.com* Ⓜ *Jaume I, Liceu.*

FAMILY **Decathlon.** Whether you're planning a trek through the Pyrenees or a beach yoga session, this mega–sports emporium should be your first port of call. From waterproof clothing to footballs to bike repairs, it caters to every conceivable sport and active hobby. Affordable and always busy, Decathlon is the best place to pick up practical travel clothing, such as that forgotten fleece jacket for a sudden cold snap. ⊠ *Canuda 20, Barri Gòtic* ☏ *93/342–6161* ⊕ *www.decathlon.es* ☾ *Closed Sun.* Ⓜ *Catalunya.*

Heritage. A compilation of luxury retro clothing matches the handsome antique storefront in this Gothic Quarter classic just a few steps from Plaça del Pi. Balenciaga, Yves Saint Laurent, and the 1950 Spanish Pertegaz label are just a few of the stars of yesteryear back in the limelight here. ⊠ *Carrer Banys Nous 14, Barri Gòtic* ☏ *93/317–8515* ⊕ *www.heritagebarcelona.com* Ⓜ *Liceu.*

L'Arca de L'Àvia. As the name ("grandmother's trunk" in English) suggests, the store sells vintage goods of all kinds, with a focus on period clothing, from shoes to gloves to hats and hairpins. Despite the found-object attitude and ambience of the place, they're not giving away these vintage baubles, so don't be surprised at the hefty price tags. You'll also find a collection of bridal gowns, newly made but in romantic, old-fashioned styles. ⊠ *Banys Nous 20, Barri Gòtic* ☏ *93/302–1598* ⊕ *www.larca.es* ☾ *Closed Sun.* Ⓜ *Liceu.*

Ojala! Born in Madrid, based in Morocco, and with a shop in Barcelona, Paloma del Pozo is one of Spain's most original and creative fashion designers. Her eclectic Renaissance-style coats, jackets, skirts, and dresses are realized in dashing, bold colors, luxurious fabrics (velvet is a favorite), and theatrical, arabesque detailing. Given the level of quality, the prices are extremely reasonable. ⊠ *Ciutat 14, Barri Gòtic* ☏ *93/165–1544* ⊕ *www.ojala.es* ☾ *Closed Sun.* Ⓜ *Jaume I.*

FOOD

Caelum. At the corner of Carrer de la Palla and Banys Nous, this café and shop sells wines and foodstuffs such as honey, biscuits, chocolates, and preserves made in convents and monasteries all over Spain. You can pop in to pick up an exquisitely packaged pot of jam, or linger longer in the tearoom, part of which is housed in an old medieval bathhouse. ⊠ *De la Palla 8, Barri Gòtic* ☎ *93/302–6993* ⊕ *www.caelumbarcelona. com* Ⓜ *Liceu, Jaume I.*

Formatgeria La Seu. Scotswoman Katherine McLaughlin has put together the Gothic Quarter's most delightful cheese-tasting sanctuary on the site of an ancient buttery. (A 19th-century butter churn is visible in the back room.) A dozen artisanal cow, goat, and sheep cheeses from all over Spain, and olive oils, can be tasted and taken home. La Seu is named for a combination of La Seu cathedral, as the "seat" of cheeses, and for cheese-rich La Seu d'Urgell in the Pyrenees. Katherine's wrapping paper, imaginatively chosen sheets of newspaper, give a final flourish to purchases. ⊠ *Dagueria 16, Barri Gòtic* ☎ *93/412–6548* ⊕ *www.format-gerialaseu.com* ۞ *Closed Sun. and Mon. and Aug.* Ⓜ *Jaume I.*

La Casa del Bacalao. This cult store decorated with cod-fishing memorabilia specializes in salt cod and books of codfish recipes. Slabs of salt and dried cod, used in a wide range of Catalan recipes (such as *esqueixada,* in which shredded strips of raw salt cod are served in a marinade of oil and vinegar) can be vacuum-packed for portability. ⊠ *Comtal 8 , just off Porta de l'Àngel, Barri Gòtic* ☎ *93/301–6539* ۞ *Closed Sun.* Ⓜ *Catalunya.*

GIFTS AND SOUVENIRS

Artesania Catalunya – CCAM. In 2010 the Catalan government created the registered trademark Empremtes de Catalunya to represent Catalan artisans and to make sure that visitors get the real deal when buying what they believe to be genuine products. The official shop now sells jewelry re-created from eras dating back to pre-Roman times, Gaudí-inspired sculptures, traditional Cava mugs, and some bravely avant-garde objects from young artisans—all officially sanctioned as fit to represent the city. ⊠ *Banys Nous 11, Barri Gòtic* ☎ *93/467–4660* ⊕ *www.artesania-catalunya.com* Ⓜ *Jaume I, Liceu.*

Coses de Casa. The 19th-century windows of this lovely corner shop overlooking Plaça del Pi burst with all sorts of home textiles—from humble, superb-quality tea towels to country-chic patchwork quilts. If they don't stock the cushion cover you're after, it probably doesn't exist, although the most unique take-home item is a gingham bread bag—a sausage-shaped carrier for your morning baguette. ⊠ *Pl. Sant Josep Oriol 5, Barri Gòtic* ☎ *93/302–7328* ⊕ *www.cosesdecasa.com* ۞ *Closed Sun.* Ⓜ *Liceu.*

Fodor's Choice ★ **Ganiveteria Roca.** Directly opposite the giant rose window of the Santa Maria del Pi church, the knife store (*ganivet* is Catalan for knife) beneath this lovely *sgraffito*-decorated facade takes cutlery culture to a new level. Knives, razors, scissors, hatchets, axes, swords, nail clippers, tweezers, and penknives are all displayed in this comprehensive cutting-edge emporium. ✉ *Pl. del Pi 3, Barri Gòtic* 🕾 *93/302–1241* ⊕ *www.ganiveteriaroca.cat* ⊘ *Closed Sun.* Ⓜ *Liceu.*

Guantería y Complementos Alonso. The storefront and interiors of this ancient little glove and accessory shop is well worth the visit. Lovely antique cabinets painstakingly stripped of centuries of paint display gloves, fans, shawls, mantillas, and a miscellany of textile crafts and small gifts. ✉ *Calle Santa Ana 27, Barri Gòtic* 🕾 *93/317–6085* ⊕ *www.tiendacenter.com* ⊘ *Closed Sun.* Ⓜ *Catalunya.*

MARKETS

Mercat Gòtic. A browser's bonanza, this interesting if somewhat pricey Thursday market for antique clothing, jewelry, and art objects occupies the plaza in front of the cathedral. ✉ *Pl. Nova, Barri Gòtic* Ⓜ *Jaume I, Urquinaona.*

Plaça del Pi. This little square fills with the interesting tastes and aromas of a natural-produce market (honeys, cheeses) throughout the month, while neighboring Plaça Sant Josep Oriol holds a painter's market every Sunday. ✉ *Pl. del Pi, Barri Gòtic* Ⓜ *Catalunya, Liceu.*

SHOES, LUGGAGE, LEATHER GOODS, AND ACCESSORIES

Fodor'sChoice   **La Manual Alpargatera.** If you appreciate old-school craftsmanship in
★   footwear and reasonable prices, visit this boutique just off Carrer Ferran. Handmade rope-sole sandals and espadrilles are the specialty, and this shop has sold them to everyone—including the Pope. The flat, beribboned, espadrilles model used for dancing the sardana is available, as are newly fashionable wedge heels with peep toes and comfy slippers. The cost of a pair of espadrilles here might put you back about $35, which is far less than the same quality shoes in the United States. ✉ *Avinyó 7, Barri Gòtic* 🕾 *93/301–0172* ⊕ *www.lamanualalpargatera.es* ⊘ *Closed Sun.* Ⓜ *Liceu, Jaume I.*

TOBACCO

Estanc Gimeno. Smoking items of every kind along with pipes and cigarettes of all sorts are sold in this tobacco sanctuary, but cigars from Havana are the top draw. ✉ *Rambla 100, Barri Gòtic* 🕾 *93/302–0983* ⊕ *www.gimenocigars.com* Ⓜ *Catalunya, Liceu.*

LA RAMBLA

Although not exactly a shopping mecca—unless you're after a Sagrada Família snow globe from one of the dozens of tacky souvenir shops—La Rambla has a few establishments that make up with convenience what they may lack in style. The diamond in the rough is La Boqueria, one of the world's great food markets.

Vinçon sells a variety of hyperdesigned home goods in a space that was once painter Ramón Casas's studio.

DEPARTMENT STORES AND MALLS

El Triangle. The Triangle d'Or or Golden Triangle at the top end of the Rambla on Plaça Catalunya is a stylish and popular complex and home for, among other stores, FNAC, where afternoon book presentations and CD launches bring together crowds of literati and music lovers. ⊠ *Pl. Catalunya 1–4, La Rambla* ☎ *93/318–0108* ⊕ *www.eltriangle.es* Ⓜ *Catalunya.*

Maremàgnum. This modern shopping complex sits on an artificial "island" in the harbor and is accessed by Rambla del Mar, a wooden swing bridge. The shops inside are fairly run-of-the-mill, but this mall is one of the few places in Barcelona where you can be sure to shop on Sunday. On the first floor, there's a good food court with fine water views. ⊠ *Moll d'Espanya, Port Vell, La Rambla* ☎ *93/225–8100* ⊕ *www.maremagnum.es* Ⓜ *Drassanes.*

FOOD

Pastelería Escribà. Barcelona's wave of creative cake makers owe a lot to Antoni Escribà, a pastry chef who elevated the craft to an art form, especially in the field of chocolate sculptures. His three sons— Cristian, Joan, and Jordi—keep his spirit alive in the Casa Figueras, a jewel box of a shop awash in mosaic murals, curly copper work, and other fanciful Art Nouveau detailing. Tortes, chocolate kisses, and candy rings are just some of the edible treasures here that delight and surprise. A second Escribà shop, which has a café area, is at Gran Vía 546 in the Eixample. ⊠ *Rambla de les Flores 83, La Rambla* ☎ *93/301–6027* ⊕ *www.escriba.es* Ⓜ *Liceu.*

EL RAVAL

Shopping in the Raval reflects the district's multicultural and bohemian vibe. Around MACBA (Barcelona Museum of Contemporary Art) you'll find dozens of designer-run start-ups selling fashion, crafts, and housewares, while the edgier southernmost section has an abundance of curious establishments chock-full of ethnic foods (along Calles Hospital and Carme) and vintage clothing (on Calle Riera Baixa).

ANTIQUES AND COLLECTIBLES

Holala! Holala! is more a lifestyle than a vintage store. Its owners travel the world in search of garments for the next trend, or wave of nostalgia. This huge space is chockablock with clothing, furniture, objects, knickknacks, and other flotsam of the distant and not-so-distant past. Hawaiian surfboards, high-waisted Levis, nobly 1980s knits—it's all put into a postmodern context at Holala!—and the kids lap it up. Holala! has a smaller shop selling clothes only at Tallers 73, also in the Raval. ⊠ *Pl. de la Castella 2, El Raval* ☎ *93/302–0593* ⊕ *www.holala-ibiza.com* Ⓜ *Catalunya.*

BOOKS

La Central del Raval. This luscious bookstore in the former chapel of the Casa de la Misericòrdia sells books amid stunning architecture and holds regular cultural events. ⊠ *Elisabets 6, El Raval* ☎ *900/802109* ⊕ *www.lacentral.com* ☾ *Closed Sun.* Ⓜ *Catalunya.*

Loring Art. This independent art and design bookshop has always prided itself on being a pioneer in Spain. Having started out with a small selection of high-quality art editions, the shop now holds about 20,000 titles covering architecture, industrial design, fashion, photography, and film and dance, among others. Whether you're looking for instructions or simple aesthetic entertainment, this shrine to beauty and creativity won't disappoint. ⊠ *Calle Floridablanca, 65–67 1°1ª, El Raval* ☎ *93/412–0108* ⊕ *www.loring-art.com* ☾ *Closed Sun.*

CLOTHING

Home on Earth. Homeware and children's clothing with a homespun sensibility are on offer in this charming store run by a Scandinavian couple. Bags made of Thai tapestries, wooden instruments, felt baskets, and handmade lamp shades are among the accessories worth checking out here. There is a second shop in the Barri Gòtic at Boqueria 14. ⊠ *Hospital 76, C. Boqueria 14, El Raval* ⊹ *Closest metro: Liceu* ☎ *93/315–8558* ⊕ *www.homeonearth.com.*

Medwinds. Made locally, this casual chic clothing for men and women is constructed with natural cotton and wool in loose silhouettes to create an effortlessly cool look loved by El Raval's armies of hipsters. Lovely leather bags and backpacks are available, too. ⊠ *Elisabets 7, El Raval* ☎ *93/619–0179* ⊕ *www.medwinds.com* ☾ *Closed Sun.*

FURNITURE

Room Service Gallery. Room Service is a commercial gallery focusing on limited-edition, handcrafted furniture by top-notch designers. Piet Hein Eeek, a Dutch cabinetmaker who champions recycled woods, is well represented. Also from the Low Countries, Maarten Baas's sinewy resin tables and chairs seem to have stepped out of a Dalían dreamscape. A small section of the gallery is put aside for emerging local design talent. ⊠ *C/dels Àngels 16, El Raval* ☎ *93/302–1016* ⊕ *www.roomsd.com* Ⓜ *Catalunya, Liceu.*

MARKETS

Flea Market BCN. Barcelona's current rage for retro and vintage reaches its pinnacle once a month on a little square behind the medieval shipyards. Flea Market BCN sees hipsters and hippies, dads and dealers empty out their wardrobes and garages. When the sun is shining, it makes for a fun morning out as you rummage through racks of last season's Zara for diamonds in the rough. Stick with it, and you may walk away with an art-deco wall clock or 1970s hand-mixer. Flea Market BCN is held on the second Sunday of every month, while the smaller Fleedonia takes places on the Plaça Salvador Seguí on the first Sunday of every month. ⊠ *Pl. Blanquerna* ⊕ *www.fleamarketbcn. com* Ⓜ *Drassanes.*

Mercat de Sant Antoni. Just outside the Raval at the end of Ronda Sant Antoni, this steel hangar colossus is an old-fashioned, food and secondhand clothing and books (many in English) market. Sunday morning is the most popular time to browse through the used-book and video game market. ⊠ *Comte d'Urgell 1, El Raval* ⊕ *www.facebook.com/mercat. dominicalsantantoni* Ⓜ *Sant Antoni.*

EIXAMPLE

Competing with the Eixample's landmarks, the best boutiques in this stylish neighborhood are destinations unto themselves. Vinçon and Nanimarquina display furnishings and objects in haute settings, while the luxe fashion flagships along the Passeig de Gràcia excel in eye-popping window displays. Ardent shoppers could easily lose themselves for a day—or a weekend—browsing in the Eixample.

ANTIQUES AND COLLECTIBLES

Bulevard dels Antiquaris. Look carefully for the stairway leading one flight up to this 73-store antiques arcade off Passeig de Gràcia. You never know what you might find: dolls, icons, Roman or Visigothic objects, paintings, furniture, cricket kits, fly rods, or toys from a century ago. Haggling is common practice—but Catalan antiques dealers are tough nuts to crack. ⊠ *Passeig de Gràcia 55, Eixample* ☎ *93/215–4499* ⊕ *www.bulevarddelsantiquaris.com* ☾ *Closed Sun.* Ⓜ *Passeig de Gràcia.*

El Recibidor. Like a scene from *Mad Men*, El Recibidor oozes mid-century modern elegance. This large split-level showroom deals in furniture and objects, mainly of European provenance, from the art deco period onward. From small ceramic figurines to dining tables, table lamps, and vintage TVs, each item has been curated and restored with a deep understanding of the period's aesthetic and value. ⊠ *Viladomat 9, Eixample* ☎ *93/530–4221* ⊕ *www.elrecibidor.com* Ⓜ *Sant Antoni.*

ART GALLERIES

Galeria Joan Prats. "La Prats" has been one of the city's top galleries since the 1920s, showing international painters and sculptors from Henry Moore to Antoni Tàpies. Barcelona painter Joan Miró was a prime force in the founding of the gallery when he became friends with Joan Prats. The motifs of bonnets and derbies on the gallery's facade are callbacks to the trade of Prats's father. José Maria Sicilia and Juan Ugalde have shown here, while Erick Beltrán, Hannah Collins, and Eulàlia Valldosera are among the regular artists on display. ⊠ *Balmes 54, Eixample* ☎ *93/216–0290* ⊕ *www.galeriajoanprats.com* ⊘ *Closed Sun.* Ⓜ *Passeig de Gràcia.*

Galeria Toni Tàpies. After the prolific Catalan painter Antoni Tàpies died in 2012, his son Toni decided to change the direction of his successful gallery and, as a touching homage, only show his late father's work, which is now on show permanently. This is complemented by periodic smaller shows and events from other leading artists, sometimes of one single piece, which have been chosen to create a "dialogue" with the Tàpies oeuvre. ⊠ *Consell de Cent 282, Eixample* ☎ *93/487–6402* ⊕ *www.tonitapies.com* ⊘ *Closed weekends* Ⓜ *Catalunya.*

Joan Gaspar. One of Barcelona's most prestigious galleries, Joan Gaspart and his father before him brought Picasso and Miró back to Catalonia during the '50s and '60s, along with other artists considered politically taboo during the Franco regime. These days you'll find leading contemporary lights such as Joan Pere Viladecans, Rafols Casamada, or Susana Solano here. ⊠ *Pl. Dr. Letamendi 1, Eixample* ☎ *93/323–0748* ⊕ *www.galeriajoangaspar.com* ⊘ *Closed Sun.; closed Sat. and Mon. in summer* Ⓜ *Universitat, Provença.*

Marlborough. This international giant occupies an important position in Barcelona's art-gallery galaxy with exhibits of major contemporary artists from around the world, as well as local stars. Recent shows featured the hyperrealist collages of Antonio López García and the contemporary designer and painter Alberto Corazón. ⊠ *Enric Granados 68, Eixample* ☎ *93/467–4454* ⊕ *www.galeriamarlborough.com* ⊘ *Closed. Sun.* Ⓜ *Passeig de Gràcia.*

N2. A relatively new kid on the block, the Galería N2 already has established its position as a beacon at the crossroads of tradition and modernity, of high- and low-brow art. The vanguard but careful selection of artists featured in six annual solo shows includes the street artist Sixeart and the Argentine surrealist Mauricio Vergara. Since N2 specializes in up-and-coming and mid-career artists, works are generally affordable yet safe to invest in, and browsing here makes for a lighthearted change from the Eixample's more serious art houses. ✉ *Enric Granados 61, Eixample* ☎ *93/452–0592* ⊕ *www.n2galeria.com.*

Projecte SD. This gallery, located in one of the Eixample's most beautiful little passages, doesn't go easy on its visitors. No show at Projecte SD can be grasped without the explanatory booklet; no piece of art can be fully appreciated in isolation. The pieces exhibited and sold here are complex, philosophical, challenging, and bleedingly conceptual—anything but simply decorative. Projecte SD is really more of a museum than a gallery. That makes every visit an experience and every purchase an audacious act of faith. ✉ *Passatge Mercader 8, Baixos 1, Eixample* ☎ *93/488–1360* ⊕ *www.projectesd.com* ☉ *Closed Sun.* Ⓜ *Diagonal, Provença.*

Sala Dalmau. An old-timer in the established Consell de Cent gallery scene, Sala Dalmau shows an interesting and heterodox range of Catalan and international artists. ✉ *Consell de Cent 349, Eixample* ☎ *93/215–4592* ⊕ *www.saladalmau.com* ☉ *Closed Sun.* Ⓜ *Passeig de Gràcia.*

BOOKS AND STATIONERY

Altaïr. Barcelona's premier travel and adventure bookstore stocks many titles in English. Book presentations and events scheduled here feature a wide range of notable authors from Alpinists to Africanists. ✉ *Gran Via 616, Eixample* ☎ *93/342–7171* ⊕ *www.altair.es* ☉ *Closed Sun.* Ⓜ *Catalunya.*

BCN Books. This midtown Eixample bookstore is a prime address for books in English, including tomes for learning Spanish and Catalan. ✉ *Roger de Llúria 118, Eixample* ☎ *93/457–7692* ⊕ *www.bcnbooks. com* Ⓜ *Verdaguer, Diagonal.*

Casa del Llibre. On Barcelona's most important shopping street, Casa del Llibre is a major book feast with a wide variety of English titles. ✉ *Passeig de Gràcia 62, Eixample* ☎ *902/026407* ⊕ *www.casadellibro. com* Ⓜ *Passeig de Gràcia.*

FNAC. For musical recordings and the latest book publications, this is one of Barcelona's most dependable and happening addresses. Regular concerts, presentations of new recordings, and art exhibits take place in FNAC, both here and its other major branch at the Triangle Shopping Center on Plaça Catalunya. Much more than a bookstore, it's an important cultural resource. ✉ *Centre Comercial L'Illa, Av. Diagonal 549, Eixample* ☎ *902/100632* ⊕ *www.fnac.es* Ⓜ *Maria Cristina, Les Corts.*

Laie. Not overly stocked with English-language titles, this bookstore boasts a very pleasant café-restaurant upstairs; the space is often used for readings and other and cultural events. Other branches of Laie are located around Barcelona, including major museums such as the Museu Picasso and Cosmocaixa. ✉ *Pau Claris 85, Eixample* ☎ *93/318–1739* ⊕ *www.laie.es* ☉ *Closed Sun. and Mon.* Ⓜ *Catalunya.*

Pepa Paper. Barcelona's most famous paper and stationery store, Pepa Paper (Pepa is a nickname for Josefina and Paper, Catalan for—you guessed it—paper), carries a gorgeous selection of stationary and more. In addition to the Balmes location, the chain has two other downtown shops including one on Avenida Diagonal and another on Avenida Paris. ⊠ *Carrer de Balmes 50, Eixample* ☎ *93/410–3754* ⊕ *pepapaper.com/ shop* ⊘ *Closed Sun.* Ⓜ *Hospital Clínic/Provença.*

CERAMICS AND GLASSWARE

Fodor'sChoice **Lladró.** This Valencia company is famed worldwide for the beauty and
★ quality of its figures. Barcelona's only Lladró factory store, this location has exclusive pieces of work, custom-designed luxury items of gold and porcelain, and classic and original works. Look for the cheeky figurines by Jaime Hayon, a young Spanish designer put in charge of injecting the 60-year-old company with some colorful postmodernism. ⊠ *Passeig de Gràcia 101, Eixample* ☎ *93/270–1253* ⊕ *www.lladro.com* ⊘ *Closed Sun.* Ⓜ *Diagonal.*

CLOTHING

Adolfo Domínguez. One of Barcelona's longtime fashion giants, this is one of Spain's leading clothes designers, with many locations around town. Famed as the creator of the Iberia Airlines uniforms, Adolfo Domínguez has been in the not-too-radical mainstream of Spanish couture for the past quarter century. ⊠ *Passeig de Gràcia 32, Eixample* ☎ *93/487–4170* ⊕ *www.adolfodominguez.com* ⊘ *Closed Sun.* Ⓜ *Passeig de Gràcia.*

Aílanto. Twin brothers Iñaki and Aitor Muñoz are the creative and business force behind Aílanto; an avant-garde fashion brand renowned for sculptural silhouettes and daring prints. Winners of various accolades and regulars at Madrid's Fashion Week, their Barcelona shop is as drama-filled as their collections, with flowering metallic lamps dangling from double-height ceilings and dressing rooms swathed in fringes and velvet. Oversized coats, heavily textured fabrics, and patterns inspired by major artistic movements have become the brand's signatures. ⊠ *C/ Enric Granados 46, Eixample* ☎ *93/451–3106* ⊕ *www.ailanto.com* Ⓜ *Provença.*

The Avant. Under her own label, Silvia Garcia Presas—the creator of El Avant—offers quietly elegant and effortlessly chic clothing for women in her simple, woody boutique at the top end of Enric Granados. Fabrics are 100% natural (organic cotton, alpaca wool, etc.), and the generous and easy cuts are transgenerational and flattering. A small room at the back displays handmade soaps, ceramic wares, home textiles, and other gifty bits sourced from across Asia and the Americas. El Avant has also has a smaller boutique in La Ribera district at Esparteria 13. ⊠ *Enric Granados 106, Eixample* ☎ *93/300–7673* ⊕ *www.theavant. com* ⊘ *Closed Sun.* Ⓜ *Diagonal.*

Carolina Herrera. Originally from Venezuela but professionally based in New York, Carolina Herrera and her international CH logo have become Barcelona mainstays. (Daughter Carolina Herrera Jr. is a Spain resident and married to former bullfighter Miguel Báez.) Fragrances for men and women and clothes with a simple, elegant line—a white blouse is the CH icon—are the staples here. Herrera's light ruffled dresses and edgy urban footwear add feminine flourishes. ⊠ *Passeig de Gràcia 87, Eixample* ☎ *93/272–1584* ⊕ *www.carolinaherrera.com* ⊗ *Closed Sun.* Ⓜ *Diagonal.*

Conti. A favorite men's fashion outlet (although women are catered to also), Conti stocks threads by top international designers. The company's shop in Ramblas Catalunya specializes in jeans, from Bikkembergs to G-Star to the more conservative Armani Jeans label. ⊠ *Rambla de Catalunya 78, Eixample* ☎ *93/215–3232* ⊕ *www.econti.com* ⊗ *Closed Sun.* Ⓜ *Diagonal.*

Erre de Raso. Popular with the uptown crowd, Erre de Raso makes clothes in bright and breezy shades and patterns. With colors ranging from electric fuchsias to bright indigo blues and materials ranging from satin (*raso*) to cottons and silks, the objective is to outfit stylish women in chameleonic outfits that look equally appropriate picking up the kids from school, dropping by an art gallery opening, and hitting a cocktail party in the same sortie. ⊠ *Aribau 69, Eixample* ☎ *93/452–3754* ⊕ *www.errederaso.com* ⊗ *Closed weekends* Ⓜ *Provença* ⊠ *València 419, Eixample* ☎ *93/487–9595* Ⓜ *Girona.*

Furest. This centenary menswear star, with four stores in town and another at the airport, markets its own designs as well as selections from Armani Jeans, Scotch & Soda, Hugo Boss, and Blackstone, as well as their own collection of dapper suits, shirts, and gentlemen's accessories. ⊠ *Passeig de Gràcia 12–14, Eixample* ☎ *93/301–2000* ⊕ *www.furest. com* Ⓜ *Catalunya.*

Loewe. Occupying the ground floor of Lluís Domènech i Montaner's Casa Lleó Morera, Loewe is Spain's answer to Hermès, a classical clothing and leather emporium for men's and women's fashions and luxurious handbags that whisper status (at eye-popping prices). Farther north along the Passeig de Gràcia at No. 91, the Galería Loewe holds stylish, sporadic fashion and costume shows. ⊠ *Passeig de Gràcia 35, Eixample* ☎ *93/216–0400* ⊕ *www.loewe.com* ⊗ *Closed Sun.* Ⓜ *Passeig de Gràcia.*

Purificación García. Known as a gifted fabric expert whose creations are invariably based on the qualities and characteristics of her raw materials, Galicia-born Purificación García enjoys solid prestige in Barcelona. Understated hues and subtle combinations of colors and shapes place this contemporary designer squarely in the camp of the less-is-more school, and although her women's range is larger and more diverse, she is one female designer who understands men's tailoring. ⊠ *Provença 292, Eixample* ☎ *93/496–1336* ⊕ *www.purificaciongarcia.com* ⊗ *Closed Sun.* Ⓜ *Diagonal.*

Santa Eulalia. The history of this luxury fashion superstore, which moved into its 2,000-square-meter premises designed by William Sofield in 2011, goes back to 1843. That year Domingo Taberner Prims opened the first shop, which would soon evolve into one of the city's first and foremost haute couture tailoring houses. Today it's run by the fourth generation of the founding family and features one of the best luxury brand selections in the country. It also regularly teams up with designers and design schools to present special collections or awards. When you're done browsing everything from Agent Provocateur to Vera Wang, refresh with some tea and cake at the fabulous café-terrace on the first floor, or head to the basement to see the in-house tailors at work on bespoke suits and men's shirts. ⊠ *Passeig de Gràcia 93, Eixample* ☎ *93/215–0674* ⊕ *www.santaeulalia.com* ⊗ *Closed Sun.* Ⓜ *Diagonal.*

Sita Murt. The local Catalan designer Sita Murt produces smart, grown-up women's wear under her own label in this minimalist space in the Eixample. Colorful chiffon dresses and light, gauzy tops and knits characterize this line of clothing popular with professional women and wedding goers. ⊠ *Mallorca 242, Eixample* ☎ *93/215–2231* ⊕ *www.sitamurt.com* ⊗ *Closed Sun.* Ⓜ *Passeig de Gràcia, Diagonal.*

Teresa Helbig. A regular at Madrid Fashion Week, Teresa Helbig designs feminine and elegant pret-a-porter women's collections. Yet she is better known, and worth visiting, for her bespoke bridal wear and evening gowns, timeless haute couture she concocts for her well-heeled clients at her Barcelona studio-showroom. It may not come cheap, but you'll be able to hand it down through generations. ⊠ *Mallorca 184, Loft, Eixample* ☎ *93/451–5544* ⊕ *www.teresahelbig.com.*

> ### CUSTO GUSTO
>
> Only Barcelona could come up with Custo, an idiosyncratic fashion line created by a couple of motorcycling brothers. Since they started the business in the 1980s, Custido and David Dalmau have parlayed their passion for colorful and original tops into an empire that now includes footwear, denim, handbags, knits, and more. With stores scattered around Barcelona and the world, Custo's quirky embroidery and metallic graphic prints have become nearly as iconic as Gaudí's organic stalagmites or Miró's colorful asteroids.

DEPARTMENT STORES AND MALLS

Bulevard Rosa. The sun has set a bit on this fashionable L-shaped arcade, but it still provides some welcome serenity from bustling Passeig de Gràcia. Worth seeking out is the deconstructed range of clothing from Lurdes Bergada (shops 41–42) or Bimba and Lola's sophisticated mid-couture (near the Passeig de Gràcia entrance). Afterward, drop by the excellent Mary's Market (at the entrance on Carrer Valencia) to admire the enormous selection of gourmet goodies and light lunch fare. ⊠ *Passeig de Gràcia 55–57, Eixample* ☎ *93/215–8331* ⊕ *www.bulevardrosa.com* Ⓜ *Passeig de Gràcia.*

El Corte Inglés. This iconic and ubiquitous Spanish department store has its main Barcelona branch on Plaça de Catalunya, with two annexes close by: one directly opposite selling mid-priced ladies' fashion and another in Porta de l'Àngel for younger fashion and sporting goods. You can find just about anything here—clothing, shoes, perfumes, electronics—and there is a wonderful supermarket and food mall on the lower-ground floor. With branches in all major cities, El Corte Inglés is Spain's only large department store and has leagues of heritage fans. Service is inconsistent, but the sale season in August is worth fighting the crowds for. ⊠ *Pl. de Catalunya 14, Eixample* ☎ *93/306–3800* ⊕ *www.elcorteingles.es* Ⓜ *Catalunya* ⊠ *Portal de l'Àngel 19–21, Barri Gòtic* ☎ *93/306–3800* ⊕ *elcorteingles.es* Ⓜ *Catalunya* ⊠ *Av. Diagonal 471, Pl. Francesc Macia, Eixample* ☎ *93/493–4800* Ⓜ *Hospital Clinic* ⊠ *Av. Diagonal 617, Diagonal Mar* ☎ *93/366–7100* ☉ *Closed Sun.* Ⓜ *Maria Cristina.*

L'Illa Diagonal. This rangy complex buzzes with shoppers swarming through more than 100 stores and shops, including food specialists, Decathlon sports gear, and Imaginarium toys, plus FNAC, Zara, Benetton, and all the usual High Street suspects. ⊠ *Av. Diagonal 557, Eixample* ☎ *93/444–0000* ⊕ *www.lilla.com* Ⓜ *Maria Cristina.*

Pedralbes Centre. This multistory conglomeration just a few blocks west of L'Illa Diagonal and next to a branch of the ubiquitous El Corte Inglés has a reasonable selection of local brands: Javier Simorra for chic ladies' apparel, Tous leather bags, and Zara Home for on-trend textiles and domestic frippery. ⊠ *Av. Diagonal 609–615, Eixample* ☎ *93/410–6821* ⊕ *www.pedralbescentre.com* ☉ *Closed Sun.* Ⓜ *Maria Cristina.*

FOOD

Cacao Sampaka. This centrally located shop is perfect for chocolate addicts. While it's perfectly possible to dash in and fill your bags with boxes of Cacao Sampaka's exquisite cocoa creations to take home with you (or nibble on the way back to your hotel), consider setting aside 30 minutes to sit down in the pleasant in-store café and order an "Azteca" hot chocolate drink. Quite possibly the best hot chocolate in Spain, a sip of this thick, rich, heaven-in-a-cup is the highlight of any Barcelona shopping spree. ⊠ *Carrer del Consell de Cent 292, Eixample* ☎ *93/410–6821* ⊕ *www.cacaosampaka.com* Ⓜ *Passeig de Gràcia.*

Oriol Balaguer. Owner Balaguer is surely running out of room to store all the "Spain's Best…" trophies he's collected over the years. He's a consultant to some of the world's most famous restaurants, and the heart of his empire is this little shop of chocolate-making magic. Bring your credit card and prepare to have your mind blown. Some of the confectionery creations are so beautiful you'll feel bad about biting into them—at least until you taste them. Balaguer has a second equally stunning boutique at Travessera de les Corts 340, which also sells bread and pastries. ⊠ *Pl. de Sant Gregori Taumaturg 2, Eixample* ☎ *93/201–1846* ⊕ *www.oriolbalaguer.com* Ⓜ *La Bonanova.*

Queviures Murria. Founded in 1890, this historic Moderniste shop, its windows decorated with Ramón Casas paintings and posters, has a superb selection of some 200 cheeses, sausages, wines, and conserves from Spain, Catalunya, and beyond. The ceramic Casas reproductions lining the interior walls are eye candy, as are all the details in this work of art–cum–grocery store (*queviures* means foodstuffs, literally, "things to keep you alive"). ⊠ *Roger de Llúria 85, Eixample* ✢ *Near metro Passeig de Gràcia* ☎ *93/215–5789* ⊕ *www.murria.cat* ☉ *Closed Sun. and Mon.* Ⓜ *Passeig de Gràcia.*

Reserva Ibérica. Purveyor of fine hams in Spain and abroad for more than 30 years, Reserva Ibérica has a shop in the Eixample where it not only sells a selection of its best, all-acorn-fed products, but also offers the opportunity for customers to taste the hams, accompanied by a glass of wine. ⊠ *Rambla de Catalunya 61, Eixample* ☏ *93/215–5230* ⊕ *www.reservaiberica.com* ⊘ *Closed Sun.*

GIFTS AND SOUVENIRS

L'Appartement. This bright and quirky design shop fits right in with this part of the Eixample, known for its abundance of gay bars. Oversized wall decals, bold '60s-inspired chairs, plastic knickknacks (some of them even useful), and sci-fi light fittings set the tone. L'Appartement has a keen eye for emerging talent, often stocking their goodies well before the big design shops catch on. ⊠ *Enric Granados 44, Eixample* ⊹ *Metro L5: estación Diagonal* ☏ *93/452–2904* ⊕ *www.lappartement. es* ⊘ *Closed Sun.* Ⓜ *Provença.*

Servei Estació. It's a hardware store, yes, but one like you've never seen before. Servei Estació is situated in a rationalist-style landmark building dating from 1962. For decades it served the city's builders and handymen with tools and materials, but more recently the huge inventory has expanded to modern design and housewares, and sells everything from ropes of string to designer shopping carts. ⊠ *Aragó 270, Eixample* ☏ *93/393–2410* ⊕ *www.serveiestacio.com* ⊘ *Closed Sun.* Ⓜ *Passeig de Gràcia.*

HOUSEHOLD ITEMS AND FURNITURE

Fins de Siècles. The third of the Fins de Siècles shops is, like its siblings in Brussels and Isle sur Sorgue, the product of the undying passion of its Belgian owners to rescue as much European design heritage from the 20th century as they can. Their particular fascination is with the art deco period ranging from the 1930s through the '50s, which they buy all over Europe and have restored and newly upholstered respecting traditional methods. Desks, sofas, vanities, and tables are shipped all over the world, but they also stock smaller (and more affordable) items like lamps, vases, rugs, and silverware. ⊠ *Enric Granados 70, Eixample* ☏ *93/511–7606* ⊕ *www.finsdesiecles-artdeco.com* ⊘ *Closed Sun.* Ⓜ *Provença.*

Jaime Beriestain Concept Store. The concept store of one of the city's hottest interior designers provides mere mortals the chance to appreciate the Beriestain groove. Reflecting his hotel and restaurant projects, the shop offers an exciting mixture of mid-century modern classics and new design pieces, peppered with freshly cut flowers (also for sale), French candles, handmade stationery, and the latest international design and architecture magazines to dress up your coffee table. The in-store café is worth a visit. ⊠ *Pau Claris 167, Eixample* ☏ *93/515–0779* ⊕ *www.beriestain.com* Ⓜ *Diagonal.*

Mar de Cava. This Aladdin's Cave of design, housewares, furniture, clothing, and accessories bursts with creativity and color. The carefully curated collection includes everything from vases by cult ceramics-maker Apparatu, cabinets rendered in Technicolor lacquers, African bead necklaces, and tables covered in antique tiles. The emphasis is more on craftsmanship than the latest trends—just about every item has an intriguing backstory. ⊠ *Valencia 293, Eixample* ☎ *93/458–5333* ⊕ *www.mardecava.com* ☉ *Closed Sun.* Ⓜ *Passeig de Gràcia.*

Nanimarquina. A lover of both traditional methods and exuberant design, Nani Marquina makes textural rugs that look just as good on a wall as they do on the floor. Some of her rugs re-create ancient Persian or Hindu styles; others are trendy compositions by designers like Sybilla or the Bouroullec brothers. Half of this large showroom—an ingenious conversion from an old private garage—accommodates Doméstico, a colorful emporium of designer objects and furniture. ⊠ *Rosselló 256/ Av. Diagonal, Eixample* ☎ *93/487–1606* ⊕ *www.nanimarquina.com* ☉ *Closed Sun.* Ⓜ *Diagonal.*

JEWELRY

Bagués Masriera. The Bagués dynasty has bejeweled barcelonins since 1839. While they stock much that glitters, the Lluís Masriera line of original Art Nouveau pieces is truly unique; intricate flying nymphs, lifelike golden insects, and other easily recognizable motifs from the period take on a new depth of beauty when executed in the translucent enameling process that Masriera himself developed. The location in Moderniste architect Puig i Cadafalch's Casa Amatller in the famous Mansana de la Discòrdia on Passeig de Gràcia is worth the visit alone, although sadly, the interior of the shop bears little of the building's exuberance. ⊠ *Passeig de Gràcia 41, Eixample* ☎ *93/216–0174* ⊕ *www. masriera.es* ☉ *Closed Sun.* Ⓜ *Catalunya.*

Puig Doria. This popular jeweler sells a full range of personal accessories of great style and taste, from neckties and watches to fashionable baubles in silver and gold. ⊠ *Rambla Catalunya 88, Eixample* ☎ *93/215–1090* ⊕ *www.puigdoria.es* ☞ *Additional location at Diagonal 612, phone 93/201–2911* Ⓜ *Diagonal.*

Zapata Joyero. The Zapata family, with five stores around town, has been prominent in Barcelona jewelry design and retail for the last half century. With original designs of their own and a savvy selection of the most important Swiss and international watch designers, this family business is now in its second generation and makes a point of taking good care of clients with large or small jewelry needs. Their L'Illa store, for example, specializes in jewelry accessible to the budgets of younger clients. In addition to their central shop on Avenida Diagpnal, they have two stores in the neighborhood of Gràcia and two in the L'illa Diagonal mall. ⊠ *Buenos Aires 60, Eixample* ☎ *93/430–6238* ⊕ *www. zapatajoyeros.com* ☉ *Closed Sun.* Ⓜ *Provença.*

MARKETS

Els Encants Vells. One of Europe's oldest flea markets, Els Encants has recently found a new home—a stunning, glittering metal canopy that protects the rag-and-bone merchants (and their keen customers) from the elements. Stalls, and a handful of stand-up bars, have become a bit more upmarket, too, although you'll still find plenty of oddities to barter over in the central plaza. Saturday is the busiest day—try going during the week for a more relaxed rummage around this fascinating slice of urban history. ⊠ *Av. Meridiana 69, Pl. de Les Glóries Catalans, Eixample* ☎ *93/246–3030* ⊕ *www.encantsbcn.com* ⊘ *Closed Sun., Tues., and Thurs.* Ⓜ *Glòries.*

SHOES

Camper. This internationally famous Spanish shoe emporium, which in Barcelona also comprises a 25-room boutique hotel of the same name and numerous branches, offers a comprehensive line of funky boots, heels, and shoes of all kinds. Both men's and women's shoes, all in line with the company's organic outdoor philosophy, are displayed against an undulating chrome-and-wood backdrop designed by architect Benedetta Tagliabue. ⊠ *Passeig de Gràcia 2–4, Eixample* ☎ *93/521–6250* ⊕ *www.camper.com* ⊘ *Closed Sun.* Ⓜ *Catalunya.*

Castañer. The rope-soled sandal, or *alpargata*, has come a long way. What started as humble farmers' treads turned to military footwear and then accessory favored by Yves Saint Laurent. Founded in 1927, the Castañer clan has seen all the chapters. Mixing tradition, craftsmanship, and modernity, the brand has elevated the espadrille to fashion must-have. Wedge-heels, booties, and flats for both men and women are on sale in this citrus-toned boutique, designed by noted architect Benedetta Tagliabue. ⊠ *Rosselló 230, Eixample* ☎ *93/414–2428* ⊕ *www.castaner. com* Ⓜ *Diagonal.*

Fodor'sChoice ★ **Norman Vilalta.** Norman Vilalta was a lawyer in Buenos Aires before he decided to move to Florence, Italy, and do something rather unusual: learn the trade of a traditional cobbler. Today he is one of a handful of people in the world who produce artisanal bespoke shoes, which take three months to make. The shoes come complete with a video showing the entire making of, and will set you back somewhere between €2,500 and €5,000. However, you will also join the ranks of the chef Ferran Adrià, the architect Oscar Tusquets, and members of the Spanish royal family as owner of a pair of Norman Vilalta shoes. And since they fit like no other and last a lifetime, you might consider it a worthy investment. For a more affordable option, Vilalta's ready-to-wear footwear is available at the high-fashion emporium Santa Eulalía on the Passeig de Gràcia. ⊠ *Enric Granados 5, Eixample* ☎ *93/323–4014* ⊕ *www. normanvilalta.com* Ⓜ *Universitat.*

Fodor'sChoice ★ **The Outpost.** A shop dedicated exclusively to men's accessories of the finest kind, the Outpost was created by a former Prada buyer who considers it his mission to bring stylishness to Barcelona men with this oasis of avant-garde fashion. The constantly changing window displays are works of art, providing a first taste of what's to be found inside: Robert Clegerie shoes, Albert Thurston suspenders, Roland Pineau belts, Yves Andrieux hats, Balenciaga ties. You enter the Outpost as a mere mortal, but leave it as a gentleman—provided you carry the necessary cash. ⊠ *Rosselló 281, bis, Eixample* ☎ *93/457–7137* ⊕ *www.theoutpostbcn. com* ☉ *Closed Sun.* Ⓜ *Diagonal, Verdaguer.*

Tascón. International footwear designers and domestic shoemakers alike fill these stores with trendy urban footwear from brands such as Camper, United Nude, and Audley, as well as more sturdy models from Timberland and the like. Models designed in-house and made locally offer high style at reasonable prices. You will find other branches of Tascón in strategic shopping hubs. ⊠ *Passeig de Gràcia 64, Eixample* ☎ *93/487–9084* ⊕ *www.tascon.es* ☉ *Closed Sun.* Ⓜ *Passeig de Gràcia.*

GRÀCIA

Cute and cozy Gràcia is steadily evolving into Barcelona's most eclectic shopping destination—it has a Brooklyn feel with a Mediterranean nonchalance. The best place to start is the Carrer d'Astúries, followed by the Carrer Verdi and Carrer Torrent d'Olla.

BEAUTY

Herbolari del Cel. Gràcia's "Herbolarium from Heaven" is widely considered among the best in Barcelona for herbal remedies, teas, spices, oils, natural cures and treatments, and cosmetics of all kinds. A mere deep breath of air here will probably cure whatever ails you. ⊠ *Travessera de Gràcia 120, Gràcia* ☎ *93/218–7331* ⊕ *www.herbolaridelcel.com* ☉ *Closed Sun.* Ⓜ *Fontana.*

FOOD

Planeta Te. With more than 1,000 products on offer, this must be widest variety of teas and infusions available in Barcelona. Planeta Te sell herbs and blends by weight from pretty tin boxes and drawers that line the walls. You will also find organic tea bags, a colorful range of teapots and other tea-making paraphernalia, and a seductive aroma as soon as you enter this sweet old-fashioned shop. ⊠ *Asturies 50, Gràcia* ☎ *93/210–3922* ⊕ *www.planetate.es* Ⓜ *Fontana.*

Tea Shop. Earl Grey, black, white, red, green: every kind of tea you've ever heard of and many you probably haven't are available at this encyclopedic tea repository on Gràcia's main drag. The Taller de Cata (Tasting Workshop) held Thursday 5:30 pm–7:30 pm will stimulate your tea culture in the event that you are interested in learning how to distinguish a Pai Mu Tan (white tea) from a Lung Ching (green tea) or how to correctly prepare and serve different varieties of this universal world brew and beverage. ⊠ *Gran de Gràcia 91, Gràcia* ☎ *93/217–4923* Ⓜ *Passeig de Gràcia.*

HOUSEHOLD ITEMS AND FURNITURE

AOO. Among the posh interior and fashion shops along the Carrer Sèneca, AOO or "Other Things" stands out for a more humble "anti-design" ethos. Started by two young creatives, AOO produces a range of predominantly pine outdoor stools, tables, and chairs in small workshops across Catalonia, giving traditional designs a contemporary twist with a splash of colorful fabric or other stylish detail. The objects can be left as is, or easily customized into unique pieces. ⊠ *Sèneca 8, Gràcia* ☎ *93/250–8254* ⊕ *www.altrescoses.cat* Ⓜ *Diagonal.*

SHOES

BBB. Any shoe store that satisfies the legendary three B requirements—*bueno, bonito,* and *barato* (good, beautiful, and cheap)—is not to be missed. Shoes in many styles from sandals to stilettos pack this popular Gràcia shoe emporium. ⊠ *Gran de Gràcia 233, Gràcia* ☎ *93/237–3514* ⊗ *Closed Sun.* Ⓜ *Fontana.*

Nagore. Yet another company of cobblers from Mallorca, Nagore carries eco-chic styles that are reminiscent of the early shoes from Camper, their larger and more famous rival. The brightly colored leathers stand out on this simple whitewashed shop interior that evokes the company's Balearic provenance. ⊠ *Astúries 50, Gràcia* ☎ *93/368–8359* ⊕ *www.nagore.es* ⊗ *Closed Sun.* Ⓜ *Fontana.*

TOYS

FAMILY **Bateau Lune.** Crafts, disguises, puzzles, games, and a thousand things to make you want to be a kid again are on display in this creative child-oriented gift shop on one of Gràcia's most emblematic squares. ⊠ *Pl. de la Virreina 7, Gràcia* ☎ *93/218–6907* ⊕ *www.bateaulune.com* ⊗ *Closed Sun.* Ⓜ *Fontana.*

SARRIÀ

Just like its residents, shops in Sarrià are smart and well-heeled. Most are along the Major de Sarrià, the main drag, and on the elegant Plaça de Sarrià. The emphasis is on kitchen gadgets and gourmet food, like what you'll find at the legendary Foix de Sarrià and a lively local fresh produce market.

BEAUTY

JC Apotecari. Downtown beauty junkies happily make the trip uptown for the hard-to-source cult products that fill the lab-like shelves of JC Apotecari. Skin and hair brands such as Australian botanical Aesop products and Dr. Jackson's are offered alongside perfumed candles from Diptyque and Tweezerman tweezers. ⊠ *Major de Sarrià 96, Sarrià* ☎ *93/205–8734* ⊕ *www.jcapotecari.com* ⊗ *Closed Sun.* Ⓜ *Sarrià.*

CERAMICS

Neo Cerámica. This is the store to visit if you need an order of handsome tiles for your kitchen back home. With some truly striking patterns and the shipping system to get them to you in one piece (each tile, that is), you can trust the Vidal-Quadras clan for care and quality. ✉ *Mandri 43, Sarrià* ☎ *93/211–8958* ⊕ *www.neoceramica.es* ⊘ *Closed Sun.* Ⓜ *Sarrià, El Putxet.*

FOOD

Big Sur La Cave. When in Sarrià, stop at this original wine cellar, tapas bar, and restaurant. With every bottle in this barrel-shaped space color-coded by taste, price, and geography, it's easy to navigate. La Cave also provides a printout of tasting notes and technical data for every bottle. ✉ *Av. J. V. Foix 80, Sarrià* ☎ *93/206–3846* ⊘ *Closed Mon.* Ⓜ *Sarrià.*

Foix de Sarrià. Pastry and poetry under the same roof merit a stop. The verses of J. V. Foix, a major Catalan poet who managed to survive the Franco regime with his art intact, are engraved in bronze on the outside wall of the Major de Sarrià location, where he was born. Excellent pastries, breads, wines, cheeses, and cavas, all available on Sunday, have made Foix de Sarrià a Barcelona landmark. There is a smaller branch nearby at Major de Sarrià 57. ✉ *Pl. Sarrià 12–13, Sarrià* ☎ *93/203–0473* ⊕ *www.foixdesarria.com* Ⓜ *Sarrià* ✉ *Major de Sarrià 57, Sarrià* ☎ *93/203–0714* ⊕ *www.foixdesarria.com* Ⓜ *Sarrià.*

Ískia. Good wine advice and a perennially changing selection of bottles make Iskia one of upper Barcelona's best wine emporiums. The proprietors speak English and are glad to talk about latest wine trends or explain their products at length. ✉ *Major de Sarrià 132, Sarrià* ☎ *93/205–0070* ⊕ *www.iskiavins.com* Ⓜ *Sarrià.*

MARKETS

Sarrià. A small Tuesday antiques markets in Sarrià's town square provides another good reason to explore this charming onetime outlying village in the upper part of the city. On other days, the nearby produce market, a mini-Boqueria, is the place for picnic fare before or after a hike over to the Monestir de Pedralbes. ✉ *Pl. de Sarrià, Sarrià* Ⓜ *Sarrià, Reina Elisenda.*

POBLENOU

For all its eye-catching architecture and creative energy, Poblenou has lacked notable retail offerings until recently. While mom-and-pop shops gather dust along Rambla de Poblenou, brave new businesses selling cutting-edge design and housewares are starting to brighten up the district.

HOUSEHOLD ITEMS AND FURNITURE

BD. Barcelona Design, a spare, cutting-edge furniture and home-accessories store, has just moved into a former industrial building near the sea. BD cofounder Oscar Tusquets, master designer and architect, gives contemporary-design star Jaime Hayon plenty of space here. The works of past giants, such as Gaudí's Casa Calvet chair, or Salvador Dalí's Gala loveseat, are also available—if your pockets are deep enough. ⊠ *Ramón Turró 126, Poblenou* ☎ *93/457–0052* ⊕ *www.bdbarcelona. com* ☾ *Closed weekends* Ⓜ *Llacuna, Bogatell.*

Noak Room. The sleek style of Scandinavian design has truly taken hold in Barcelona, as seen in the cafés and restaurants of the Born and Eixample. Started by a couple who are passionate about retro and vintage pieces from northern Europe, this large, loftlike locale stocks a large selection of upcycled and renovated lamps, sofas, chairs, and mirrors from the 1950s to the '70s. International shipping can be arranged. ⊠ *Rec Boronat 69, Poblenou* ☎ *93/309–5300* ⊕ *www.noakroom.com* ☾ *Closed Sun. and Mon.*

MARKETS

Palo Alto Market. This old factory complex in the Poblenou district was one of the first to be become a creative space. Nineteen designers have studios here, including the legendary Javier Mariscal. With 19th-century industrial architecture (the "palo alto" refers to a towering chimney) and a verdant garden, it is something of an island in this newly developed district. One weekend a month, the Palo Alto Market invites the public to view this urban oddity with live music, food trucks, and dozens of stalls selling goods. Check their website for dates and get there around 11 am, as queues to get in can often snake around the block. ⊠ *Pellaires 30, Poblenou* ☎ *93/159–6670* ⊕ *www.paloaltomarket.com* Ⓜ *Selva del Mar.*

Tutusaus. With an anthological selection of cheeses, hams, pastries, and delicacies of all kinds, this famous café, restaurant, and delicatessen is a hallowed upper Barcelona hangout just off Turo Park. Whether for coffee, a taste of cheese or foie gras, or a full meal composed of a selection of delicacies, this little hideaway is superb. ⊠ *Francesc Perez Cabrero 5, Sant Gervasi* ☎ *93/209–8373* ⊕ *www.tutusaus.com* Ⓜ *La Bonanova.*

CATALONIA, VALENCIA, AND THE COSTA BLANCA

WELCOME TO CATALONIA, VALENCIA, AND THE COSTA BLANCA

TOP REASONS TO GO

★ **Girona:** Explore a city where the monuments of Christian, Jewish, and Islamic cultures that coexisted for centuries are just steps apart.

★ **Valencia reborn:** The past 20 years has seen a transformation of the Turia River into a treasure trove of museums, concert halls, parks, and architectural wonders.

★ **Great restaurants:** Foodies argue that the fountainhead of creative gastronomy has moved from France to Spain— and in particular to the great restaurants of the Empordà and Costa Brava.

★ **Dalí's home and museum:** "Surreal" doesn't begin to describe the Teatre-Museu Dalí in Figueres or the wild coast of the artist's home at Cap de Creus.

★ **Las Fallas festival:** Valencia's Las Fallas in mid-March, a week of fireworks and solemn processions with a finale of spectacular bonfires, is one of the best festivals in Europe.

1 Northern Catalonia.

Inland and westward from the towns of Girona and Figueres is perhaps the most dramatic and beautiful part of old Catalonia; it's a land of medieval villages and hilltop monasteries, volcanic landscapes, and lush green valleys. The ancient city of Girona, often ignored by people bound for the Costa Brava, is an easy and interesting day trip from Barcelona. The upland towns of Besalú and Vic are Catalonia at its most authentic.

2 The Costa Brava.

Native son Salvador Dalí put his mark on the northeasternmost corner of Catalonia, where the Costa Brava begins, especially in the fishing village of Cadaqués and the coast of Cap de Creus. From here, south and west toward Barcelona, lie beaches, historical settlements, and picturesque towns like Sant Feliu de Guixols that draw millions of summer visitors to the region.

3 Southern Catalonia and Around Valencia.

Spain's third-largest city, rich in history and tradition, Valencia is now a cultural magnet for its modern art museum and its space-age City of Arts and Sciences complex. The Albufera Nature Park to the south is an important wetland and wildlife sanctuary. North of Valencia, the monastery of Montserrat is a popular pilgrimage; Sitges has a lovely beach, and Santes Creus and Poblet are beautiful Cistercian monasteries. Roman ruins, chief among them the Circus Maximus, are the reason to go to Tarragona. The Middle Ages added wonderful city walls and citadels here.

4 The Costa Blanca.

Culturally and geographically diverse, the Costa Blanca's most populated coastal resorts stretch north from the provincial capital of Alicante to Dénia. Alicante's historic center and vibrant night-owl scene occupy the hub of a rich agricultural area punctuated by towns like Elche, a UNESCO World Heritage Site. Dénia, capital of the Marina Alta region and a port for ferries to the Balearic Islands, is a charming destination and has a well-deserved reputation for gastronomy.

GETTING ORIENTED

Year-round, Catalonia is the most visited of Spain's autonomous communities. The Pyrenees, which separate it from France, provide some of the country's best skiing, and the rugged Costa Brava in the north and the Costa Dorada to the south are havens for sunseekers. The interior is full of surprises, too: an expanding rural tourism industry and the region's growing international reputation for food and wine give Catalonia a broad-based appeal. Excellent rail, air, and highway connections link Catalonia to the beach resorts of Valencia, its neighbor to the south.

8

EATING AND DRINKING WELL IN CATALONIA, VALENCIA, AND THE COSTA BLANCA

Both Catalonia and Valencia cuisine have classic Mediterranean dishes, and Catalans feel right at home with *paella valenciana* (Valencian paella). Fish preparations are similar along the coast, though inland favorites vary from place to place.

Top left: Paella valenciana in a classic paella pan; Top right: Fresh calçots; Bottom right: Suquet of fish, potatoes, onions, and tomatoes

The grassy inland meadows of Catalonia's northern Alt Empordà region put quality beef on local tables; from the Costa Brava comes fine seafood, such as anchovies from L'Escala and *gambas* (jumbo shrimp) from Palamós, both deservedly famous. *Romesco*—a blend of almonds, peppers, garlic, and olive oil—is used as a fish and seafood sauce in Tarragona, especially during the *calçotadas* (spring onion feasts) in February. *Allioli*, garlicky mayonnaise, is another popular topping. The Ebro Delta is renowned for fresh fish and eels, as well as *rossejat* (fried rice in a fish broth). Valencia and the Mediterranean coast are the homeland of *paella valenciana*. *Arròs a banda* is a variant in which the fish and rice are cooked separately.

CALÇOTS

The *calçot* is a sweet spring onion developed by a 19th-century farmer who discovered how to extend the edible portion by packing soil around the base. It is grilled on a barbecue, then peeled and dipped into romesco sauce. In January, the town of Valls holds a *calçotada* where upward of 30,000 people gather for meals of onions, sausage, lamb chops, and red wine.

RICE

Paella valenciana is one of Spain's most famous gastronomic contributions. A simple country dish dating to the early 18th century, "paella" refers to the wide frying pan with short, sturdy handles that's used to cook the rice. Anything fresh from the fields that day, along with rice and olive oil, traditionally went into the pan, but paella valenciana has particular ingredients: short-grain rice, chicken, rabbit, *garrofó* (a local legume), tomatoes, green beans, sweet peppers, olive oil, and saffron. Artichokes and peas are also included in season. *Paella marinera* (seafood paella) is a different story: rice, cuttlefish, squid, mussels, shrimp, prawns, lobster, clams, garlic, olive oil, sweet paprika, and saffron, all stewed in fish broth. Many other paella variations are possible, including *paella negra*, a black rice dish made with squid ink; *arròs a banda* made with peeled seafood; and *fideuà*, paella made with noodles in place of rice.

SEAFOOD STEWS

Sèpia amb pèsols is a vegetable and seafood *mar i muntanya* ("surf and turf") beloved on the Costa Brava: cuttlefish and peas are stewed with potatoes, garlic, onions, tomatoes, and a splash of wine. The *picadillo*—the finishing touches of flavors and textures—includes parsley, black pepper, fried bread, pine nuts, olive oil, and salt. *Es niu* ("the nest") of game fowl, cod, tripe, cuttlefish, pork, and rabbit is another Costa Brava favorite. Stewed for a good five hours until the darkness of the onions and the ink of the cuttlefish have combined to impart a rich chocolate color to the stew, this is a much-celebrated wintertime classic. You'll also find *suquet de peix*, the Catalan fish stew, at restaurants along the Costa Brava.

FRUITS AND VEGETABLES

Valencia and the eastern Levante region have long been famous as Spain's *huerta*, or garden. The alluvial soil of the littoral produces an abundance of everything from tomatoes to asparagus, peppers, chard, spinach, onions, artichokes, cucumbers, and the whole range of Mediterranean bounty. Catalonia's Maresme and Empordà regions are also fruit and vegetable bowls, making this coastline a true cornucopia of fresh produce.

WINES

The Penedès wine region west of Barcelona has been joined by new wine Denominations of Origin from all over Catalonia. Alt Camp, Tarragona, Priorat, Montsant, Costers del Segre, Pla de Bages, Alella, and Empordà all produce excellent reds and whites to join Catalonia's sparkling *cava* on local wine lists; the rich, full-bodied reds of Montsant and Priorat, especially, are among the best in Spain.

Updated by
Elizabeth
Prosser

The long curve of the Mediterranean from the French border to Cabo Cervera below Alicante encompasses the two autonomous communities of Catalonia and Valencia, with the country's second- and third-largest cities (Barcelona and Valencia, respectively). Rivals in many respects, the two communities share a language, history, and culture that set them apart from the rest of Spain.

Girona is the gateway to Northern Catalonia's attractions—the Pyrenees, the volcanic region of La Garrotxa, and the beaches of rugged Costa Brava. Northern Catalonia is memorable for the soft, green hills of the Empordà farm country and the Alberes mountain range at the eastern end of the Pyrenees. Across the landscape are *masías* (farmhouses) with staggered-stone roofs and square towers that make them look like fortresses. Even the tiniest village has its church, arcaded square, and *rambla*, where villagers take their evening *paseo* (stroll).

Salvador Dalí's deep connection to the Costa Brava is enshrined in the Teatre-Museu Dalí in Figueres: he's buried in the crypt beneath it. His wife Gala is buried in his former home, a castle in Púbol. His summer home in Port Lligat Bay, north of Cadaqués, is now a museum of his life and work.

The province of Valencia was incorporated into the Kingdom of Aragón, Catalonia's medieval Mediterranean empire, when it was conquered by Jaume I in the 13th century. Along with Catalonia, Valencia became part of the united Spanish state in the 15th century, but defenders of its separate cultural and linguistic identity still resent the centuries of Catalan domination. The Catalan language prevails in Tarragona, a city and province of Catalonia, but Valenciano—a dialect of Catalan—is spoken and used on street signs in the Valencian provinces.

The *huerta* (a fertile, irrigated coastal plain) is devoted mainly to citrus and vegetable farming, which lends color to the landscape and fragrance to the air. Arid mountains form a stark backdrop to the lush coast. Over the years these shores have entertained Phoenician, Greek, Carthaginian, and Roman visitors; the Romans stayed several centuries and left archaeological remains all the way down the coast, particularly in Tarragona, the capital of Rome's Spanish empire by 218 BC. Rome's dominion did not go uncontested, however; the most serious challenge came from the Carthaginians of North Africa. The three Punic Wars, fought over this territory between 264 and 146 BC, established the reputation of the Carthaginian general Hannibal.

The coastal farmland and beaches that attracted the ancients now call to modern-day tourists, though in parts, a number of "mass-tourism" resorts have marred the shore. Inland, however, local culture survives intact. The rugged and beautiful territory is dotted with small fortified towns, several of which bear the name of Spain's 11th-century national hero, El Cid, commemorating the battles he fought here against the Moors some 900 years ago.

PLANNING

WHEN TO GO

Come for the beaches in the hot summer months, but expect crowds and serious heat—in some places up to 40°C (104°F). The Mediterranean coast is more comfortable in May and September.

February and March are the peak months for skiing in the Pyrenees. Winter travel in the region has other advantages: Valencia still has plenty of sunshine, and if you're visiting villages and wineries in the countryside you might have the place all to yourself. Note that many restaurants outside the major towns may close on weekdays in winter, so call ahead. Many museums and sites close early in winter (6 pm).

The Costa Brava and Costa Blanca beach areas get hot and crowded in summer, and accommodations are at a premium. In contrast, spring is mild and an excellent time to tour the region, particularly the rural areas, where blossoms infuse the air with pleasant fragrances and wild-flowers dazzle the landscape.

PLANNING YOUR TIME

Not far from Barcelona, the beautiful towns of Vic, Girona, and Cada-qués are easily reachable from the city by bus or train in a couple of hours. Figueres is a must if you want to see the Teatre-Museu Dalí. Girona makes an excellent base from which to explore La Garrotxa—for that, you'll need to rent a car. Allot a few days to explore Tarragona, easily reached from Barcelona by train or a 1½-hour' drive. If you're driving, take a detour to the wineries in the Penedès region; most of Spain's cava comes from here. Explore Tarragona's Roman wonders on foot, and stop for a meal at any of the fine seafood restaurants in the Serallo fishing quarter.

Valencia is three hours by express train from Barcelona; stop in Tarragona on your way if you have time. From Tarragona, it's a comfortable hour-long train ride to Valencia; if driving, stop off for a meal or stroll in one of the coastal towns like Castellon. Historic Valencia and the Santiago Calatrava–designed City of Arts and Sciences complex can be covered in two days, but stay longer and indulge in the city's food and explore the nightlife in the Barrio del Carmen.

Travel agencies in Alicante can arrange tours of the city and bus and train tours to Guadalest, the Algar waterfalls, the Peñón de Ifach (Calpe) on the Costa Blanca, and inland to Elche.

FESTIVALS

In Valencia, **Las Fallas** fiestas begin March 1 and reach a climax between March 15 and El Día de San José (St. Joseph's Day) on March 19, Father's Day in Spain. Las Fallas originated from St. Joseph's role as patron saint of carpenters; in medieval times, carpenters' guilds celebrated the arrival of spring by cleaning out their shops and making bonfires with scraps of wood. These days it's a 19-day celebration ending with fireworks, floats, carnival processions, and bullfights. On March 19, huge wood and papier-mâché effigies of political figures and other personalities (the result of a year's work by local community groups), are torched to end the fiestas.

GETTING HERE AND AROUND

AIR TRAVEL

El Prat de Llobregat in Barcelona is the main international airport for the Costa Brava; Girona is the closest airport to the region, with bus connections directly into the city and to Barcelona. Valencia has an international airport with direct flights to London, Paris, Brussels, Lisbon, Zurich, and Milan as well as regional flights from Barcelona, Madrid, Málaga, and other cities in Spain. There is a regional airport in Alicante serving the Valencian region and Murcia.

BOAT AND FERRY TRAVEL

Many short-cruise lines along the coast offer the chance to view the Costa Brava from the sea. Visit the port areas in the main towns and you'll quickly spot several tourist cruise lines. Plan to spend around €15–€27, depending on the length of the cruise. Many longer cruises include a stop en route for a swim. The glass-keel Nautilus boats for observation of the Medes Islands underwater park cost €19 and run daily April–October and weekends November–March.

The shortest ferry connections to the Balearic Islands originate in Dénia. Balearia sails from there to Ibiza, Formentera, and Mallorca.

Boat and Ferry Information Balearia. ☎ 902/160180, 966/428700 *from abroad* ⊕ www.balearia.com. **Nautilus.** ✉ Passeig Marítim 23, L'Estartit ☎ 972/751489 ⊕ www.english.nautilus.es.

BUS TRAVEL

Private companies run buses down the coast and from Madrid to Valencia, and to Alicante. ALSA is the main bus line in this region; check local tourist offices for schedules. Sarfa operate buses from Barcelona to Blanes, Lloret, Sant Feliu de Guixols, Platja d'Aro, Palamos, Begur, Roses, L'Escala, and Cadaqués.

Contacts ALSA. ☎ 902/422242 ⊕ www.alsa.es. **Moventis Sarfa.** ✉ Estació del Nord, Alí Bei 80, Barcelona ☎ 902/302025 ⊕ compras.moventis.es/en-GB/trayectos-barcelona.html Ⓜ Arc de Triomf. **Sagalés.** ☎ 902/130014 *tickets* ⊕ www.sagales.com. **Sagalés AirportLine.** ☎ 902/130014 ⊕ www.sagalesairportline.com.

CAR TRAVEL

A car is necessary for explorations inland, where drives are smooth and scenic. Catalonia and Valencia have excellent roads; the only drawbacks are the high cost of fuel and the high tolls on the *autopistas* (highways, usually designated by the letters "AP"). The national roads (starting with the letter N) can get clogged, however, so you're often better off on toll roads if your time is limited.

TRAIN TRAVEL

Most of the Costa Brava is not served directly by railroad. A local line runs up the coast from Barcelona to Blanes, then turns inland and connects at Maçanet-Massanes with the main line up to France. Direct trains stop only at major connections, such as Girona, Flaçà, and Figueres. To visit one of the smaller towns in between, you can take a fast direct train from Barcelona to Girona, for instance, then get off and wait for a local to come by. The stop on the main line for the middle section of the Costa Brava is Flaçà, where you can take a bus or taxi to your final destination. Girona and Figueres are two other towns with major bus stations that feed out to the towns of the Costa Brava. The train serves the last three towns on the north end of the Costa Brava: Llançà, Colera, and Portbou.

Express intercity trains reach Valencia from all over Spain, arriving at the new Joaquin Sorolla station; from there, a shuttle bus takes you to the Estación del Norte, the terminus in the center of town, for local connections. From Barcelona there are 15 trains a day, including the fast train TALGO, which takes 3½ hours. There are 22 daily trains to Valencia from Madrid; the high-speed train takes about 1 hour 40 minutes.

For the Costa Blanca, the rail hub is Alicante; for southern Catalonia, make direct train connections to Tarragona from either Barcelona or Valencia.

Contacts RENFE. ☎ *902/320320* ⊕ *www.renfe.com.*

TOURS

Hiking, cycling, and walking tours are available around Valencia and the Costa Blanca.

Riding schools in a number of towns in the region provide classes and trekking opportunities. Pick up brochures at local tourist offices.

Learn to sail in most of the major resorts. For kitesurfing or windsurfing, gear is available for rent at many of the beaches, including Roses and Santa Pola. Many companies offer scuba-diving excursions; in the smaller coastal towns it's possible to dive in the protected waters of offshore nature reserves if you book ahead.

This region is a bird-watcher's paradise, especially in the salt pans of Santa Pola and Albufera Lake. The main coastal plain is a migratory highway for thousands of birds winging their way between Europe and Africa.

CONTACTS

Abdet. The Sierra Mariola and Sierra Aitana regions are both easily accessible from the Costa Blanca resorts. Abdet, near Guadalest, offers itineraries and traditional self-catering guesthouses amid breathtaking scenery. ⊕ *www.abdet.com* ✉ *From €350 for 1-wk accommodation.*

Ciclo Costa Blanca. If pedal power is your thing, Ciclo Costa Blanca is a good place to start, with both guided and self-guided tours. ⊠ *Meta Bike Cafe Comercio Enara 2, Calle Vell de Altea 24, Alicante* ☎ *966/868104* ⊕ *www.ciclocostablanca.com* ✉ *From €499 for 7 nights (self-guided, includes bike hire).*

Julià Travel. Bus tours from Barcelona to Girona and Figueres (including Teatre-Museu Dalí) are run by Julià Travel. Buses leave Barcelona Tuesday–Sunday at 8:30 am and return around 6. ⊠ *Carrer de Balmes 5, Barcelona* ☎ *93/402–6900* ⊕ *www.juliatravel.com* ✉ *From €78.*

Mountain Walks. Self-guided or guided bird-watching, mountain-walking, and cycling tours are customized to suit your requirements, with picturesque cottage accommodations, meals, and transportation included in the price. ⊠ *San Gregorio 4, Quatretondeta, Alicante* ☎ *965/511044* ⊕ *www.mountainwalks.com* ✉ *From €630 (including accommodations and meals), from €120 (guided walking tour only).*

FARMHOUSE STAYS IN CATALONIA

Dotted throughout Catalonia are farmhouses (*casas rurales* in Spanish, and *cases de pagès* or *masíes* in Catalan), where you can spend a weekend or longer. Accommodations vary from small rustic homes to spacious luxurious farmhouses with fireplaces and pools. Stay in a guest room at a bed-and-breakfast, or rent an entire house and do your own cooking. Most tourist offices, including the main Catalonia Tourist Office, have information and listings. Several organizations in Spain have detailed listings and descriptions of Catalonia's farmhouses.

Contacts Agroturisme.org. ☎ *932/680900* ⊕ *www.agroturisme.org.* **CatalunyaRural.info.** ⊕ *www.catalunyarural.info.*

RESTAURANTS

Catalonia's eateries are deservedly famous. Girona's Celler de Can Roca was voted Best Restaurant in the World in 2015 in the annual critics' poll conducted by British magazine *Restaurant,* and a host of other first-rate establishments continue to offer inspiring fine dining in Catalonia, which began in the hinterlands at the legendary Hotel Empordà. Yet you needn't go to an internationally acclaimed restaurant to dine well. Superstar chef Ferran Adrià of the former foodie paradise elBulli dines regularly at dives in Roses, where straight-up fresh fish is the attraction. Northern Catalonia's Empordà region is known for seafood and rich assortment of inland and upland products. Beef from Girona's verdant pastureland is prized throughout Catalonia, while wild mushrooms from the Pyrenees and game from the Alberes range offer seasonal depth to menus across the region. From a simple beachside paella or *llobarro* (sea bass) at a *chiringuito* (beach shack) with tables on the sand, to the splendor of a meal at El Celler de Can Roca, playing culinary hopscotch through Catalonia is a good way to get to know the city.

CLOSE UP

Beaches of the Costa Brava and Costa Blanca

COSTA BRAVA BEACHES
The beaches on the Costa Brava range from stretches of fine white sand to rocky coves and inlets; summer vacationers flock to **Tossa de Mar, Roses,** and **Calella de Palafrugell;** in all but the busiest weeks of July and August, the tucked-away coves of **Cap de Creus National Park** are oases of peace and privacy. **Valencia** has a long beach that's wonderful for sunning and a promenade lined with paella restaurants; for quieter surroundings, head farther south to **El Saler.**

COSTA BLANCA BEACHES
The southeastern coastline of the Costa Blanca varies from the long stretches of sand dunes north of **Dénia** and south of **Alicante** to the coves and crescents in between. The benign climate permits lounging on the beach at least eight months of the year. **Altea,** popular with families, is busy and pebbly, but the old town has retained a traditional pueblo feel with narrow cobbled streets and attractive squares. **Calpe's** beaches have the scenic advantage of the sheer outcrop Peñón de Ifach (Cliff of Ifach), which stands guard over stretches of sand to either side. Dénia has family-friendly beaches to the north, where children paddle in relatively shallow waters, and rocky inlets to the south.

HOTELS
Lodgings on the Costa Brava range from the finest hotels to spartan pensions. The better accommodations have splendid views of the seascape. If you plan to visit during the high season (July and August), be sure to book reservations well in advance at almost any hotel in the area; the Costa Brava remains one of the most popular summer resort areas in Spain. Many Costa Brava hotels close down in the winter season (November–March).

Restaurant and hotel reviews have been shortened. For full information, visit Fodors.com.

WHAT IT COSTS IN EUROS			
	$	$$	$$$	$$$$
Restaurants	under €12	€12–€17	€18–€22	over €22
Hotels	under €90	€90–€125	€126–€180	over €180

Prices are per person for a main course, or a combination of small plates, at dinner, and for two people in a standard double room in high season, excluding tax.

NORTHERN CATALONIA

For many, Northern Catalonia is *the* reason to visit Spain. The historic center of Girona, its principal city, is a labyrinth of climbing cobblestone streets and staircases, with remarkable Gothic and Romanesque buildings at every turn. El Call, the Jewish Quarter, is one of the best preserved in Europe, and the Gothic cathedral is an architectural masterpiece. Streets in the modern part of the city are lined with smart shops and boutiques, and the overall quality of life in Girona is considered among the best in Spain.

Nearby towns Besalú and Figueres are vastly different. Figueres is unremarkable town made exceptional by the Dalí Museum. Besalu is a picture-perfect Romanesque village on a bluff overlooking the Riu Fluvià, with one of the most prestigious restaurants in Catalonia. Lesser known are the medieval towns in and around La Garrotxa: Vic, Rupit, and Olot boast the best produce in the region.

GIRONA

97 km (60 miles) northeast of Barcelona.

At the confluence of four rivers, Girona (population: 97,000) keeps intact the magic of its historic past; with its brooding hilltop castle, soaring cathedral, and dreamy riverside setting, it resembles a vision from the Middle Ages. Today, as a university center, Girona combines past and vibrant present: art galleries, chic cafés, and trendy boutiques have set up shop in many of the restored buildings of the old quarter, known as the Força Vella (Old Fortress), which is on the east side of the Riu Onyar. Built on the side of the mountain, it presents a tightly packed labyrinth of medieval buildings and monuments on narrow cobblestone streets with connecting stairways. You can still see vestiges of the Iberian and Roman walls in the cathedral square and in the patio of the old university. In the central quarter is El Call, one of Europe's best-preserved medieval (12th- to 15th-century) Jewish communities and an important center of Kabbalistic studies.

The main street of the Força Vella is Carrer de la Força, which follows the old Via Augusta, the Roman road that connected Rome with its provinces.

Explore Girona on foot. As you wander through the old quarter, you will be surprised by new discoveries. One of Girona's treasures is its setting, high above where the Onyar merges with the Ter; the latter flows from a mountain waterfall that can be glimpsed in a gorge above the town. Walk first along the west bank of the Onyar, between the train trestle and the Plaça de la Independència, to admire the classic view of the old town, with its pastel waterfront facades. Many of the windows and balconies—always draped with colorful drying laundry—are adorned with fretwork grilles of embossed wood or delicate iron tracery. Cross Pont de Sant Agustí over to the old quarter from under the arcades in the corner of Plaça de la Independència and find your way to the Punt de Benvinguda tourist office, to the right at Rambla Llibertat 1. Work your way up through the labyrinth of steep streets, using the cathedral's huge baroque facade as a guide.

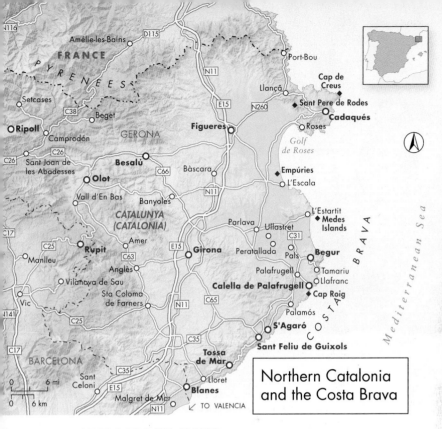

Northern Catalonia
and the Costa Brava

GETTING HERE AND AROUND

There are more than 20 daily trains from Barcelona to Girona (continuing on to the French border). Bus service to the city center is limited, but there are frequent Sagales buses to the Girona airport; they take an average of 75 minutes and cost €16 one-way, €25 round-trip. Getting around the city is easiest on foot or by taxi; several bridges connect the historic old quarter with the more modern town across the river.

DISCOUNTS AND DEALS

The GironaMuseus discounts admission to all the city's museums. ■TIP→ Some are free on the first Sunday of every month. Check the tourist office or at the Punt de Benvinguda welcome center, which can also arrange guided tours.

ESSENTIALS

Bus Information Sagalés AirportLine. ☎ 902/130014 ⊕ www.barcelona-bus.com.

Visitor Information Girona Office of Tourism. ⊠ Rambla de la Llibertat 1 ☎ 972/226575 ⊕ www.girona.cat/turisme. **Punt de Benvinguda.** ⊠ Carrer Berenguer Carnisser 3 ☎ 972/211678 ⊕ www.gironabooking.com/eng/index.asp.

There's more to Girona's cathedral than the 90 steps to get to it; inside there's much to see, including the Treasury.

EXPLORING
TOP ATTRACTIONS

Fodor's Choice
★

Cathedral. At the heart of the Força Vella, the cathedral looms above 90 steps and is famous for its nave—at 75 feet, the widest in the world and the epitome of the spatial ideal of Catalan Gothic architects. Since Charlemagne founded the original church in the 8th century, it has been through many fires and renovations. Take in the rococo-era facade, "eloquent as organ music" and impressive flight of 17th-century stairs, which rises from its own *plaça*. Inside, three smaller naves were compressed into one gigantic hall by the famed architect Guillermo Bofill in 1416. The change was typical of Catalan Gothic "hall" churches, and it was done to facilitate preaching to crowds. Note the famous silver canopy, or *baldaquí* (baldachin). The oldest part of the cathedral is the 11th-century Romanesque **Torre de Carlemany** (Charlemagne Tower).

The cathedral's exquisite 12th-century cloister has an obvious affinity with the cloisters in the Roussillon area of France. Inside the Treasury there's a variety of precious objects. They include a 10th-century copy of Beatus's manuscript *Commentary on the Apocalypse* (illuminated in the dramatically primitive Mozarabic style), the Bible of Emperor Charles V, and the celebrated *Tapís de la Creació* (*Tapestry of the Creation*), considered by most experts to be the finest tapestry surviving from the Romanesque era (and, in fact, thought to be the needlework of Saxons working in England). It depicts the seven days of Creation as told in Genesis in the primitive but powerful fashion of early Romanesque art and looks not unlike an Asian mandala. Made of wool, with predominant colors of green, brown, and ocher, the tapestry once hung behind the main altar as a pictorial Bible lesson. Representations of time and nature circle around a central figure, likening paradise to the eternal cosmos presided over by Christ. The bottom band (which appears to have been added at a later date) contains two *iudeis,* or Jews, dressed in the round cloaks they were compelled to wear to set them apart from Christians. This scene is thought to be the earliest portrayal of a Jew (other than biblical figures) in Christian art. ⊠ *Pl. de la Catedral s/n* ☎ *972/427189* ⊕ *www.catedraldegirona.org* ✑ *€7, includes audio guide.*

El Call. Girona is especially noted for its 13th-century Jewish Quarter, El Call, which branches off Carrer de la Força, south of the Plaça Catedral. The quarter is a network of lanes that crisscross above one another, and houses built atop each other in disorderly fashion along narrow stone medieval streets. With boutique shopping, artsy cafés, and lots of atmospheric eateries and bars, there is plenty to explore.

The word *call* (pronounced "kyle" in Catalan) may come from an old Catalan word meaning "narrow way" or "passage." Others suggest that it comes from the Hebrew word *qahal,* meaning "assembly" or "meeting of the community." The earliest presence of Jews in Girona is uncertain, but the first historical mention dates from 982, when a group of 25 Jewish families moved to Girona from nearby Juïgues. Owing allegiance to the Spanish king (who exacted tribute for this distinction) and not to the city government, this once-prosperous Jewish community—one of the most flourishing in Europe during the Middle Ages—was, at its height, a leading center of learning. ⊠ *Girona.*

WORTH NOTING

Banys Arabs (*Arab Baths*). A misnomer, the Banys Arabs were actually built by Morisco craftsmen (workers of Moorish descent) in the late 12th century, long after Girona's Islamic occupation (714–797) had ended. Following the old Roman model that had disappeared in the West, the custom of bathing publicly may have been brought back from the Holy Land with the Crusaders. These baths are sectioned off into three rooms in descending order: a *frigidarium,* or cold bath, a square room with a central octagonal pool and a skylight with cupola held up by two stories of eight fine columns; a *tepidarium,* or warm bath; and a *caldarium,* or steam room, beneath which is a chamber where a fire was kept burning. Here the inhabitants of old Girona came to relax, exchange gossip, or do business. It is known from another public bathhouse in Tortosa, Tarragona, that the various social classes came to bathe by sex and religion on fixed days of the week: Christian men on one day, Christian women on another, Jewish men on still another, Jewish women (and prostitutes) on a fourth, Muslims on others. ⊠ *Carrer Ferran el Catòlic s/n* ☎ *972/190969* ⊕ *www.banysarabs.org* ✑ *€2.*

Monestir de Sant Pere de Galligants. The church of St. Peter, across the Galligants River, was finished in 1131, and is notable for its octagonal Romanesque belfry and the finely detailed capitals atop the columns in the cloister. It now houses the **Museu Arqueològic** (Museum of Archaeology), which documents the region's history since Paleolithic times and includes some artifacts from Roman times. ⊠ *Carrer Santa Llúcia 8* ☎ *972/202632* ✑ *€4.50* ۞ *Closed Mon.*

Museu d'Art. The Episcopal Palace near the cathedral contains the wide-ranging collections of Girona's main art museum. You'll see everything from superb Romanesque *majestats* (carved wood figures of Christ) to reliquaries from Sant Pere de Rodes, illuminated 12th-century manuscripts, and works of the 20th-century Olot school of landscape painting. ✉ *Pujada de la Catedral 12* ☎ *972/203834* 🌐 *www.museuart.com* 🎟 *€4.50* 🕒 *Closed Mon. except holidays.*

Museum of Jewish History. Housed in a former synagogue and dedicated to the preservation of Girona's Jewish heritage, this center organizes conferences, exhibitions, and seminars and contains 21 stone tablets, one of the finest collections in the world of medieval Jewish funerary slabs. These came from the old Jewish cemetery of Montjuïc, revealed when the railroad between Barcelona and France was laid out in the 19th century. Its exact location, about 1½ km (1 mile) north of Girona on the road to La Bisbal and known as La Tribana, is being excavated. The center also holds the **Institut d'Estudis Nahmànides,** with an extensive library of Judaica. ✉ *Carrer de la Força 8* ☎ *972/216761* 🌐 *www.girona.cat/call/eng/museu.php* 🎟 *€4.*

Passeig Arqueològic. The landscaped gardens of this stepped archaeological walk are below the restored walls of the Força Vella (which you can walk, in parts) and have good views from belvederes and watchtowers. From there, climb through the Jardins de la Francesa to the highest ramparts for a view of the cathedral's 11th-century Torre de Carlemany. ✉ *Girona.*

WHERE TO EAT

$$$$ CATALAN

🍴 **Bubbles Gastrobar.** Excellent Catalan cuisine with Mediterranean-fusion touches is served here in an elegant setting just across the river from the Força Vella. Try the innovative tapas, or choose the dinner tasting menu for €45. **Known for:** €45 tasting menu; innovative tapas; great lunch spot. [$] *Average main: €25* ✉ *Passeig José Canalejas 6* ☎ *972/226002* 🌐 *www.gastrobubbles.com* 🕒 *Closed Sun. and Mon.*

$$$ CATALAN

🍴 **Cal Ros.** Tucked under the arcades just behind the north end of Plaça de la Llibertat, this restaurant combines ancient stone arches with crisp, contemporary furnishings and cheerful lighting. The menu changes regularly, featuring organically raised local produce in season, and fresh fish in updated versions of traditional Catalan cuisine. **Known for:** rice dishes. [$] *Average main: €20* ✉ *Carrer Cort Reial 9* ☎ *972/219176* 🕒 *Closed Mon. and Tues. No dinner Sun.*

$$$$ CONTEMPORARY Fodor's Choice ★

🍴 **El Celler de Can Roca.** Annointed in 2013 and 2015 by an international panel of food critics and chefs as the best restaurant in the world, El Celler de Can Roca is a life-changing experience for anybody persistent enough to get a reservation. The Roca brothers, Joan, Josep, and Jordi, showcase their masterful creations in two tasting menus, at €155 and €190; consider your visit blessed if yours includes signature dishes like lobster *parmentier* with black trumpet mushrooms, or suckling Iberian pig with pepper sauce and garlic and quince terrine, or Dublin Bay prawns with curry smoke (the Rocas pioneered the technique of roasting in the aromas of spices during the cooking process). **Known for:** extensive wine selection. [$] *Average main: €180* ✉ *Can Sunyer 48* ☎ *972/222157* 🌐 *cellercanroca.com* 💳 *No credit cards* 🕒 *Closed 1 wk in Aug. No lunch Sun.–Tues.*

WHERE TO STAY

$$$$ ⊡ **Alemanys 5.** Award-winning architect Anna Noguera and partner
RENTAL   Juan-Manuel Ribera transformed a 16th-century house steps from the
FAMILY   cathedral into two extraordinary apartments: one for up to five people,
Fodor's Choice   the other for six. **Pros:** perfect for families or small groups; ideal loca-
★   tion. **Cons:** difficult to reach by car; minimum stay required. $ *Rooms
from: €275* ⊠ *Carrer Alemanys 5* ☎ *649/885136* ⊕ *www.alemanys5.
com* ⊟ *No credit cards* ⊅ *2 apartments* ⦶ *No meals.*

$ ⊡ **Bellmirall.** This pretty little *hostal* (guesthouse) in the old city, on the
B&B/INN   edge of El Call, makes up in value and location what it lacks in amenities and services; when there's no staff on call, you come and go with
your own key. **Pros:** steps from the important sites; charming sitting
room; good value. **Cons:** bedrooms are small. $ *Rooms from: €87*
⊠ *Carrer de Bellmirall 3* ☎ *972/204009* ⊕ *www.bellmirall.eu* ⊟ *No
credit cards* ⊙ *Closed Jan.* ⊅ *7 rooms* ⦶ *Breakfast.*

$$ ⊡ **Hotel Històric.** Perfectly placed for exploring El Call, this boutique
HOTEL   hotel occupies a 9th-century house, with remnants of a 3rd-century
Fodor's Choice   Roman wall and a Roman aqueduct on the ground floor and in one of
★   the apartments. **Pros:** good location; historical features; top amenities
and comforts. **Cons:** rooms and apartments are a little cramped; dif-
ficult access by car; no pets. $ *Rooms from: €114* ⊠ *Carrer Bellmirall
4A* ☎ *972/223583* ⊕ *www.hotelhistoric.com* ⊅ *6 rooms, 7 apartments,
2 suites* ⦶ *No meals.*

$$ ⊡ **Hotel Peninsular.** In a handsomely restored early-20th-century build-
HOTEL   ing across the Riu Onyar, with views into Girona's historic Força Vella,
this modest but useful hotel occupies a strategic spot at the end of the
Pont de Pedra (Stone Bridge), a Girona landmark in the center of the
shopping district. **Pros:** good location at the hub of Girona life; near
the stop for the bus from Girona airport. **Cons:** smallish rooms; can
be noisy on Friday and Saturday nights. $ *Rooms from: €90* ⊠ *Carrer
Nou 3, Av. Sant Francesc 6* ☎ *972/203800* ⊕ *www.novarahotels.com*
⊅ *48 rooms* ⦶ *No meals.*

NIGHTLIFE

Girona is a university town, so the night scene is especially lively during
the school year.

Nou Plàtea. This nightspot, popular with students and visitors alike, has
both disco and live bands in concert, depending on the day of the week.
⊠ *Carrer Jeroni Real de Fontclara 4* ☎ *972/227288.*

SHOPPING

BOOKS AND TOYS

La Carpa. All manner of masks, dolls, toys, and other crafts are available here. ⊠ *Carrer Ballesteries 37* ☎ *972/212002* ⊕ *www.lacarpa.cat.*

Llibreria 22. Girona's best bookstore has a large travel-guide section and
a small selection of English fiction. ⊠ *Carrer Hortes 22* ☎ *972/212395*
⊕ *www.llibreria22.net.*

CLOTHING AND SHOES

Despiral. Young people stock up on threads at Despiral, from lines
including Citizens of Humanity, Bellerose, and American Vintage.
⊠ *Carrer Santa Clara 43* ☎ *972/213004* ⊕ *www.despiral.com.*

With its picturesque rivers, Girona is often called the Spanish Venice.

Peacock. For a good range of shoes, from Crocs and sneakers to strappy high heels and Armani moccasins, go to one of Peacock's four Girona locations—the others are at Carrer Migdia 18, and Carrer Pare Claret 29. ⊠ *Carrer Nou 15* ☎ *972/226848* ⊕ *www.peacock.cat.*

FOOD AND CANDY

Gluki. This chocolatier and confectioner has been in business since 1870. ⊠ *Carrer Santa Clara 44* ☎ *972/201989* ⊕ *www.gluki.cat.*

Rocambolesc. Couldn't get a table at El Celler de Can Roca? Keep trying, but in the meantime there's Rocambolesc, the latest of the Roca family culinary undertakings. This ice-cream kiosk in the heart of the city serves up master confectioner Jordi Roca's exquisite *helados* and takeaway desserts. Expect long lines. There are no seats, so enjoy the ice cream on the go. ⊠ *Carrer Santa Clara 50* ☎ *972/416667* ⊕ *www.rocambolesc.com.*

Torrons Victoria Candela. Tasty nougat is the specialty here. ⊠ *Carrer Anselm Clavé 3* ☎ *972/211103.*

JEWELRY

Baobab. A lot of designer Anna Casal's original jewelry seems at first sight to be rough-hewn; it takes a second careful look to realize how sophisticated it really is. This shop doubles as her studio. ⊠ *Carrer de les Hortes 18* ☎ *972/410227.*

FIGUERES

37 km (23 miles) north of Girona.

Figueres is the capital of the *comarca* (county) of the Alt Empordà, the bustling county seat of this predominantly agricultural region. Local people come from the surrounding area to shop at its many stores and stock up on farm equipment and supplies. Thursday is market day, and farmers gather at the top of La Rambla to do business and gossip, taking refreshments at cafés and discreetly pulling out and pocketing large rolls of bills, the result of their morning transactions. What brings the tourists to Figueres in droves, however, has little to do with agriculture and everything to do with Salvador Dalí's jaw-droppingly surreal "theater-museum"—one of the most visited museums in Spain.

Artist Salvador Dalí is Figueres's most famous son. With a painterly technique that rivaled that of Jan van Eyck, a flair for publicity so aggressive it would have put P. T. Barnum to shame, and a penchant for the shocking (he loved telling people Barcelona's historic Barri Gòtic should be knocked down), Dalí, whose most lasting image may be the melting watches in his iconic 1931 painting *The Persistence of Memory*. enters art history as one of the foremost proponents of surrealism, the movement launched in the 1920s by André Breton. The artist, who was born in Figueres and died there in 1989, decided to create a museum-monument to himself during the last two decades of his life. Dalí often frequented the Cafeteria Astòria at the top of La Rambla (still the center of social life in Figueres), signing autographs for tourists or just being Dalí: he once walked down the street with a French omelet in his breast pocket instead of a handkerchief.

GETTING HERE AND AROUND

Figueres is one of the stops on the regular train service from Barcelona to the French border. Local buses are also frequent, especially from nearby Cadaqués, with more than eight schedules daily. If you're driving, take the AP7 north from Girona. The town is small enough to explore on foot.

ESSENTIALS

Visitor Information Figueres. ✉ *Pl. de l'Escorxador 2* ☎ *972/503155* ⊕ *en.visitfigueres.cat.*

EXPLORING

Castell de Sant Ferran. Just a minute's drive northwest of Figueres is this imposing 18th-century fortified castle, one of the largest in Europe—only when you start exploring can you appreciate how immense it is. The parade grounds extend for acres, and the arcaded stables can hold more than 500 horses; the perimeter is roughly 4 km (2½ miles around). This castle was the site of the last official meeting of the Republican parliament (on February 1, 1939) before it surrendered to Franco's forces. Ironically, it was here that Lieutenant Colonel Antonio Tejero was imprisoned after his failed 1981 coup d'état in Madrid. ■TIP→ Call a day ahead and arrange for the two-hour Catedral de l'Aiguas guided tour in English (€15), which includes a trip

The Dalí Museum in Figueres is itself a work of art. Note the eggs on the exterior: they're a common image in his work.

through the castle's subterranean water system by Zodiac pontoon boat. ☒ *Pujada del Castell s/n* ☎ *972/506094* ⊕ *www.lesfortaleses-catalanes.info* ☒ *€3.*

FAMILY **Museu del Joguet de Catalunya.** Hundreds of antique dolls and toys are on display here—including collections owned by, among others, Salvador Dalí, Federico García Lorca, and Joan Miró. It also hosts Catalonia's only *caganer* exhibit (mid-December–mid-January, in odd-numbered years). These playful little figures answering nature's call have long had a special spot in the Catalan *pessebre* (Nativity scene). Farmers are the most traditional figures, squatting discreetly behind the animals, but these days you'll find Barça soccer players and politicians, too. Check with the museum for exact dates. ☒ *Carrer de Sant Pere 1* ☎ *972/504585* ⊕ *www.mjc.cat* ☒ *€6* ☉ *Closed Mon. and mid-Jan.–mid–Feb.*

Fodor'sChoice **Teatre-Museu Dalí.** "Museum" was not a big enough word for Dalí, so
★ he christened his monument a theater. In fact, the building was once the Força Vella theater, reduced to a ruin in the Spanish civil war. Now topped with a glass geodesic dome and studded with Dalí's iconic egg shapes, the multilevel museum pays homage to his fertile imagination and artistic creativity. It includes gardens, ramps, and a spectacular drop cloth Dalí painted for Les Ballets de Monte Carlo. Don't look for his greatest paintings here, although there are some memorable images, including *Gala at the Mediterranean,* which takes the body of Gala (Dalí's wife) and morphs it into the image of Abraham Lincoln once you look through coin-operated viewfinders. The sideshow theme continues with other coin-operated pieces, including

Taxi Plujós (*Rainy Taxi*), in which water gushes over the snail-covered occupants sitting in a Cadillac once owned by Al Capone, or *Sala de Mae West*, a trompe-l'oeil vision in which a pink sofa, two fireplaces, and two paintings morph into the face of the onetime Hollywood sex symbol. Fittingly, another "exhibit" on view is Dalí's own crypt. When his friends considered what flag to lay over his coffin, they decided to cover it with an embroidered heirloom tablecloth instead. Dalí would have liked this unconventional touch if not the actual site: he wanted to be buried at his castle of Púbol next to his wife, but the then-mayor of Figueres took matters into his own hands. The summer night session is a perfect time to browse through the world's largest surrealist museum. ✉ *Pl. Gala-Salvador Dalí 5* ☎ *972/677500* 🌐 *www.salvador-dali.org* 🎟 *€14* 🕓 *Closed Mon. Oct.–May.*

WHERE TO STAY

$$ HOTEL 🏨 **Hotel Duràn.** Dalí had his own private dining room in this former stagecoach relay station, and you can take a meal amid pictures of the great surrealist. **Pros:** good central location; family-friendly. **Cons:** rooms lacks character; parking inconvenient; no pets. [$] *Rooms from: €107* ✉ *Carrer Lasauca 5* ☎ *972/501250* 🌐 *www.hotelduran.com* 🛏 *65 rooms* 🍴 *No meals.*

$$ HOTEL Fodor'sChoice ★ 🏨 **Hotel Empordà.** Just 1½ km (1 mile) north of town, this hotel houses the elegant restaurant run by Jaume Subirós that's been hailed as the birthplace of modern Catalan cuisine and has become a beacon for gourmands. **Pros:** historic culinary destination; convenient to the Teatre-Museu Dalí. **Cons:** on an unprepossessing roadside lot beside the busy N11 highway. [$] *Rooms from: €113* ✉ *Av. Salvador Dalí i Domènech 170* ☎ *972/500562* 🌐 *www.hotelemporda.com* 🛏 *39 rooms, 3 suites* 🍴 *No meals.*

BESALÚ

34 km (21 miles) northwest of Girona, 25 km (15 miles) west of Figueres.

Besalú, the capital of a feudal county until power was transferred to Barcelona at the beginning of the 12th century, remains one of the best-preserved medieval towns in Catalonia. Among its main sights are the 12th-century Romanesque fortified bridge over the Riu Fluvià; two churches—Sant Vicenç (set on an attractive, café-lined plaza) and Sant Pere—and the ruins of the convent of Santa Maria on the hill above town.

GETTING HERE AND AROUND

With a population of less than 2,500, the village is easily small enough to stroll through—restaurants and sights are within walking distance of each other. There is bus service to Besalú from Figueres and the surrounding Costa Brava resorts.

ESSENTIALS

Visitor Information **Besalú Tourist Office.** ✉ *Carrer del Pont 1* ☎ *972/591240* 🌐 *www.besalu.cat.*

EXPLORING

Convent de Santa Maria. The ruins of the Santa Maria Convent, on a hill just outside of town, make a good walk and offer a panoramic view over Besalú. ✉ *Besalú.*

Església de Sant Pere. This 12th-century Romanesque church is part of a 10th-century monastery, still in an excellent state of preservation. ✉ *Pl. de Sant Pere s/n.*

Església de Sant Vicenç. Founded in 977, this pre-Romanesque gem contains the relics of St. Vincent as well as the tomb of its benefactor, Pere de Rovira. La Capella de la Veracreu (Chapel of the True Cross) displays a reproduction of an alleged fragment of the True Cross brought from Rome by Bernat Tallafer in 977 and stolen in 1899. ✉ *Pl. Sant Vicenç s/n.*

Jewish ritual baths. The remains of this 13th-century *mikvah,* or Jewish ritual bath, were discovered in the 1960s. It's one of the few surviving in Spain. A stone stairway leads down into the chamber where the water was drawn from the river, but little else indicates the role that the baths played in the medieval Jewish community. Access is by guided tour only (organized through the tourist office). ✉ *Calle de Pont Vell* ☎ *972/591240* 🎟 *€3.*

Pont Fortificat. The town's most emblematic feature is this Romanesque 11th-century fortified bridge with crenellated battlements spanning the Riu Fluvià. ✉ *Besalú.*

WHERE TO EAT

$$$$ CATALAN Fodor's Choice ★

🍴 **Els Fogons de Can Llaudes.** A faithfully restored 10th-century Romanesque chapel holds proprietor Jaume Soler's outstanding restaurant—one of Catalonia's best. A typical dish could be *confitat de bou i raïm glacejat amb el seu suc* (beef confit au jus with glacé grapes), but the menu changes weekly. **Known for:** rotating menu; excellent decor. [$] *Average main: €80* ✉ *Plaça de Prat de Sant Pere 6* ☎ *972/590858* 🕒 *Closed Tues. and last 2 wks of Nov.*

OLOT

21 km (13 miles) west of Besalú, 55 km (34 miles) northwest of Girona.

Capital of the *comarca* (administrative region) of La Garrotxa, Olot is famous for its 19th-century school of landscape painters and has several excellent Art Nouveau buildings, including the Casa Solà-Morales, which has a facade by Lluís Domènech i Montaner, architect of Barcelona's Palau de la Música Catalana. The Sant Esteve church at the southeastern end of Passeig d'en Blay is famous for its El Greco painting *Christ Carrying the Cross* (1605).

WHERE TO EAT

$$$$ CATALAN

🍴 **Ca l'Enric.** Chefs Jordi and Isabel Juncà have become legends in the town of La Vall de Bianya just north of Olot, where symposia on culinary matters such as woodcock preparation have inspired prizewinning books. Cuisine firmly rooted in local products, starring game of all sorts, truffles, and wild mushrooms, is taken to another level here. **Known for:** local ingredients; rotating menu.

Besalú contains astonishingly well-preserved medieval buildings.

$ *Average main: €32* ✉ *Ctra. de Camprodon s/n, La Vall de Bianya* ✚ *Nacional 260, Km 91* ☎ *972/290015* ⊕ *www.restaurantcalenric. cat* ⊗ *Closed Mon. and Jan. 1–17 and 1st 2 wks of July (can vary). No dinner Sun.–Wed.*

$$$$
CATALAN
✗ **Les Cols.** Off the road east to Figueres, Fina Puigdevall has made this ancient *masia* (Catalan farmhouse) a design triumph. The sprawling 18th-century rustic structure is filled with glassed-in halls, intimate gardens, and wrought-iron and steel details. **Known for:** local ingredients; seasonal menu; incredible decor. $ *Average main: €50* ✉ *Mas les Cols, Ctra. de la Canya s/n* ☎ *972/269209* ⊕ *www. lescols.com* ⊗ *Closed Mon. and 1st 3 wks of Jan. No dinner Sun. and Tues.*

EN ROUTE
Vall d'En Bas. The villages of Vall d'En Bas lie south of Olot, off the C153. A freeway cuts across this countryside to Vic, but you'll miss a lot by taking it. The twisting old road leads you through rich farmland past farmhouses with dark wooden balconies bedecked with bright flowers. Turn off for Sant Privat d'En Bas and Els Hostalets d'En Bas. Farther on, the picturesque medieval village of Rupit has excellent restaurants serving the famous *patata de Rupit*, potato stuffed with duck and beef, while the rugged Collsacabra mountains offer some of Catalonia's most pristine landscapes.

THE COSTA BRAVA

The Costa Brava (Wild Coast) is a nearly unbroken series of sheer rock cliffs dropping down to clear blue-green waters, punctuated by innumerable coves and tiny beaches on narrow inlets, called *calas*. It basically begins at Blanes and continues north along 135 km (84 miles) of coastline to the French border at Portbou. Although the area does have spots of real-estate excess, the rocky terrain of many pockets (Tossa, Cap de Begur, and Cadaqués) has discouraged overbuilding. On a good day here, the luminous blue of the sea contrasts with red-brown headlands and cliffs, and the distant lights of fishing boats reflect on wine-color waters at dusk. Small stands of umbrella pine veil the footpaths to many of the secluded coves and little patches of white sand—often, the only access is by boat.

GETTING HERE AND AROUND

From Barcelona, the fastest way to the Costa Brava by car is to start up the inland AP7 tollway toward Girona, then take Sortida 10 (Exit 10) for Blanes, Lloret de Mar, Tossa de Mar, Sant Feliu de Guíxols, S'Agaró, Platja d'Aro, Palamós, Calella de Palafrugell, and Palafrugell. From Palafrugell, you can head inland for La Bisbal and from there on to Girona, in the heart of Northern Catalonia. To head to the middle section of the Costa Brava, get off at Sortida 6, the first exit after Girona; this will point you directly to the Iberian ruins of Ullastret. To reach the northern part of the Costa Brava, get off the AP7 before Figueres at Sortida 4 for L'Estartit, L'Escala, Empúries, Castelló d'Empúries, Aïguamolls de l'Empordà, Roses, Cadaqués, Sant Pere de Rodes, and Portbou. Sortida 4 will also take you directly to Figueres, Peralada, and the Alberes mountains. The old national route, N11, is slow, heavily traveled, and more dangerous, especially in summer.

BLANES

60 km (37 miles) northeast of Barcelona, 45 km (28 miles) south of Girona.

The beaches closest to Barcelona are at Blanes. The Costa Brava begins here with five different beaches, running from Punta Santa Anna on the far side of the port—a tiny cove with a pebbly beach at the bottom of a chasm encircled by towering cliffs, fragrant pines, and deep blue-green waters—to the 2½-km-long (1½-mile-long) S'Abanell beach, which draws the crowds. Small boats can take you from the harbor to Cala de Sant Francesc or the double beach at Santa Cristina May–September.

The castle of Sant Joan, seated on a mountain overlooking the town, dates back to the 11th century. The watchtower on the coast was built in the 16th century to protect against Barbary pirates. Most travelers skip the working port of Blanes.

DID YOU KNOW?

The artist Marc Chagall loved to vacation in Tossa de Mar and felt inspired by its vivid-blue ocean seascape.

FESTIVALS

FAMILY **Els Focs de Blanes** (*Fireworks Competition*). The summer event in Blanes that everyone waits for is the fireworks competition, held every night at 11, around July 23–26 (dates can vary year to year; check the website for the exact schedule), which coincides with the town's annual festival. The fireworks are launched over the water from a rocky outcropping in the middle of the seaside promenade known as Sa Palomera while people watch from the beach and surrounding area as more gunpowder is burned in a half hour than at the battle of Trafalgar. ⊠ *Blanes* ⊕ *www.blanes.cat/focs.*

TOSSA DE MAR

80 km (50 miles) northeast of Barcelona, 41 km (25 miles) south of Girona.

The next stop north from Blanes on the coast road—by way of the mass-market resort of Lloret de Mar—is Tossa de Mar, christened "Blue Paradise" by painter Marc Chagall, who summered here for four decades. Tossa's walled medieval town and pristine beaches are among Catalonia's best.

Set around a blue buckle of a bay, Tossa de Mar is a symphony in two parts: the Vila Vella (Old Town) and the Vila Nova (New Town), the latter a lovely district open to the sea and threaded by 18th-century lanes. The Vila Vella is a knotted warren of steep, narrow, cobblestone streets with many restored buildings, some dating back to the 14th century. It sits on the Cap de Tossa promontory that juts out into the sea, and is girdled by 12th-century walls and towers, which line the water's edge and are a local pride and joy—the only example of a fortified medieval town on the entire Catalan coast.

Ava Gardner filmed the 1951 British drama *Pandora and the Flying Dutchman* here (a statue dedicated to her stands on a terrace on the medieval walls). Things may have changed since those days, but this beautiful village retains much of the unspoiled magic of its past. The primary beach at Tossa de Mar is the Platja Gran (Big Beach) in front of the town beneath the walls, and just next to it is Mar Menuda (Little Sea), where the small, colorfully painted fishing boats—maybe the same ones that caught your dinner—pull up onto the beach.

GETTING HERE AND AROUND

The main bus station (the local tourist office is here) is on Plaça de les Nacions Sense Estat. Take Avinguda Ferran and Avinguda Costa Brava to head down the slope to the waterfront and the Vila Vella, which you enter via the Torre de les Hores, and head to the Vila Vella's heart—the Gothic church of Sant Vicenç—for a journey back in time to the Middle Ages.

EXPLORING

Museu Municipal. In a lovingly restored 14th-century house, this museum is said to be Catalonia's first dedicated to modern art. It is home to one of the only three Chagall paintings in Spain, *Celestial Violinist.* ⊠ *Pl. Pintor Roig i Soler 1* ☎ *972/340709* ⊕ *www.tossademar.com/museu* ⊠ *€3* ⊙ *Closed Mon.*

BEACHES

Mar Menuda (*Little Sea*). Just north of the town center, this gentle 460-foot sandy crescent is a pleasant Blue Flag beach that's popular with local families. The sand is coarse, but the sparkling, calm, shallow waters make it ideal for children to bathe. Fishing boats bob peacefully in the water nearby after completing their morning's work. At the top of the beach there is a second cove called La Banyera de Ses Dones (the women's bathtub), which provides ideal conditions for diving, though if the sea is not calm, it is dangerous for swimmers. By day there is little natural shade, so bring adequate sunblock and a parasol if you plan a long beach session. It gets extremely busy in high season. **Amenities:** none. **Best for:** snorkeling; sunset; swimming. ✉ *Av. Mar Menuda.*

Platja Gran (*Big Beach*). Sweeping past the Vila Vella, this well-maintained, soft-sand beach runs along the front of town to meet the base of the Cap de Tossa. One of the most photographed coastlines in this area of Spain, it is also, at the height of summer, one of the busiest. Conditions are normally fine for swimming (any warnings are announced via loudspeaker). A rising number of motorboats is impacting on the water quality, but for now it retains its Blue Flag status. Running behind the beach, there is no shortage of cafés and kiosks selling ice cream and snacks. There is no natural shade but you can rent deck chairs and umbrellas. **Amenities:** food and drink; lifeguards; showers; toilets; water sports. **Best for:** snorkeling; sunset; swimming. ✉ *Av. Palma 1.*

WHERE TO EAT AND STAY

$$$$ CATALAN
🍴 **La Cuina de Can Simon.** Elegantly rustic, this restaurant right beside Tossa del Mar's medieval walls serves a combination of classical Catalan cuisine with up-to-date innovative touches. The menu changes with the season; two tasting menus (€65 and €98) provide more than enough to sample. **Known for:** top-notch service; seasonal menu; welcoming tapa and cava upon entrance. [$] *Average main: €25* ✉ *Carrer del Portal 24* ☎ *972/341269* 🕒 *Closed Mon. and Tues.*

$$ HOTEL
🏨 **Hotel Capri.** Located on the beach, this hotel is in hailing distance of the old quarter in the medieval fortress. **Pros:** family-friendly; perfect location; good value. **Cons:** rooms are small; minimal amenities; no private parking. [$] *Rooms from: €97* ✉ *Passeig del Mar 17* ☎ *972/340358* 🌐 *www.hotelcapritossa.com* 🕒 *Closed Nov.–end Feb.* 🛏 *22 rooms* 🍽 *Breakfast.*

$$$$ HOTEL
Fodor's Choice ★
🏨 **Hotel Diana.** Built in 1906 by architect Antoni Falguera i Sivilla, disciple of Antoni Gaudí, this Moderniste gem sits on the square in the heart of the Vila Vella, steps from the beach. **Pros:** attentive service; ideal location. **Cons:** minimal amenities; room rates unpredictable. [$] *Rooms from: €265* ✉ *Pl. de Espanya 6* ☎ *972/341886* 🌐 *www.hotelesdante.com* 🕒 *Closed Nov.–Mar.* 🛏 *19 rooms, 2 suites* 🍽 *Breakfast.*

$$ HOTEL
🏨 **Hotel Sant March.** This family hotel in the center of town is two minutes from the beach. **Pros:** warm personal touch; good value. **Cons:** no elevator; rooms a bit small; few exterior views. [$] *Rooms from: €110* ✉ *Av. Pelegrí 2* ☎ *972/340078* 🌐 *www.hotelsantmarch.com* 🕒 *Closed Oct. 15–end Mar.* 🛏 *29 rooms* 🍽 *Breakfast.*

SANT FELIU DE GUIXOLS

23 km (14 miles) northeast of Tossa de Mar.

The little fishing port of Sant Feliu de Guixols is set on a small bay; Moderniste mansions line the seafront promenade, recalling a time when the cork industry made this one of the wealthier towns on the coast. In front of them, a long crescent beach of fine white sand leads around to the fishing harbor at its north end. Behind the promenade, a well-preserved old quarter of narrow streets and squares leads to a 10th-century gateway with horseshoe arches (all that remains of a pre-Romanesque monastery); nearby stands a church that combines Romanesque, Gothic, and baroque styles.

GETTING HERE AND AROUND

To get here, take the C65 from Tossa del Mar—though adventurous souls might prefer the harrowing hairpin curves of the G1682 coastal corniche.

EXPLORING

Museu d'Història de la Ciutat. The Romanesque Benedictine monastery houses this museum, which contains interesting exhibits about the town's cork and fishing trades, and displays local archaeological finds. ✉ *Pl. del Monestir s/n* ☎ *972/821575* 🌐 *www.museu.guixols.cat* 🎫 €2.

WHERE TO EAT AND STAY

$ CATALAN — 🍴 **Can Segura.** Half a block in from the beach at Sant Feliu de Guixols, this restaurant serves home-cooked seafood and upland specialties; the *pimientos de piquillos rellenos de brandada* (sweet red peppers stuffed with codfish mousse) are first-rate, as are the rice dishes and the *escudella* (traditional winter soup with meatballs, vegetables, and pasta). The dining room is always full, with customers waiting their turn in the street, but the staff is good at finding spots at the jovially long communal tables. **Known for:** first-rate seafood specialties; communal dining; excellent rice dishes. [$] *Average main: €11* ✉ *Carrer de Sant Pere 11* ☎ *972/321009.*

$$ SEAFOOD FAMILY — 🍴 **El Dorado Mar.** Around the southern end of the beach at Sant Feliu de Guixols, perched over the entrance to the harbor, this superb family restaurant offers fine fare at unbeatable prices. Whether straight seafood such as *lubina* (sea bass) or *dorada* (gilt-head bream) or *revuelto de setas* (eggs scrambled with wild mushrooms), everything served here is fresh and flavorful. **Known for:** affordable cuisine; knockout egg scramble; fresh seafood. [$] *Average main: €15* ✉ *Passeig Irla 15* ☎ *972/326286* 🌐 *www.grupeldorado.com* 🕒 *Closed Wed. Oct.–May.*

$$$$ CATALAN — 🍴 **Villa Mas.** This Moderniste villa on the coast road from Sant Feliu to S'Agaró, with a lovely turn-of-the-20th-century zinc bar, serves up typical Catalan and seasonal Mediterranean dishes like *arròs a la cassola* (deep-dish rice) with shrimp brought fresh off the boats in Palamos, just up the coast. The terrace is a popular and shady spot just across the road from the beach. **Known for:** dining on terrace; across from beach; fresh catches. [$] *Average main: €28* ✉ *Passeig de Sant Pol 95* ☎ *972/822526* 🌐 *www.restaurantvillamas.com* 🕒 *Closed Mon. and mid-Dec.–mid-Jan. No dinner Tues.–Thurs. and Sun. during Oct.–Mar. June–Aug. open every day lunch and dinner.*

$$ ⌂ **Hostal del Sol.** Once the summer home of a wealthy family, this Mod-
HOTEL erniste hotel has a grand stone stairway and medieval-style tower, as
FAMILY well as a garden and a lawn where you can relax by the pool. **Pros:**
family-friendly; good value. **Cons:** bathrooms a bit claustrophobic;
far from the beach; on a busy road. $ *Rooms from: €120* ⌷ *Ctra. a
Palamós 194* ☎ *972/320193* ⊕ *www.hostaldelsol.cat/en* ⊟ *No credit
cards* ⊘ *Closed mid-Oct.–Easter* ⇌ *41 rooms* ⦿ *No meals.*

S'AGARÓ

3 km (2 miles) north of Sant Feliu.

S'Agaró is an elegant gated community on a rocky point at the north
end of the cove. The 30-minute walk along the **sea wall** from Hostal
de La Gavina to Sa Conca Beach is a delight, and the one-hour hike
from Sant Pol Beach over to Sant Feliu de Guixols offers a views of the
Costa Brava at its best.

WHERE TO STAY

$$$$ ⌂ **L'Hostal de la Gavina.** Orson Welles, who used to spend weeks at a
HOTEL time here, called this the finest resort hotel in Spain. **Pros:** in a gated
Fodor's Choice community; impeccable service and amenities; sea views. **Cons:** hard
★ on the budget *and* habit-forming. $ *Rooms from: €515* ⌷ *Pl. Roserar
s/n* ☎ *972/321100* ⊕ *www.lagavina.com* ⊘ *Closed Nov.–Easter* ⇌ *51
rooms, 23 suites* ⦿ *Breakfast.*

CALELLA DE PALAFRUGELL AND AROUND

25 km (15½ miles) from S'Agaró.

Up the coast from S'Agaró, the C31 brings you to Palafrugell and
Begur; to the east are some of the prettiest, least developed inlets of the
Costa Brava. One road leads to **Llafranc,** a small port with waterfront
hotels and restaurants, and forks right to the fishing village of **Calella
de Palafrugell,** known for its July habaneras festival. (The *habanera* is
a form of Cuban dance music brought to Europe by Catalan sailors
in the late 19th century; it still enjoys a nostalgic cachet here.) Just
south is the panoramic promontory of **Cap Roig,** with views of the
barren Formigues Isles.

North along the coast lie **Tamariu, Aiguablava, Fornell, Platja Fonda,** and
(around the point at Cap de Begur) **Sa Tuna** and **Aiguafreda.** There's not
much to do in any of these hideaways (only Llafranc has a long enough
stretch of seafront to accommodate a sandy beach), but you can luxuri-
ate in wonderful views and the soothing quiet.

WHERE TO EAT AND STAY

$$$ ✕ **Pa i Raïm.** "Bread and Grapes" in Catalan, this excellent restaurant
CATALAN in Josep Pla's ancestral family home in Palafrugell has one rustic dining
Fodor's Choice room as well as another in a glassed-in winter garden. In summer the leafy
★ terrace is the place to be. **Known for:** traditional country cuisine; contemporary fare; standout prawns tempura. $ *Average main: €20* ⌷ *Torres
i Jonama 56, Palafrugell* ☎ *972/304572* ⊕ *www.pairaim.com* ⊘ *Closed
Mon., late Mar.–early Apr. (dates can vary). No dinner Sun.–Thurs.*

$$$$ B&B/INN FAMILY 🏨 **El Far Hotel-Restaurant.** Rooms in this 17th-century hermitage attached to a 15th-century watchtower have original vaulted ceilings, hardwood floors, and interiors accented with floral prints. **Pros:** friendly service; graceful architecture; spectacular views. **Cons:** distance from the beach; pricey for the value. [$] *Rooms from: €270* ✉ *Muntanya de Sant Sebastia, Carrer Uruguai s/n, Llafranc* ☎ *972/301639* 🌐 *www.elfar.net* 🕓 *Closed Jan.* 🛏 *8 rooms, 1 suite* 🍴 *Breakfast.*

BEGUR AND AROUND

11 km (7 miles) from Calella de Palagrugell.

From Begur, go east through the calas or take the inland route past the rose-colored stone houses and ramparts of the restored medieval town of **Pals.** Nearby **Peratallada** is another medieval fortified town with a castle, tower, palace, and well-preserved walls. North of Pals there are signs for **Ullastret,** an Iberian village dating to the 5th century BC. **L'Estartit** is the jumping-off point for the spectacular natural park surrounding the Medes Islands, famous for its protected marine life and consequently for diving and underwater photography.

EXPLORING

Empúries. The Greco-Roman ruins here are Catalonia's most important archaeological site. This port is one of the most monumental ancient engineering feats on the Iberian Peninsula. As the Greeks' original point of arrival in Spain, Empúries was also where the Olympic Flame entered Spain for Barcelona's 1992 Olympic Games. ✉ *Calle Puig i Cadafalch s/n* ☎ *972/770208* 🌐 *www.mac.cat/seus/empuries* 🎫 *€5.*

Medes Islands (*Underwater Natural Park*). The marine reserve around the Medes Islands, an archipelago of several small islands, is just off the coastline of L'Estartit, and is touted as one of the best places in Spain to scuba dive. Thanks to its protected status, the marine life—eels, octopus, starfish, and grouper—is tame, and you can expect high visibility unless the weather is bad. If diving doesn't appeal, you can take one of the glass-bottomed boats that frequent the islands from the mainland and view from above.

WHERE TO EAT AND STAY

$$$ CATALAN ✕ **Restaurant Ibèric.** This excellent pocket of authentic Costa Brava cuisine serves everything from snails to wild boar in season. Wild mushrooms scrambled with eggs or stewed with hare are specialties, as are complex and earthy red wines made by enologist Jordi Oliver (of the Oliver Conti vineyard in the Alt Empordà's village of Capmany). **Known for:** eclectic cuisine. [$] *Average main: €20* ✉ *Carrer Valls 11, Ullastret* ☎ *972/757108* 🌐 *www.restaurantiberic.com* 🕓 *Closed Mon. No dinner Tues.–Thurs. and Sun.*

$$$$ HOTEL 🏨 **El Convent Hotel and Restaurant.** Built in 1730, this elegant former convent is a 10-minute walk to the beach at the Cala Sa Riera—the quietest and prettiest inlet north of Begur. **Pros:** outstanding architecture; quiet and private. **Cons:** minimum stay in summer. [$] *Rooms from: €239* ✉ *Ctra. de la Platja del Racó 2, Begur* ☎ *972/623091* 🌐 *www.hotelconventbegur.com* 🛏 *24 rooms, 1 suite* 🍴 *Breakfast.*

$$$$ HOTEL FAMILY Fodor's Choice ★ 🏨 **Hotel Aigua Blava.** What began as a small hostal in the 1920s is now a sprawling luxury hotel, run by the fourth generation of the same family. **Pros:** impeccable service; gardens and pleasant patios at every turn; private playground. **Cons:** no elevator; no beach in the inlet. [$] *Rooms from: €361* ✉ *Platja de Fornells s/n, Begur* ☎ *972/622058* 🌐 *www.aiguablava.com* ⏲ *Closed Nov.–Mar.* 🛏 *66 rooms, 19 suites* 🍴 *Breakfast.*

CADAQUÈS AND AROUND

70 km (43 miles) from Begur.

Spain's easternmost town, Cadaqués, still has the whitewashed charm that transformed this fishing village into an international artists' haunt in the early 20th century. Salvador Dalí's house, now a museum, is at Port Lligat, a 15-minute walk north of town.

EXPLORING

Fodor's Choice ★ **Cap de Creus.** North of Cadaqués, Spain's easternmost point is a fundamental pilgrimage, if only for the symbolic geographical rush. The hike out to the lighthouse—through rosemary, thyme, and the salt air of the Mediterranean—is unforgettable. The Pyrenees officially end (or rise) here. New Year's Day finds mobs of revelers awaiting the first emergence of the "new" sun from the Mediterranean. Gaze down at heart-pounding views of the craggy coast and crashing waves with a warm mug of coffee in hand or fine fare on the table at **Bar Restaurant Cap de Creus,** which sits on a rocky crag above the Cap de Creus. On a summer evening, you may be lucky and stumble upon some live music on the terrace.

Casa Museu Salvador Dalí. This was Dalí's summerhouse and a site long associated with the artist's notorious frolics with everyone from poets Federico García Lorca and Paul Eluard to filmmaker Luis Buñuel. Filled with bits of the surrealist's daily life, it's an important point in the "Dalí triangle," completed by the castle at Púbol and the Teatre-Museu Dalí in Figueres. You can get here by a 3-km (2-mile) walk north along the beach from Cadaqués. Only small groups of visitors are admitted at any given time, and reservations are required. ✉ *Port Lligat s/n, Cadaqués* ☎ *972/251015* 🌐 *www.salvador-dali.org* 🎟 *€11* ⏲ *Closed Mon. and Jan. 9–Feb. 11* ☞ *Reservations essential.*

Castillo Gala Dalí de Púbol. Dalí's former home is now the resting place of Gala, his perennial model and mate. It's a chance to wander through another Dalí-esque landscape: lush gardens, fountains decorated with masks of Richard Wagner (the couple's favorite composer), and distinctive elephants with giraffe's legs and claw feet. Two lions and a giraffe stand guard near Gala's tomb. ✉ *Pl. Gala Dalí s/n, on Rte. 255, about 15 km (9 miles) east of the A7 toward La Bisbal, Púbol* ☎ *972/488655* 🌐 *www.salvador-dali.org* 🎟 *€8* ⏲ *Closed Mon. and Jan. 9–mid Mar.*

Fodor's Choice ★ **Sant Pere de Rodes.** The monastery of Sant Pere de Rodes, 7 km (4½ miles) by car (plus a 20-minute walk) above the pretty fishing village of El Port de la Selva, is a spectacular site. Built in the 10th and 11th centuries by Benedictine monks—and sacked and plundered repeatedly since—this Romanesque monolith, recently restored, commands

8

The popular harbor of Cadaqués

a breathtaking panorama of the Pyrenees, the Empordà plain, the sweeping curve of the Bay of Roses, and Cap de Creus. (Topping off the grand trek across the Pyrenees, Cap de Creus is a spectacular six-hour walk from here on the well-marked GR11 trail.) **■ TIP→ In July and August, the monastery is the setting for the annual Festival Sant Pere (www.festivalsantpere.com), drawing top-tier classical musicians from all over the world.** Find event listings online (in Catalan); phone for reservations or to book a post-concert dinner in the monastery's refectory-style restaurant: ☎ *972/194233 or 610/310073.* ✉ *Camí del Monestir s/n, El Porte de la Selva* ☎ *972/387559* 🌐 *www.mhcat.cat* 🎫 *€4.50* 🕒 *Closed Mon.*

WHERE TO EAT AND STAY

$$$$
SEAFOOD
Fodor's Choice ★

🍴 **Casa Anita.** Simple, fresh, and generous dishes are the draw at this informal little eatery, an institution in Cadaqués for nearly half a century. It sits on the street that leads to Port Lligat and Dalí's house. **Known for:** no menu; communal dining; famous clientele. [$] *Average main: €25* ✉ *Carrer Miquel Rosset 16, Cadaqués* ☎ *972/258471* 🕒 *Closed Mon., and Oct.–1st wk in Dec.*

$$$$
HOTEL

🏨 **Hotel Playa Sol.** On the cove of Es Pianc, just a five-minute walk from the village center, this hotel, in business for more than 50 years, has rooms that are light and airy, with modern furnishings; all but two have a balcony or terrace, and some have wonderful views of the sea. **Pros:** attentive, friendly service; family-friendly; great views. **Cons:** decor could be more colorful; rooms with balcony and sea views are harder to book. [$] *Rooms from: €247* ✉ *Riba Es Pianc 3, Cadaqués* ☎ *972/258100* 🌐 *www.playa-sol.com* 🕒 *Closed Nov.–mid-Feb.* 🛏 *48 rooms* 🍽 *No meals.*

$$$ HOTEL 🏨 **Llané Petit.** This intimate, typically Mediterranean bay-side hotel caters to people who want to make the most of their stay in the village and don't want to spend too much time in their hotel. **Pros:** semiprivate beach next to hotel. **Cons:** small rooms; somewhat lightweight beds and furnishings. [$] *Rooms from: €142* ✉ *Pl. Llane Petit s/n, Cadaqués* ☎ *972/251020* 🌐 *www.llanepetit.com* ⏲ *Closed Nov.–Mar.* 🛏 *37 rooms* 🍴 *Breakfast.*

SOUTHERN CATALONIA AND AROUND VALENCIA

South of the Costa Brava, the time machine takes you back some 20 centuries. Tarragona, the principal town of southern Catalonia, was in Roman times one of the finest and most important outposts of the empire. Its wine was already famous and its population was the first *gens togata* (literally, the toga-clad people) in Spain, which conferred on them equality with the citizens of Rome. Roman remains, chief among them the Circus Maximus, bear witness to Tarragona's grandeur, and to this the Middle Ages added wonderful city walls and citadels.

Farther south lies Valencia, Spain's third-largest city and the capital of its region and province, equidistant from Barcelona and Madrid. If you have time for a day trip (or you decide to stay in the beach town of El Saler), make your way to the Albufera, a scenic coastal wetland teeming with native wildlife, especially migratory birds.

TARRAGONA

98 km (61 miles) southwest of Barcelona, 251 km (156 miles) northeast of Valencia.

With its vast Roman remains and medieval Christian monuments, Tarragona has been designated a UNESCO World Heritage Site. The city today is a vibrant center of culture and art, a busy fishing and shipping port, and a natural jumping-off point for the towns and pristine beaches of the Costa Daurada, 216 km (134 miles) of coastline north of the Costa del Azahar.

Though modern Tarragona is very much an industrial and commercial city, it has preserved its heritage superbly. Stroll along the town's cliffside perimeter and you'll see why the Romans set up shop here: Tarragona is strategically positioned at the center of a broad, open bay, with an unobstructed view of the sea. As capital of the Roman province of Hispania Tarraconensis (from 218 BC), Tarraco (as it was then called) formed the empire's principal stronghold in Spain. St. Paul preached here in AD 58, and Tarragona became the seat of the Christian church in Spain until it was superseded by Toledo in the 11th century.

Entering the city from Barcelona, you'll pass the **Triumphal Arch of Berà,** dating from the 3rd century BC, 19 km (12 miles) north of Tarragona; and from the Lleida (Lérida) autopista, you can see the 1st-century **Roman aqueduct** that helped carry fresh water 32 km (20 miles) from the Gaià River. Tarragona is divided clearly into old and new by Rambla Vella; the old town and most of the Roman remains are to the north, while modern Tarragona spreads out to the south. Start your visit at acacia-lined Rambla Nova, at the end of which is a balcony overlooking the sea, the **Balcó del Mediterràni.** Then walk uphill along Passeig de les Palmeres; below it is the ancient amphitheater, the curve of which is echoed in the modern, semicircular Imperial Tarraco hotel on the promenade.

GETTING HERE AND AROUND

Tarragona is well connected by train: there are half-hourly express trains from Barcelona (1 hour 20 minutes; prices from €8.05) and regular train service from other major cities, including Madrid.

Seven to 10 buses leave Barcelona's Estació del Nord every day. Connections between Tarragona and Valencia are frequent. There are also bus connections with the main Andalusian cities, plus Alicante, Madrid, and Valencia.

The €18 Tarragona Card, valid for two days, gives free entry to all the city's museums and historical sites, free rides on municipal buses, and discounts at more than 100 shops, restaurants, and bars. It's sold at the main tourist office and at most hotels.

Tours of the cathedral and archaeological sites are conducted by the tourist office, located just below the cathedral.

ESSENTIALS

Visitor Contacts Visitor Information Tarragona. ⊠ *Carrer Major 37* ☎ *977/250795* ⊕ *www.tarragonaturisme.cat/en.*

EXPLORING

TOP ATTRACTIONS

Amphitheater. Tarragona, the Emperor Augustus's favorite winter resort, had arguably the finest amphitheater in Roman Iberia, built in the 2nd century AD for gladiatorial and other contests. The remains have a spectacular view of the sea. You're free to wander through the access tunnels and along the tiers of seats. In the center of the theater are the remains of two superimposed churches, the earlier of which was a Visigothic basilica built to mark the bloody martyrdom of St. Fructuós and his deacons in AD 259. ■TIP➔ **€7.40 buys a combination ticket valid for all Tarragona's Roman sites.** ⊠ *Parc de l'Amphiteatre Roma s/n* ☎ *977/242579* ⊒ *€3.30* ☉ *Closed Mon.*

Catedral. Built between the 12th and 14th century on the site of a Roman temple and a mosque, this cathedral shows the transition from Romanesque to Gothic style. The initial rounded placidity of the Romanesque apse gave way to the spiky restlessness of the Gothic—the result is somewhat confusing. If no Mass is in progress, enter the cathedral through the cloister, which houses a collection of artistic and religious treasures. The main attraction here is the 15th-century Gothic alabaster altarpiece of Sant Tecla by Pere Joan, a richly detailed depiction of the life of Tarragona's patron saint. Converted by Sant Paul and subsequently persecuted by local pagans, Sant Tecla was repeatedly saved from demise through divine intervention. ⊠ *Pl. Pla de la Seu s/n* ☎ *977/226935* ⊕ *www.catedraldetarragona.com* ⊒ *€5 (cathedral and museum)* ☉ *Closed Sun. in winter.*

Tarragona's cathedral is a mix of Romanesque and Gothic styles.

Roman Circus. Students have excavated the vaults of the 1st-century AD Roman arena, near the amphitheater. The plans just inside the gate show that the vaults now visible formed only a small corner of a vast space (350 yards long), where 23,000 spectators gathered to watch chariot races. As medieval Tarragona grew, the city gradually engulfed the circus. ✉ *Pl. del Rei, Rambla Vella s/n* ☎ *977/251515* ✉ *€3.30, €7.40 combination ticket with Praetorium and Amphitheatre* ⊙ *Closed Mon.*

WORTH NOTING

El Serrallo. The always-entertaining fishing quarter and harbor are below the city near the bus station and the mouth of the Francolí River. Attending the afternoon fish auction is a golden opportunity to see how choice seafood starts its journey toward your table in Barcelona or Tarragona. Restaurants in the port offer no-frills fresh fish in a rollicking environment. ✉ *Tarragona.*

Gaudí Centre. In this small museum showcasing the life and work of the city's most illustrious son, there are copies of the models Gaudí made for his major works and a replica of his studio. His original notebook—with English translations—is filled with his thoughts on structure and ornamentation, complaints about clients, and calculations of cost-and-return on his projects. A pleasant café on the third floor overlooks the main square of the old city and the bell tower of the Church of Sant Pere. The Centre also houses the **Tourist Office**; pick up information here about visits to two of Domènech's most important buildings, the Casa Navàs (by appointment, €10) and the Institut Pere Mata (€5). ✉ *Pl. del Mercadal 3, Reus* ☎ *977/010670* ⊕ *www.gaudicentre.cat/en* ✉ *€9.*

Museu Paleocristià i Necrópolis (*Early-Christian Museum and Necropolis*). Just uphill from the fish market is the early Christian necropolis and museum. In 1923, the remains of this burial ground were discovered during the construction of a tobacco factory. The excavations on display—more than 2,000 tombs, sarcophagi, and funeral objects—allow visitors a fascinating insight into Roman funeral practices and rituals. ✉ *Av. Ramon y Cajal 84* ☎ *977/251515* 💶 *€4.50 combined ticket with Museu Nacional Arqueològic (MNAT) de Tarragona* 🕐 *Closed Mon.*

Museu Pau Casals. The family house of renowned cellist Pau (Pablo) Casals (1876–1973) is on the beach at Sant Salvador, just east of the town of El Vendrell. Casals, who left Spain in self-imposed exile after Franco seized power in 1939, left a museum of his possessions here, including several of his cellos, original music manuscripts, paintings, and sculptures. Other exhibits describe the Casals campaign for world peace ("Pau," in Catalan, means both Paul and peace), his speech and performance at the inauguration of the United Nations in 1958 (at the age of 95), and his haunting interpretation of *El Cant dels Ocells* (*The Song of the Birds*), his homage to his native Catalonia. Across the street, the Auditori Pau Casals holds frequent concerts and, in July and August, a classical music festival. ✉ *Av. Palfuriana 67* ☎ *977/684276* 🌐 *www.paucasals.org* 💶 *€7* 🕐 *Closed Mon.*

Passeig Arqueològic. A 1½-km (1-mile) circular path skirting the surviving section of the 3rd-century-BC Ibero-Roman ramparts, this walkway was built on even earlier walls of giant rocks. On the other side of the path is a glacis, a fortification added by English military engineers in 1707 during the War of the Spanish Succession. Look for the rusted bronze of Romulus and Remus. ✉ *Access from Via de l'Imperi Romà.*

Praetorium. This towering building was Augustus's town house, and is reputed to be the birthplace of Pontius Pilate. Its Gothic appearance is the result of extensive alterations in the Middle Ages, when it housed the kings of Catalonia and Aragón during their visits to Tarragona. ✉ *Pl. del Rei* ☎ *977/221736, 977/242220* 💶 *€3.30, €7.40 combined ticket with Tarragona's other Roman sites* 🕐 *Closed Mon.*

WHERE TO EAT AND STAY

$$$$
CATALAN
✕ **Les Coques.** If you have time for only one meal in the city, take it at this elegant little restaurant in the heart of historic Tarragona. The menu is bursting with both mountain and Mediterranean fare. **Known for:** mountain fare; bargain prix-fixe lunch. 💲 *Average main: €24* ✉ *Carrer Sant Llorenç 15* ☎ *977/228300* 🌐 *www.les-coques.com* 🕐 *Closed Sun.*

$$
CATALAN
Fodor's Choice
★
✕ **Les Voltes.** Built into the vaults of the Roman Circus, this unique spot serves a hearty cuisine within one of the oldest sites in Europe. You'll find Tarragona specialties, mainly fish dishes, as well as international recipes, with *calçotadas* (spring onions, grilled over a charcoal fire) in winter. (For the calçotadas, you need to reserve a day—preferably two or more—in advance.) **Known for:** reserve one or two days in advance; Tarragona specialties; historic locale. 💲 *Average main: €13* ✉ *Carrer Trinquet Vell 12* ☎ *977/230651* 🌐 *www.restaurantlesvoltes.cat* 🕐 *Closed Mon. No dinner Sun.*

$ 🔲 **Plaça de la Font.** The central location and the cute rooms at this
HOTEL budget choice just off the Rambla Vella in the Plaça de la Font make
for a practical base in downtown Tarragona. **Pros:** easy on the budget;
comfortable, charming rooms. **Cons:** rooms are on the small side;
rooms with balconies can be noisy on weekends. **$** *Rooms from: €75*
✉ *Pl. de la Font 26* ☎ *977/240882* ⊕ *www.hotelpdelafont.com* ⮐ *20
rooms* ⦵ *No meals.*

NIGHTLIFE AND PERFORMING ARTS

Nightlife in Tarragona takes two forms: older and quieter in the upper
city, younger and more raucous down below. There are some lovely
rustic bars in the Casc Antic, the upper section of Old Tarragona. Port
Esportiu, a pleasure-boat harbor separate from the working port, has
another row of dining and dancing establishments; young people flock
here on weekends and summer nights.

El Galliner de L'Antiquari. For a dose of culture with your cocktail, this
laid-back bar and restaurant hosts readings, live music, art exhibits,
and occasional screenings of classic or contemporary movies. ✉ *Carrer
Santa Anna 3* ☎ *977/241843* ⊕ *www.elgallinerdelantiquari.com.*

Museum Cafe. Here you can relax and have a drink and a reviving tapa
in the heart of the old city. ✉ *Carrer Sant Llorenç 5* ☎ *977/222587.*

Teatre Metropol. Tarragona's center for music, dance, theater, and cultural
events stages performances ranging from *castellers* (human-castle formations, usually performed in August and September) to folk dances.
✉ *Rambla Nova 46* ☎ *977/244795.*

SHOPPING

Carrer Major. You have to haggle for bargains, but Carrer Major has
some exciting antiques stores. They're worth a thorough rummage, as
the gems tend to be hidden. ✉ *Tarragona.*

MONTSERRAT

50 km (31 miles) west of Barcelona.

A popular side trip from Barcelona is a visit to the shrine of La Moreneta (the Black Virgin of Montserrat) and the dramatic sawtooth peaks
of Montserrat, as memorable for its strange topography as it is for
its religious treasures. The views over the mountains that stretch all
the way to the Mediterranean and, on a clear day, to the Pyrenees are
breathtaking, and the rugged, boulder-strewn terrain makes for exhila-
rating walks and hikes.

GETTING HERE AND AROUND

By car, follow the A2/A7 autopista on the upper ring road (Ronda de
Dalt), or from the western end of the Diagonal as far as Salida 25 to
Martorell. Bypass this industrial center and follow signs to Montserrat.
Or, take the FGC train from the Plaça d'Espanya metro station (hourly
7:36 am–5:41 pm, connecting with the funicular, which leaves every 15
minutes), or go on a guided tour with Pullmantur or Julià (*see Tours in
Planning in this chapter*).

EXPLORING

Fodor's Choice ★ **La Moreneta.** The shrine of La Moreneta, one of Catalonia's patron saints, resides in a Benedictine monastery high in the Serra de Montserrat, surrounded by jagged peaks that have given rise to countless legends: here St. Peter left a statue of the Virgin Mary carved by St. Luke, Parsifal found the Holy Grail, and Wagner sought musical inspiration. The monastic complex is dwarfed by the grandeur of sheer peaks, and the crests above bristle with chapels and hermitages. The hermitage of Sant Joan can be reached by funicular. Although a monastery has stood on the same site in Montserrat since the early Middle Ages, the present 19th-century building replaced the rubble left by Napoléon's troops in 1812. The shrine is world famous and one of Catalonia's spiritual sanctuaries—honeymooning couples flock here by the thousands seeking La Moreneta's blessing on their marriages, and twice a year, on April 27 and September 8, the diminutive statue of Montserrat's Black Virgin becomes the object of one of Spain's greatest pilgrimages. Only the basilica and museum are regularly open to the public. The basilica is dark and ornate, its blackness pierced by the glow of hundreds of votive lamps. Above the high altar stands the polychrome statue of the Virgin and Child, to which the faithful can pay their respects by way of a separate door. ■TIP➜ The famous Escolania de Montserrat boys' choir sing the Salve and Virulai from the liturgy weekdays at 1 pm and Sunday at noon. ☎ No *phone* ⊕ *www. montserratvisita.com* ☑ €16.

SITGES, SANTES CREUS, AND SANTA MARIA DE POBLET

This trio of attractions south and west of Barcelona can be seen in a day. Sitges is the prettiest and most popular resort in Barcelona's immediate environs, with an excellent beach and a whitewashed and flowery old quarter. It's also one of Europe's premier gay resorts. Monolithic Romanesque architecture and beautiful cloisters characterize the Cistercian monasteries west of here, at Santes Creus and Poblet.

GETTING HERE AND AROUND

By car, head southwest along Gran Vía or Passeig Colom to the freeway that passes the airport on its way to Castelldefels. From here, the freeway and tunnels will get you to Sitges in 20–30 minutes. From Sitges, drive inland toward Vilafranca del Penedès and the A7 freeway. The A2 (Lleida) leads to the monasteries. Regular trains leave Sants and Passeig de Gràcia for Sitges; the ride takes a half hour. To get to Santes Creus or Poblet from Sitges, take a Lleida-bound train to L'Espluga de Francolí, 4 km (2½ miles) from Poblet; there's one direct train in the morning at 7:37 and four more during the day with transfers at Sant Vicenç de Calders. From L'Espluga, take a cab to the monastery.

SITGES

43 km (27 miles) southwest of Barcelona.

The fine white sand of the Sitges beach is elbow-to-elbow with sun-worshippers April–September. On the eastern end of the strand is an alabaster statue of the 16th-century painter El Greco, usually associated with Toledo, where he spent most of his professional career. The artist Santiago Rusiñol is responsible for this surprise; he was such a Greco fan that he not only installed two of his paintings in his Museu Cau Ferrat but also had this sculpture planted on the beach.

Just over 30 minutes by train (€3.80 each way), there's regular service from all three Barcelona stations. Buses, roughly the same price, run at least hourly from Plaza Espanya and take about 45 minutes, depending how many stops they make. If you're driving head south on the C32.

EXPLORING

Cau Ferrat. This is the most interesting museum in Sitges, established by the bohemian artist and cofounder of the Quatre Gats café in Barcelona, Santiago Rusiñol (1861–1931), and containing some of his own paintings together with two by El Greco. Connoisseurs of wrought iron will love the beautiful collection of *cruces terminales,* crosses that once marked town boundaries. Next door is the **Museu Maricel de Mar,** with more artistic treasures. ✉ *Carrer Fonollar s/n, Sitges* ☎ *938/940364* 🌐 *www.museusdesitges.com* 🎟 *€10, includes Cau Ferrat and Museu Maricel de Mar* 🕓 *Closed Mon.*

WHERE TO EAT

$$$$ SEAFOOD

🍴 **Vivero.** Perched on a rocky point above the bay at Playa San Sebastián, east of the city center, Vivero specializes in paellas and seafood; try their *mariscada,* a meal-in-itself ensemble of lobster, mussels, and prawns. Inside, the dining areas are geared up for banquets and large groups, but, weather permitting, the best seats in the house are on the terraces, with their wonderful views of the water—especially on the night of August 23, when the *fiesta major* of Sitges is ushered out with a spectacular display of fireworks. **Known for:** outdoor dining; excellent mariscada; wonderful water views. [$] *Average main: €24* ✉ *Passeig Balmins s/n, Playa San Sebastián, Sitges* ☎ *938/942149* 🌐 *www.elviverositges.com* 💳 *No credit cards.*

EN ROUTE

Bodegas Torres. After leaving Sitges, make straight for the A2 autopista by way of Vilafranca del Penedès. Wine buffs may want to stop here for a tour or to taste some excellent Penedès wines. ✉ *Finca "El Maset", Ctra. BP2121 (direction Sant Martí Sarroca), Vilafranca del Penedès* ☎ *938/177330* 🌐 *www.torres.es* 🎟 *€9 includes tour and wine tasting.*

SANTES CREUS

95 km (59 miles) west of Barcelona.

Sitges, with its summer festivals of dance and music, film and fireworks, is anything but solemn. Head inland, however, some 45 minutes' drive west, and you discover how much the art and architecture—the very tone of Catalan culture—owes to its medieval religious heritage.

It takes about 45 minutes to drive to Santes Creus from Sitges. Take the C32 west, then get onto the C51 and TP2002.

EXPLORING

Montblanc. The ancient gates are too narrow for cars, and a walk through its tiny streets reveals Gothic churches with stained-glass windows, a 16th-century hospital, and medieval mansions. ✉ *Off A2, Salida 9.*

Santes Creus. Founded in 1157, Santes Creus is the first of the monasteries you'll come upon as the A2 branches west toward Lleida; take Exit 11 off the highway. Three austere aisles and an unusual 14th-century apse combine with the newly restored cloisters and the courtyard of the royal palace. ⊠ *Pl. Jaume el Just s/n, Santes Creus* ☎ *977/638329* 🎟 *€4.50* ⊘ *Closed Mon.*

SANTA MARIA DE POBLET

8 km (5 miles) west of Santes Creus.

This splendid Cistercian monastery, located at the foot of the Prades Mountains, is one of the great masterpieces of Spanish monastic architecture. Declared a UNESCO World Heritage Site, the cloister is a stunning combination of lightness and size, and on sunny days the shadows on the yellow sandstone are extraordinary.

The Barcelona–Lleida train can drop you at L'Espluga de Francolí, from where it's a 4-km (2½-mile) walk to the monastery. Buses from Tarragona or Lleida will get you a little closer, with a 2¾-km (1½-mile) walk. The drive from Sitges takes about an hour, via the C32 and AP2.

EXPLORING

Fodor's Choice ★ **Santa Maria de Poblet.** Founded in 1150 by Ramón Berenguer IV in gratitude for the Christian Reconquest, the monastery first housed a dozen Cistercians from Narbonne. Later, the Crown of Aragón used Santa Maria de Poblet for religious retreats and burials. The building was damaged in an 1836 anticlerical revolt, and monks of the reformed Cistercian Order have managed the difficult task of restoration since 1940. Today, a community of monks and novices still pray before the splendid retable over the tombs of Aragonese rulers, restored to their former glory by sculptor Frederic Marès; they also sleep in the cold, barren dormitory and eat frugal meals in the stark refectory. ⊠ *Off A2 (Salida 9 from Barcelona, Salida 8 from Lleida)* ☎ *977/870089* ⊕ *www.poblet.cat* 🎟 *€7.50.*

Valls. This town, famous for its early spring calçotada held on the last Sunday of January, is 10 km (6 miles) from Santes Creus and 15 km (9 miles) from Poblet. Even if you miss the big day, calçots are served November–April at rustic and rambling farmhouses such as **Cal Ganxo** in nearby Masmolets (*Carrer Església 13* ☎ *977/605960*). Also, the **Xiquets de Valls,** Catalonia's most famous *castellers* (human castlers), might be putting up a living skyscraper.

VALENCIA

351 km (218 miles) southwest of Barcelona, 357 km (222 miles) southeast of Madrid.

Valencia, Spain's third-largest municipality, is a proud city with a thriving nightlife and restaurant scene, quality museums, and spectacular contemporary architecture, juxtaposed with a thoroughly charming historic quarter, making it a popular destination year in and year out. During the civil war, it was the last seat of the Republican Loyalist government (1935–36), holding out against Franco's National forces until the country fell to 40 years of dictatorship. Today it represents the essence of contemporary Spain—daring design and architecture along with experimental cuisine—but remains deeply conservative and proud of its traditions. Although it faces the Mediterranean, Valencia's history and geography have been defined most significantly by the Turia River and the fertile huerta that surrounds it.

The city has been fiercely contested ever since it was founded by the Greeks. El Cid captured Valencia from the Moors in 1094 and won his strangest victory here in 1099: he died in the battle, but his corpse was strapped into his saddle and so frightened the besieging Moors that it caused their complete defeat. In 1102 his widow, Jimena, was forced to return the city to Moorish rule; Jaume I finally drove them out in 1238. Modern Valencia was best known for its frequent disastrous floods until the Turia River was diverted to the south in the late 1950s. Since then the city has been on a steady course of urban beautification. The lovely bridges that once spanned the Turia look equally graceful spanning a wandering municipal park, and the spectacularly futuristic Ciutat de les Arts i les Ciències (City of Arts and Sciences), most of it designed by Valencia-born architect Santiago Calatrava, has at last created an exciting architectural link between this river town and the Mediterranean. If you're in Valencia, an excursion to Albufera Nature Park is a worthwhile day trip.

GETTING HERE AND AROUND

By car, Valencia is about 3½ hours from Madrid via the A3 motorway, and about the same from Barcelona on the AP7 toll road. Valencia is well connected by bus and train, with regular service to and from cities throughout the country, including nine daily AVE high-speed express trains from Madrid, making the trip in 1 hour 40 minutes, and six Euromed express trains daily from Barcelona, taking about 3½ hours. Valencia's bus station is across the river from the old town; take Bus No. 8 from the Plaza del Ayuntamiento. Frequent buses make the four-hour trip from Madrid and the five-hour trip from Barcelona. Dozens of airlines, large and small, serve Valencia airport, connecting the city with dozens of cities throughout Spain and the rest of Europe.

Once you're here, the city has an efficient network of bus, tram, and metro service. For timetables and more information, stop by the local tourist office. The double-decker Valencia Bus Turístic runs daily 9:45–7:45 (until 9:15 in summer) and departs every 20–30 minutes from the Plaza de la Reina. It travels through the city, stopping at most of the main sights: 24- and 48-hour tickets (€17 and €19, respectively) let you get on and off at eight main boarding points, including the Institut Valencià d'Art Modern, the Museo de Bellas Artes, and the Ciutat de les Arts i les Ciències. The same company also offers a two-hour guided trip (€16) to Albufera Nature Park, including an excursion by boat through the wetlands, departing from the Plaza de la Reina. In summer (and sometimes during the rest of the year) Valencia's tourist office organizes tours of Albufera. You see the port area before continuing south to the lagoon itself, where you can visit a traditional *barraca* (thatch-roof farmhouse).

ESSENTIALS

Bus Contact Valencia Bus Station. ✉ *Av. Menendez Pidal 11* ☎ *963/466266.*

Visitor Information Valencia Tourist Office. ✉ *Pl. del Ayuntamiento 1* ☎ *963/524908* ⊕ *www.visitvalencia.com/en.*

TOURS

Valencia Bus Turístic. Valencia's tourist bus allows you to hop on and hop off as you please, while audio commentary introduces the city's history and highlights. The three different routes cover the historical center; the marina, beaches, and City of Arts and Sciences; or Albufera Natural Park. ⊠ *Pl. de la Reina 8* ☎ *963/414400, 699/982514* ⊕ *www.valenciabusturistic.com* 🎫 *From €17.*

FESTIVALS

Gran Fira de València (Great Valencia Fair). Valencia's monthlong festival, in July, celebrates theater, film, dance, and music. ⊠ *Valencia* ⊕ *www.granfiravalencia.com.*

Fodor'sChoice **Las Fallas.** If you want nonstop nightlife at its frenzied best, come dur-
★ ing the climactic days of this festival, March 15–19, when revelers throng the streets and last call at many of the bars and clubs isn't until the wee hours, if at all. ⊠ *Valencia* ⊕ *www.visitvalencia.com/en/whats-on-offer-valencia/festivities/the-fallas.*

EXPLORING
TOP ATTRACTIONS

Fodor'sChoice **Cathedral.** Valencia's 13th- to 15th-century cathedral is the heart
★ of the city. The building has three portals—Romanesque, Gothic, and rococo. Inside, Renaissance and baroque marble was removed to restore the original Gothic style, as is now the trend in Spanish churches. The Capilla del Santo Cáliz (Chapel of the Holy Chalice) displays a purple agate vessel purported to be the Holy Grail (Christ's cup at the Last Supper) and thought to have been brought to Spain in the 4th century. Behind the altar is the left arm of **St. Vincent**, martyred in Valencia in 304. Stars of the cathedral **museum** are Goya's two famous paintings of St. Francis de Borja, Duke of Gandia. Left of the entrance is the octagonal tower **El Miguelete,** which you can climb (207 steps) to the top: the roofs of the old town create a kaleidoscope of orange and brown terra-cotta, with the sea in the background. It's said that you can see 300 belfries from here, many with bright-blue cupolas made of ceramic tiles from nearby Manises. The tower was built in 1381 and the final spire added in 1736. ■TIP➔ The Portal de los Apostoles, on the west side of the cathedral, is the scene every Thursday at noon of the 1,000-year-old ceremony of the Water Tribunal: the judges of this ancient court assemble here, in traditional costume, to hand down their decisions on local irrigation-rights disputes. ⊠ *Pl. Almoina s/n, Ciutat Vella* ☎ *963/918127* ⊕ *www.catedraldevalencia.es* 🎫 *€7, includes audio guide* ⊗ *Closed Sun. Nov.–Mar.*

FAMILY **Ciutat de les Arts i les Ciències.** Designed mainly by native son Santiago
Fodor'sChoice Calatrava, this sprawling futuristic complex is the home of Valen-
★ cia's **Museu de les Ciències Príncipe Felipe** (Prince Philip Science Museum), **L'Hemisfèric** (Hemispheric Planetarium), **L'Oceanogràfic** (Oceanographic Park), and **Palau de les Arts** (Palace of the Arts). With resplendent buildings resembling combs and crustaceans, the Ciutat is a favorite of architecture buffs and curious kids. The Science Museum has soaring platforms filled with lasers, holograms, simula-tors, hands-on experiments, and a swell "zero gravity" exhibition on

Valencia

space exploration. The eye-shape planetarium projects 3-D virtual voyages on its huge IMAX screen. At l'Oceanogràfic (the work of architect Felix Candela), the largest marine park in Europe, you can take a submarine ride through a coastal marine habitat. Other attractions include an amphitheater, an indoor theater, and a chamber-music hall. ⊠ *Av. del Profesor López Piñero 7* ☎ *902/100031* ⊕ *www.cac. es* ⊠ *Museu de les Ciències €8, L'Oceanogràfic €29.10, L'Hemisfèric €8.80; combination ticket L'Oceanogràfic and L'Hemisfèric €31.40; Museu de les Ciències and L'Oceanogràfic €30.80.*

Lonja de la Seda (*Silk Exchange*). On the Plaza del Mercado, this 15th-century building is a product of Valencia's golden age, when the city's prosperity as one of the capitals of the Corona de Aragón made it a leading European commercial and artistic center. The Lonja was constructed as an expression of this splendor. Widely regarded as one of Spain's finest civil Gothic buildings, its facade is decorated with ghoulish gargoyles, complemented inside by high vaulting and slender helicoidal (twisted) columns. Opposite the Lonja stands the **Iglesia de los Santos Juanes** (Church of the St. Johns), gutted during the 1936–39 Spanish civil war, and, next door, the Moderniste **Mercado Central** (Central Market, ⇨ *see Shopping*), with its wrought-iron girders and stained-glass windows. ⊠ *Lonja 2, Ciutat Vella* ☎ *962/084153* ⊠ *€2.*

FodorśChoice   **Museo de Bellas Artes.** Valencia was a thriving center of artistic activity
★   in the 15th century—one reason that the city's Museum of Fine Arts, with its lovely palm-shaded cloister, is among the best in Spain. To get here, cross the old riverbed by the Puente de la Trinidad (Trinity Bridge) to the north bank; the museum is at the edge of the **Jardines del Real** (Royal Gardens; open daily 8–dusk), with its fountains, rose gardens, tree-lined avenues, and small zoo. The permanent collection of the museum includes many of the finest paintings by Jacomart and Juan Reixach, members of the group known as the Valencian Primitives, as well as work by Hieronymus Bosch—or El Bosco, as they call him here. The ground floor has a number of the brooding, 17th-century Tenebrist masterpieces by Francisco Ribalta and his pupil José Ribera, a Diego Velázquez self-portrait, and a room devoted to Goya. Upstairs, look for Joaquín Sorolla (Gallery 66), the Valencian painter of everyday Spanish life in the 19th century. ⊠ *Calle San Pío V 9, Trinitat* ☎ *963/870300* ⊕ *www.museobellasartesvalencia.gva.es* ⊠ *Free* ☉ *Closed Mon.*

Palacio del Marqués de Dos Aguas (*Ceramics Museum*). This building near Plaza Patriarca has gone through many changes over the years and now has elements of several architectural styles, including a fascinating baroque alabaster facade. Embellished with carvings of fruits and vegetables, the facade was designed in 1740 by Ignacio Vergara. It centers on the two voluptuous male figures representing the Dos Aguas (Two Waters), a reference to Valencia's two main rivers and the origin of the noble title of the Marqués de Dos Aguas. Since 1954, the palace has housed the **Museo Nacional de Cerámica,** with a magnificent collection of local and artisanal ceramics. Look for the Valencian kitchen on the second floor. ⊠ *Rinconada Federico García Sanchiz 6* ☎ *963/516392* ⊠ *Palace and museum €3; free Sat. 4–8 and Sun.* ☉ *Closed Mon.*

WORTH NOTING

Institut Valencià d'Art Modern (IVAM). Dedicated to modern and contemporary art, this blocky, uninspired building on the edge of the old city—where the riverbed makes a loop—houses a permanent collection of 20th-century avant-garde painting, European Informalism (including the Spanish artists Antonio Saura, Antoni Tàpies, and Eduardo Chillida), pop art, and photography. ⊠ *Carrer de Guillem de Castro 118, Ciutat Vella* ☎ *963/176600* ⊕ *www.ivam.es* 🖅 *€6; free Sun.* ☉ *Closed Mon.*

Plaza de Toros. Adjacent to the train station, this bullring is one of the oldest in Spain. The best bullfighters are featured during Las Fallas in March, particularly on March 18 and 19. ⊠ *Calle Xátiva 28, Ciutat Vella* ☎ *902/107777* ⊕ *www.torosvalencia.com.*

Plaza del Ayuntamiento. With the massive baroque facades of the Ayuntamiento (City Hall) and the Correos (central Post Office) facing each other across the park, this plaza is the hub of city life. The Ayuntamiento itself houses the municipal tourist office and a museum of paleontology. ■TIP➔ **Pop in just for a moment to marvel at the Post Office, with its magnificent stained-glass cupola and ring of classical columns. They don't build 'em like that any more.** ⊠ *Plaza del Ayuntamiento 1* ☎ *963/525478* ⊕ *www.visitvalencia.com* ☉ *Closed weekends.*

Real Colegio del Corpus Christi (*Iglesia del Patriarca*). This seminary, with its church, cloister, and library, is the crown jewel of Valencia's Renaissance architecture. Founded by San Juan de Ribera in the 16th century, it has a lovely Renaissance patio and an ornate church, and its museum holds works by Juan de Juanes, Francisco Ribalta, and El Greco. ⊠ *Calle de la Nave 1* ☎ *963/514176* ⊕ *www.seminariocorpuschristi.org* 🖅 *€3.*

San Nicolás. A small plaza contains Valencia's oldest church, once the parish of the Borgia Pope Calixtus III. The first portal you come to, with a tacked-on, rococo bas-relief of the Virgin Mary with cherubs, hints at what's inside: every inch of the originally Gothic church is covered with exuberant ornamentation. ⊠ *Calle Caballeros 35* ☎ *963/913317* ⊕ *www.sannicolasvalencia.com* 🖅 *Free.*

BEACHES

Playa las Arenas. This wide (nearly 450 feet) and popular grand municipal beach stretches north from the port and the America's Cup marina more than a kilometer (½ mile), before it gives way to the even busier and livelier Platja de Malvarrosa. The Paseo Marítimo promenade runs the length of the beach and is lined with restaurants and small hotels, including the **Neptuno.** There's no shade anywhere, but the fine golden sand is kept pristine and the water is calm and shallow. There are three lifeguard posts and first-aid stations. Brisk off-shore winds can make this ideal for windsurfing and small-craft sailing; there's a sailing school on the beach to meet the demand. **Amenities:** food and drink; lifeguards; showers; toilets; water sports. **Best for:** sunset; swimming; walking; windsurfing. ⊠ *Valencia* ⊕ *www.playadelasarenas.com.*

Valencia's L'Oceanogràfic (Ciutat de les Arts i les Ciències) has amazing exhibits, as well as an underwater restaurant.

WHERE TO EAT

$$$$
SPANISH

✗ **La Pepica.** Locals regard this bustling informal restaurant, on the promenade at El Cabanyal beach, as the best in town for seafood paella. Founded in 1898, the walls of the establishment are covered with signed pictures of appreciative visitors, from Ernest Hemingway to King Juan Carlos and the royal family. **Known for:** locally revered seafood paella; delectable tarts; historic locale. $ *Average main: €25* ⊠ *Paseo Neptuno 6* ☎ *963/710366* ⊕ *www.lapepica.com* ☾ *Closed last 2 wks in Nov. No dinner Sun.–Thurs.*

$$
SPANISH

✗ **La Riuà.** A favorite of Valencia's well-connected and well-to-do since 1982, this family-run restaurant a few steps from the Plaza de la Reina specializes in seafood dishes like *anguilas* (eels) prepared with *all i pebre* (garlic and pepper), *pulpitos guisados* (stewed baby octopus), and traditional paellas. Lunch begins at 2 and not a moment before. **Known for:** specialty eel dish; award-winning dining; family-run. $ *Average main: €13* ⊠ *Calle del Mar 27, bajo* ☎ *963/914571* ⊕ *www.lariua.com* ☾ *Closed Mon., Easter wk, last 2 wks in Aug., and 1st wk in Sept. (dates can vary). No dinner Sun.*

WHERE TO STAY

$$
HOTEL

▦ **Ad Hoc Monumental.** This nicely designed 19th-century town house sits on a quiet street at the edge of the old city, a minute's walk from the Plaza Almoina and the cathedral in one direction, and steps from the Turia gardens in the other. **Pros:** close to sights but quiet; courteous, helpful staff; great value. **Cons:** parking can be a nightmare; not especially family-oriented. $ *Rooms from: €124* ⊠ *Carrer Boix 4, Ciutat Vella* ☎ *963/919140* ⊕ *www.adhochoteles.com* ⇌ *28 rooms* ⏺ *No meals.*

$ B&B/INN Fodor'sChoice ★ **Antigua Morellana.** Run by four convivial sisters, this 18th-century town house provides the ultimate no-frills accommodations in the heart of the old city. **Pros:** friendly service; excellent location; complimentary tea in the lounge. **Cons:** no parking; soundproofing leaves much to be desired. [$] *Rooms from: €85* ✉ *Calle En Bou 2, Ciutat Vella* ☎ *963/915773* 🌐 *www.hostalam.com* 🛏 *18 rooms* 🍴 *No meals.*

$$$ HOTEL Fodor'sChoice ★ **Caro Hotel.** A triumph of design, opened in 2012, this elegant modern hotel is seamlessly wedded to an important historical property: a 14th-century Gothic palace, built on the 12th-century Arabic wall and over the Roman circus, fragments of which, discovered during the renovation, are on show. **Pros:** good location, a few minutes' walk from the cathedral; spot-on, attentive service; oasis of quiet. **Cons:** the two top-floor rooms have low, slanted ceilings; valet parking is rather pricey; decidedly not family-friendly. [$] *Rooms from: €176* ✉ *Carrer Almirante 14* ☎ *963/059000* 🌐 *www.carohotel.com* 💳 *No credit cards* 🛏 *24 rooms, 2 suites* 🍴 *No meals.*

$$$ HOTEL FAMILY **Neptuno Hotel.** This beachfront hotel is a slick, modern addition to the city's accommodations options. **Pros:** superb restaurant; great location for families; hydromassage baths and showers. **Cons:** extremely long walk to the historic center; gets booked up early in the summer. [$] *Rooms from: €176* ✉ *Paseo de Neptuno 2* ☎ *963/567777* 🌐 *www.hotelneptunovalencia.com* 🛏 *48 rooms, 2 suites* 🍴 *Breakfast.*

$$$$ HOTEL **Palau de la Mar.** In a restored 19th-century palace, this boutique hotel looks out at the Porta de La Mar, which marked the entry to the old walled quarter of Valencia. **Pros:** big bathrooms with double sinks; great location. **Cons:** top-floor rooms have low, slanted ceilings. [$] *Rooms from: €240* ✉ *Av. Navarro Reverter 14, Ciutat Vella* ☎ *963/162884, 902/254255* 🌐 *www.hospes.com* 🛏 *61 rooms, 5 suites* 🍴 *Breakfast.*

$$$$ HOTEL **Westin Valencia.** Built in 1917 as a cotton mill, with successive recyclings as a fire station and a stable for the mounted National Police Corps, this classic property was transformed in 2006 into the odds-on premier luxury hotel in Valencia. **Pros:** attentive, professional, multilingual staff; location steps from the metro that connects directly to the airport; pet-friendly. **Cons:** rates are high—and climb to astronomical levels during special events like Las Fallas and Formula One races. [$] *Rooms from: €227* ✉ *Av. Amadeo de Saboya 16, Pl. del Reial* ☎ *963/625900* 🌐 *www.westinvalencia.com* 🛏 *124 rooms, 11 suites* 🍴 *No meals.*

NIGHTLIFE AND PERFORMING ARTS

Valencianos have perfected the art of doing without sleep. The city's nocturnal way of life survives even in summer, when locals vie for space on the beach amid hordes of tourists. Nightlife in the old town centers on Barrio del Carmen, a lively web of streets that unfolds north of Plaza del Mercado. Popular bars and pubs dot Calle Caballeros, starting at Plaza de la Virgen; the Plaza del Tossal also has some popular cafés, as does Calle Alta, off Plaza San Jaime.

Some of the funkier, newer places are in and around Plaza del Carmen. Across the river, look for appealing hangouts along Avenida Blasco Ibáñez and on Plaza de Cánovas del Castillo. Out by the sea, Paseo Neptuno and Calle de Eugenia Viñes are lined with clubs and bars, lively in summer. The monthly English-language nightlife and culture magazine *24/7 Valencia* (⊕ *www.247valencia.com*) is free at tourist offices and various bars and clubs; leisure guides in Spanish include *Hello Valencia* (⊕ *www.hellovalencia.es*) and *La Guía Go* (⊕ *www.laguiago.com*).

NIGHTLIFE

BARS AND CAFÉS

Café del Duende. For a taste of *el ambiente andaluz* (Andalusian atmosphere), stop by this flamenco club in the heart of the Barrio del Carmen. It's open Thursday–Saturday from 10 pm (performances start at 11 pm). On Sunday performances start at 10 pm. Get there early to secure a seat. ⊠ *Carrer Túria 62, El Carmen* ☎ 630/455289.

Café Tertulia 1900. A *tertulia* is a social gathering or a group discussion; lots of Valencianos start here on a night out, and plan the rest of the evening over a mojito or one of the café's 18 different gin-tonics. ⊠ *Carrer de Dalt 4, El Carmen* ☎ 600/029201.

DANCE CLUBS

Calcatta. Need tangible proof that Valencia never sleeps? Find it at this Barrio del Carmen disco (Friday and Saturday only, from midnight), where a younger crowd parties to pop, R&B, and house music in a restored 17th-century palacio. Even if you drop by at 6 am, Calcutta will still be open. ⊠ *Calle Reloj Viejo 6, La Seu* ☎ 637/488505.

Las Animas. This is the center-city location of Las Ánimas discos and pubs scattered around Valencia. ⊠ *Pizarro 31* ☎ 902/108527 ⊕ *www.grupolasanimas.com*.

MUSIC CLUBS

Jimmy Glass Jazz Bar. Aficionados of modern jazz gather at this bar (open Tuesday–Thursday 8:15 pm–2:30 am, and Friday and Saturday 9 pm–3:30 am), which books an impressive range of local and international combos and soloists. Cover charge usually runs €10–€20. ⊠ *Carrer Baja 28, El Carmen* ⊕ *www.jimmyglassjazz.net*.

Radio City. The airy, perennially popular, bar–club–performance space at Radio City offers eclectic nightly shows featuring music from flamenco to Afro-jazz fusion. ⊠ *Carrer Santa Teresa 19, Ciutat Vella* ☎ 963/914151 ⊕ *www.radiocityvalencia.com*.

PERFORMING ARTS

CINEMA

Filmoteca. The Filmoteca has changing monthly programs of films in their original language (look for "*v.o.*" for *versión original*) and an artsy haunt of a café. ⊠ *Pl. del Ayuntamiento 17* ☎ 963/539300 ⊕ *www.ivac.gva.es/la-filmoteca*.

THEATER

Palau de la Música. Home of the Orquesta de Valencia, the main hall also hosts touring performers from around the world, including chamber and youth orchestras, opera, and an excellent concert series featuring early, baroque, and classical music. For concert schedules, pick up a Turia guide or one of the local newspapers at any newsstand, or check the website. ⊠ *Passeig de l'Albereda 30* ☎ 963/375020 ⊕ *www.palaudevalencia.com*.

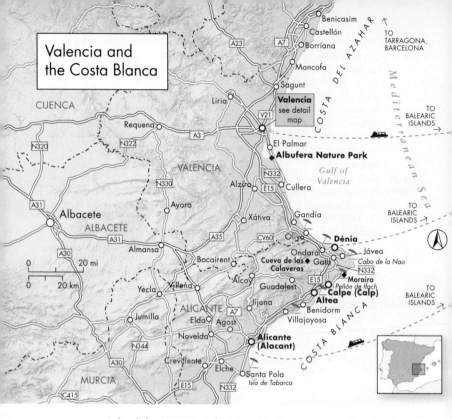

Palau de les Arts Reina Sofía. This visually arresting performing arts venue and concert hall hosts a rich calendar of opera and classical music throughout the year. ✉ *Av. del Profesor López Piñero (Historiador de la Medicina) 1* ☎ *961/975800* ⊕ *www.lesarts.com.*

SHOPPING

A few steps from the cathedral, off the upper end of Calle San Vicente Mártir, the newly restored **Plaza Redonda** ("Round Square") is lined with stalls selling all sorts of souvenirs and traditional crafts.

Lladró. The world-famous porcelain figurines of Lladró originated in Valencia, and are still made not far from here. Tour the factory and museum in Tavernes Blanques for free (reservations required: ☎ 963/187000), or visit the flagship salesroom in the old town. ✉ *Calle Poeta Querol 9, Ciutat Vella* ☎ *963/511625* ⊕ *www.lladro.com.*

Mercado Central (Central Market). The bustling food market (at nearly 88,000 square feet, one of the largest in Europe) is open Monday–Saturday 7 am–3 pm. Locals and visitors alike line up at the 1,247 colorful stalls to shop for fruit, vegetables, meat, fish, and confectionery. The market is closed on Sunday. ✉ *Pl. Ciudad de Brujas s/n* ☎ *963/829100* ⊕ *www.mercadocentralvalencia.es.*

Nela. Browse here, in the heart of the old city, for *abanicos* (traditional silk folding fans), hand-embroidered *mantillas* (shawls), and parasols. ⊠ *Calle San Vicente Màrtir 2, Ciutat Vella* ☎ *963/923023.*

ALBUFERA NATURE PARK

11 km (7 miles) south of Valencia.

South of Valencia, Albufera Nature Park is one of Spain's most spectacular wetland areas. Home to the largest freshwater lagoon on the peninsula, this protected area and bird-watcher's paradise is bursting with unusual flora and fauna, such as rare species of wading birds. Encircled by a tranquil backdrop of rice fields, it's no surprise that the villages that dot this picturesque place have some of the best options in the region for trying classic Valencian paella or *arròs a banda* (rice cooked in fish stock).

GETTING HERE AND AROUND

From Valencia, buses depart from the corner of Sueca and Gran Vía de Germanías every hour, and every half hour in summer, 7 am–9 pm daily.

EXPLORING

Albufera Nature Park. This beautiful freshwater lagoon was named by Moorish poets—*albufera* means "the sun's mirror." The park is a nesting site for more than 250 bird species, including herons, terns, egrets, ducks, and gulls. Admission is free. Bird-watching companies offer boat rides all along the Albufera. For maps, guides, and tour arrangements, start your visit at the park's information center, the Centre d'Interpretació Raco de l'Olla in El Palmar. ⊠ *Ctra. de El Palmar s/n, El Palmar* ☎ *963/868050* ⊕ *www.albufera.com.*

El Palmar. This is the major village in the area, with restaurants specializing in various types of paella. The most traditional kind is made with rabbit or game birds, though seafood is also popular in this region because it's so fresh.

WHERE TO EAT

$$ ✕ **La Matandeta.** With its white garden walls and rustic interior, this
SPANISH restaurant is a culinary island in the rice paddies. Valencian families come here on Sunday, when many of the city's restaurants are closed. **Known for:** Sunday dinner; signature paella de pato, pollo, y conejo; 50 types of olive oil. Ⓢ *Average main: €16* ⊠ *Carretera Alfafar–El Saler, Km 4, Valencia* ☎ *962/112184, 608/306009* ⊕ *www.lamatandeta.es* ☾ *Closed Mon. and Tues. Dinner by reservation only.*

THE COSTA BLANCA

The stretch of coastline known as the Costa Blanca (White Coast) begins at Dénia, south of Valencia, and stretches down roughly to Torrevieja, below Alicante. It's best known for its magical vacation combo of sand, sea, and sun, with popular beaches and more secluded coves and stretches of sand. Alicante itself has two long beaches, a charming old quarter, and mild weather most of the year.

DÉNIA

Dénia is the port of departure on the Costa Blanca for the ferries to Ibiza, Formentera, and Mallorca—but if you're on your way to or from the islands, stay a night in the lovely little town in the shadow of a dramatic cliff-top fortress. Or, spend a few hours wandering in the Baix la Mar, the old fishermen's quarter with its brightly painted houses, and exploring the historic town center.

GETTING HERE AND AROUND

Dénia is linked to other Costa Blanca destinations via Line 1of the Alicante–Benidorm narrow-gauge TRAM train. There's also regular bus service from major towns and cities, including Madrid (7¼–9 hours) and Valencia (1¾–2½ hours). Local buses can get you around all of the Costa Blanca communities.

ESSENTIALS

Visitor Information Visitor Information Dénia. ⊠ *Pl. Oculista Buigues 9* ☎ *966/422367* ⊕ *www.denia.net.*

EXPLORING

Castillo de Dénia. The most interesting architectural attraction here is the castle overlooking the town, and the **Palau del Governador** (Governor's Palace) inside. On the site of an 11th-century Moorish fortress, the Renaissance-era palace was built in the 17th century and was later demolished. A major restoration project is underway. The fortress has an interesting archaeological museum as well as the remains of a Renaissance bastion and a Moorish portal with a lovely horseshoe arch. ⊠ *Av. del Cid–Calle San Francisco s/n* ☎ *966/422367* 💲 *€3 (includes entrance to archeological museum).*

FAMILY **Cueva de las Calaveras** (*Cave of the Skulls*). Inland from Dénia, this 400-yard-long cave was named for the 12 Moorish skulls found here when it was discovered in 1768. The cave of stalactites and stalagmites has a dome rising to more than 60 feet and leads to an underground lake. ⊠ *Ctra. Benidoleig–Pedreguera, Km 1.5, Benidoleig* ☎ *966/404235* ⊕ *www.cuevadelascalaveras.com* 💲 *€3.90.*

WHERE TO EAT

$$ ✕ **El Port.** In the old fishermen's quarter just across from the port, this
SEAFOOD classic dining spot features all kinds of fish fresh off the boats. There are also shellfish dishes and a full range of rice specialties, from *arròs negre* (rice with squid ink) to a classic paella marinera. **Known for:** busy summer season; local favorite; ample tapas. 💲 *Average main: €12* ⊠ *Carrer de Bellavista 11* ☎ *965/784973* ⊕ *www.restaurantedeniaelport.com* ⊘ *Closed Thurs.*

$$$ ✕ **El Raset.** Across the harbor, this Valencian favorite has been serving
SEAFOOD traditional cuisine with a modern twist for more than 30 years. From a terrace with views of the water you can choose from an array of excellent seafood dishes. **Known for:** excellent seafood dishes; reasonably priced set menu; tasty paella. 💲 *Average main: €20* ⊠ *Calle Bellavista 7* ☎ *965/785040* ⊕ *www.grupoelraset.com.*

Dénia's massive fort overlooks the harbor and provides a dramatic element to the skyline, with the Montgü mountains in the background.

8

$$$ SPANISH Fodor's Choice ★ 🍴 **La Seu.** Under co-owners Fede and Diana Cervera and chef Xicu Ramón, this distinguished restaurant in the center of town continues to reinvent and deconstruct traditional Valencian cuisine. The setting is an architectural tour de force: a 16th-century town house transformed into a sunlit modern space with an open kitchen and a three-story-high wall sculpted to resemble a billowing white curtain. **Known for:** creative tapas; midweek menu prices unbeatable; inventive take on Valencian cuisine. [$] *Average main: €20* ✉ *Calle Loreto 59* ☎ *966/424478* 🌐 *www.laseu.es* ⏲ *Closed Mon. and early Jan.–early Feb.*

WHERE TO STAY

$ B&B/INN 🏨 **Art Boutique Hotel Chamarel.** Ask the staff and they'll tell you that *chamarel* means a "mixture of colors," and this hotel, built as a grand family home in 1840, is certainly an eccentric blend of styles, cultures, periods, and personalities. **Pros:** friendly staff; individual attention; pet-friendly. **Cons:** no pool; not on the beach. [$] *Rooms from: €85* ✉ *Calle Cavallers 13* ☎ *966/435007* 🌐 *www.hotelchamarel.com* 🛏 *10 rooms, 5 suites* 🍽 *Breakfast.*

$ HOTEL Fodor's Choice ★ 🏨 **Hostal Loreto.** Travelers on tight budgets will appreciate this basic yet impeccable lodging, on a central pedestrian street in the historic quarter just steps from the Town Hall. **Pros:** great location; good value; broad comfy roof terrace. **Cons:** no elevator; no amenities. [$] *Rooms from: €88* ✉ *Calle Loreto 12* ☎ *966/435419* 🌐 *www.hostalloreto.com* 🛏 *43 rooms* 🍽 *Breakfast.*

$$$
B&B/INN
Fodor'sChoice
★

Hotel El Raset. Just across the esplanade from the port, where the Balearia ferries depart for Mallorca and Ibiza, this upscale boutique hotel has amenities that few lodgings in Dénia offer. **Pros:** staff is friendly, attentive, and multilingual; good location. **Cons:** no pool; dim overhead lighting in rooms; pricey private parking. $ *Rooms from: €152* ✉ *Calle Bellavista 1, Port* ☎ *965/786564* ⊕ *www.hotelelraset.com* ↪ *20 rooms* ⏐◯⏐ *Breakfast.*

$$$$
HOTEL

La Posada del Mar. A few steps across from the harbor, this hotel in the 13th-century customs house has an inviting rooftop terrace and rooms with views. **Pros:** serene environment; close to center of town. **Cons:** pricey parking; no pool. $ *Rooms from: €193* ✉ *Pl. de les Drassanes 2, Port* ☎ *966/432966* ⊕ *www.laposadadelmar.com* ↪ *20 rooms, 11 suites* ⏐◯⏐ *Breakfast.*

EN
ROUTE

The Playa del Arenal, a tiny bay cut into the larger one, is worth a visit in summer. You can reach it via the coastal road (CV736) between Dénia and Jávea.

CALPE (CALP)

35 km (22 miles) south of Dénia.

Calpe has an ancient history, as it was chosen by the Phoenicians, Greeks, Romans, and Moors as a strategic point from which to plant their Iberian settlements. The real-estate developers were the latest to descend upon it: much of Calpe today is overbuilt with high-rise resorts and *urbanizaciónes*. But the old town is a delightful maze of narrow streets and small squares, archways and cul-de-sacs, houses painted in Mediterranean blue, red, ocher, and sandstone; wherever there's a broad expanse of building wall, you'll likely discover a mural. Calpe is a delightful place to wander.

The narrow-gauge TRAM railway from Dénia to Alicante also serves Calpe, as do local buses.

ESSENTIALS

Visitor Information Visitor Information Calpe. ✉ *Av. Ejércitos Españoles 44, Calp* ☎ *965/836920* ⊕ *www.calpe.es.*

EXPLORING

Fish Market. The fishing industry is still very important in Calpe, and every evening the fishing boats return to port with their catch. The subsequent auction at the fish market can be watched from the walkway of La Lonja de Calpe. ✉ *Port, Calp* ☉ *Closed weekends.*

Mundo Marino. Choose from a wide range of sailing trips, including cruises up and down the coast. Glass-bottom boats make it easy to observe the abundant marine life. ✉ *Calle Joan Fuster 2, Calp* ☎ *966/423066* ⊕ *eventos.mundomarino.es.*

Peñón d'Ifach. The landscape of Calpe is dominated by this huge calcareous rock more than 1,100 yards long, 1,090 feet high, and joined to the mainland by a narrow isthmus. The area is rich in flora and fauna, with more than 300 species of plants and 80 species of land and marine birds. A visit to the top is not for the fainthearted; wear shoes with traction for the hike, which includes a trip through a tunnel to the summit. The views are spectacular, reaching to the island of Ibiza on a clear day. Check with the local visitor information center (Centro de Interpretación, Calle Isla de Formentera s/n ☎ 965/837596 or 679/195912) about guided tours for groups. ✉ *Calp.*

WHERE TO EAT

$$$ ✕ **Patio de la Fuente.** In an intimate little space with wicker chairs and
MEDITERRANEAN pale mauve walls, this restaurant in the old town serves a bargain three-course prix-fixe dinner, wine included. Try the warm salad of bacon, potato, asparagus, avocado, and tomato with lime dressing, or the crispy duck confit with ginger and plum sauce. **Known for:** outdoor dining; cheap three-course dinner; divine Scotch egg. $ *Average main: €18* ✉ *Carrer Dos de Mayo 16, Calp* ☎ *965/831695* ⊕ *www. patiodelafuente.com* ⊙ *Closed Sun. and Mon. No lunch.*

ALTEA

11 km (7 miles) southwest of Calpe.

Perched on a hill overlooking a bustling beachfront, Altea (unlike some of its neighboring towns) has retained much of its original charm, with an atmospheric old quarter laced with narrow cobblestone streets and stairways, and gleaming white houses. At the center is the striking church of Nuestra Señora del Consuelo, with its blue ceramic-tile dome, and the Plaza de la Iglesia in front.

GETTING HERE AND AROUND
Also on the Dénia–Alicante narrow-gauge TRAM train route, Altea is served by local buses, with connections to major towns and cities.

ESSENTIALS
Visitor Information **Visitor Information Altea.** ✉ *Calle Sant Pere 14* ☎ *965/844114* ⊕ *www.visitaltea.es.*

WHERE TO EAT

$$$ ✕ **La Costera.** This popular restaurant focuses on fine French fare, with
CATALAN such specialties as house-made foie gras, roasted lubina, and fondue bourguignonne. There's also a variety of game in season, including venison and partridge. **Known for:** bucolic outdoor terrace; in-season game; fine French fare. $ *Average main: €18* ✉ *Costera Mestre de Música 8* ☎ *965/840230* ⊕ *www.lacosteradealtea.es.*

$$ ✕ **Oustau de Altea.** In one of the prettiest corners of Altea's old town,
EUROPEAN this eatery was formerly a cloister and a school. Today the dining room and terrace combine contemporary design gracefully juxtaposed with a rustic setting. **Known for:** polished French cuisine; dishes named after classic films; contemporary artwork. $ *Average main: €14* ✉ *Calle Mayor 5, Casco Antiguo* ☎ *965/842078* ⊕ *www.oustau.com* ⊙ *Closed Mon. and Feb. No lunch Oct.–June.*

8

DID YOU KNOW?

The town of Altea (from the Moorish name Althaya, which means "health to all") has a popular seafront promenade. The church is easily recognized by its blue-tile domes.

ALICANTE (ALACANT)

82 km (51 miles) northeast of Murcia, 183 km (114 miles) south of Valencia, 52 km (32 miles) south of Alctea.

The Greeks called it Akra Leuka (White Summit) and the Romans named it Lucentum (City of Light). A crossroads for inland and coastal routes since ancient times, Alicante has always been known for its luminous skies. The city is dominated by the 16th-century grande dame castle, **Castillo de Santa Bárbara**, a top attraction. The best approach is via the elevator cut deep into the mountainside. Also memorable is Alicante's grand **Esplanada**, lined with date palms. Directly under the castle is the city beach, the Playa del Postiguet, but the city's pride is the long, curved Playa de San Juan, which runs north from the Cap de l'Horta to El Campello.

GETTING HERE AND AROUND

Alicante has two train stations: the main Estación de Madrid and the local Estación de la Marina, from which the local FGV line runs along the Costa Blanca from Alicante to Dénia. The Estación de la Marina is at the far end of Playa Postiguet and can be reached by Buses C1 and C2 from downtown.

The narrow-gauge TRAM train goes from the city center on the beach to El Campello. From the same open-air station in Alicante, the Line 1 train departs to Benidorm, with connections on to Altea, Calpe, and Dénia.

ESSENTIALS

Visitor Information Tourist Information Alicante. ✉ *Rambla Méndez Núñez 41, Alicante* ☎ *965/200000* ⊕ *www.alicanteturismo.com.* **TRAM.** ✉ *Av. Villajoyosa 2, Alicante* ☎ *900/720472* ⊕ *www.tramalicante.es.*

EXPLORING

OLD TOWN

Ayuntamiento. Constructed between 1696 and 1780, the town hall is a beautiful example of baroque civic architecture. Inside, a gold sculpture by Salvador Dalí of San Juan Bautista holding the famous cross and shell rises to the second floor in the stairwell. Ask gate officials for permission to explore the ornate halls and rococo chapel on the first floor. ✉ *Pl. de Ayuntamiento, Alicante* ☎ *965/149100.*

Basílica de Santa María. Constructed in a Gothic style over the city's main mosque between the 14th and 16th century, this is Alicante's oldest house of worship. The main door is flanked by beautiful baroque stonework by Juan Bautista Borja, and the interior highlights are the golden rococo high altar, a Gothic image in stone of St. Mary, and a sculpture of Sts. Juanes by Rodrigo de Osona. ✉ *Pl. de Santa María s/n, Alicante* ☎ *965/216026.*

Concatedral of San Nicolás de Bari. Built between 1616 and 1662 on the site of a former mosque, this church (called a *con*catedral because it shares the seat of the bishopric with the Concatedral de Orihuela) has an austere facade designed by Agustín Bernardino, a disciple of the great Spanish architect Juan de Herrera. Inside, it's dominated by a dome nearly 150 feet high, a pretty cloister, and a lavish baroque side chapel,

Alicante's Esplanada de España, lined with date palms, is the perfect place for a stroll. The municipal brass band offers concerts on the bandstand of the Esplanada on Sunday evenings in July and August.

the Santísima Sacramento, with an elaborate sculptured stone dome of its own. Its name comes from the day that Alicante was reconquered (December 6, 1248), the feast day of St. Nicolás. ⊠ *Pl. Abad Penalva 2, Alicante* ☎ *965/212662* ⊗ *Closed Mon.*

Museo de Bellas Artes Gravina. Inside the beautiful 18th-century Palacio del Conde de Lumiares, MUBAG—as it's best known—has some 500 works of art ranging from the 16th to the early 20th century. ⊠ *Calle de Gravina 13–15, Alicante* ☎ *965/146780* ⊕ *www.mubag.org* ✉ *Free* ⊗ *Closed Mon.*

OUTSIDE OLD TOWN

Fodor's Choice
★

Castillo de Santa Bárbara (*Saint Barbara's Castle*). One of the largest existing medieval fortresses in Europe, Castillo de Santa Bárbara sits atop 545-foot-tall Monte Benacantil. From this strategic position you can gaze out over the city, the sea, and the whole Alicante plain for many miles. Remains from civilizations dating from the Bronze Age onward have been found here; the oldest parts, at the highest level, are from the 9th through 13th century. The castle is most easily reached by first walking through a 200-yard tunnel entered from Avenida Jovellanos 1 along Playa del Postiguet by the pedestrian bridge, then taking the elevator up 472 feet to the entrance. Guided tours (€3) are offered Monday–Saturday at 11 and 12:30, and in summer, a "theatrical tour" (€5), with performers in costume interpreting the history of the castle take place on Sunday at noon (performed in Spanish only). ⊠ *Monte Benacantil s/n, Alicante* ☎ *965/147160* ⊕ *www.castillodesantabarbara. com* ✉ *Elevator €2.70 (runs 10–7:45).*

Museo Arqueológico Provincial. Inside the old hospital of San Juan de Dios, this museum has a collection of artifacts from the Alicante region dating from the Paleolithic era to modern times, with a particular emphasis on Iberian art. The MARQ, as it is known, has won recognition as the European Museum Forum's European Museum of the Year. ✉ *Pl. Dr. Gómez Ulla s/n, Alicante* ☎ *965/149000* 🌐 *www.marqalicante.com* 🎟 *€3* 🕒 *Closed Mon.*

Museo de Hogueres. Bonfire festivities are popular in this part of Spain, and the effigies can be elaborate and funny, including satirized political figures and celebrities. Every year the best *ninots* (effigies) are saved from the flames and placed in this museum, which also has an audiovisual presentation of the festivities, scale models, photos, and costumes. ✉ *Calle Teniente Álvarez Soto s/n (on the corner with Rambla Méndez Núñez), Alicante* ☎ *965/146828* 🌐 *www.hogueras.org* 🎟 *Free* 🕒 *Closed Mon.*

WHERE TO EAT AND STAY

$$ TAPAS

🍴 **Cervecería Sento.** The bar and the grill behind it are the center of attention at this historic eatery just off the Rambla, serving up what many claim are the town's best tapas and *montaditos* (bite-size sandwiches). Join the throng trying melt-in-your-mouth *solomillo con foie* (sirloin with foie gras) or the sandwich made with marinated pork, mushrooms, and red peppers, accompanied by a glass of red from the excellent wine cellar. **Known for:** historic; great tapas; delicious montaditos. [$] *Average main: €12* ✉ *Calle Teniente Coronel Chapuli s/n, Alicante* ☎ *646/932213.*

$$$ TAPAS Fodor's Choice ★

🍴 **La Taberna del Gourmet.** This comfortable restaurant and wine bar in the heart of the *casco antiguo* (old town) earns high marks from locals and international visitors alike. Two dining rooms in back are furnished with thick butcher-block tables and dark brown leather chairs, and the subdued lighting adds to the casual yet elegant dining experience. **Known for:** excellent wine list; fresh seafood tapas; reservations essential. [$] *Average main: €20* ✉ *Calle San Fernando 10, Alicante* ☎ *965/204233* 🌐 *www.latabernadelgourmet.com.*

$$$$ HOTEL Fodor's Choice ★

🏨 **Eurostars Mediterránea Plaza.** You'll find this elegant hotel tucked under the arches in the central plaza. **Pros:** spacious bedrooms; double-glazed French windows; gym and sauna; good value. **Cons:** no lobby space to speak of; private parking a bit steep; no pets. [$] *Rooms from: €200* ✉ *Pl. del Ayuntamiento 6, Alicante* ☎ *902/932424* 🌐 *www.eurostarsmediterraneaplaza.com* 🛏 *49 rooms* 🍽 *Breakfast.*

$ HOTEL

🏨 **Hostal Les Monges Palace.** In a restored 1912 building, this family-run hostal in Alicante's central casco antiguo features lovingly preserved exposed stone walls, ceramic tile floors, and rooms furnished with eccentric artwork and quirky charm. **Pros:** personalized service; ideal location; lots of character. **Cons:** all services cost extra (breakfast is €6); must book well in advance. [$] *Rooms from: €70* ✉ *Calle San Agustín 4, Alicante* ☎ *965/215046* 🌐 *www.lesmonges.es* 🛏 *22 rooms, 2 suites* 🍽 *No meals.*

NIGHTLIFE

El Barrio, the old quarter west of Rambla de Méndez Núñez, is the prime nightlife area of Alicante, with music bars and discos every couple of steps. In summer, or after 3 am, the liveliest places are along the water, on Ruta del Puerto and Ruta de la Madera.

El Coscorrón. It's an Alicante tradition to start an evening out here, with El Coscorrón's generous mojitos. ✉ *Calle Tarifa 5, Alicante* ☎ *965/212727.*

UNDERSTANDING BARCELONA

SPANISH VOCABULARY

WORDS AND PHRASES

	ENGLISH	SPANISH	PRONUNCIATION
BASICS			
	Yes/no	Sí/no	see/no
	Please	Por favor	pohr fah-vohr
	Thank you (very much)	(Muchas) gracias	(moo-chas) grah-see-as
	You're welcome	De nada	deh nah-dah
	Excuse me	Con permiso/perdón	con pehr-mee-so/ pehr-dohn
	Pardon me/ what did you say?	¿Perdón?/Mande?	pehr-dohn/mahn-deh
	I'm sorry	Lo siento	lo see-en-to
	Good morning!	¡Buenos días!	bway-nohs dee-ahs
	Good afternoon!	¡Buenas tardes!	bway-nahs tar-dess
	Good evening!	¡Buenas noches!	bway-nahs no-chess
	Goodbye!	¡Adiós!/ ¡Hasta luego!	ah-dee-ohss/ ah-stah-lwe-go

NUMBERS

	1	un, uno	oon, oo-no
	2	dos	dohs
	3	tres	tress
	4	cuatro	kwah-tro
	5	cinco	sink-oh
	6	seis	saice
	7	siete	see-et-eh
	8	ocho	o-cho
	9	nueve	new-eh-veh
	10	diez	dee-es
	20	veinte	vain-teh
	50	cincuenta	seen-kwen-tah
	100	cien	see-en
	200	doscientos	doh-see-en-tohss
	500	quinientos	keen-yen-tohss

ENGLISH	SPANISH	PRONUNCIATION

USEFUL PHRASES

ENGLISH	SPANISH	PRONUNCIATION
Do you speak English?	¿Habla usted inglés?	ah-blah oos-ted in-glehs
I don't speak Spanish	No hablo español	no ah-bloh es-pahn-yol
I don't understand (you)	No entiendo	no en-tee-en-doh
I understand (you)	Entiendo	en-tee-en-doh
Yes, please/	Sí, por favor/	see pohr fah-vor/
No, thank you	No, gracias	no grah-see-ahs
When?	¿Cuándo?	kwahn-doh
What?	¿Qué?	keh
Where is … ?	¿Dónde está … ?	dohn-deh es-tah
.. the subway station?	.. la estación del metro?	la es-ta-see-on del meh-tro
.. the hospital?	.. el hospital?	el ohss-pee-tal
.. the bathroom?	.. el baño?	el bahn-yoh
Here/there	Aquí/allá	ah-key/ah-yah
Open/closed	Abierto/cerrado	ah-bee-er-toh/ ser-ah-doh
I'd like …	Quisiera …	kee-see-ehr-ah
How much is this?	¿Cuánto cuesta?	kwahn-toh kwes-tah
I am ill	Estoy enfermo(a)	es-toy en-fehr- moh(mah)
Please call a doctor	Por favor llame un médico	pohr fah-vor ya- meh oon med-ee-koh
Help!	¡Ayuda!	ah-yoo-dah

DINING OUT

ENGLISH	SPANISH	PRONUNCIATION
Bill/check	La cuenta	lah kwen-tah
Is the tip included?	¿Está incluida la propina?	es-tah in-cloo-ee- dahah pro-pee-nah
Menu	La carta, el menú	lah cart-ah, el meh-noo
Please give me …	Por favor déme …	pohr fah-vor deh-meh

TRAVEL SMART
BARCELONA

GETTING HERE AND AROUND

With some planning, finding your way around in Barcelona can be simple. All of Barcelona's Ciutat Vella (Old City), including the Barri Gòtic (Gothic Quarter), can be explored on foot. Your transport needs will be mainly to get to Sarrià, Gràcia, Park Güell, Gaudí's Sagrada Família, Montjuïc, and the Auditori near Plaça de les Glòries. The metro system will normally get you wherever you need to go. The commuter trains on the Catalan regional government's FGC system are also handy. The municipal metro lines are useful, air-conditioned, and safe. Buses are practical for certain runs, and taxis are rarely much more than €15 for a complete crosstown ride.

Modern Barcelona, above Plaça de Catalunya, is built on a grid system. The Old City, however, from Plaça de Catalunya to the port, is a labyrinth of narrow streets, so you'll need a good street map (or GPS) and a good pair of shoes to explore it. Whenever possible, it's best to avoid driving in the city. *(For information about driving, see Car Travel.)* Maps of the bus and metro routes are available free from the main Tourist Information office on Plaça de Catalunya.

▌ AIR TRAVEL

Transatlantic flying time to Barcelona's El Prat Airport averages about 7 hours and 30 minutes from New York's JFK Airport. Other U.S. cities with direct flights to Barcelona are Atlanta, Chicago, Miami, Newark, and Philadelphia. Low-cost carrier Norwegian Airlines will introduce additional direct routes from Fort Lauderdale, Oakland, Newark, and Los Angeles in fall 2017. Flying from other cities in North America usually requires a connection.

Nonstop flights from London to Barcelona average 2 hours and 30 minutes. Flights from the United Kingdom to a number of destinations in Spain are frequent and offered at competitive fares, particularly on low-cost carriers such as Ryanair or easyJet. There are no direct flights to Barcelona or anywhere in Spain from Australia or New Zealand.

Flying from Sydney, the best one-stop connections are via Dubai (14 hours, 30 minutes), with a layover, and then direct to Barcelona/El Prat (7 hours, 20 minutes).

For air travel within the regions covered in this book there are numerous regular flights, but rates tend to be high, so consider alternative ways of getting around. Bilbao, Pamplona, and San Sebastián all have small airports, and flights do run from Barcelona to each of them. For travel between those cities, given the short distances involved, most people elect to go by train or car.

Iberia operates a shuttle, the *puente aereo,* between Barcelona and Madrid from 6:50 am to 9:45 pm; planes depart from Terminal 1 hourly, and more frequently in the morning and afternoon commuter hours. Flying time is about an hour and a half; given the time you need for airport transfers, many commuters now prefer the high-speed rail connection between Estació de Sants in Barcelona and Atocha Station in Madrid. *(For information, see Train Travel.)* You don't need to reserve ahead for the shuttle flight; you can buy your tickets at the counter when you get to the airport.

Charter flights of varying prices routinely fly in and out of El Prat Airport. Top charter companies include NetJets, Global Jet Concept, and Luxaviation.

Arriving three hours in advance for international flights is more than enough for Spanish security. Arriving fewer than 40 minutes in advance is no longer possible for either domestic or international flights.

Airline Security Issues European Commission. ⊕ *www.ec.europa.eu/transport/modes/air/safety.*

AIRPORTS

Most connecting flights arriving in Spain from the United States and Canada pass through Madrid's Barajas Airport (MAD), but the major gateway to Catalonia and other regions in this book is Spain's second-largest airport, Barcelona's spectacular glass, steel, and marble El Prat del Llobregat (BCN). The second of two terminals, the T1 terminal, which opened in 2009, is a sleek ultramodern facility that uses solar panels for sustainable energy and offers a spa, a fitness center, restaurants and cafés, and VIP lounges. This airport is about 12 km (7½ miles) southwest from the center of Barcelona and is served by numerous international carriers, but Catalonia also has two other airports that handle passenger traffic, including charter flights. One is Girona-Costa Brava Airport (GRO) 12½ km (8 miles) southwest of Girona, 90 km (56 miles) north of Barcelona and convenient to the resort towns of the Costa Brava. Bus and train connections from Girona to Barcelona are convenient and affordable, provided you have the time. The other Catalonia airport is the tiny Reus Airport (REU), 110 km (68 miles) south of Barcelona and a gateway to neighboring Tarragona, Port Adventura theme park and the beaches of the Costa Daurada. Both airports are considerably smaller than El Prat and offer the bare essentials: a limited number of duty-free shops, restaurants, and car hire services. Flights to and from the major cities in Europe and Spain also fly into and out of Bilbao's Loiu (BIL) airport. For information about airports in Spain, consult ⊕ *www.aena.es.*

Airport Information Aeroport de Girona–Costa Brava (*GRO*). ⊠ *17185 Vilobi de Onyar, Girona* ☎ *913/211000* ⊕ *www.girona-airport.cat.* **Aeropuerto de Madrid (Adolfo Suárez Madrid-Barajas)** (*MAD*). ⊠ *Av. de la Hispanidad s/n, Madrid* ☎ *902/404704, 913/211000 general info on Spanish airports* ⊕ *www.aeropuertomadrid-barajas.com/eng.* **Aeropuerto de Reus** (*REU*). ⊠ *Autovía Tarragona–Reus, Reus* ☎ *902/404704*

English-language airport information from Aena ⊕ *www.aena.es/en/reus-airport/index.html.* **Aeropuerto Internacional de Bilbao** (*BIO*). ⊠ *Loiu 48180, Bilbao* ☎ *913/211000,* ⊕ *www.aeropuertodebilbao.net/en.* **Barcelona El Prat de Llobregat** (*BCN*). ☎ *902/404704, 91/321–1000 general info on Spanish airports* ⊕ *www.aeropuertobarcelona-elprat.com.*

GROUND TRANSPORTATION

Check first to see if your hotel in Barcelona provides airport-shuttle service. If not, visitors typically get into town by train, bus, taxi, or rental car.

The quickest and most convenient way to and from the airport is by taxi, though buses and trains are more economical. Official yellow cab stands are available at both airport terminals. Never get into a taxi that does not have a meter and the driver's ID card on the dashboard. As of 2017, all Barcelona taxicabs are required to carry a portable credit card machine.

Cab fare from the airport into town is €30–€35, depending on traffic, the part of town you're heading to, and the amount of baggage you have (there's a €3.10 surcharge for airport pickups/drop-offs, and a €1 surcharge for each suitcase that goes in the trunk). If you're driving your own car, follow signs to the Centre Ciutat, from which you can enter the city along Gran Vía. For the port area, follow signs for the Ronda Litoral. The journey to the center of town can take 25–45 minutes, depending on traffic.

If you have to get to the airport by car or taxi during rush hour, allow yourself plenty of extra time, as the ring roads are likely to be jammed.

The Aerobus leaves Terminal 1 at the airport for Plaça de Catalunya every 10 minutes 5:35–7:20 am and 10:25 pm–1:05 am, and every 5 minutes 7:30 am–10:20 pm. From Plaça de Catalunya the bus leaves for the airport every 5 or 10 minutes between 5 am and 12:10 am. The fare is €5.90 one-way and €10.20 round-trip. Aerobuses for terminals 1 and 2 pick up and drop off passengers at the same stops en route, so if you're outward bound make sure that you board the right one. The A1 Aerobus for Terminal 1 is two-tone light and dark blue; the A2 Aerobus for Terminal 2 is dark blue and yellow.

The train's only drawback is that it's a 10- to 15-minute walk from your gate through Terminal 2 over the bridge. From Terminal 1 a shuttle bus drops you at the train. Trains leave the airport every 30 minutes between 5:42 am and 11:38 pm, stopping at Estació de Sants, for transfer to the Arc de Triomf, then at Passeig de Gràcia and finally at El Clot–Aragó. Trains going to the airport begin at 5:21 am from El Clot, stopping at Passeig de Gràcia at 5:27 am, and Sants at 5:32 am. The trip takes about half an hour, and the fare is €4.10. But the best bargain is the T10 subway card; it gives you free connections within Barcelona plus nine more rides, all for €9.95. Add an extra hour if you take the train to or from the airport.

TRANSFERS BETWEEN AIRPORTS

To get to Girona Airport from Barcelona Airport by train you have to first catch the RENFE train that leaves from the airport and then change at Barcelona Sants station. From Barcelona Sants you need to catch the train for Figueres and get off at Girona, two stops before. Travel times vary between 38 minutes and 2 hours 10 minutes depending on the train line, with a cost of €11.25 for the faster AVE and Avant lines. From there you will have to take a 30-minute bus ride for €2.75, or a 17-minute taxi ride to the airport for around €25–€30. Allow yourself 30 minutes from the RENFE Girona station to the airport.

Sagales runs the Barcelona Bus shuttle buses between Girona airport and El Prat (€17 one-way or €27 round-trip; valid 30 days). The trip takes about 1 hour and 15 minutes. The schedules, set up to coincide with RyanAir arrivals and departures at Girona, are a bit tortuous; consult the Sagales website or call *902/130014* for bus information.

Contact Aerobus. ⊠ *Av. Joan Carles I, 50* ☎ *902/100104* ⊕ *www.aerobusbcn.com.* **Metropolitan Area Taxis.** ☎ *932/235151* ⊕ *www.taxi.amb.cat.* **Sagales.** ☎ *902/130014* ⊕ *www.sagales.com/en.*

FLIGHTS

If you are traveling from North America, consider flying a British or other European carrier, especially if you are traveling to Barcelona or Bilbao. Though you may have to change planes in London, Paris, Amsterdam, Zurich, or even Rome, savings can be significant.

The least expensive airfares to Barcelona are priced for round-trip travel and must usually be purchased in advance. Airlines generally allow you to change your return date for a fee; most low-fare tickets, however, are nonrefundable.

On certain days of the week, Iberia offers minifares (*minitarifas*), which can save you 40% on domestic flights. Tickets must be purchased at least two days in advance, and you must stay over at your destination on a Saturday night.

American, United/Continental, Delta, and Iberia fly to Madrid and Barcelona; Norwegian Air Shuttle flies to Barcelona from San Francisco, Los Angeles, New York, Miami, and Orlando; US Airways and Air Europa fly to Madrid. Within Spain, Iberia is the main domestic airline; two independent airlines, Air Europa and Vueling, fly a number of domestic routes at somewhat lower prices.

▌ BOAT TRAVEL

There are regular ferry services between the United Kingdom and northwestern Spain. Brittany Ferries sails from Portsmouth to Bilbao and Santander. The trip is more than 24 hours, so not practical unless you love the ocean and have some extra time on your hands. Spain's major ferry line, Trasmediterránea, links mainland Spain (including Barcelona) with the Balearics and the Canary Islands. This ferry's fast catamaran service takes half the time of the standard ferry, but catamarans are often canceled because they can navigate only in very calm waters. Trasmediterránea and Balearia operate overnight ferries from Barcelona, Valencia, and Dénia to the islands of Majorca, Menorca, and Ibiza. Formentera can be reached from Ibiza via Balearia and Transmapi, a local ferry company. At 7 hours, 30 minutes from Barcelona via ferry crossing, Mallorca is the closest island. Long-stretch ferries are equipped with a choice of seating options including sleepers, a restaurant, several bars, and small shopping area.

You can pick up schedules and buy tickets at the ferry ticket office in the port.

From the U.K. Brittany Ferries. ☎ *0330/159–7000 in U.K., 902/108147 Bilbao port office, Spain* ⊕ *www.brittany-ferries.com.*

In Spain Trasmediterránea. ☎ *902/454645* ⊕ *www.trasmediterranea.es.*

CRUISE TRAVEL
Barcelona is Europe's busiest cruise port, and the fourth largest in the world. Vessels dock at the Port Vell facility, which has seven terminals catering to cruiseship traffic. All terminals are equipped with duty-free shops, telephones, bar/restaurants, information desks, and currency-exchange booths. The ships docking closest to the terminal entrance are a 10-minute walk from the southern end of Las Ramblas (the Rambla), but those docked at the farthest end require passengers to catch a shuttle bus (the Autobús Azul, a distinctive blue bus) to the port entrance. The shuttle, which runs every 20 minutes, links all terminals with the public square at the bottom of the Rambla. If you walk up Las Ramblas, after about 10 minutes you'll reach Drassanes metro station for onward public transport around the city. The shuttle runs about every 30 minutes. A single metro or bus ticket is €2.15; a 10-ticket pass (T-10) is €9.95.

If you intend to explore Barcelona, don't rent a car. Public transportation and taxis are by far the most sensible options. City buses run daily from 5:30 am to 11:30 pm; all-night buses (designated with the prefix N) depart from Plaça Catalunya on a limited number of routes roughly from 11 pm to 5 am. The FGC (Ferrocarril de la Generalitat) train and the ATM metro are comfortable commuter trains that get you to within walking distance of nearly everything in Barcelona. The Barcelona Tourist Bus is another excellent way to tour the city. Three routes (Red, Blue, and Green) cover just about every place you might want to visit, and you can hop on and off whenever you want. Buses run from 9 am to 7 pm (8 pm in summer), and a one-day ticket costs €29; you can also buy advance tickets online at ⊕ *www.barcelonabusturistic.cat* for 10% off.

If you plan to explore the Spanish coast or countryside, you would probably prefer a car, but even an economy model (diesel, manual transmission), with the cost of fuel and highway tolls, will set you back at least €50 a day. Allow for plenty of time to get back to your ship, as Barcelona traffic is always heavy.

GETTING TO THE AIRPORT
Barcelona's main airport is El Prat de Llobregat, 14 km (9 miles) south of Barcelona. If you opt not to buy airport transfers from your cruise line, the simplest way to get from the airport to the cruise port is by taxi (about €35). There are public transport options, but transfers between bus, metro, or rail stations do involve up to 10 minutes of walking, and this may be impractical with many pieces of luggage. If you only have light baggage, this will certainly be a less expensive option.

The RENFE airport train is inexpensive and efficient, but runs only every 30 minutes. From the airport, the RENFE station is a 10- to 15-minute walk (with moving walkway) from the port gates. Trains run between 5:42 am and 12:38 am, stopping at the Estació de Sants. The one-way fare is €4.10.

■ BUS TRAVEL

Barcelona's main bus station for intra-Spain routes is Estació del Nord, a few blocks east of the Arc de Triomf. Buses also depart from the Estació de Sants for long-distance and international routes, as well as from the depots of Barcelona's various private bus companies. Spain's major national long-haul company is Alsa-Enatcar. Grup Sarbus serves Catalonia and, with its subsidiary Sarfa, the Costa Brava. Bus timetables are complicated and confusing; trying to get information by phone will probably get you put on interminable hold. Better to plan your bus trip online or through a local travel agent, who can quickly book you the best way to your destination.

Within Spain, private companies provide comfortable and efficient bus services between major cities. Fares are lower than the corresponding train fares, and service is more extensive: if you want to get somewhere not served by rail, you can be sure a bus will go there. *See the planner section in Chapter 8 for companies serving Catalonia.*

Most larger bus companies have buses with comfortable seats and adequate legroom; on longer journeys (two to three hours or more) a movie is shown on board, and earphones are provided. Except for smaller, regional buses that travel short hops, buses have bathrooms on board. Smoking is prohibited. Most long-haul buses stop at least once every two to three hours for a snack and bathroom break. Although buses are subject to road and traffic conditions, highways in Catalonia and the Basque Country, particularly along major routes, are well maintained. That may not be the case in more rural areas, where you could be in for a bumpy ride.

You can get to Spain by bus from London, Paris, Rome, Frankfurt, Prague, and other major European cities. It is a long journey, but the buses are modern and inexpensive. Eurolines, the main carrier, connects many European cities with Barcelona.

Alsa-Enatcar, Spain's largest national bus company, has two luxury classes in addition to its regular coach services. The top of the line is Supra Clase, with roomy leather seats, free Wi-Fi Internet connection, and onboard meals; in this class you also have the option of *asientos individuales,* single-file seats along one side of the bus. The next class is the Eurobus, with comfy seats and plenty of legroom, but no asientos individuales or onboard meals. The Supra Clase and Eurobus cost up to 1/3 and 1/4 more, respectively, than the regular coaches.

Some smaller, regional bus lines (Sarfa, for example, which connects Barcelona to destinations on the Costa Brava) offer multi-trip bus passes, which are worthwhile if you plan on making multiple trips between two destinations. Generally, these tickets offer a savings of 20% per journey; you can buy them only in the bus station (not on the bus).

The general rule for children is that if they occupy a seat, they pay.

In Barcelona you can pick up schedule and fare information at the tourist information offices in Plaça de Catalunya, Plaça Sant Jaume, or at the Sants train station. A better and faster solution is to check online at ⊕ *www.barcelonanord.com.*

At bus-station ticket counters, major credit cards (except for American Express) are universally accepted. You must pay in cash for tickets purchased on the bus. Traveler's checks are almost never accepted.

During peak travel times (Easter, August, and Christmas), it's always a good idea to make a reservation at least three to four days in advance.

City buses run daily 5:30 am–11:30 pm. Route maps are displayed at bus stops. Note that those with a red band always stop at a central square—Catalunya, Universitat, or Urquinaona—and blue, with an N prefix on the bus number, indicates a night bus. Barcelona's 17 night buses generally run until about 5 am.

Bus Information Alsa. 📞 *902/422242*
🌐 *www.alsa.es.* **Grup Sarbus.** ✉ *Estació
d'Autobusos Barcelona–Nord, Carrer d' Alí Bei
80, Eixample* 📞 *902/302025* 🌐 *www.sarfa.com*
Ⓜ *L1 Arc de Triomf.* **Julià Travel.** ✉ *Carrer
Balmes 5, Eixample* 📞 *93/317–6454* 🌐 *www.
juliatravel.com.*

Bus Terminals Estació del Nord. ✉ *Carrer
d'Ali Bei 80, Eixample* 📞 *902/260606* 🌐 *www.
barcelonanord.com.* **Estació de Sants.**
✉ *Pl. dels Països Catalans s/n, Eixample*
📞 *902/432343, 902/240505 bookings and
sales* Ⓜ *L3/L5 SantsEstació.*

International Bus Companies Alsa.
✉ *Estación de Barcelona Nord, Carrer d'Alí Bei
80* 📞 *902/422242* 🌐 *www.alsa.es.* **Eurolines.**
✉ *Estación de Autobuses Barcelona Sants,
Carrer de Viriat s/n, Eixample* 📞 *93/367–4400,
902/405040 information and reservations*
🌐 *www.eurolines.es* ✉ *Estación de Autobuses
Barcelona Nord, Carrer d'Alí Bei 80, Eixample*
📞 *932/650788* 🌐 *www.eurolines.es.* **Linebus.**
✉ *Estació del Nord, Carrer d' Alí Bei 80,
Eixample* 📞 *932/650700* 🌐 *www.linebus.es.*

▮ CABLE CAR AND FUNICULAR TRAVEL

The Montjuïc Funicular is a cog railway
that runs from the junction of Avinguda
Paral.lel and Nou de la Rambla (Ⓜ *Paral.
lel*) to Montjuïc Castle, with stops en
route at Parc de Monjuic and Miramar.
It operates weekdays 7:30 am–8 pm and
weekends 9 am–9 pm; the fare is €2.15,
or one ride on a T10 card.

A Transbordador Aeri del Port (Harbor
Cable Car) runs between Miramar and
Montjuïc across the harbor to Torre de
Jaume I, on Barcelona's *moll* (quay), and
on to Torre de Sant Sebastià, at the end of
Passeig Joan de Borbó in Barceloneta. You
can board at either stage. One-way fare
is €11; round-trip fare is €16.50. The car
runs every eight minutes, November–Feb-
ruary 11 am–5:30 pm, March–May and
September and October 11 am–7 pm, and
June–August 11 am–8 pm.

To reach the summit of Tibidabo, take
the metro to Avinguda de Tibidabo, then
the Tramvía Blau (€5.50 one-way) to Peu
del Funicular, and finally the Tibidabo
Funicular (€7.70 round-trip; €4.10 with
purchase of admission to the Tibidabo
Amusement Park) from there to the top.
The Tramvia runs daily March–December, and weekends only in February.
Generally it runs every 15–30 minutes,
beginning at 10 am and finishing at
dusk (around 6 pm in winter and 8 pm
in summer).

▮ CAR TRAVEL

Major routes throughout Spain bear
heavy traffic, especially in peak holiday
periods, so be extremely cautious; Spain
has one of the highest traffic accident
rates in Europe, and the roads are shared
by a mixture of local drivers, immigrants
en route elsewhere from eastern Europe
and north Africa, and non-Spanish
travelers on vacation, some of whom
are more accustomed to driving on the
left-hand side of the road. Watch out for
heavy truck traffic on national routes.
Expect the near-impossibility of on-
street parking in the major cities. Parking garages are common and affordable,
and provide added safety to your vehicle
and possessions.

The country's main cities are well
connected by a network of four-lane
autovías (freeways). The letter N stands
for a national route (*carretera nacional*),
either four- or two-lane. An *autopista*
(AP) is a toll road. At the tollbooth
plazas (the term in Castilian is *peaje*;
in Catalan, *peatge*), there are three
systems to choose from—*automàtic,*
with machines for credit cards or coins;
manual, with an attendant; or *telepago,*
an automatic chip-driven system mostly
used by Spanish drivers.

GETTING AROUND AND OUT OF BARCELONA

Arriving in Barcelona by car from the north along the AP7 autopista or from the west along the AP2, follow signs for the Ronda Litoral (the coastal ring road—but beware: it's most prominently marked "Aeroport," which can be misleading) to lower and central Barcelona along the waterfront, or the Ronda de Dalt (the upper-ring road) along the edge of upper Barcelona to Horta, the Bonanova, Sarrià, and Pedralbes. For the center of town, take the Ronda Litoral and look for Exit 21 ("Paral.lel–Les Ramblas") or 22 ("Barceloneta–Via Laietana–Hospital de Mar"). If you are arriving from the Pyrenees on the C1411/E9 through the Tunel del Cadí, the Tunels de Vallvidrera will put you on the upper end of Via Augusta with off-ramps to Sarrià, Pedralbes, and La Bonanova. The Eixample and Ciutat Vella are 10–15 minutes farther if traffic is fluid. Watch out for the new variable speed limits on the approaches to Barcelona. While 80 kph (48 mph) is the maximum speed on the rondas, flashing signs over the motorway sometimes cut the speed limit down to 40 kph (24 mph) during peak hours.

Barcelona's main crosstown traffic arteries are Diagonal (running diagonally through the city) and the midtown avenues, Carrer d'Aragó, and Gran Via de les Corts Catalanes, both cutting northeast–southwest through the heart of the city. Passeig de Gràcia, which becomes Gran de Gràcia above Diagonal, runs all the way from Plaça de Catalunya up to Plaça Lesseps, but the main up-and-down streets, for motorists, are Balmes, Muntaner, Aribau, and Comtes d'Urgell. The general urban speed limit is 50 kph (30 mph).

Getting around Barcelona by car is generally more trouble than it's worth. It's better to walk or travel via subway, taxi, or bus.

Leaving Barcelona is not difficult. Follow signs for the *rondas,* do some advance mapping, and you're off.

Follow signs for Girona and França for the Costa Brava, Girona, Figueres, and France. Follow Via Augusta and signs for Tunels de Vallvidrera or E9 and Manresa for the Tunel del Cadí and the Pyrenean Cerdanya valley. Follow Diagonal west and then the freeway AP7 signs for Lleida, Zaragoza, Tarragona, and Valencia to leave the city headed west. Look for airport, Castelldefells, and Sitges signs to head southwest down the coast for these beach points on the Costa Daurada. This C32 freeway to Sitges joins the AP7 to Tarragona and Valencia.

For travel outside Barcelona, the freeways to Girona, Figueres, Sitges, Tarragona, and Lleida are surprisingly fast. The distance to Girona, 97 km (58 miles), is a 45-minute shot. The French border is an hour away. Perpignan, at 188 km (113 miles) away, is an hour and 20 minutes.

GASOLINE

There are some 60 gas stations in Barcelona and environs, often open 24 hours, especially around Barcelona's rondas. Virtually all stations are self-service, though prices are the same as those at full-service stations. At the tank, punch in the amount of gas you want (in euros, not in liters), unhook the nozzle, pump the gas, and then pay. At night, however, you must pay before you fill up. Some stations allow for credit cards at the pump. Most pumps offer unleaded gas and diesel fuel, so be careful to pick the right one for your car. Unleaded gas (*gasolina sin plomo*) is available in two grades, 95 and 98 octanes. Prices per liter (⊕ *www.elpreciodelagasolina.com*) vary little between stations: €1.23 for sin plomo (95 octane) and €1.34 for unleaded (98 octane). Diesel fuel, known as *gas-oleo*, is about €1.12 a liter and, what's more, gets you farther per liter, so renting a car with a diesel engine will save you major fuel money.

PARKING

Barcelona's underground parking lots (posted "Parking" and symbolized by a white P on a blue background) are generally safe and convenient. Garage prices vary; expect close to €4 an hour and €25–€40 per 24-hour day. Airport parking runs from €5.48 for up to two hours to €18.75 per day for up to four days and €15 per day thereafter. The long-term parking located between Terminal 1 (T1) and Terminal 2 (T2) costs €87 up to 20 days and €3 per day after that.

Barcelona's street-parking system runs 9 am–2 pm and 4 pm–8 pm (with on-call attendants) weekdays and all day Saturday. Park in the specially marked blue spaces (about €2.60 per hour in the most expensive zones), and look for a nearby ticket vending machine. Tickets are valid for one, two, or three hours, but renewable in half-hour increments. The ticket must be displayed on the front dashboard. On the streets, do not park where the pavement edge is yellow or where there is a private entry (*gual* or *vado*). Parking signs marked "1–15" or "15–30" signify you can park on those dates of the month on the side of the street where indicated. Whenever you feel you have found an open space, be alert for triangular yellow stickers on the pavement that indicate a tow-away zone—all the spot might not be so lucky after all. If your car is towed in Barcelona, you will find one of these yellow triangles, with the phone number and address of the municipal car deposit where your vehicle now resides, on the pavement where you left your car. A taxi will know where to take you to get it back.

The fine and towing charges, with taxes and storage fees, can set you back as much as €175, depending on the make and model of the car, and where and when you've parked illegally. Note that you will need to bring your passport and produce the vehicle registration documents at the pound. To avoid risking this annoying and expensive catastrophe, park in a parking lot or garage. If your car is towed in Bilbao, contact the *ayuntamiento*, or town hall.

Towing Contact Information Ayuntamiento de Barcelona (Town Hall). ✉ *Carrer d'Avinyó 15* ☎ *93/402–7000* ⊕ *ajuntament.barcelona. cat/es.* **Barcelona.** ☎ *901/513151 information on parking fines, impoundings.*

RENTAL CARS

Currently, one of the best ways to rent a car, whether you arrange it from home or during your travels, is through the company's website—the rates are the best and the arrangements the easiest.

Generally you'll get a better deal if you book a car before you leave home. Avis, Hertz, Budget, and the European agency Europcar all have counters at the airports in Barcelona, Bilbao, and other cities. National companies work through the Spanish agency Atesa. Smaller, local companies offer lower rates. Cars with automatic transmission are less common, so specify your need for one in advance. A SatNav system programmable in English is likely to be well worth the cost of the option. Rates for pickup at Barcelona airport can start as low as €13 a day and €30 a week for an economy car with air-conditioning, manual transmission and unlimited mileage, booked online, but commonly run at least twice that amount. This does not include the tax on car rentals, which is 21%.

Your own driver's license is valid in Spain, but you may want to get an International Driver's Permit (IDP) for extra assurance. Permits are available from the American or Canadian Automobile Association, or, in the United Kingdom, from the Automobile Association or Royal Automobile Club. Check the AAA website for more info as well as for IDPs ($15) themselves.

If you are stopped you will be asked to present your license and passport (or a photocopy). In Spain anyone over 18 with a valid license can drive; however, some rental companies will not rent a car to drivers under 21.

The cost for a child's car seat is €3.50 a day; the cost per day for an additional driver is approximately €4.50 per day.

Automobile Associations American Automobile Association (AAA). ☎ *800/222–3395, 407/444–8000 association headquarters* ⊕ *www.aaa.com.*

Local Agencies in Barcelona Enterprise Rent-A-Car. ✉ *Aeropuerto El Prat, Prat De Llobregat, El Prat del Llobregat* ☎ *93/521–9095* ⊕ *www.enterprise.es* ✉ *Barcelona City Centre, Carrer Muntaner 45, Eixample* ☎ *93/323–0701* ⊕ *www.enterprise.es* Ⓜ *L1/ L2 Universitat.* **Vanguard Rent.** ✉ *Carrer Londres 31, Eixample* ☎ *93/439–3880* ⊕ *www.vanguardrent.com/en.*

Major Agencies Avis. ✉ *Estació de Sants, Carrer Rector Triad 104, Eixample* ☎ *902/110293* ⊕ *www.avis.com* ✉ *Carrer Còrsega 293–295, Eixample* ☎ *902/110275* ⊕ *www.avis.es* Ⓜ *Provença (FGC).* **Europcar.** ✉ *Aeropuerto El Prat, Eixample* ☎ *93/439–8403* ⊕ *www.europcar.es* ✉ *Estació de Sants, Pl. Paises Catalanes s/n, Eixample* ☎ *902/105055* ⊕ *www.europcar.es* Ⓜ *L3/ L5 Sants Estació.* **Hertz.** ✉ *Estació de Sants, Carrer Viriat 45, Eixample* ☎ *902/998707* ⊕ *www.hertz.com* Ⓜ *L3/L5 Estació Sants* ✉ *Centro Comercial L'Illa, Av. Diagonal 622, Eixample* ☎ *93/410–1034* ⊕ *www.hertz.com.*

ROAD CONDITIONS

You can reach all major cities and destinations by high-speed *autopistas*—two- and three-lane freeways where 110 kph (63 mph) is the legal speed limit, and vehicles that cannot reach at least 60 kph are banned. Tolls are steep, sometimes as high as €20 for two- to three-hour sections, but these freeways are spectacular touring tracks with terrific views of the countryside (billboards are prohibited, *and* they make the Iberian Peninsula into a relatively small piece of geography. Once you are off these major roads, all bets are off. Trucks can hold up long lines of traffic, and averaging 60 kph (36 mph) can be challenging. Still, the scenery remains superb.

Signage on autopistas can be erratic and the lettering too small to decipher early enough to make decisions. Add to this the different languages (Spanish, Catalan, Euskera) appearing on road signs within a few hours of each other, and a certain amount of confusion is guaranteed. Only slower speeds can alleviate this problem by giving motorists more time to react.

Traffic jams (*atascos*) can be a problem in and around Barcelona, where the travel on the rondas slows to a standstill at peak hours. If possible, avoid the rush hours, which can last from 7 am until 9:30 am, and from 7 pm to 9 pm.

Long weekends, called *puentes* (literally, bridges), particularly those that start on a Friday, routinely provoke delays leaving Barcelona. Avoiding the rondas in favor of the Tunels de Vallvidrera (straight out Via Augusta) can save time if you're headed north. Most of Barcelona vacation during August, so if you're hitting the road at the beginning or end of this month you'll likely encounter lots of traffic, particularly on the roads heading up or down the coast.

ROADSIDE EMERGENCIES

The rental agencies Hertz and Avis have 24-hour breakdown service. If you belong to an auto club (AAA or CAA), you can get emergency assistance from their Catalan counterpart, the Reial Automovil Club de Catalunya (RACC), or the Spanish branch Real Automovil Club de España (RACE). There are emergency telephones on all autopistas, every 2 km (1 mile), with service stations generally found every 40 km (25 miles).

Traveling with a European cell phone is essential for safety and convenience, keeping in mind that coverage in the mountains is erratic.

If your rental car breaks down, be especially wary of anyone who stops to help you on the road: highway robbery has been known to be all too literal here on occasion, as bands of thieves puncture tires and steal belongings (nearly always on toll roads and freeways, sometimes at knife- or gunpoint) while pretending to offer assistance.

Emergency Services Real Automovil Club de Catalunya (*RACC*). ✉ *Diagonal 687, Diagonal Mar* ☎ *93/495–5058, 902/156156 emergency aid* ⊕ *www.racc. es* Ⓜ *L3 Zona Universitária*. **Real Automovil Club de España** (*RACE Asistencia*). ✉ *Carrer Muntaner 107, Eixample* ☎ *93/451–1551, 900/112222 for emergency aid* ⊕ *www.race. es* Ⓜ *Provença (FGC)*.

RULES OF THE ROAD

In Spain, motorists drive on the right. Horns are technically banned in cities, but are still often heard on the roads.

Children under 12 may not ride in the front seat, and seat belts are compulsory. Speed limits are 50 kph (31 mph) in cities; 100 kph (62 mph) on N roads; 120 kph (72 mph) on the autopistas and autovías (highways); and, unless otherwise signposted, 70 kph (44 mph) on secondary roads. Barcelona's rondas now limit motorists to 80 kph (48 mph) and sometimes, at peak hours, cut the speed limit down to 40 kph (24 mph). If you're caught driving over the limit by 10 kph (6 mph), you can expect a substantial fine.

Right turns on red are not permitted. In the cities people are more often stopped for petty rule-breaking such as crossing a solid line or doing a U-turn than for speeding. However, Spanish highway police are especially vigilant regarding speeding and illegal passing, generally interpreted as crossing the solid line; fines start at €100 and can go as high as €600; in the case of foreign drivers, police are empowered to demand payment on the spot.

It is illegal to use a handheld phone, headphones, or earphones while driving. If you're traveling with an infant or a young child, you can be fined for not having a carrier seat of approved design.

On freeway ramps, expect to come to a full stop at the red stop (not yield) triangle at the end of the on-ramp and wait for a break in the traffic. Expect no merging to the left lane, especially from trucks, which, by law, must remain in the right lane.

Drunk-driving tests are becoming more prevalent. It is illegal to drive with an alcohol level that exceeds 0.5% BAC (blood-alcohol count) or 0.25 on a breath test; this is about three medium-size glasses of wine or three beers for a man of average height and weight, but it's best to be extra cautious. Penalties vary from one region of Spain to another; in the worst-case scenario, you can be fined as much as €1,000 or wind up in jail for three to eight months.

▌ METRO TRAVEL

In Barcelona the underground metro, or subway, is the fastest, cheapest, and easiest way to get around. Metro lines run Monday–Thursday and Sunday 5 am–midnight, Friday to 2 am, Saturday and holiday evenings all night. The FGC trains run 5 am to just after midnight on weekdays and to 1:52 am on weekends and the eves of holidays. Sunday trains run on weekday schedules.

Transfers from a metro line to the FGC (or vice versa) are free within an hour and 15 minutes. Note that in many stations, you need to validate your ticket at both ends of your journey. Maps showing bus and metro routes are available free from the Tourist Information office in Plaça de Catalunya.

TICKET/PASS	PRICE
Single Fare	€2.15
10-Ride Pass	€9.95

Subway Info Transports Metropolitans de Barcelona (*TMB*). ☎ *93/214–8000, 93/298–7000* ⊕ *www.tmb.cat/en/home*.

▌ TAXI TRAVEL

In Barcelona taxis are black and yellow and show a green rooftop sign on the front right corner when available for hire. The meter currently starts at €2.10 and rises in increments of €1.07 every kilometer. These rates apply 6 am–10 pm weekdays. At hours outside of these, the rates rise 20%. There are official supplements of €1 per bag for luggage.

Trips to or from a train station entail a supplemental charge of €2.10; a cab to or from the airport, or the Barcelona Cruise Terminal, runs add a supplemental charge of €4.20, as do trips to or from a football match. The minimum price for taxi service to or from the Barcelona airport is €20 for terminals T1, T2, and T3, and €39 from T4. There are cabstands (*parades*, in Catalan) all over town, and you can also hail cabs on the street, though if you are too close to an official stand they may not stop. You can call for a cab by phone 24 hours a day. Drivers do not expect a tip, but rounding up the fare is standard.

Taxi Companies **Barna Taxi.** ☎ 93/322222, 93/300–2314 ⊕ www.barnataxi.com. **Cooperativa Radio Taxi.** ☎ 93/225–1734, 93/225–0000 to call a cab ⊕ www.radiotax-ibcn.cat/en. **Taxi Class Rent.** ☎ 93/307–0707 ⊕ www.taxiclassrent.com/en.

I TRAIN TRAVEL

International overnight trains to Barcelona arrive from many European cities, including Paris, Grenoble, Geneva, Zurich, and Milan; the four-a-day high-speed trains to and from Paris take about 5½ hours, and advance-purchase tickets online start at €59 (€118 round-trip), making the downtown-to-downtown journey by train competitive with a flight. Almost all long-distance trains arrive at and depart from Estació de Sants, though many make a stop at Passeig de Gràcia that comes in handy for hotels in the Eixample or in the Ciutat Vella. Estació de França, near the port, handles only a few regional trains within Catalonia. Train service connects Barcelona with most other major cities in Spain; in addition a high-speed Euromed route connects Barcelona to Tarragona and Valencia.

Spain's intercity services (along with some of Barcelona's local train routes) are the province of the government-run railroad system—RENFE (Red Nacional de Ferrocarriles Españoles). The high-speed AVE train now connects Barcelona and Madrid (via Lleida and Zaragoza) in less than three hours. (Spain has more high-speed tracks in service than any other country in Europe.) The fast TALGO and ALTARIA trains are efficient, though local trains remain slow and tedious. The Catalan government's FGC (Ferrocarril de la Generalitat de Catalunya) also provide train service, notably to Barcelona's commuter suburbs of Sant Cugat, Terrassa, and Sabadell.

Smoking is forbidden on all RENFE trains.

Information on the local/commuter lines (*rodalies* in Catalan, *cercanias* in Castilian) can be found at ⊕ www.renfe.es/cercanias. Rodalies go, for example, to Sitges from Barcelona, whereas you would take a regular RENFE train to, say, Tarragona. It's important to know whether you are traveling on RENFE or on *rodalies* (the latter distinguished by a stylized C), so you don't end up in the wrong line.

Both Catalonia and the Basque Country offer scenic railroad excursions. The day train from Barcelona to Madrid runs through bougainvillea-choked towns before leaping out across Spain's central *meseta* (plateau) via Zaragoza, most trains arriving at Atocha Station in Madrid in about 2½ hours. The train from Barcelona's Plaça de Catalunya north to Sant Pol de Mar and Blanes runs along the edge of the beach.

First-class train service in Spain, with the exception of the *coche-cama* (Pullman) overnight service, barely differs from second class or *turista*. The TALGO or the AVE trains, however, are much faster than second-class carriers like the slow-poke Estrella overnight from Barcelona to Madrid, both with limited legroom and general comforts. The AVE is the exception: these sleek comfortable bullet trains travel between Barcelona and Madrid or between Madrid and Sevilla. Some 30 AVE trains a day connect Barcelona and Madrid, with departures from 5:50 am to 9:15 pm. Ticket prices in tourist class start at €66.75 (purchased online) and go up during peak hours. Trips take from 2 hours 30 minutes to 3 hours 10 minutes.

After buses, trains are the most economical way to travel. Within the RENFE pricing system, there are 20% discounts on long-distance tickets if you buy a round-trip ticket, and there are 20% discounts for students and senior citizens (though they usually have to carry cards issued by the local government, the Generalitat, so they are not intended for tourists).

If you're planning extensive train travel, look into rail passes. If Spain is your only destination, consider a Spain Flexipass. Prices begin at $234 for four journeys in second-class coach within a one-month period and $324 for first class. Other passes cover more days and longer periods. The 10-journey pass costs $492 in second class, $672 in first class. (Beware when you order online; brokers' quotations can vary considerably.)

Spain is one of 17 European countries in which you can use Eurail Global Passes, which buy you unlimited first- or second-class rail travel in all participating countries for the duration of the pass. If you plan to rack up the miles and go between countries, get a standard pass; these are available for 5 days ($496) and 7 days ($632) to be used within one month; 10 days ($777) and 15 days ($1020) to be used within two months; 15 days ($595), 22 days ($852), one month ($1046), two months ($1,474), and three months ($1,817) to be used continuously. If your needs are more limited, look into a Regional Pass, which costs less than a Eurail Pass and buys you a limited number of travel days in a limited number of countries (France, Italy, and Spain, for example), during a specified time period.

In addition to standard Eurail Passes, Rail Europe sells the Eurail Youthpass (for those under age 26), the Eurail Saverpass (which gives a discount for two or more people traveling together), a Eurail Flexipass (which allows a certain number of travel days within a set period), the Euraildrive Pass (four days of train travel and two days of Avis or Hertz car rental), and the Europass Drive (which combines three days travel by train and two by rental car). Whichever pass you choose, remember that you must buy your pass before you leave for Europe.

■ TIP➔ **Even if you're using the rail pass, you still will need to reserve seats in advance.** Seat reservations are required on some European trains, particularly high-speed trains, and are wise on any train that might be crowded. You'll also need a reservation if you want sleeping accommodations. All reservations require an extra fee.

For schedules and fares, call RENFE. The easiest way for non–Spanish speakers to get schedule information is to go the RENFE website (⊕ *www.renfe.es*).

Train services to Barcelona from the United Kingdom are not as frequent, fast, or affordable as flights, and you have to change trains (and stations) in Paris. From Paris it's worth paying extra for a TALGO express to avoid having to change trains again at the Spanish border. Journey time to Paris (from London via Eurostar through the Channel Tunnel) is around 3 hours; from Paris to Barcelona takes 5½ hours more. Allow at least 2 hours in Paris for changing trains.

Although overnight trains have comfortable sleeper cars for two or four in coche-cama, first-class fares that include a sleeping compartment are comparable to airfares.

For shorter, regional train trips, you can often buy your tickets directly from machines in the main train stations. For a one-way ticket, ask for, in Catalan, *anada* (in Spanish it's *ida*); or for a round-trip ticket, *anada i tornada*, or *ida y vuelta* in Spanish.

Most travel agencies can sell you train tickets (though not for same-day travel), which saves standing in line at the station *taquilla* (ticket office).

Lines at Sants can be long. Look for the counters marked *salida inmediata* (next departure), where you can buy same-day tickets more quickly.

Visa and MasterCard are universally accepted at station ticket counters.

During peak travel times (Easter, August, and Christmas), it's important to make a reservation weeks or even months in advance; on routes between major cities (Barcelona to Bilbao or Madrid, for example), it's a good idea to reserve well in advance, especially for overnight trips.

You can make reservations over the phone by calling RENFE, online, or by waiting at the station ticket counter, preferably in Barcelona's Passeig de Gràcia, where lines are often shorter.

The easiest way to make reservations is to use the TIKNET service on the RENFE website. When you make the reservation, you will be given a car and seat assignment and a *localizador* (translated as "localizer" on the English version of the site). Print out the reservations page or write down car number, seat number, and localizer. When traveling, go to your assigned seat on the train. When the conductor comes around, give him the localizer, and he will issue the ticket on the spot. You will need your passport and, in most cases, the credit card you used for the reservation. The AVE trains check you in at the gate to the platform, where you provide the localizer. You can review your pending reservations online at any time.

Caveats: the first time you use TIKNET, you must pick up the tickets at a RENFE station; you can go to a RENFE booth at the airport as you get off your plane. A 15% cancellation fee is charged if you cancel more than two hours after making the reservation. You cannot buy tickets online for certain regional lines or for commuter lines (*cercanias*). Station agents cannot alter TIKNET reservations: you must do this yourself online. If the train is already full the system does not notify you immediately; reserve in advance to guarantee a seat.

To purchase advance tickets at the station, take a number and wait until it is called. Ticket clerks at stations rarely speak English, so for help or advice in planning a more complex train journey, stop by a travel agency that displays the blue-and-yellow RENFE sign. A small commission (American Express Viajes charges €3.75) should be expected.

General Information Estació de França. ⊠ *Av. Marquès de l'Argentera 1, Born-Ribera* ☎ *902/432343 station info, 902/320320 RENFE general info* ⊕ *www.renfe.es* Ⓜ *L4 Barceloneta.* **Estació de Passeig de Gràcia.** ⊠ *Passeig de Gràcia/Carrer Aragó, Eixample* ☎ *902/432343 station info, 902/320320 RENFE general info* ⊕ *www.adif.es* Ⓜ *L2/L3/L4 Passeig de Gràcia.* **Estació de Sants.** ⊠ *Pl. dels Països Catalans s/n, Les Corts* ☎ *902/157507 customer service (English), 902/320320 RENFE general info* ⊕ *www.renfe.com* Ⓜ *L3/L5 Sants Estació.* **Ferrocarrils de la Generalitat de Catalunya (FGC).** ⊠ *Carrer Vergos 44, Sarrià* ☎ *93/366–3000* ⊕ *www.fgc.cat/eng/index.asp* Ⓜ *Sarrià (FGC).* **RENFE.** ☎ *902/240202, 902/320320* ⊕ *www.renfe.es.*

Information and Passes Eurail. ⊕ *www.eurail.com.* **Rail Europe.** ☎ *800/622–8600* ⊕ *www.raileurope.com* ☎ *800/361–7245 in Canada* ⊕ *www.raileurope.ca.*

From the U.K. Eurostar. ☎ *01233/617575 in U.K.* ⊕ *www.eurostar.co.uk.* **Voyages-sncf.** ⊠ *193 Piccadilly, London* ☎ *0844/848–5484 in U.K.* ⊕ *uk.voyages-sncf.com/en.*

Channel Tunnel Car Transport Eurotunnel. ☎ *8443/353535 in U.K., 902/307315 in Spain, 810/630304 in France* ⊕ *www.eurotunnel.com.*

Channel Tunnel Passenger Service Eurostar. ☎ *03432/186186 in U.K., 1233/617575 outside U.K.* ⊕ *www.eurostar.co.uk.* **Rail Europe.** ☎ *800/622–8600 in U.S., 08448/484064 in U.K.* ⊕ *www.raileurope.com.*

ESSENTIALS

■ ADDRESSES

Abbreviations used in the book for street names are Av. for *avinguda* in Catalan; *avenida* in Spanish, and Ctra. for *carreter* (or *carretera* in Spanish). The letters *s/n* following an address mean *sin número* (without a street number). *Carrer* (*calle* in Spanish) is often dropped entirely or not abbreviated at all. *Camí* (*camino* in Spanish) is abbreviated to *C. Passeig* (*paseo* in Spanish) is sometimes abbreviated as P., but is usually written out in full. Plaça/ plaza is usually not abbreviated (in this book it is abbreviated as Pl.).

Addresses in Barcelona may include the street name, building number, floor level, and apartment number. For example, Carrer Balmes 155, 3°, 1ª indicates that the apartment is on the *tercero* (third) floor, *primera* (first) door. In older buildings, the first floor is often called the *entresuelo*; one floor above it is *principal* (sometimes called the *planta baja*), and above this, the first floor (*primera*). The top floor of a building is the *ático*; occasionally there is a floor above that, called the *sobreàtico*. In more modern buildings there is often no *entresuelo* or *principal*.

■ COMMUNICATIONS

INTERNET

Internet access via Wi-Fi is available in virtually all Barcelona hotels. In addition, many cafés and bars are Internet hot spots and have signs indicating it in their windows. An important piece to pack is the adapter that translates flat-edged plugs or triple plugs to round dual ones. Wi-Fi is common throughout Barcelona.

Cybercafé Resources Friends on Line.
✉ *Carrer Còrsega 197, Eixample* ☎ *93/363-0754* Ⓜ *L5 Hospital Clinic.*

PHONES

Calling out to anywhere from your hotel almost always incurs a hefty surcharge. Prepaid cards can help you keep costs to a minimum, but only if you purchase them locally. Your best bet is to use messaging or call services over Wi-Fi on your cell phone.

The country code for Spain is 34. Dialing 00 gets you an international line; country codes are 1 for the United States and Canada, 61 for Australia, 64 for New Zealand, and 44 for the United Kingdom.

CALLING WITHIN SPAIN

Spain's telephone system is efficient, and direct dialing is the norm everywhere. Only cell phones conforming to the European GSM standard will work in Spain.

All Spanish area codes begin with a 9; for instance, Barcelona is 93 and Bilbao is 94. The 900 code indicates a toll-free number. Numbers that begin with 901 and 902 charge the caller for the call. Numbers starting with a 6 indicate a cellular phone; note that calls from landlines to cell phones (and vice versa) are significantly more expensive.

For general information in Spain, dial 1–18–18. The operator for international information and assistance is at 1–18–25 (some operators speak English). Barcelona information of all kinds, including telephone information, is available at 010, where many operators speak English.

Calls within Spain require dialing 8, 9, or 10 digits (beginning with a 2- or 3-digit regional code), even within the same area code.

Making a long-distance call within Spain simply requires dialing the 8, 9, or 10-digit number including the provincial area code and number.

Between phone booths (ask for a *cabina telefónica*) and public phones in bars and restaurants, telephone communication in Spain functions as well as anyplace in the world. Many phones have digital screens, so you can see how much the call is costing. You need at least €0.20 in coin for a local call, €1 to call another province. Pick up the phone, wait for the dial tone, and only then insert coins before dialing. Rates are reduced on weekends and after 8 pm on weekdays.

CALLING OUTSIDE SPAIN

The best way to make calls outside the country is to use a public phone that accepts prepaid cards (available from tobacconists and most newsagents) or make your call from a *locutorio* (phone center). The best thing about the locutorio is the quiet, private booth. If the call costs more than €5, you can often pay with Visa or MasterCard.

To make an international call yourself, dial 00, then the country code, then the area code and number. Ask at a tourist office for a list of locutorios and Internet centers that include phone service.

Before you go, find out your long-distance company's access code in Spain.

Access Codes AT&T. ☎ *900/990011 toll-free access from Spain.* **MCI WorldPhone.** ☎ *800/099357 toll-free access from Spain.* **Sprint International Access.** ☎ *900/990013 toll-free access from Spain.*

CALLING CARDS

Pay phones work with a prepaid card (*tarjeta telefónica*), of which there are several varieties that you can buy at any tobacco shop (*tabac*) or newsagent. The Euro Hours Card, sold at many tobacco shops for €6, is good for 350 minutes' worth of international calls.

MOBILE PHONES

If you have a multiband phone and your service provider uses the world-standard GSM network (as do T-Mobile, AT&T, and Verizon), you can probably use your phone almost anywhere abroad—roaming fees can be steep, however, and overseas, you can get stuck with toll charges for incoming calls. It's almost always cheaper (but confirm with your carrier) to send a text message than to make a

call, because text messages have a low set fee (often less than €0.05). To avoid roaming fees completely, select airplane mode or turn off data roaming until you are in a Wi-Fi hot spot, where you can check email or use the Web at much lower costs (often free). If you were to do either while roaming, your bill would show it: an email with a five-megapixel photo, for example, would require your phone to download about 2 megabytes of data at a cost of about $20 per MB from either Verizon or AT&T.

If you just want to make local calls, consider buying a new SIM card (note that your provider may have to unlock your phone for you to use a different card) and a prepaid service plan in your destination.

Cell Phone Rentals Telecon Iberica. ☎ *93/228–9110* ⊕ *www.telecon.es.*

Contacts Cellular Abroad. ☎ *800/287–5072 in U.S.* ⊕ *www.cellularabroad.com.* **Mobal.** ☎ *888/888–9162* ⊕ *www.mobal-rental.com.* **Planet Fone.** ☎ *888/988–4777* ⊕ *www.planetfone.com.*

▌ ELECTRICITY

The electrical current in Spain is 220 volts, 50 cycles alternating current (AC); wall outlets take Continental-type plugs, with two round prongs. An adapter from flat to round prongs is a must for computers and hair dryers.

▌ EMERGENCIES

You can expect local residents to be helpful if you have an emergency. For assistance, dial the pan-European emergency phone number 112, which can connect you to an English-speaking operator. Otherwise, dial the emergency numbers below for national police, local police, fire department, or medical services. On the road, there are emergency phones at frequent regular intervals on autovías and autopistas. They are marked S.O.S.

If your documents are stolen, contact both the police and your consulate or embassy. If you lose a credit card, phone the issuer immediately.

To find out which pharmacies are open late at night or 24 hours on a given day, look on the door of any pharmacy or in any local newspaper under *"Farmacias de Guardia"* or dial 010.

In Barcelona, Tourist Attention, a service provided by the local police, can help if you're the victim of a crime or need medical assistance. English interpreters are on hand.

▌ MAIL

The postal system in Spain is called *Correos*; though reliable, delivery times can vary widely. An airmail letter to the United States may take anywhere from four days to two weeks to reach its destination. Mail to the United Kingdom may range from overnight delivery to four days. Delivery to other places worldwide is equally unpredictable. Sending letters by special delivery (*urgente*) will ensure speedier delivery.

Post offices are usually open 8:30–8:30 on weekdays, and 9:30–1 on Saturday. Barcelona's main post office, on Plaça Antonio López at the port end of Via Laietana, is open 8:30 am–9:30 pm on weekdays, and 8:30–2 on Saturdays.

Airmail letters to Australia, New Zealand, the United States, and Canada cost €1 up to 20 grams. Letters to the United Kingdom and other EU countries cost €0.90 up to 20 grams. Postcard rates are identical. An urgente sticker costs €2.96. Letters within Spain are €0.42. You can buy stamps at post offices and at licensed tobacco shops.

To have mail held at the Barcelona post office, have it addressed to *Lista de Correos* (the equivalent of Poste Restante), Oficina Central de Correus i Telecomunicacions, Plaça Antonio López 1, 08002. Provincial postal addresses should include the name of the province in parentheses, for example, Figueres (Girona). For Barcelona, this is not necessary.

Main Branch **Oficina Carrer Aragó.** ⊠ *Carrer Aragó 282, Eixample* ☎ *93/216–0453* Ⓜ *L2/L3/L4 Passeig de Gràcia.*

▌ MONEY

Barcelona has long been an expensive city, but prices are still lower than they are an hour north across the French border. Coffee or beer in a bar generally costs €1.50 (standing) or €1.75 (seated). Small glass of wine in a bar: around €2:50. Soft drink: €2 to €3 a bottle. Ham-and-cheese sandwich: €5 to €8. Two-kilometer (1-mile) taxi ride: about €5, but the meter keeps ticking in traffic jams. Local bus or subway ride: €2.15. Movie ticket: €9.70. Foreign newspaper: €4.20 to €6.50.

Prices throughout this guide are given for adults. Substantially reduced fees are almost always available for children, students, and senior citizens.

▌ TIP➔ Banks never have every foreign currency on hand, and it may take as long as a week to order. Plan in advance to exchange funds.

CREDIT CARDS

If you plan to use your credit card for cash advances, apply for a PIN at least two weeks before your trip.

Dynamic currency conversion (DCC) programs are becoming increasingly widespread. You can specify whether you want to be charged in dollars or the local currency, but merchants do not always ask; there may be additional surcharges as well. With American Express cards, DCC isn't an option. In Spain, many restaurants do not accept American Express.

Reporting Lost Cards American Express. ☎ *800/528–4800 in U.S., 336/391111 collect from abroad* ⊕ *www.americanexpress.com.* **Diners Club.** ☎ *800/234–6377 in U.S., 303/799–1504 collect from abroad* ⊕ *www.dinersclub.com.* **MasterCard.** ☎ *800/627–8372 in U.S., 636/722–7111 collect from abroad* ⊕ *www.mastercard.com.* **Visa.** ☎ *800/847–2911 in U.S., 301/967–1096 collect from abroad* ⊕ *www.visa.com.*

CURRENCY AND EXCHANGE

On January 1, 2002, the European monetary unit, the euro (€), went into circulation in Spain and the other countries that have adopted it (Austria, Belgium, Cyprus, Estonia, Finland, France, Germany, Greece, Ireland, Italy, Latvia, Lithuania, Luxembourg, Malta, the Netherlands, Portugal, Slovakia, and Slovenia). Euro notes come in denominations of 5, 10, 20, 50, 100, 200, and 500 euros; coins are in denominations of 1 cent (100 cents—in Spain, *centimos*—to the euro), 2 cents, 5 cents, 10 cents, 20 cents, 50 cents, 1 euro, and 2 euros. (€500 notes don't really circulate. Shops and restaurants won't accept them, and they tend to carry a whiff of the underground economy; many shops will refuse to handle €200 notes as well.) All coins have one side with the value of the euro on it; the other side has each country's own national symbol. Banknotes are the same for all European Union countries. At this writing exchange rates were U.S. $1.11, U.K. £0.85, Australian $1.49, Canadian $1.51, New Zealand $1.60, and 14.97 South African rands to the euro.

■TIP→ Even if a currency-exchange booth has a sign promising no commission, there's going to be a fee. You're better off getting foreign currency at an ATM.

Currency Conversion XE.com.
⊕ *www.xe.com.*

■ PASSPORTS

Visitors from the United States, Australia, Canada, New Zealand, and the United Kingdom need a valid passport to enter Spain. No visa is required for U.S. passport holders for a stay of up to three months; for stays exceeding three months, contact the Consulate of Spain nearest you. Australians require a visa for stays longer than one month; you should obtain it from the Spanish Embassy before you leave.

■ TAXES

Value-Added Tax (similar to sales tax) is called IVA (for *Impuesto sobre el valor añadido*) in Spain. It is levied on services, such as hotels and restaurants, and on consumer products. When in doubt about whether tax is included, ask, "*Está incluido el IVA* ("ee-vah")?"

The IVA rate for hotels and restaurants is 10%. Menus will generally say at the bottom whether tax is included (*IVA incluido*) or not (*más 7% IVA*). While food and basic necessities are taxed at the lowest rate, most consumer goods are taxed at 21%. In shops displaying the Tax-Free Shopping sticker, non–EU citizens can request a Tax-Free Cheque on purchases of at least €90.16. ■TIP→ The great majority of shops you're likely to visit have signed on to the Tax Free Shopping Service, even if they don't display the sticker. Ask before you buy, and note that the service only applies to goods you intend to take home with you. The paperwork must be stamped at the airport Civil Guard office *before* you check your luggage in, on the third floor of the Terminal 1 departure hall. After this is done, present it to one of the Caixa or Banco de España offices in the airport. The bank issues a certified check or credits its amount to your credit card.

If you're leaving Spain by ship, you need to get a VAT Reclaim envelop (in Spanish *sobre*) at the shop where you bought your goods. Have the Tax-Free Cheques stamped at the port customs office, put them in the envelope, and when you return home mail the envelope to the indicated claim office in Madrid, along with the form where you specify how you want to receive your refund. A direct wire transfer to your bank is best. The whole process is complicated and time-consuming, but if you've made any hefty purchases, the 21% you get back is well worth it.

Global Blue is a Europe-wide service with 225,000 affiliated stores and more than 700 refund counters at major airports and border crossings. Its refund form, called a Tax-Free Cheque, is the most common across the European continent. The service issues refunds in the form of cash, check, or credit-card adjustment. The company's offices are in the departure lobby of Terminal 1 (third floor) and Terminal 2 (ground floor) at Barcelona's El Prat airport. Note that Global Blue takes a handling fee for processing your refund.

V.A.T. Refunds Global Blue. ⊠ *Aeroport de Barcelona El Prat, El Prat del Llobregat* ☎ *93/297-2430 Terminal I, 3F, 93/298-3265 Terminal 2, 0F* ⊕ *www.globalblue.com.*

▌TIPPING

While tipping isn't expected in Spain, it is always welcome, and if you feel so inclined you can be sure that your contribution will be appreciated. On the other hand, if you experience bad or surly service, don't feel obligated to leave a tip.

Restaurant checks always include service. The bill may not tell you that the service is included, but it is. An extra tip of 5% to 10% of the bill is icing on the cake. Leave tips in cash, even if paying by credit card. If you eat tapas or sandwiches at a bar, just round up the bill to the nearest euro. Tip cocktail servers €0.50 a drink, depending on the bar. In a fancy establishment, leave no more than a 10% tip even though service is included—likewise if you had a great time.

Taxi drivers expect no tip and are happy if you round up in their favor. A tip of 5% of the total fare is considered generous. Long rides or extra help with luggage may merit a tip, but if you're short of change, you'll never hear a complaint. On the contrary, your driver may sometimes round down in *your* favor instead of ransacking his pockets for exact change.

Tip hotel porters €1 a bag, and the bearer of room service €1. A doorman who calls a taxi for you gets €1. If you stay in a

hotel for more than two nights, tip the maid about €1 per night. A concierge should receive a tip for service, from €1 for basic help to €5 or more for special assistance such as getting reservations at a popular restaurant.

Tour guides should be tipped about €2, barbers €1, and women's hairdressers at least €2 for a wash and style. Restroom attendants (though you won't see many of them today) are tipped €1 or whatever loose change is at hand.

▌TOURS

SPECIAL-INTEREST TOURS
ART TOURS
The Ruta del Modernisme (Moderniste Route), a self-guided tour, provides an excellent guidebook (available in English) that interprets 116 Moderniste sites from the Sagrada Família and the Palau de la Música Catalana to Art Nouveau building facades, lampposts, and paving stones. The €12 Guide, sold at the Pavellons Güell and the Institut Municipal del Paisatge Urbà (*Av. Drassanes* 6), comes with a book of vouchers good for discounts up to 50% on admission to most of the Moderniste buildings and sites in the Guide in Barcelona and 13 other towns and cities in Catalonia, as well as free guided tours in English at Pavellons Güell (daily 10:15 and 12:15) and the Hospital de Sant Pau (daily at 10, 11, noon, and 1).

The Palau de la Música Catalana offers guided tours in English every hour on the hour from 10 to 3:30. Sagrada Família guided tours cost extra. Casa Milà offers one guided tour daily (6 pm weekdays, 11 am weekends). Architect Dominique Blinder of Urbancultours specializes in explorations of the Barcelona Jewish Quarter but can also provide tours of the Sagrada Família or virtually any architectural aspect of Barcelona.

Contacts Centre del Modernisme, Pavellons Güell. ⊠ *Av. de Pedralbes 7, Pedralbes* ☎ *93/317-7652, 93/256-2504 for guided*

visits ⊕ *www.rutadelmodernisme.com*
Ⓜ *L3 Palau Real, Maria Cristina.* **Recinte Modernista de Sant Pau** (*Hospital de la Santa Creu i Sant Pau*). ✉ *Carrer Sant Antoni Maria Claret 167, Eixample* ☎ *93/553–7801* ⊕ *www.santpaubarcelona.org/en* Ⓜ *L5 Sant Pau/Dos de Maig.* **Urbancultours.** ⊕ *www.urbancultours.com.*

CULINARY

Aula Gastronómica (Cooking Classroom) has different culinary tours, including tours of the Boqueria and Santa Catarina markets with breakfast, cooking classes, and tastings, for €12 per person and up. The locals you'll meet on the tours may struggle a bit in English, but between the guides and the help of fellow travelers, everyone manages. Jane Gregg, founder of Epicurean Ways, offers gourmet and wine tours of Barcelona and Catalonia. Teresa Parker of Spanish Journeys organizes cooking classes, seasonal specials, custom cultural or culinary tours, corporate cooking retreats, or off-the-beaten-path travel.

Contacts Aula Gastronómica. ✉ *Carrer Sagristans 5, Entresuelo, Barri Gòtic* ☎ *93/301–1944* ⊕ *www.aulagastronomica. com/cooking-classes* Ⓜ *L4 Jaume I.* **Epicurean Ways.** ✉ *714 Graves St., Downtown* ☎ *434/738–2293 in U.S., 93/802–2688 in Spain* ⊕ *www.epicureanways.com.* **Spanish Journeys.** ☎ *508/349–9769* ⊕ *www.spanishjourneys.com.*

DAY TOURS AND GUIDES
BOAT TOURS

Golondrina harbor boats make short trips from the Portal de la Pau, near the Columbus monument. The fare is €7.50 for a 40-minute "Barcelona Port" tour of the harbor and €15 for the "Barcelona Sea" 90-minute ride out past the beaches and up the coast to the Fòrum at the eastern end of Diagonal. Departures are spring and summer (Easter week–September), daily 11:15 am–5:15 pm for the Port tour, 12:30 pm and 3:30 pm for the Sea tour; fall and winter, weekends and holidays only, 11 am–5 pm. It's closed mid-December–early January.

Fees and Schedules Las Golondrinas. ✉ *Pl. Portal de la Pau s/n, Moll de les Drassanes, La Rambla* ☎ *93/442–3106* ⊕ *www.lasgolondrinas.com/en* Ⓜ *L3 Drassanes.*

BUS TOURS

The Bus Turístic (9 or 9:30 am to 7 or 8 pm every 5–25 minutes, depending on the season), sponsored by the tourist office, runs on three circuits with stops at all the important sights. The blue route covers upper Barcelona; the red route tours lower Barcelona; and the green route runs from the Port Olímpic along Barcelona's beaches to the Fòrum at the eastern end of Diagonal (April through September only). A one-day ticket can be bought online (with a 10% discount) for €26.10 (a two-day ticket is €35.10). An additional €11.25 ticket (for sale on the same website) covers the fare for the Tramvía Blau, funicular, and Montjuïc cable car across the port. You receive a booklet with discount vouchers for various attractions. The blue and red bus routes start at Plaça de Catalunya near Café Zurich. The green route starts at Port Olímpic next to the Hotel Arts. Passengers can jump off and catch a later bus at any stop along the way; some stops are "hubs" where you can switch to a bus on one of the other routes. Audio coverage is provided in 10 languages. A competing bus tour, Barcelona Tours, also leaves from Plaça de Catalunya near the corner of Ronda de la Universitat.

The product and prices are all but identical, though the Bus Turístic is the official Tourist Office tour, offering discount vouchers and superior service. In the event of long lines or delays on the Bus Turístic, Barcelona Tours is a good alternative.

Contacts Bus Turístic. ✉ *Pl. de Catalunya 3* ☎ *93/285–3832* ⊕ *www.barcelonabusturistic.cat* Ⓜ *Catalunya.* **Julià Travel.** ✉ *Carrer Balmes 5, Eixample* ☎ *93/402–6900* ⊕ *www.juliatravel.com/destinations/barcelona* Ⓜ *Catalunya, L1/L2 Universitat.*

PRIVATE GUIDES

Guides from the organizations listed below are generally competent, though the quality of language skills and general showmanship may vary. For customized tours, including access to some of Barcelona's leading chefs, architects, art historians, and artists, Heritage Tours will set it all up from New York.

Contacts Barcelona Guide Bureau. ⊠ *Via Laietana 54, 2-2, Born-Ribera* ☎ *93/268–2422, 667/419140 on weekends* ⊕ *www. barcelonaguidebureau.com* Ⓜ *Urquinaona.* **Heritage Tours.** ⊠ *121 W. 27th St., Suite 1201, New York* ☎ *800/378-4555 toll-free in U.S., 212/206-8400 in U.S.* ⊕ *www.htprivatetravel.com.*

SEGWAY TOURS

Barcelona Segway Tours, with an office near the cathedral, puts you up on one of its futuristic two-wheelers for a two-hour tour (€55) of the Barri Gòtic, La Rambla, and the seafront; its longer three-hour excursion (€75) includes the Ciutadella Park as well. Tours depart daily at 9:30 and 10 am, and 12:30, 3, 4:30, and 6 pm; the Early Bird tour, at 8 am, includes breakfast. Helmets are provided; children must be more than 10 years of age; learn more at ⊕ *www. barcelonasegwaytour.com.*

WALKING TOURS

Turisme de Barcelona offers weekend walking tours of the Barri Gòtic, the Waterfront, Picasso's Barcelona, Modernisme, a shopping circuit, and Gourmet Barcelona in English (at 10:30 am). Prices range from €15 to €21, with 10% discounts for purchases online. For private tours, Julià Travel and Pullmantur *(Bus Tours)* both lead walks around Barcelona. Tours leave from their offices, but you may be able to arrange a pickup at your hotel. Prices per person are €35 for half a day and €90 for a full day, including lunch.

For the best English-language walking tour of the medieval Jewish Quarter, Dominique Tomasov Blinder, of Urbancultours *(Art Tours)* is an architect with 13 years experience in Jewish heritage. Her tour of Jewish Barcelona is a unique combination of history, current affairs, and personal experience; learn more at ⊕ *www.urbancultours.com.*

Contact Turisme de Barcelona. ⊠ *Pl. de Catalunya 17, soterrani, Eixample* ☎ *93/285–3834* ⊕ *bcnshop.barcelonaturisme.com/ tours–visits* Ⓜ *Pl. de Catalunya.*

▌ VISITOR INFORMATION

The Tourist Office of Spain and its website provides valuable practical information about visiting the country. Turisme de Barcelona has two main locations: Plaça de Catalunya, in the center of town, open daily 8:30–8:30; and Plaça Sant Jaume in the Gothic Quarter, open weekdays 8:30–8, Saturday 9–7, and Sunday 9–2. Other tourist information stands are near the top of La Rambla just below Carrer Tallers, at the port end of La Rambla (just beyond the Columbus monument) and at the main entrance of the Sagrada Família. There are smaller facilities at the Sants train station, open daily 8–8; the Palau de la Virreina, open Monday–Saturday 9–9 and Sunday 10–2; the Glories tourist point in the center of the @22 district, open Monday, Wednesday, Friday, and Saturday 10–5; and the Palau de Congressos, open daily 10–8 during trade fairs and conventions only. For general information in English, dial *010* between 8 am and 10 pm any day except for Sunday.

El Prat Airport has an office with information on Catalonia and the rest of Spain, open Monday–Saturday 9:30–8 and Sunday 9:30–3. The tourist office in Palau Robert, open Monday–Saturday 10–7, specializes in provincial Catalonia. From June to mid-September, information aides patrol the Barri Gòtic and La Rambla area 9–9. They travel in pairs and are recognizable by their red shirts, white trousers or skirts, and badges.

Barcelona Tourist Offices Plaça Sant Jaume. ✉ *Carrer de la Ciutat 2, Ajuntament de Barcelona, Barri Gòtic* ☎ *93/285–3834* ⊕ *www.barcelonaturisme.com* Ⓜ *L3 Liceu, L4 Jaume I.* **Sants Estació.** ✉ *Pl. dels Països Catalans s/n, Eixample* ☎ *93/285–3834* ⊕ *www.barcelonaturisme.com* Ⓜ *L3/L5 Sants Estació.* **Servei d'Informació Cultural–Palau de la Virreina** (*Tiquet Rambles*). ✉ *Rambla 99, La Rambla* ☎ *93/316–1000, 93/316–1111* ⊕ *lameva.barcelona.cat/ tiquetrambles* Ⓜ *Catalunya, L3 Liceu.*

Regional Tourist Offices El Prat-Barcelona Airport. ✉ *El Prat de Llobregat, El Prat del Llobregat* ☎ *93/478–4704 Terminal 1, 93/378–8149 Terminal 2* ⊕ *www.barcelonaturisme.com.* **Palau Robert.** ✉ *Oficina Turistica de Catalunya, Passeig de Gràcia 107, Eixample* ☎ *93/238–8091* ⊕ *palaurobert.gencat.cat/en/oficina_de_turisme.*

INDEX

PHOTO CREDITS

Front cover: Stefano Politi Markovina/ AWL Images Ltd. [Description: Central light well inside Casa Batllo, Barcelona, Spain]. **Back cover, from left to right:** Dudau | Dreamstime.com; Masterlu | Dreamstime.com; robertpaulyoung, Fodors.com member. **Spine:** Jacekkadaj | Dreamstime.com. 1, Bjorn Svensson/age fotostock. 2-3, Joan Miro Foundation, Barcelona. Catalonia, Spain. 5, Solodovnikova Elena/Shutterstock. **Chapter 1: Experience Barcelona:** 8-9, Ingenui/iStockphoto. 18 (left), Steven NeWton/Shutterstock. 18 (top center), Quim Roser/age fotostock. 18 (bottom center), Xcaballe/Wikipedia.org. 18 (right), David Davies/Flickr. 19 (top left), Javier Larrea/age fotostock.19 (bottom left), Andoni Canela/age fotostock. 19 (bottom center), Ken Welsh/age fotostock. 19 (right), Astroid | Dreamstime.com. 24, Oso Media/Alamy. 25, Pavel Kirichenko/iStockphoto. 26 (top left), Public Domain. 26 (bottom left), Alfonso de Tomás/Shutterstock. 26 (top right), Zina Seletskaya/ Shutterstock. 26 (center right), Amy Nichole Harris/Shutterstock. 26 (bottom right), Luis M. Seco/ Shutterstock. 27 (left), IWona Grodzka/Shutterstock. 27 (top right), zvonkomaja/Shutterstock. 27 (center right), Public Domain. 27 (bottom right), Smackfu/Wikipedia.org. 28 (top left), synes/Flickr. 28 (bottom left), rubiphoto/Shutterstock. 28 (right), Solodovnikova Elena/Shutterstock. 29 (top), Quim Roser/age fotostock. 29 (bottom), Jan van der Hoeven/Shutterstock. **Chapter 2: Exploring Barcelona:** 33, Brzozowska/iStockphoto. 34, GARDEL Bertrand/age fotostock. 36, Bruno Perousse/age fotostock. 39, Wolfcomm/Flickr. 40, Matz Sjöberg/age fotostock. 43, JACQUES Pierre/age fotostock. 46, böhringer friedrich/Wikipedia.org. 49, böhringer friedrich/Wikipedia.org. 51, Xavier Caballé/Wikipedia.org. 55, Rafael Campillo/age fotostock. 57, travelstock44/LOOK/age fotostock. 59, Lalupa/Wikipedia.org. 60, Rafael Campillo/ age fotostock. 62, BORGESE Maurizio/age fotostock. 64, Yearofthedragon/Wikipedia.org. 67, Mikhail Zahranichny/Shutterstock. 68 and 71, Ken Welsh/age fotostock. 75, Vinicius Tupinamba/Shutterstock. 77, Philip Lange/Shutterstock. 78, Petr Svarc/age fotostock. 81, Juergen Richter/age fotostock. 83, Juergen Richter/age fotostock. 85, Yuriy Chertok/Shutterstock. 87, Marco Cristofori/age fotostock. 90, Astroid | Dreamstime.com. 91, Robert Harding Productions/age fotostock. 92 (left), Jose Fuste Raga/age fotostock. 92 (top right), Sylvain Grandadam/age fotostock. 92 (center right), Javier Larrea/age fotostock. 92 (bottom right), Siobhan O'Hare. 93 (top), ccchan 19/Flickr. 93 (bottom), Pep Daudé/Temple de la Sagrada Família. 94 (top), Jsome1/Flickr. 94 (bottom), Pepe Navarro/ Temple de la Sagrada Família. 95 (top), Hans Blosseyimagebro / age fotostock. 95 (bottom), Achimhb | Dreamstime.com. 96 (top), Jose Antonio Sanchez/Shutterstock. 96 (2nd from top), Rafael Campillo/ age fotostock. 96 (3rd from top), MM Images/age fotostock. 96 (bottom) and 97 (top), Temple de la Sagrada Família. 97 (2nd from top), Harmonia Amanda/Wikipedia.org. 97 (3rd from top), Achim Prill/iStockphoto. 97 (bottom), ARCO/P Svarc/age fotostock. 98, Wikipedia.org. 101, peresanz/ Shutterstock. 103, Jan van der Hoeven/Shutterstock. 106, Factoria Singular/age fotostock. 109, posztos (colorlab.hu)/Shutterstock. 111, Canaan/Wikipedia.org. 114, Solodovnikova Elena/Shutterstock. 118, Jordi Puig/age fotostock. 119, Elan Fleisher/age fotostock.121, Philip Lange/Shutterstock. 122, Jordi Puig/age fotostock. **Chapter 3: Where to Eat:** 125, robertpaulyoung/Flickr. 126, Elan Fleisher/age fotostock. 127 (top), jynus/Wikipedia. org. 127 (bottom), Javier Lastras/ Wikipedia. org. 128, atanas.dk/Shutterstock. 138, OSOMEDIA/age fotostock. 149, Ioseba Egibar/age fotostock. 150, Javier Larrea/age fotostock. 152 (top left), Daniel P. Acevedo/age fotostock. 152 (bottom left), Sam Bloomberg-Rissman/age fotostock. 152 (right), Javier Larrea/age fotostock. 153, J.D. Dallet/age fotostock. 154 (top), PHB.cz (Richard Semik)/Shutterstock. 154 (2nd from top), Javier Larrea/age fotostock, 154 (3rd from top), Jakub Pavlinec/Shutterstock, 154 (4th from top), J.D. Dallet/age fotostock. 154 (5th from top), Fresnel/Shutterstock. 154 (6th from top), J.D. Dallet/age fotostock. 154 (bottom), Marta Menéndez/Shutterstock. 155 (top left), Mauro Winery. 155 (top 2nd from left), Cephas Picture Library/Alamy. 155 (top 3rd from left), Alvaro Palacios Winery. 155 (top right), Mas Martinet Winery. 155 (bottom), Mike Randolph/age fotostock. **Chapter 4: Where to Stay:** 175, Albert Font/2 Primero Primera. 176, Rafael Vargas. **Chapter 5: Nightlife and the Arts:** 195, alterna2/Flickr. 196, Rene Mattes/age fotostock. 197 (top), Juan David Ferrando Subero/ Shutterstock. 197 (bottom), Hemis / Alamy. 198, Josep Renalias/Wikipedia.org. **Chapter 6: Sports and the Outdoors:** 223, sportgraphic/Shutterstock. 224, Mikhail Zahranichny/ Shutterstock. 225 (top), Regien Paassen/Shutterstock. 225 (bottom), Philip Lange/Shutterstock. 226, Carlos Neto/Shutterstock. **Chapter 7: Shopping:** 233, Peter Horree/Alamy. 234, Courtesy of La Manual Alpargatera/Joan Carles "Vei" Tasies. 241, Xavier Subias/age fotostock. **Chapter 8: Catalonia, Valencia and The Costa Blanca:** 257, Robwilson39 | Dreamstime.com. 259, VRoig/Flickr. 260, Patty Orly/Shutterstock. 261 (top), Mauricio Pellegrinetti/Flickr. 261 (bottom), Ana Abadla/age fotostock. 262, Helio San Miguel. 270, Oscar García Bayerri/age fotostock. 274, Carlos S. Pereyra/age fotostock. 276, B&Y Photography Inc./age fotostock. 279, Oscar García Bayerri/age fotostock. 281, José Fuste Raga/age fotostock. 288, Helio San Miguel. 291, Alberto Paredes/age fotostock. 302, Nils-Johan Norenlind/age fotostock. 304, Igor Gonzalo Sanz/age fotostock. 309, Charles Bowman/age fotostock. 312, Hidalgo & Lopesino/age fotostock. 314, Alan Copson/Jon Arnold/age fotostock.

About Our Writers: All photos are courtesy of the writers.

NOTES

ABOUT OUR WRITERS

Jared Lubarsky is a university teacher and freelance travel journalist who has been writing for Fodor's since 1997, first on Japan, where he lived for 30 years, and more recently—having relocated to Barcelona—on Spain. His credits include in-flight and general interest travel magazines, guidebooks, and newspapers. Jared updated our Experience, Exploring, Where to Stay, and Travel Smart chapters.

Malia Politzer is a freelance journalist and travel writer based out of Granada, Spain, where she has been living for the past several years. She has also lived in India, China, and Mexico. Apart from Fodor's Travel, she has written for the *Wall Street Journal*, *Foreign Policy*, *Far Eastern Economic Review*, *The Village Voice*, and *Vogue India*, among others.

Originally from the cloudy north of England, **Elizabeth Prosser** has embraced sunnier climes since she emigrated to Barcelona, Spain, in 2007. While indulging her passion for food and travel, she works as a freelance writer and editor for a range of print and online publications. Elizabeth updated the Catalonia, Valencia and the Costa Blanca, and Sports and Outdoors chapters.

Steve Tallantyre is a British journalist and copywriter. He moved from Italy to Barcelona in the late 1990s. Married to a Catalan native, with two "Catalangles" children, Steve writes about the region's restaurants, and food culture for leading international publications. He also owns a popular blog about Barcelona cuisine (⊕ *www.foodbarcelona.com*) and is the founder of a copywriting agency (⊕ *www.BCNcontent.com*). Steve updated our Where to Eat and Nightlife chapters.

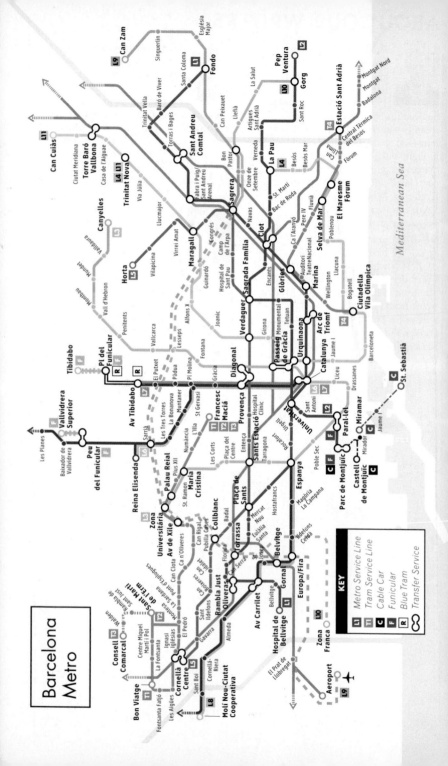

Barcelona Metro

KEY

- **L1** Metro Service Line
- **T1** Tram Service Line
- **C** Cable Car
- **R** Funicular
- ∞ Blue Tram
- ⊂⊃ Transfer Service

Mediterranean Sea